Ceramic Millennium

Critical Writings on Ceramic History, Theory, and Art

Garth Clark
Clement Greenberg
Nancy Selvage
Doris Shadbolt
Philip Rawson
John Bentley Mays
Paul Greenhalgh
Michael McTwigan
Mark Pennings
Justin Clemens
George Woodman

David Hamilton
Susan Tunick
Edward Lebow
Gerry Williams
Léopold L. Foulem
Graham McLaren
Tanya Harrod
Janet Koplos
Gabi Dewald
David McFadden
Edmund de Waal

Edited by Garth Clark

The Press of the Nova Scotia
College of Art and Design

NSCAD UNIVERSITY THE PRESS

The Press of the Nova Scotia College of Art and Design
5163 Duke Street
Halifax Nova Scotia B3J 3J6 Canada

The Press of the Nova Scotia College of Art and Design was established in 1972 as a vehicle to publish books by and about leading contemporary artists. Between 1972 and 1987, 26 titles by such artists as Michael Snow, Steve Reich, Gerhard Richter and Yvonne Rainer were published. Re-launched in 2002, The Press will once again establish the university as a source for the publishing of primary documents and scholarly works in the fields of contemporary art, craft and design.

NSCAD University is a university of the visual arts singularly dedicated to the pursuit of excellence in the training of professional practitioners, in the conducting of research and in the production of works of art in all media.

© 2006 Garth Clark, The Press of the Nova Scotia College of Art and Design, and the authors.

All rights reserved. No part of this publication maybe reproduced, stored in a retrieval system, or transmitted, in any form or by any means, without the prior permission in writing of The Press of the Nova Scotia College of Art and Design, or as expressly permitted by law, or under terms agreed with the appropriate reprographic rights organizations. Enquiries concerning reproduction outside the scope of the above should be sent to The Press of the Nova Scotia College of Art and Design at the address above.

Editorial Director: Susan McEachern
Manager: Christopher McFarlane
Graphic Design: Arthur Carter, AustenHouse
Printed and bound in Canada

Available through D.A.P./Distributed Art Publishers
155 Sixth Avenue, 2nd Floor, New York, N.Y. 10013
Tel (212) 627-1999 Fax (212) 627-9484

Library and Archives Canada Cataloguing in Publication

   Ceramic millennium : critical writings on ceramic history, theory and art / Garth Clark ... [et al.] ; edited by Garth Clark.

Selection of papers from 8 conferences held over a period of 20 years.
Includes bibliographical references and index.
ISBN-13: 978-0-919616-45-5
ISBN-10: 0-919616-45-3

   1. Ceramics--History. I. Clark, Garth, 1947-
NK3930.C46 2006   738'.09   C2005-906712-8
Printed in Canada

Contents

Acknowledgments viii

Preface ix
Paul Greenhalgh

Introduction: 8 x 20: A Personal Recollection xi
Garth Clark

Section One:
Status of Clay 1

Chapter 1
Status of Clay 3
Clement Greenberg

Chapter 2
Art Versus Craft: The Issue of Craftsmanship in Twentieth Century Art 10
Nancy Selvage

Chapter 3
The Transparency of Clay 24
Doris Shadbolt

Chapter 4
Analogy and Metaphor in Ceramic Art 35
Philip Rawson

Chapter 5
The Mud File 53
John Bentley Mays

SECTION TWO:
CERAMICS AND MODERNISM 63

CHAPTER 6
RADICAL ORNAMENT:
CERAMICS AT THE *FIN DE SIÈCLE* 64
PAUL GREENHALGH

CHAPTER 7
MODERNISM AND CERAMICS TODAY: AN OVERVIEW 77
MICHAEL MCTWIGAN

CHAPTER 8
CERAMICS AND MODERNISM: EUROPE 1910-1940 92
GARTH CLARK

CHAPTER 9
MODERNISM AND CERAMICS 115
MARK PENNINGS

CHAPTER 10
POSTMODERNITY, OR "THE BREAKING OF THE VESSELS" 129
JUSTIN CLEMENS

SECTION THREE:
THE DECORATIVE 141

CHAPTER 11
CERAMIC DECORATION AND THE CONCEPT
OF CERAMICS AS DECORATIVE ART 142
GEORGE WOODMAN

Chapter 12
The Decorative Vessel   154
George Woodman

Chapter 13
Discourse and Decoration:
The Struggle for Historical Space   163
Paul Greenhalgh

Section Four:
Architecture   169

Chapter 14
License to Decorate   170
David Hamilton

Chapter 15
Architectural Terra Cotta:
Preserving the Inheritance   176
Susan Tunick

Chapter 16
Architectural Ceramics   186
Edward Lebow

Section Five:
History and Tradition   195

Chapter 17
The Role of the Traditional Potter
in Contemporary Society   196
Gerry Williams

CHAPTER 18
ECHOES: AN INTRODUCTION   207
PHILIP RAWSON

CHAPTER 19
THE PRIMAL VESSEL: EXPLORATIONS
IN HISTORY, TRADITION, AND TIME   219
GARTH CLARK

CHAPTER 20
THE USE OF CERAMICS HISTORY
IN CONTEMPORARY CERAMICS   231
LÉOPOLD FOULEM

SECTION SIX:
EDUCATION   245

CHAPTER 21
STILL A SURE TOUCHSTONE:
THE FUTURE OF CERAMIC HISTORY
WITH ART AND DESIGN EDUCATION   246
GRAHAM MCLAREN

CHAPTER 22
STUDIOS, ACADEMIES, AND WORKSHOPS:
CERAMIC EDUCATION FROM THE
MID-NINETEENTH CENTURY TO WORLD WAR II   259
TANYA HARROD

SECTION SEVEN:
STATE OF THE ART   277

Chapter 23
Ceramics and Art Criticism 278
Janet Koplos

Chapter 24
Of the Undead and Desires: About the Undead and Desires for a Definition of the Craft Arts. For Example: Ceramics, an Example of Futility 289
Gabi Dewald

Chapter 25
Patronage 301
David McFadden

Chapter 26
Homer, Ceramics, and Marketplace Anxieties 317
Garth Clark

Chapter 27
Guess Who's Coming to Lunch 337
Léopold Foulem

Chapter 28
Not Ideas But in Things 350
Edmund de Waal

Chapter 29
The Aesthetics of Function 362
Edward Lebow

List of Awardees 373
Biographies 376
Index 394

Acknowledgements

Firstly, my gratitude to Paul Greenhalgh for his early commitment to publish these papers and his patience as the volume was compiled. Without his confidence, I doubt that this volume would have been published. John Pagliaro put these texts (often in chaotic states, as papers delivered at conferences often are) into a serviceable format, bringing to this compilation his distinctive, deft touch that preserves the authentic voice of the speakers. Christopher Dowdell, CAF's intern (we thank CDS International for sponsoring his work visa) completed the task, and given that he is a graduate of NSCAD University, has created a warm, working partnership between the great people at NSCAD and CAF. My thanks to Osvaldo Da Silva for training Pagliaro and Dowdell in the alchemy of optical character recognition. The NSCAD University Press must be thanked for transforming the manuscript into a magnificent book. This process was well run by Christopher McFarlane, the Manager of the Press and the designer and production manager, Arthur Carter. Ulli Walker thoroughly copyedited the text with an eye to academic precision. Susan McEachern, the Editorial Director was responsible for overseeing the visual and academic content. The papers exist because of the speakers and their willingness to do hard work for meager payment. Also, my thanks go to the organizing directors of the various symposia: Anne Mortimer (1979 and 1983), Mark Del Vecchio (1981 and 1999), Lennie Berkowitz (1981), Marge Malouf (1983), John Huntingford (1986), Barbara Perry (1989), Tom Piche (1993), and Dawn Bennett (1999). Amongst the heroes in this brief history are all the artists who contributed to *Night of 101 Cups*, a fund-raiser that provided all of the seed money to get the eighth symposium off the ground. Lastly, I am dedicating this book to Mark Del Vecchio, who has played a crucial role in every CAF event since 1981, often without credit and always as a volunteer, and to svelte and super efficient Dawn Bennett, our "goad and whip," without whom *Ceramic Millennium: A Leadership Congress for the Ceramics Arts*, our crowning glory to date, would never have happened. Their creativity, dedication, and sacrifice over five years has produced scholarly fruit that the field is still harvesting and will provide intellectual sustenance for decades to come.

Garth Clark

Preface

Between 1972 and 1987 the NSCAD Press published numerous volumes and came to distinguish itself as a principal vehicle in North America for the publication of artists' writings. In 2002 the NSCAD University Press was relaunched, and in 2004 we reissued some of our classic volumes and published our first new works. It is our intention, in our reborn condition, not simply to publish original documentation and writings on the fine arts, but on all areas of visual culture. This volume is indicative of that intention. We at the university are deeply indebted to our Press Editorial Director, Susan McEachern, to our Press Manager, Chris McFarlane, and to Professor Walter Ostrom, the champion behind this book.

In the humanities generally, but emphatically in the visual arts, disciplines are drastically affected by what is said and written about them. The fate of the individual genres within the visual arts has been mediated by the way that their history has been constructed for them. The way we see painting, sculpture, or architecture, for example, is heavily informed by the way we read about them; similarly, the way we see ceramics has been shaped by what has been written. Sadly, this shaping has not always been a positive one.

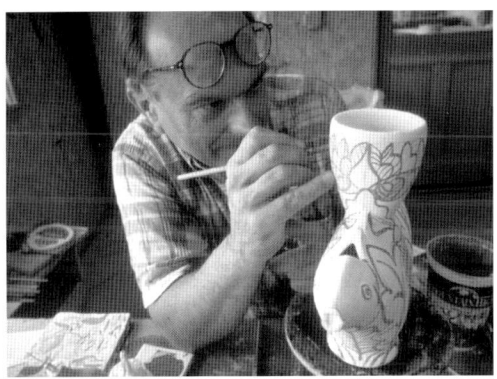

WALTER OSTRAM, PROFESSOR, NSCAD UNIVERSITY.
PHOTO: ANDERSON RANCH ARTS CENTRER, COLORADO.

Of course, it would be wrong not to acknowledge that there has been some very significant writing on ceramics. But there should be more. This volume, our first on an applied arts theme, aims to add to the literature on modern ceramics, and also to act as a catalyst to further volumes. This group of previously unpublished lectures uncovers an extensive terrain, but it has a single unifying theme that emerges clearly in virtually every piece: the identity of ceramic practice in the modern world. Most of the writers address the problem of ceramics and modernity.

There are very few fields in the humanities where one individual has made a bigger contribution than Garth Clark has to the world of ceramics. As a writer, editor, historian, curator, conference organizer, and dealer, he has contributed spectacularly to the ceramics world over the last four decades. Indeed, it is difficult for many of us to imagine how the North American ceramics scene would look in the absence of Garth's extraordinary contribution. This volume simply could not have happened without his indescribable energy and commitment. And needless to say, the friendship and warmth he showed to colleagues at the university made the task of creating the book into a joy.

Paul Greenhalgh
President, NSCAD University

Introduction: 8 x 20
A Personal Recollection

Garth Clark

My apologies if this introduction is too personal; but most of the eight events have, in a sense, been my children, tenderly nursed into life, carefully shaped and guided, and always funded against the odds. Collectively, they have attracted an audience of thousands of writers, critics, artists, and others, gathering to learn, challenge the status quo, and expand the boundaries of what is a fundamentally conservative art form given to evolution rather than revolution. What I would like to make clear from the outset, is that when I write in this introduction about the success, elegance, professionalism, and impact of the various events, I am not suffering from hubris. Symposia are team events; so I am not praising myself but those many individuals who put the events together, those who spoke, and those from the audience who spurred debate and, with their fees, paid for the bulk of symposia's cost. But I make no bones about the fact that I am proud of what the Ceramic Arts Foundation (CAF) has achieved in its eight symposia and twenty years. It is an impressive legacy, and CAF remains the only organization dedicated to raising the bar for criticism and history in this field.

Let us first dispense with a few background details. The Institute for Ceramic History (ICH) was founded in 1979 by me, Anne Mortimer, and Margie Hughto, with goal of promoting scholarship in modern and contemporary ceramic arts through a single conference. In 1995 it was renamed the Ceramics Art Foundation and restructured as a tax-exempt, not-for-profit corporation. ICH and CAF have organized and presented six major symposia at the following venues: Syracuse University, 1979; Waldorf-Astoria, New York City, 1981; Contemporary Art Society / Nelson Atkins Museum, Kansas City, 1983; Ontario Institute for Studies and Education, Toronto, 1985; Victoria and Albert Museum, London, 1986. The Everson Museum presented the sixth and seventh symposia (1991 and 1993) in Syracuse, New York. CAF reclaimed the event to produce the Ceramic Millennium, Leadership Congress for the Ceramic Arts, the eighth international symposium in this series and a huge, million-dollar event with national delegations from sixty-three countries and over 3,500 participants.

CAF has also been the catalyst of several cornerstone exhibitions including: *Michael Cardew: A Retrospective Portrait*, Wichita, 1982; *Ceramic Echoes: Historical References in Contemporary Ceramic Art*, Kansas City, 1983; *Hans Coper: Works in North American Collections*, Toronto, 1985; *American Potters Today*, London, 1986; and major art festivals in Toronto and Europe. The latter involved over seventy museums and galleries throughout Europe. CAF has also begun to involve itself in publishing, putting together the award-winning *Shards: Garth Clark on Ceramic Art* published by Distributed Art Publishing in 2002. (The royalties were all donated to CAF, which in turn paid for some of the work on this volume.)

CAF has a unique way of operating. It awakens when a project is being planned and goes dormant in between events, so it is only consuming funds when a project is active, a highly cost effective model. One ceramist, amusingly, referred to us as "the grizzly bear of clay." (We think it was a compliment.) CAF employs no permanent staff and has no ongoing overheads when it is in its "sleep mode." Its officers have never been paid, not an achievement of which we are unduly proud but, in our cash-starved medium, a reality we have accepted. The decision to operate in this manner, which proved to have drawbacks as well as advantages, was taken early because we did not want CAF to evolve into a self-perpetuating bureaucracy, which often causes non-profits to lose their edge. We are, as a result, not beholden to any particular funding sources in the long run. We could—and have—taken controversial stands on issues without offending our base because, aside from those who attend our symposia (and there are some who have been at every one of the eight), we do not have a funding base and, as a result, have no political pressures taking up residence and distorting our vision.

Each of the symposia has had a different goal (aside from the umbrella issue of improving scholarship) as CAF's own goals have changed over the years, gradually setting higher and higher standards. To better understand this, each of the eight symposia is discussed briefly to give a context. But before we deal with these events, I would like to explain some of the thinking behind the selection of the papers.

We could not publish them all, and so a selection had to be made. My first exclusion was papers on individual artists or artist presentations, as we wanted this compilation to deal with broader issues. Then, too, I decided to omit transcribed panel debates for a number of reasons. Making the final cut amongst the eligible papers was always painful (such as when two or more papers of relatively similar quality discussed the same subject and only one could be chosen). Some omissions come from speakers who, despite many requests, never delivered their written papers. There are also a few gaps. Certain symposia did not generate publishable papers, and the reasons for this are explained more fully below. You will also note that not all papers are presented in scholarly form. Many of those in ceramics who have recorded, written, and critiqued are not from academia but are artists, dealers, and others. So some papers lack institutional formality; citations have never been footnoted or, in some cases, were not even identified. We have added those we could locate. Also, I gave a major paper at every symposium. It seemed strange to omit those from the proceedings, and so I have included the ones that seemed relevant, not out of vanity, but for completeness's sake.

FIRST INTERNATIONAL CERAMICS SYMPOSIUM, 1979
A CENTURY OF CERAMICS IN THE UNITED STATES 1878-1979

The first symposium was planned as a one-shot deal. We never anticipated that it would have the history it has today. It took place because Margie Hughto and I were the curators for the exhibition, *A Century of Ceramics in the United States 1878-1978*, organized for the Everson Museum of Art, Syracuse, New York. The Everson was then the most active museum, ceramic-wise, in America. We were ambitious, and the exhibition grew like Topsy. By the time it opened on May 5, 1979, it comprised 450 objects, some the size of a cup and others weighing hundreds of pounds, and we ended up occupying every gallery in the museum. The exhibition spawned a film narrated by Orson Welles; *Earth, Fire and Water: A Century of Cermaics in the United States*, which was sponsored by Phillip Morris and became a PBS (Public Broadcasting System) mainstay. The exhibition traveled the USA for four years. The book that accompanied the exhibition sold exceptionally well and went through numerous printings. The overall impact of the *Century* show, as it became known, was immense, in part because of perfect timing, arriving as the field was in the process of coming of age. Margie and I have often talked about this perfect chemistry of the moment and debated whether it could have had the same success five years earlier or later.

The *Century* show was the first attempt to give the unruly modern history of

USA ceramics shape, context and a properly researched chronology. The preparation for the show was a highly charged subject in the hermetic politics of the clay world. Our biggest conflict was over whether work should be included because an individual was an important teacher or a good artist. We argued for the latter; the field argued for the former. Artists actively lobbied to be included. Others played hard to get but also wanted inclusion. Artists such as Roy Lichtenstein, Isamu Noguchi, and others loved the show's concept and actively participated in getting us works on loan. (I remember a call from Lichtenstein to Leo Castelli's wife that changed her tune from "I will never lend this piece to an exhibition" to "I would love to lend.")

It had become an inadvertent, 800-pound gorilla, benign to some, frightening to others, redrawing the comfortable lines of pedagogy and university-based patronage that then passed for history. As we drew closer to the opening, the interest (and controversy) grew, and it was apparent that this event needed to have a forum other than the exhibition itself, where critical voices could be heard, where the premise of the exhibition could be questioned, and where a wealth of historical information—too much to be explored fully in the exhibition or its accompanying book—could be expanded upon, and the aesthetic issues faced by American ceramists today could be analyzed.

Marjie and I took the idea of a major three-day symposium to Ron Kuchta, director of the Everson Museum. He had watched the *Century* show grow from a modest survey into an epic of Cecil B. De Mille proportions. Concerned about his two seemingly out-of-control curators and seeing us as a threat to the museum's troubled bottom line, he reasonably refused to let the museum be the organizer for the symposium. (We did land the funding for the full exhibition tour and the book, however, and eventually created a substantial profit for museum operating costs.)

Ann Mortimer, a Canadian friend and one of her county's most skilled and effective organizers for the crafts, joined us, and we decided to go ahead anyway. Overnight the Institute for Ceramic History was born to gather funds, create, and run the event. Mortimer was our organizing director, and she proved to be an exceptional worker, planner, and diplomat. Funding came in bits and pieces, and in the early months, all three of us charged up our credit cards to their limit in order get this off the ground. Our first bit of good luck came when National Endowment for the Arts surprised us with a modest grant which gave us credibility as well as cash.

Syracuse University was generous in providing the facilities for the event (including low-cost housing in the dormitories), and so the basics were in place. Gambling that income from delegate fees would balance the budget, the flyers went out announcing the event.

I could say that the planning of the symposium's program took years to put together. Margie and I had been working on the *Century* show for three years by the time the work began on the symposium. We knew where to find the best speakers, historians, and critics in the field, and we understood which topics most urgently needed to be debated. But actually putting together the ambitious three-day program took only forty-eight hours.

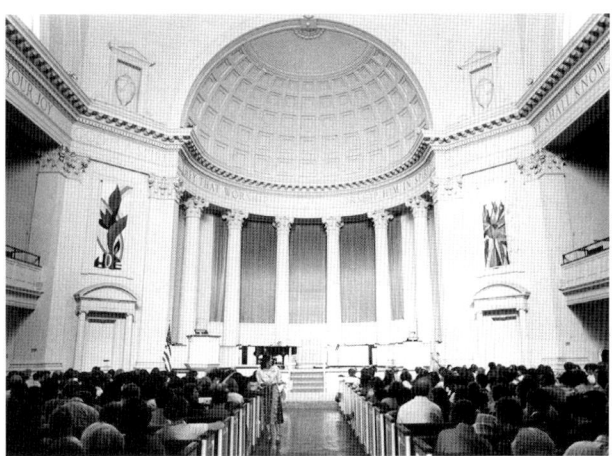

HENDRICK'S CHAPEL JUST BEFORE THE KEYNOTE ADDRESS, *FIRST INTERNATIONAL CERAMICS SYMPOSIUM*, SYRACUSE UNIVERSITY.

Margie and Anne flew out to my home in Claremont, California, for a weekend. On Saturday we sketched out the program, and then the three of us picked up our address books and hit the phones. By Sunday night, ninety percent of the speakers were confirmed, and the First International Ceramics Symposium was on its way.

Five hundred delegates from all over the USA and Canada, as well as a sprinkling of delegates from abroad, signed up. This was the field's first symposium devoted to history, criticism, and aesthetics, and the pent-up hunger for this material was palpable. We banished the two usual staples of ceramic symposia from the program—personality and process—in search of broader content. CAF's twenty-year life began portentously at 9 a.m. on June 1, 1979, in the Henricks Chapel of Syracuse University with Clement Greenberg's keynote address. The domed chapel was a singular setting: a serious, reverent space that reinforced the fact that the symposium was meant to be a serious engagement, an act of faith for ceramics as an undervalued aesthetic in American art.

It was a coup to have Greenberg, this legendary figure—one of most influential writers and thinkers on American fine art in the twentieth century—open the symposium. Margie Hughto talked Greenberg into taking on the assignment. However, he did not treat this as a favour to a friend, to be dispensed with in a standard speech. He approached the task with rigour. Greenberg obtained the proof sheets for the *Century* book and read them carefully, often calling into question a point or premise. He requested other books, asked many questions, and even visited the exhibition twice while we were installing it, spending many hours scrutinizing and commenting on the work.

Yet we were nervous. By now Greenberg had become the target for every minor postmodernist trying to pose as a giant slayer. He had a reputation for being a poor speaker, not in the content of his talks, but in his indifferent and, at times, arrogant style of presentation. He sometimes became antagonistic and riled his audiences, or became so esoteric that he made little sense. Many were predicting a Greenbergian embarrassment and, while still impressed, questioned our judgment. But he arrived relaxed and in an excellent mood, speaking beautifully in smooth cadences. While he did not annoy the assembled ceramists, he certainly did not pander to them either, noting that he found ceramists to be more concerned with opinion than with achievement. He concluded by pointing out that good art trumps all criticism—good or bad—and that the best new art of any era is often not

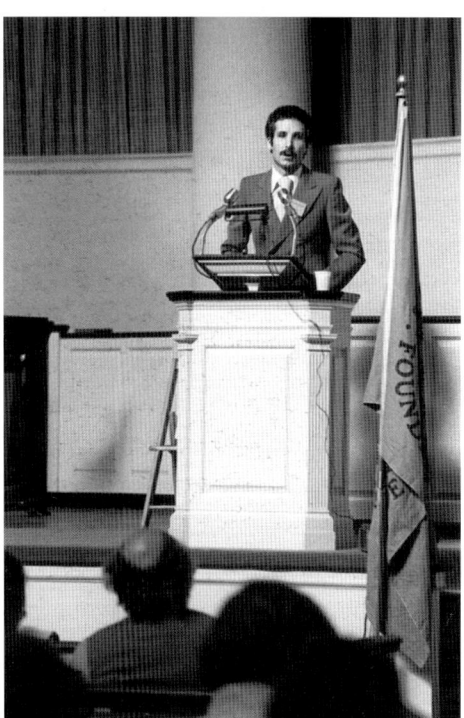

GARTH CLARK WELCOMING DELEGATES TO THE *FIRST INTERNATIONAL CERAMICS SYMPOSIUM*, HENDRICKS CHAPEL, SYRACUSE UNIVERSITY, JUNE 1, 1979.

recognized early, and so ceramics may "have to wait backstage for a while."

Ceramists felt that they had been backstage for too long already, but Greenberg's careful language and the lack of paternalism in his discussion of ceramics set the perfect tone. The crowd poured out into a bright summer day, talking excitedly and heading off to the various lecture halls (we had three operating concurrently). They were ready to engage the speakers and confront their historical heritage. We all had the feeling that at last ceramics had begun to shift away from the narrow dialogues that had dominated critical intercourse up to that point. It was a rare but empowering moment, when one suddenly realized that one was participating in what would become known as an historic moment.

Part of the magic was that the symposium was paired with the huge *Century* show at the Everson. Delegates were shuttled between the university campus and the museum to see the works being discussed "in the flesh." Janet Koplos, associate editor of *Art in America*, recalled attending the conference: "I had only been writing about art then for three years, and I essentially knew no one at the conference. I drank it all in and found what I heard enormously useful in my thinking and writing."[1]

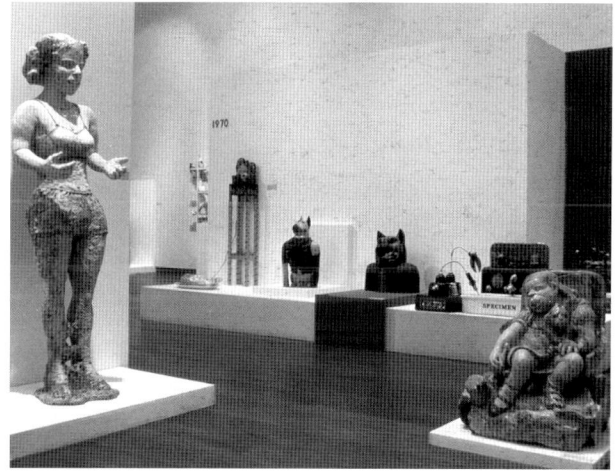

VIEW OF THE EXHIBITION, *A CENTURY OF CERAMICS IN THE UNITED STATES: 1878-1978*, AT THE EVERSON MUSEUM OF ART, SYRACUSE, NY, MAY 5 - SEPTEMBER 23, 1979.

The event ended with an awards dinner and dance honouring the writings of Michael Cardew, Bernard Leach, Susan Peterson, Daniel Rhodes and Rose Slivka, the organizing genius of Jean Delius, the vision of the collector Fred Marer, and the nurturing energies of Anna Wetherill Olmstead, who launched the Ceramic Nationals that the Everson had run for decades. The award, known by the awkward title of the International Ceramics Symposium Award, has continued to go to a distinguished list of recipients (see appendix). This it was renamed the Ostracon Award. Ostracon is the Greek word for pottery shards that were used two thousand years ago to write notes, to send messages, or as ballot "cards" for voting. Paper, then made from papyrus, was too costly for casual scribbling, so plentiful shards became the Post-Its of their time. This relationship between a ceramic fragment and language seemed perfect for an award that has been given primarily for writing and criticism.

SECOND INTERNATIONAL CERAMICS SYMPOSIUM, 1981
CERAMICS AND MODERNISM

The first symposium settled its bills and left a small surplus. Part of that was used to publish the papers—a small nightmare as it turned out—due to untested new developments in computerizing typesetting. We had not planned on continuing the symposium as a regular event, but the interest in a second meeting was high, and the Syracuse conference had really only nudged the doors of inquiry open a crack. The symposium had created a wave of discussion that reached out beyond the United States, and many of the papers were published and republished in various journals. We had momentum on our side, or so we thought. With a young (twenty-year old) Mark Del Vecchio as the able and courageous (he says naïve) organizing director, we set off to produce symposium number two. The focus was *Ceramics and Modernism*, again a first. Modernism, the defining art movement of the twentieth century, had been dismissive of the crafts and of anything associated with that term. Without addressing this difficult schism, ceramics could not achieve closure on the persistent art vs. craft debate. This symposium was the first to address this subject head-on.

The symposium opened on July 2 at the Waldorf Astoria in New York. The venue, like the theme, was carefully chosen. I was tired of attending ceramic symposia at community colleges or other minor (read "free") venues. I wanted to take this medium, which was producing such extraordinary work, into a high-profile city and space. We were surprised that the Waldorf was so accommodating to such a small group and that the costs were so reasonable. Not being as much of an American as I am today (I became a naturalized citizen in 1985), I did not understand how important a holiday the July 4th weekend was for most Americans. Nor did I realize how intolerable New York weather could be at that time of year. The hotel welcomed any group that was either courageous or foolish enough to brave this weekend. They found one other—a Bavarian-American cultural group—but more about that later.

About a month before the event, Mark and I were walking to ICH's offices on Sunset Boulevard in Hollywood when I let him know that, as of that moment, as a result of disappointing registration, ICH was currently $55,000 in debt, and we had thirty days to close up the gap. Since knowing Mark, I had never seen his face paler than it was at that moment. Eventually, registrations picked up, and we had just over four hundred delegates but still hundred fewer than we needed. What saved us was a group of ceramists who agreed to donate works to an auction at the Waldorf to benefit the event, and the monies from that brought us within two thousand dollars of our goal. Mark and I paid off the remaining money from our own pockets.

The symposium itself was everything we had hoped for; great papers and panels by David Queenberry, David Hamilton, Michael McTwigan, Philip Rawson, and others. There was an imbalance in favour of British speakers this time, mainly because they were better schooled and more erudite on the subject at hand. The audience of writers, curators, artists, dealers, and others, made up for in intensity and sophistication that which it lacked in numbers. Alas, the weather was appalling. The city was gripped by a record-breaking heat wave. It was like being in a kiln, a metaphor that was too close to home for comfort. Then, too, there was a bizarre disruption late on Saturday night.

The Bavarian cultural group, resplendent in their costume dirndls and lederhosen (leather, even for shorts, was a poor fashion choice in hundred-degree weather), ran amok at midnight after their annual celebration. Those of us who were not kept awake by the fighting, singing, and all-night revelry—scores of our delegates were moved in the early hours of the morning by hotel staff to floors that were quieter and safer—woke up Sunday morning to an extraordinary sight. Police and insurance adjustors moved through the hotel, nudging awake the naked and semi-naked men who were unconscious in the corridors and stairwells, removing lederhosen from the most improbable places, hosing half-digested meals from the walls, and assessing the serious damage to their rooms. By contrast, the only trace of our presence was the occasional but ubiquitous white footprints left on the carpets from clay-covered shoes.

THIRD INTERNATIONAL CERAMICS SYMPOSIUM, 1983
HISTORICAL REFERENCES IN CONTEMPORARY CERAMIC ART

Soon after the New York event, we were contacted by the Contemporary Art Society (CAS) of Kansas City, an active, progressive group that decided that ceramics and its emerging role in the fine arts was a topic ripe for serious attention—thanks in part to Ken Ferguson (the head of the ceramics department at the Kansas City Art Institute), who tirelessly promoted the medium. The carrot they offered was a large exhibition at the Nelson Atkins Museum of Art (then America's fifth largest art museum.) I was invited to be its curator; and the exhibition's title, *Ceramic Echoes: Historical References in Contemporary Ceramic Art*, became the logical focus for the symposium. This time it was Lennie Berkowitz, a member of the CAS, who took on the role of organizing director. Over seven hundred delegates showed up with a stronger international contingent than ever before.

The exhibition was large, well received, and beautifully installed in the museum's soaring neo-classical galleries, taking full advantage of the fact that the Nelson-Atkins had two particular plums in their holdings of ceramics: a rich, broad collection of Asian ceramics, and the huge Burnap Collection of early British ceramics, particularly strong in Delftwares and slipwares. Contemporary artists were paired with pieces from centuries and millennia ago that inspired their work, an exercise both in continuity and transformation. The four-day symposium, from October 14th to 16th, took place at the Hilton-Plaza Hotel, a mere five-minute walk to the museum.

At the symposium, speakers navigated the difficult line between historicism and postmodernist appropriation: a problematic divide in ceramics, where the temptation is often to fall back on imitating the past instead of using it to engage the present. The organization, thanks to Berkowitz and her team of volunteers, was exemplary. From the opening ceremony (a charming award ceremony honouring Beatrice Wood, and a masterful keynote address entitled, "The Echoing '80s: Hierarchal Breakdown and Media Confusion" by Patterson Simms (then the curator of the permanent collection, Whitney Museum of American Art) to the closing paper by Philip Rawson, ran without a hitch.

The only sour note was an exchange between Michael McTwigan and myself. McTwigan was speaking on a panel, "The Future of Clay," on Sunday, the last day of the program. My angry public response to McTwigan's remarks, just before I introduced Philip Rawson's closing keynote, was excessive and discomforting for the audience no matter whose side of the brouhaha they took. It is one of those moments in life that, if life were a film, one would have preferred to have left on the floor of the editing studio.

This symposium highlighted the dangers of not having a permanent home for the CAF. The archives were left in the hands of the CAS, and one of their members accidentally threw out the boxes of delegates' registration forms, photographs, tapes of the speakers, and all written papers, including a handwritten copy of the closing address by Philip Rawson—a terrible loss, although his catalogue text, used here, is close to the original. A few papers have survived, courtesy of the exhibition catalogue and other sources; but despite contacting the speakers, little has been recovered. This was partly due to the fact that few papers were presented as written documents, partly because many of the speakers were artists (Joe Bova, Rick Dillingham, Adrian Saxe, Betty Woodman) who did not follow academic protocols and yet had fascinating information to pass along.

FOURTH INTERNATIONAL CERAMICS SYMPOSIUM, 1985
EDGES: IN THOUGHT, IN HISTORY, IN CLAY

Ann Mortimer proved the "never say never" rule when she surprised us by suggesting that the next symposium take place in Toronto, with her and Marge Malouf as the organizing directors. After our first event in Syracuse, Ann had sworn that she would never take on a job like that again. But being a loyal Canadian, she wanted her country's ceramists to benefit from the presence and excitement that came with the International Symposium. Entitled *Edges: In Thought, In History, In Clay*, it attracted over five hundred delegates (a more international audience than before) to Toronto from October 17th to 20th. They came, not just for the speakers, but also for the enormous arts festival, with dozens of exhibitions, including the first retrospective show of Hans Coper's work on the American continent at the Gardiner Museum of Ceramic Art.

It was, again, a triumph of organization and content, due to Mortimer's experience and Malouf's dedication and energy. It comprised seventeen papers, sixteen panel discussions, forty-eight exhibitions, and seventeen new films on ceramics. There were many exciting moments: from Doris Shadbolt quoting Léopold

Foulem's dictum during her keynote address that "craft is what you piss in—art is what your piss on"[2] to Ed Lebow using words like scalpels to objectively dissect the oeuvre of Ken Price. In one of the moving highlights, sculptor George Jeanclos, opened his talk with the line, "I am French and a Jew."[3] He left much of his audience in tears after his moving presentation about his aesthetic journey as a French-Jewish artist who, as a teenager lived for nearly a year in the forests to evade the Vichy police, foraging for food and living like animal.

Martin Smith, another speaker, wrote of his experience at the symposium in *Crafts*, noting that, while the event was international, what impressed him most was the state of Northern American culture. As he put it, North American culture

> …is in a much healthier state than British. Attitudes are more open and opportunities greater, but the most significant difference is the level of debate, which revolves around quality and intention, in contrast to our own parochial hang-ups about the proper work of the potter.[4]

In a lengthy and rigorous examination of the event for *ArtsAtlantic*, Astrid Brunner wrote,

> The audience was guided with fervour, sadness, alacrity, irony... .*Edges* was very sotto voce, civilized, and understated. The philosophers discoursed, the historians narrated, the poets sang....There was an accord about something named, perhaps no one noticed. The accord came from the deep—a kind of *zeitgeist*, if one still talked that way—that had to do with a great expectation to find a new discourse for what is taking place in clay.[5]

FIFTH INTERNATIONAL CERAMICS SYMPOSIUM, 1986
AMERICAN CERAMICS TODAY

In 1985, David Queensberry, who had been my supervising professor at the Royal College of Art, suggested that I assist the Victoria and Albert Museum (V&A) in putting together a collection of ceramics. Its holding of American ceramics at that time was embarrassingly slight. Mark and I approached all the galleries dealing with ceramics in the United States and some collectors who had a record of being generous donors to museums. A collection of forty pieces, then valued at around a quarter of a million dollars (including work by Peter Voulkos, Betty Woodman, Adrian Saxe and others) was assembled, and the V&A produced both an exhibition of the gift (curated by Oliver Watson, the keeper of ceramics) and a modest, popular book.

It seemed a perfect opportunity for the next symposium, the fifth, but with a twist. Even though the bias of CAF was towards scholarly papers, this time we decided to create a casual forum (organized by John Huntingford) for American ceramists to enter into an unscripted dialogue with their British counterparts, hence the absence of any papers from this symposium in the selection. The symposium on May 14th and 15th attracted a capacity crowd in the V&A's distinctive, august auditorium, with its life-size nineteenth-century portraits of greats from the arts and sciences arrayed around the theater. Many ceramic students attended, their registration fees paid for by American collectors from a fund assembled for this purpose.

Interestingly, this outburst of generosity and sharing, did not have quite the effect we had anticipated. The students were very open and excited to experience a different kind of ceramic culture through the speakers—Susanne Stephenson, Ken Ferguson, Betty Woodman, Jerry Rothman, Adrian Saxe, Anna Silver, Bill Daley,

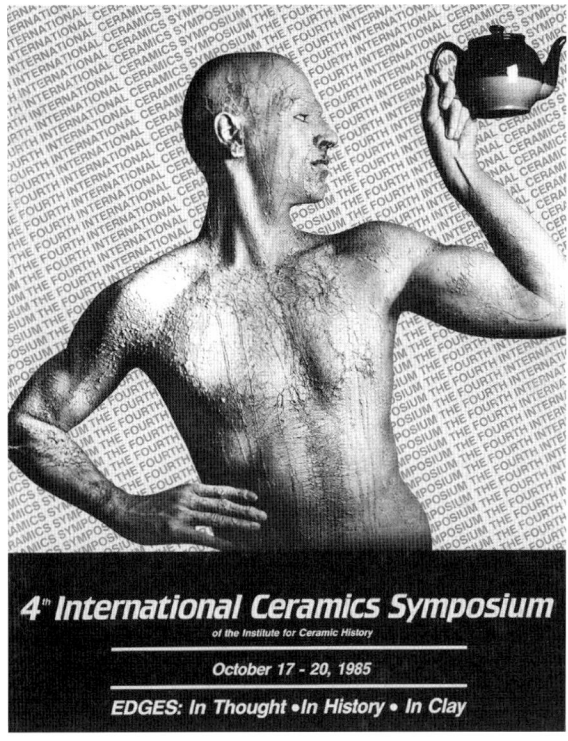

PROGRAM COVER, *FOURTH INTERNATIONAL CERAMICS SYMPOSIUM*, VICTORIA & ALBERT MUSEUM, LONDON, OCTOBER, 1985.

and non-artists Michael McTwigan and me—but many leading ceramists of this island state were clearly in a defensive mood. It was as though the marines had occupied the London offices of the Craftsman Potter's Association. We thought it was an exchange. They saw it as an invasion. Had the same event taken place in reverse, the response would have been more welcoming, and it left us puzzled.

Peter Dormer spotted this and wrote in a review that "some of our own and best people were jealous" of the Americans, their access to real critics, their certainty in being artists, and the fact that "anyone raising the art/craft distinction was shot down in a hail of Coke cans." He was at his teasing best in his comments,

It was a Budweiser kind of session. At times this successful symposium was like a USAF reunion of World War II veterans: "Hell, me and the boys took off out of Otis and zapped the clay around some. But that Voulkos was the meanest Daddy of us all." We were treated to some wonderful pots (and some shockers), and the audience swayed to the Glenn Miller confidence and assertiveness in pottery.[6]

SIXTH INTERNATIONAL CERAMICS SYMPOSIUM, 1991
EAST AND WEST

The burden of overseeing the international symposia and running a gallery and writing books had become too great for me to continue, so we passed this baton on to the Everson Museum, which with its large collection of twentieth-century ceramics, seemed to be the perfect permanent home for this ongoing event. Barbara Perry, the curator of the ceramics collection, took on the job of organizer. The symposium was now well established, drawing a serious audience of over five to seven hundred delegates for each conference. The Everson produced an elegant exhibition, *Influence of Japanese Art*, and explored the subject further in the conference.

While we had given over control to the Everson, CAF had an emotional investment in the future of this event; and as we began to quarrel over plans, it became an interesting clash between the pragmatism of our small group and the ivory-tower culture of the museum world. We became concerned as the planning evolved. The prospectus came out too late, just three months before the symposium, whereas international conferences need at least a year to nine months' advance notice. The subject, while important, has been dealt with in so many other exhibitions and conferences that it excited little interest. We began to ring alarm bells but were dismissed as meddlers and rebuked in a letter from the museum that claimed, wrongly I believe, that the museum world was not in show business. Our concerns proved real. Less than fifty delegates signed up for the event, less than a tenth of our usual audience. No papers of consequence were delivered.

SEVENTH INTERNATIONAL CERAMICS SYMPOSIUM, 1993
HISTORY AND ITS ROLE IN CONTEMPORAPY CERAMICS ART CRITICISM, SCHOLARSHIP, EDUCATION

Fences were mended, and with the new curator, Tom Piche, as organizer, a more energetic effort went into the seventh symposium. It attracted slightly over a hundred delegates and this time produced several memorable papers, notably those by Paul Greenhalgh who bristled with energy, intelligence, and insight, and the always-edgy Léopold Foulem. The talk by Foulem, the uncontested *agent provocateur* of Canadian ceramics, was wickedly uncompromising, dealing with homosexual content in ceramics (a margin within the marginalized); and his remarks about the growing gay sensibility in clay as an honest, authentic counterpoint to "scenes of insipid heterosexuality" in court porcelains provoked a walkout by several audience members. While the symposium had improved, it was clear that the Everson, while it had the best of intentions, was not the ideal home. The International Ceramics Symposium was atrophying, and so we reached an amicable agreement to return the symposium to CAF.

EIGHTH INTERNATIONAL CERAMICS SYMPOSIUM, 1999
CERAMIC MILLENNIUM: A LEADERSHIP CONGRESS FOR THE CERAMIC ARTS

Ceramic Millennium: A Leadership Conference for the Ceramic Arts was, from the outset, conceived as a blockbuster event. It was our first symposium on the European continent. Amsterdam was chosen as the host city for a variety of reasons: the openness of the Dutch to ceramic art, the generosity of their government in supporting cultural events (particularly those that explored new ground), the warmth of its people, its long history of openness and internationalism, and its accessibility. It proved to be a perfect choice.

Encouraged and advised by the late Benno Premsela, the Netherlands' unofficial minister of the arts—and with a sister non-profit corporation to CAF (or a *stichting* in Dutch) in Holland created for this event—we set out to raise funds and begin to gather an audience with the somewhat cheeky catch-line of our advertisements reading: "After July, 1999, there will only be two kinds of people in the ceramic arts: those who attended the *Ceramic Millennium* and those who did not."

Our *stichting* was lead by two capable men: briefly by Geert Dales and then by an effective, down-to-earth Friso Broeksma. Preparation for this event took five years and one million dollars, attracting 3,500 participants and sixty-five national delegations from around the world. It had five components: the symposium, an art fair, a major ceramics film festival (produced from Hollywood by Tony Marsh and Patti Marcus and which has since travelled to four continents), and an arts festival of seventy-three exhibitions throughout Europe overseen by Yvonne Joris[7] and, lastly, the Caravans. These were tours, following the symposium, to Germany's salt-glaze region, with its plethora of ceramics museums; Faenza, Italy, to view the fiftieth Concorso Internationale della Ceramica, amongst other treats; Stoke-on-Trent, which was enormously rich in information and the sleeper of the Caravans; and, lastly, Barcelona. Also, the faithful Anne Mortimer, our organizing council member-at-large was an important contributor, as was Susan Tunick, one of the members of a forty-one nation World Advisory Committee.

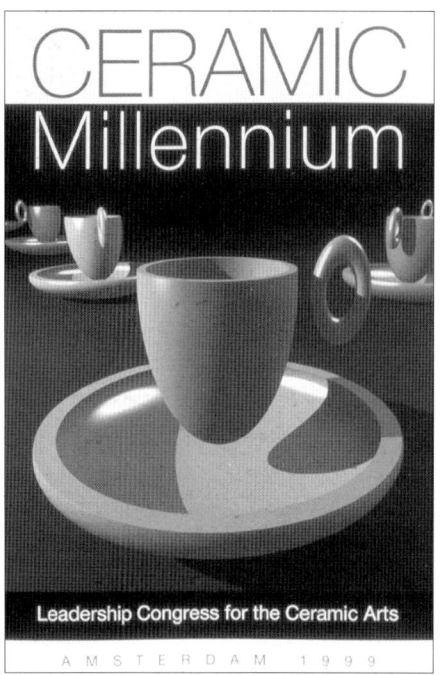

PROGRAM COVER, *EIGHTH INTERNATIONAL CERAMICS SYMPOSIUM*, AMSTERDAM, 1999.

We were able to pull this off, in part, because of CAF's unconventional approach. Usually these events are produced by large committees that become bogged down in politics and personality. While we had an army of valued advisors from around the world, the American side of this project was developed, promoted, and managed by a three-person team: me, Mark Del Vecchio (veteran of all of the symposia since 1981), with Dawn Bennett as the organizing director. We met every week early on, then every day, and enjoyed perfect working chemistry for a trio of opinionated and independent thinkers. We were each given a great deal of freedom to make decisions unilaterally and so could move at speed and were a highly efficient team. Bennett was a hard taskmaster, and her travel itineraries were the equivalent of forced marches. She sent me off on one mission—to develop the Caravans—that took me from New York to ten cities and back in seven days! On another occasion she agreed to us being at six meetings in three Dutch cities on the same day, and we were on time for each, thanks to the Netherlands' reliable intercity train service.

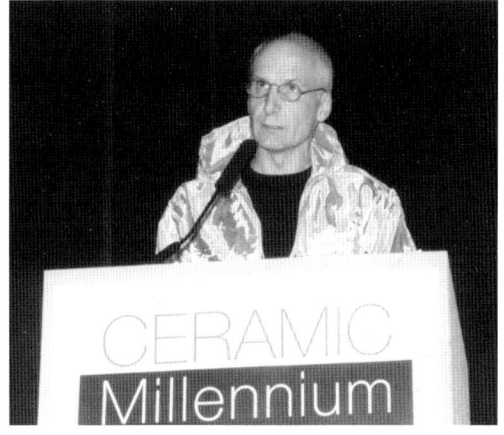

GARTH CLARK SPEAKING AT THE OPENING CEREMONY OF *EIGHTH INTERNATIONAL CERAMICS SYMPOSIUM, AMSTERDAM*, JULY 13, 1999. HIS JACKET, MADE FROM NYLON, ALUMINUM, AND MICROSCOPIC CERAMIC BEADS, LOOKED LIKE LIQUID MERCURY UNDER THE LIGHTS AND CAUSED AS MUCH COMMENT AS ANY MOMENT IN THE CONFERENCE.

Delegates arrived in the evening at the RAI Conference Centre's huge auditorium and were greeted by giant *Ceramic Millennium* flags fluttering in a semi circle at the entrance to this complex, the seventh largest conference center in Europe. The evening began with the lights dimming, and swelling music introducing a widescreen digital fanfare by Jeroen Bechtold, in which a fleet of flying cups and saucers raced out of space and formed the event's logo. What followed was meat enough for a conference in itself. The Dutch minister of culture, Dr. Rick Van der Ploeg, opened the event. With typical Dutch bluntness, he observed that he first found the event's title "rather pompous." But he went on to say:

On further reflection, I find it appropriate. For thousands of years, from the beginnings of civilization around the world, human beings have transformed the elements of clay, water, fire, and air into dwellings, produced pots, and designed the sacred objects and items that we now call art.[8]

Ten awardees were honoured. Broeksma, in his welcome to the delegates, showed a slide taken thirty years ago of one of the honourees, the architect and designer Ettore Sottsass, which showed him seated in the same auditorium and in exactly the same seat, a charming, unexpected moment. He repeated that same procedure with Claes Oldenburg, one of the keynote speakers. Then the film *Pot-Shots* by Roger Law was screened. We had commissioned this for the opening ceremony (for an unreasonably small amount of money—but all that we had). Law is the founder of *Spitting Image*, a satiric spoof using puppets that was one of Britain's highest rated TV programs and the feared bane of the political establishment. He did not disappoint those who knew and loved his "take-no-prisoners" approach. His film, *Pot-Shots*, featured the comedian and failed potter, Johnny Vegas (who later made a live appearance in the program). It was a wild twenty minutes (the latter coming as a surprise, as it was agreed that it would be seven minutes in a evening already too long) in which Vegas, depressed by his failure as an artist, took out his frustration on a room full of pots by Britain's top potters.

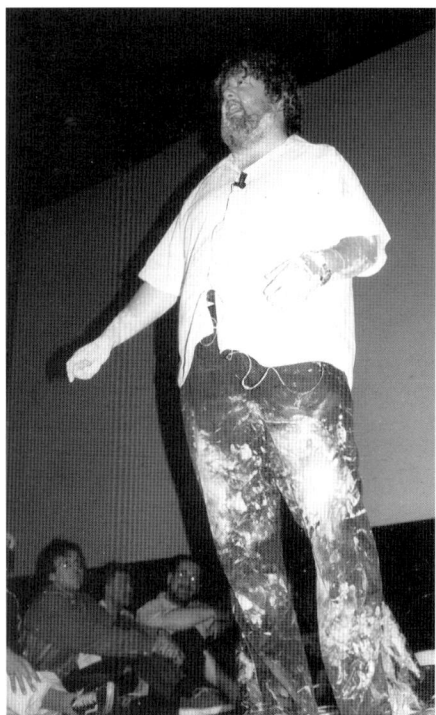

JOHNNY VEGAS AT THE *EIGHTH INTERNATIONAL CERAMICS SYMPOSIUM*, AMSTERDAM, 1999.

The artists had all given Law pots to smash, mostly vessels with flaws and little actual value but clearly recognizable to this audience as their work. Also, he had made a few ersatz pots, seemingly by Hans Coper and Lucie Rie, to add further anxiety to the destruction derby, which was, admittedly, shocking to witness. This morphed into scenes showing a sex-crazed George E. Ohr at work (à la *Ghost*) and then reached its high point (or nadir for many in this partly conservative clay audience) when Vegas, now playing the French Mannerist, Bernard Palissy, having run out of fuel for his kiln, tossed his infant child into the flames to keep the temperature stable!

The husband-and-wife team of Oldenburg and Koosje van Bruggen gave a memorable talk, a yin-yang, left brain-right brain kind of experience. Oldenburg was casual, relaxed, and funny as he took us through a catalogue of his rejected City projects, while van Bruggen, a tough intellectual, spoke eloquently but formally on theory, both buttressing their art, handing the microphone backwards and forwards to each other in an ongoing dialogue. It should have been schizophrenic and disjointed, but actually, it was a seamless conversation that made more and more sense as their presentation progressed. Finally, the program ended almost an hour behind schedule, long but not boring, and we moved into the entrance hall in search of Dutch beer and Genever and a buffet of *bitterbollen* and other national treats.

We were buoyed by the same frisson that many of us had felt in Syracuse: that sure knowledge that something remarkable was beginning to happen, and the next three days proved that the feeling was warranted. It will be unfair to single out any of the speakers. The quality was remarkable, as the papers reproduced here attest. Artists' presentations on their own work were kept brief (twenty minutes) and were riveting, interspersed like a taste of sorbet between longer courses of more formal presentations. The richness of information was at times overwhelming.

Delegates were summoned back to the auditorium after the coffee and lunch breaks by the sound of further violence being done to ceramics. This had inadvertently become the leitmotif of the event. (Out with the old, in with the new?) Del Vecchio had noticed that, every time the camera caresses a pot in a film, it means only one thing: that pot has only a few minutes to live. His *Smashing Pots* assembled these moments of ceramic carnage from the great movies into several five-minutes assemblages, with Judy Garland, Jackie Chan, Michael Jackson, Eddie Murphy, and Kathleen Turner amongst the movie-star destroyers of vases, dinnerware, and Staffordshire figures. We ran each segment just before the start of a new session, often bringing delegates back a few minutes early, determined not to miss one minute of Del Vecchio's compilations (done with the assistance of Arthur Williams and Tape House, his post-production service company).

Mention does need to be made of the performance by Johnny Vegas (a.k.a. Michael Pennington). Vegas failed in his ambitions to become a potter and, looking for a career, turned to stand-up comedy. Winner of the coveted Perrier Award, one of Britain's great honours for comedy, he admits to being the only show-business star whose dream is to be on the cover of *Ceramic Review*. He performs behind a wheel, throwing pots and dragging unsuspecting members from the audience onto the stage, bantering incessantly and creating his signature one-minute teapots that are literally thrown and assembled in sixty seconds. (The one he produced onstage that afternoon was acquired by the Victoria and Albert Museum.) He treated the assembled audience, mainly ceramists, to an over-the-edge, manic and hilarious routine, just this side of chaos, that, as Chris Staley commented to me afterwards, was like sitting through a marathon psychotherapy session devised specifically to treat the disorders, fears, and dreams of the ceramic artist.

The official symposium program ended with the screening of *Seni's Children*, the Gold Award winner for the best new film on ceramic art. It was a portrait by director Philip Hass and producer Fernando Trueba of of Seni Camara, a self-taught Senegalese artist who made bizarre half-human, half-creature figures from clay. Then, worn out by the talks, issues, debates, semantics, and theory, we got together later for the Mud Ball at the Kransapolsky Hotel, with Andy Anderson of New York's famed Roxy imported for the event. It proved to be the perfect way to decompress, and Anderson kept the crowd sweating and moving until the very early hours of the morning.

On Saturday morning a number of focus meetings were held at various venues around the city, where small groups of professionals in specific fields could discuss various issues arising from the proceedings. These low-key gatherings, bleary eyed and exhausted as we were (not just from the dancing but also a week of parties given every night by various museums and public galleries), gave an interesting and intimate closure to a momentous week that was often larger than life.

It could not have worked better. Our vision set the course, and our energy provided the engine; but this event was again a triumph of a ceramics movement reaching a new maturity, and the labours of a vast team. Two hundred people are thanked in the program brochure for their various contributions, and the final number of those who assisted was probably closer to three hundred. Again, ceramics proved that it did not have to be the stepchild of the arts but could produce a gathering of its clans equal in its professionalism and sophistication to anything any other art medium could put together. It has left, aside from the ongoing intellectual stimulation that it initiated, a legacy of affirmation for ceramics as an art form.

A Tenth Symposium?
Ceramic Canon

A tenth symposium? That suggestion, if made within twenty-four months of the *Ceramic Millennium*, would have been ridiculed. But all wounds heal eventually, and we slowly began to realize that CAF's job, as much as we wanted to ignore the fact, was not yet done. Astrid Brunner's comments about the *Edges* conference in 1983 still resonated. As she pointed out, while the Toronto conference searched for that "new discursive language" it did not find exactly what it sought. With each succeeding conference, we came closer. But there remains, for all our efforts and those of others, a missing core to our scholarship that deals with language and canon. So *Ceramic Canon* is now in the early stage of preparation. No date has been selected as yet, although either 2007 or 2008 are likely. Nor has a venue been chosen for the planning conferences.

This is going to be a symposium unlike any other. It will be preceded by a dozen invitation-only mini-conferences for writers, critics, and historians to argue how ceramic achievement should be evaluated and—even more controversially—to select who the "greats" of the twentieth century are and why. The results of the dozen working sessions will be presented at a public symposium in New York City. But even at this final stage, it will be different from other events. Any delegate registering must, as a condition of attendance, provide us with their own list of twentieth-century masters and then will be called upon to vote for or against candidates for canonization during the symposium itself. After the inevitable clamour of controversy and debate that such a process must provoke (and the book of proceedings has gone to press) CAF may choose terminal dormancy as its future. It will have fulfilled its own role in the greater mission, and we never wanted it to become a permanent institution. Closure is part of CAF's plan. Good entrances are crucial. So, too, are good exits. And because they happen last, they are remembered longer.

1. This quotation is from the introductory remarks to Janet Koplos's talk at the *Ceramic Millennium* in Amsterdam, which is not part of her paper.
2. From Doris Shadlbolt's address reproduced in this volume.
3. Quoted in Astrid Brunner's "Edges in Thought, In History, In Clay," *ArtsAtlantic* (Spring, 1986) 53.
4. Martin Smith, "International Ceramics Symposium," *Crafts*. Issue number not available.
5. Brunner, 52.
6. Peter Dormer, "Commentary," *Crafts* (July/August, 1986) 198.
7. These exhibitions included Anthony Gormley's *Ceramic Fields: a Survey of Ceramics by the CoBrA Group*; the huge, spacious *541 Pots* at the Stedelijk Museum, Amsterdam; and various other group, theme, and solo shows with works by George E. Ohr, Peter Voulkos, Geert Lap, Colenbrander, Pablo Picasso, Ken Price, Ron Nagle, Lucie Rie, and Wouter Dam.
8. Rick Van der Ploeg, "Speech on the occasion of the opening of the *Ceramic Millennium*, Tuesday, 13 July, 1999." Manuscript in the archives of the Ceramic Arts Foundation, unpaginated.

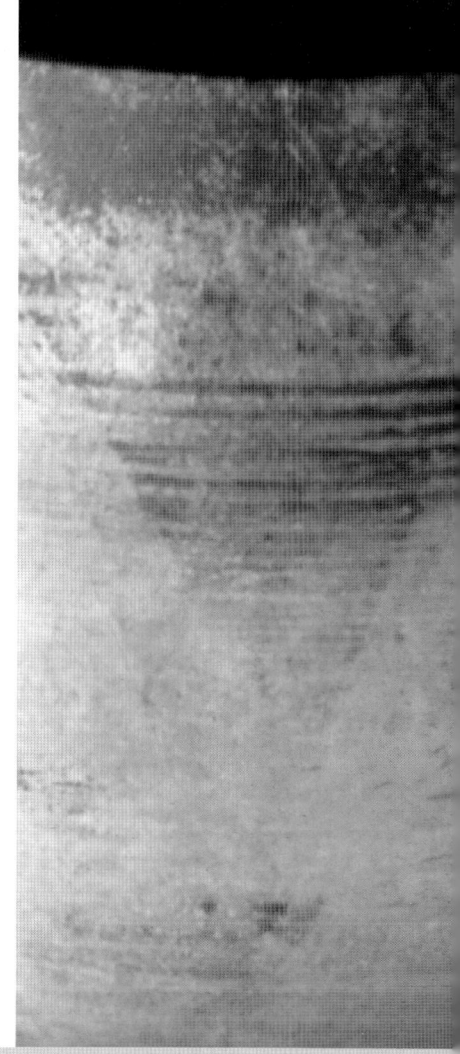
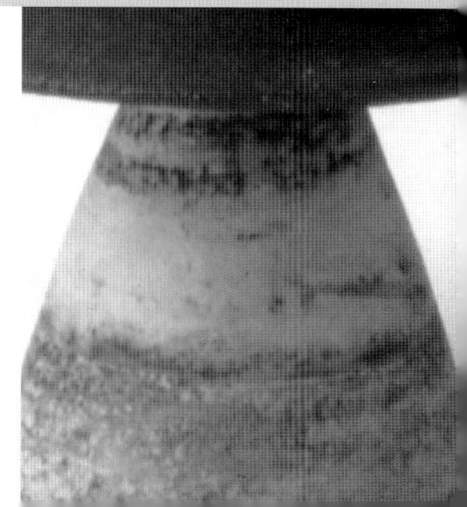

SECTION ONE
STATUS OF CLAY

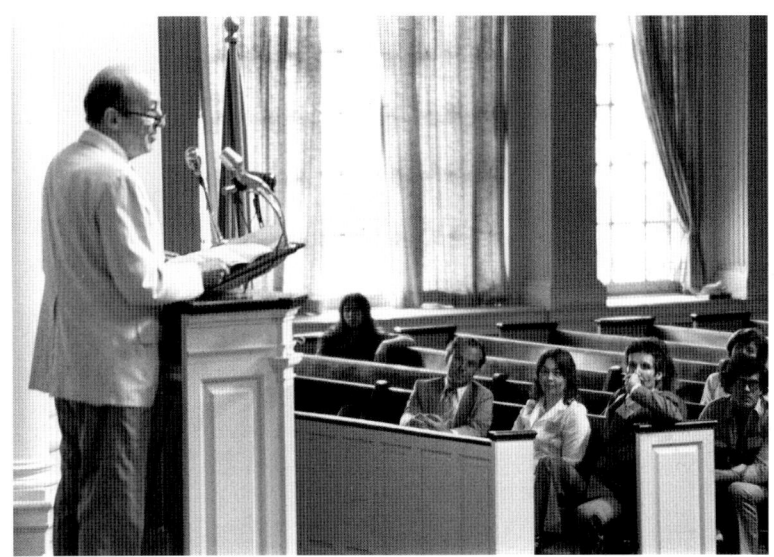

Clement Greenberg delivering the keynote address at the *First International Ceramics Symposium*, Hendricks Chapel, Syracuse University, June 1, 1979.

CHAPTER 1

STATUS OF CLAY

CLEMENT GREENBERG

Well, is ceramics getting—or going to get—as photography has, the benefit of this recent levelling of status? The question requires two different answers. The one has to do with opinion, the other with actual achievement, with aesthetic results.

Presented at *The Ceramics Symposium*, 1979, Syracuse

Of course, I'm flattered to have been asked to talk on this occasion, and to talk first, no less. But I remain diffident for a very good reason. I haven't had that much experience of clay. Yes, I know what I like, and knowing what you like is where art starts from, for both beholder and artist. But where art starts from isn't quite enough. Where it continues may matter more; by "continues" I mean the development, through sustained experience, of your eye, your taste as regards the given medium, in this case, clay.

What I have to admit is that I haven't sought out ceramic art as I have painting and sculpture and literature, too, and even photography and music. I haven't made a point of consorting with, hanging around, ceramic art. Not that I'm complacent about this, far from it. I haven't paid all that much attention to architecture, and I'm not complacent about that either.

The fact is that I did in the past give in, as other people have, to the notion that ceramics was largely craft, and that craft was just craft. I didn't hold this notion consciously, and I do remember feeling that I couldn't get the aesthetic force of a vase or bowl from a photograph, as I felt I could do with most other utilitarian objects. But still I didn't visit most of the clay shows within reach. Though at the time I admired Shang and Chou bronzes enormously (knowing the clay prototypes that lay behind them), I was also entranced by Persian pottery of the Islamic period, especially the colour that went into its decoration.

I'd intended to talk here about the state of visual art in general at this time, but then I read Garth Clark's catalogue text. It set many things going in my mind that hadn't been there before. It also awakened echoes of my experience in other arts, other mediums.

Ceramists worry about the status of their art. I remember when photographers did that too. Photography's status had had many ups and downs, with some of the latter going even further down, maybe, than ceramics' status. There were so many times when photography was written off as being too mechanical to qualify as art. After being more or less up in the 1920s, 1930s, and in the latter 1940s, art photography faded from serious critical attention, at least that's my impression. I know that I, myself, didn't feel called on to review photography as often as I had before then. Whether this was photography's fault or my own, I can't really say. I'd like to think it wasn't my own.

Well, what happened towards the end of the 1960s (when I was no longer reviewing regularly) changed this situation. Medium–scrambling and medium–mixing came in, between painting and sculpture at first, and then between these and other mediums. The idea of the sanctity of the boundaries between the different mediums lost its hold. At the same time painting and sculpture proper—in the sense of tradition—began to lose something of their status in relation to other arts (environmental, "earth," decorative, etc., etc.). I won't say that medium–scrambling, in itself, is either good or bad. It's but a means, and means in themselves don't pertain in art, only results do. Maybe most of the results of recent medium–scrambling haven't turned out so well, but this may change. One beneficial, if rather indirect, outcome of medium–scrambling has been, by levelling the hierarchy of the visual arts, to re-enhance the aesthetic status of photography. People no longer ask, as they used to, whether photography is "really" art. The whole question of the relative status of the different mediums or arts is being phased out (to use current jargon). For instance, it can now be more readily admitted that Rembrandt often drew and etched better than he painted (especially, as I think, in his last years); that is, that his papers can be better than his canvases.

Well, is ceramics getting—or going to get—as photography has, the benefit of this recent levelling of status? The question requires two different answers. The one has to do with opinion; the other with actual achievement, with aesthetic results. I won't venture to say that photography has gained as much, lately, in terms of such results as it has in those of attention and opinion. Maybe it has; maybe it hasn't needed to. Maybe photography did far better during the decades in which initiated opinion was turned away from it, far better qua art, than now. (I can't tell; I haven't paid enough attention to photography these past years.)

But back to ceramic art. It seems to me that it's getting more serious attention of late. But still not enough (which "enough" includes me). The question still asks for more than one answer. Attention is a matter of opinion. Is that what ceramists want most: favourable opinion? Or are achievements, aesthetic results, what are wanted most, regardless of opinion? And then, too, the answer, with its question, breaks down into two further parts in a way particular to the nature of ceramics. Mr. Clark's text reminded me that there is ceramics as vessel making: functional and utilitarian; and there is ceramics as free, "fine" art. He writes: "Despite the hopes of the 1960s, ceramics has not emerged as a convincing sculptural genre."[1] Emerged how? As opinion convincing or as actual achievement, as aesthetic results? I say that the second is, by far, the more important question, just as it's been with photography. Are ceramists to bother about whether they're put down as potters or hailed as sculptors? Should they—and we—care about nomenclature? Opinion changes; achievement stays. Achievement also erases the difference between the utilitarian, the vessels and fine-art sculpture. Once again, results experienced, not discussed or debated, are all that count when it comes to art as art.

Clay has been an ongoing medium for sculpture all along, long before the terra cottas of Tanagra, and ever since. In France from the eighteenth century on, sculptors like Hudson, Clodion, and Carpeaux were, I myself find, far better in terra cotta than in any other material. I think Degas's clay or putty maquettes are even better than his finished bronzes. But since these artists didn't make vessels, they can't be brought under the heading of ceramists. A worry about terms, nothing more.

So let ceramists proper (to earn that appellation would they have to make vessels too?) contribute to sculpture proper. Let clay be a final, definitive medium for sculpture proper instead of it serving as paper used to serve painting proper (I'm not sure the analogy is a just one). And let's suppose that ceramic art, done by artists who were clay handlers before anything else, got accepted as sculpture proper—that and nothing less. Would this redound to the credit of ceramics? I altogether doubt it. I don't need precedent in order to prophesy here that the ceramics accepted as sculpture would be altogether lost to the art of clay as far as opinion and nomenclature were concerned; it would simply be assimilated to sculpture as such, sculpture as always. The artists responsible would no longer be called ceramists but sculptors *tout court*, like Donatello and Rodin and David Smith. That this hasn't quite happened yet, or only half-happened is, as I think, because no full-fledged ceramist of this or recent time has yet managed to take himself seriously as a sculptor, that is, as distinct from an object maker. The case has been different, ironically enough, for certain sculptors and even painters who are strictly amateurs in clay.

In Mrs. Hughto's *New Clay Project* (worked at here in Syracuse, at the University, and shown at the Everson) sculptors proper and painters, too, took part. They were all more or less strangers to clay. That was the idea. Some of them, the sculptors particularly, but also one or two painters, found new openings for their own art in the process. And, lo and behold, look what they did with their openings and discoveries. Caro and Steiner, to name two, ended up by translating them into bronze, where they were lost to ceramics, lost utterly and irrevocably to sculpture proper; that is, if we go by nomenclature, by the naming of names, by fidelity to classifications and labels. Ceramics gets left, abandoned, to the lowly vessel maker: *ceramics* proper, that is. But let the vessel maker not despair. There's nothing that says that a great pot can't match a great statue in aesthetic value. Let the vessel maker show us that. There are no rules or prescriptions or laid–down–in–advance categories of value in art.

Mr. Clark's next sentence after the one quoted earlier reads: "The ceramist still lacks a platform for contemporary appreciation at depth."[2] Margie Hughto, in her preface, writes: "There still is a realm of the unknown, in terms of judging the quality of ceramics. The number of ceramists working continues to expand and yet the criticism evaluating the work doesn't."[3] I don't believe these complaints to be all that justified or, to be more exact, necessary. So much of the best art of the past got along without written, publicized criticism. The question for ambitious ceramists is not so much formal criticism but attention. Does what the ceramists do, whether creating vessels or "fine" art, get noticed and talked about enough? Without these—attention and the talk that reflects attention—no art or artist fares well. Here, with respect to informal, to what I'd call "private" criticism, Mr. Clark and Mrs. Hughto may have a real point.

After my visit to the show at the Everson, I'm persuaded that they do. For *me* that show raises the issue of aesthetic quality in ceramic art as it's never been raised before. Mr. Clark pays tactful heed to this issue in his catalogue text. But is it raised enough elsewhere? I can't tell, being the outsider I am. But I can tell that ceramics as high art is caught up in the situation of art in general in this time. A review of the past would help to throw light on that situation.

My knowledge may be a little shaky, but it seems to me a fact that the ceramic art of the past began to get its due in our Western culture—its larger due—only some hundred–odd years ago. Vases and bowls and cups and dishes began to be taken more seriously as art, and no longer as just curiosities or as things, precious mostly for their historical or exotic origins (Greek vases have been the exception, but that was because of their rather undecorative decoration). This was also when Western taste, as well as art making, began to open up to exotic traditions as no other tradition of taste before had opened up to what was exotic itself. And again, it was also when Western taste began repairing past omissions of taste. All kinds of art, Western and non–Western, have since then been rescued from neglect and inattention.

Modernism didn't set this trend off, but it has done the most maybe, to keep it expanding—Modernism, which insists on expanding taste in general, on opening it to any and everything that can be experienced aesthetically. Well, how did, how has, ceramics as an ongoing, contemporary endeavor made out under this new dispensation? According to Mrs. Hughto and Mr. Clark, not so well in terms of serious critical attention. But how about actual achievement, whether noticed or not? Maybe that remains, for the time being, an open question. If so, it's due to another aspect of the new situation that Modernism brought about.

The best taste has, since the arrival of urban culture, almost always belonged, by and large, to an elite. In the mid–nineteenth century, it became more or less the monopoly of an elite within the elite, of an elite of insiders so to speak, not just of cultivated people. Since Manet, since Baudelaire, just when and while the best neglected extant art of the past was being brought back into the open, the best new art of the present was becoming more and more closed off from cultivated taste at large, becoming more and more the affair of insiders. This paradox would get resolved, and so far has always gotten resolved, with the passing of time, usually in the space of a short generation. Then the best new art, no longer so new, would settle into the continuity of tradition, lose its startlingness, and become accepted by cultivated taste at large. But this would happen, I repeat, only when the new had lost enough of its newness, when it was past the moment of challenge. This situation and this process haven't changed since the mid–nineteenth century. The best new art continues to get resisted and rejected in its own present moment as much today as ever.

The best new art has usually been major art, at least over the last thousand years in the West. Nothing says that ceramics can't produce major art. It already has, in the Far East, in Persia, in pre-Columbian America. I don't know about the West: I'll have to be instructed there. But no matter. What matters is whether ceramic art of major quality is going to be produced here and now, and that's up to ceramists themselves. They can't wait for serious critical attention to get demonstrated in print. Their art, by its strength, will have to compel such attention. But maybe ceramic art of major quality is already being made in the here and now, and has been in the recent past too. (The Everson show does more than hint that.) I myself can't really tell, or even if I could, I wouldn't feel confident saying so. That's because, to repeat, I'm an outsider to clay and, like all outsiders since the advent of Modernism, have to wait a while in order to recognize the genuinely new. The same situation pertains to painting and sculpture (where I don't feel myself an outsider): there, too, the outsiders still have to wait before becoming able to recognize the genuinely new. Meanwhile, the best new painting and sculpture stay in the background. They, too, get little serious formal criticism—not as little as clay does—yet the difference isn't all that great (and ceramists might well congratulate themselves on being spared what mostly passes for serious public criticism of painting and sculpture nowadays).

I say again: let ceramists not bother themselves so much about the lack of serious formal or public criticism in their field. Just let them make their art good enough. And let them resign themselves to the expectation that their best art will get no earlier recognition or acceptance than the best new art in almost every other medium has over the past hundred and thirty years. It will have to wait backstage for a while.

1 Garth Clark, *A Century of Ceramics in the United States 1878-1978* (New York: E.P. Dutton, 1979) 206.
2 Clark, 206.
3 Margie Hughto, Preface, in Garth Clark, *A Century of Ceramics in the United States 1878-1978* (New York: E.P. Dutton, 1979) xvi.

CHAPTER 2

Art Versus Craft: The Issue of Craftsmanship in Twentieth-Century Art

Nancy Selvage

The abstract expressionist approach to ceramics involved a very aggressive manipulation of the clay; in an approach which has been labelled process art, we find a sensibility which may be closer, in some respects, to Zen aesthetics. An artist such as Larry Shep is involved with exploring the inherent qualities of his raw material in conjunction with time. In order to investigate this, it is necessary to keep manipulative intervention to a minimum and to work out a system of organization so skillfully that it is apparent only as a counterpoint to the clay. This approach does not use traditional methods of craftsmanship; rather, it relies on devising an effective, circumscribed situation within which nature can take its course.

Presented at *The Ceramics Symposium*, 1979, Syracuse

As an undergraduate I majored in art history. After four years of looking at masterpieces, prefaced by a colouring-book approach to art in secondary school, I was convinced that being an artist involved inheriting a God-given talent which enabled one to draw with vivid realism at a very early age, based on the conception there was no hope of my becoming an artist. But I did have a desire to form something and finally decided that making pottery might provide me with an appropriate medium. Certainly, I could make bowls and plates, since, presumably, that wouldn't require any aesthetic genius. I guess I must have been under the impression that there was some sort of a universal pottery tradition that one could just plug into. Needless to say, there wasn't; and as I sat at that potter's wheel, I was confronted with a vast range of aesthetic choices.

My dilemma at that wheel was integral to issues involved in the art-versus-craft controversy. These issues have been a subject of concern for well over a century, and they stem from the changing role of the craftsman in an industrial society and from important developments in twentieth-century art—developments which have challenged the traditional concept of craftsmanship. Aspects of these issues have been examined in the panel discussions yesterday and this morning, but I hope that what I have to say about craftsmanship* in relation to issues in twentieth-century art will give us another handle on this subject.

First I would like to briefly deal with issues of function. Function has often been used to determine the boundary between art and craft. If an individual is to support him or herself as a potter, it may be important that the work functions well; but I do not think that this functional need is any more central to the potter's concerns and intent than the need for a painting to be flat or for a sculpture to be of a particular size and orientation in order for it to be effective in its setting. Today very few first-world potters make a pot because they or their clientele have a practical need for a container. Industry has long ago taken care of this level of necessity. The studio potter is presumably working towards satisfying needs beyond those of functional necessity. Whether one makes vessels, graven images, or conceptual investigations, the range of formal choices is equally extensive and the possibility of a quality result equally elusive.

The contemporary American potter, like all fellow artists, is an educated individual, self-conscious of personal identity and capable of certain choices of lifestyle. Being a potter, as does being an artist, involves aesthetic choices, commitment, and risk. Even if a potter believes that one can escape from this competitive, individualistic society by embracing the role of the relatively anonymous craftsman creating simple utilitarian objects, the potter does so in order to realize a personal conception of a good lifestyle. This self-realization, as it has developed from the pioneer experience in America and from attitudes in modern psychology, would have been a liability for the traditional craftsman in tightly circumscribed situations; and it is this concept of self expression that separates the contemporary potter from the field's romanticized past and allies the contemporary potter to contemporary craft.

* Please accept the word "craftsman" and the word "his" as implicitly referring to both genders.

Aesthetic as well as practical impulses emanate from function. We must accept the art-craft dialectic as an integral matrix in all our endeavors.

Early in the twentieth century many important artists accepted pottery as a valid expressive medium. Herbert Read, an extremely insightful critic, wrote in 1930:

> Pottery is at once the simplest and the most difficult of all the arts. It is the simplest because it is the most elemental; it is the most difficult because it is the most abstract. Pottery is pure art; it is art freed from any imitative intention.[1]

This point of view is very interesting to me in light of the fact that it was at the point that artists began to use a more abstract vocabulary that pottery was accepted into the fine arts curriculum and became an important medium for such major artists as Picasso, Miró, and Malevich.

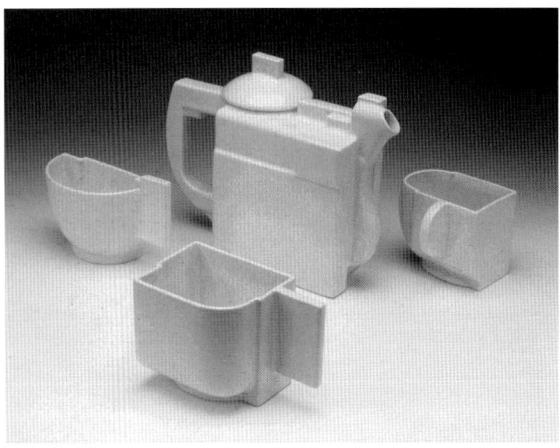

KASIMIR MALEVICH, *SUPREMATIST TEAPOT AND THREE CUPS,*
C.1923. PORCELAIN, 16.5 X 24.1 X 9.1 CM.
COLLECTION: GLORIA AND SONNY KAMM
PHOTO: TONY CUNHA

In Russia between 1918 and 1921, Malevich, Lissitzky, and other young artists designed utilitarian ceramic pieces that were related to their work in painting and sculpture. This interest in pottery and other areas of applied art was philosophically supported by their proletarian conscience which rejected the myth of the artist genius and embraced the art of the people. Malevich learned to knit and embroider, and compared his painting to weaving. This attitude was politically tied to ideas championed by the earlier Arts and Crafts Movement in England; however, the results looked very different, since the Russian avant-garde had incorporated an acceptance of industrial forms with an aesthetic commitment to pure geometry. John Ruskin and William Morris had rejected industry in the name of the people, but Lissitzky accepted the machine in the name of revolution and democracy. For a brief time, purely abstract imagery was accepted by the state as an expression of the new revolutionary spirit; but soon it was denounced in painting and sculpture as non-utilitarian decadence, and many artists migrated to Western Europe. In the meantime pottery probably provided an acceptable utilitarian medium in which artists could explore abstract principles.

In Western Europe artists were also involved with abstraction and excited by technological possibilities. Rayner Banham theorizes that the accessibility of the motor car after 1900 provided artists and intellectuals, for the first time, with personal command over a very powerful machine and that this experience was crucial for the subsequent development of attitudes.[2] Futurist writings are full of impassioned praises of the automobile and the machine and strong denunciations of handicraft. Marinetti wrote: "Nothing is more beautiful that a great humming power-station, holding back the hydraulic pressures of a whole mountain range."[3] In 1912 he attacked John Ruskin and the Arts and Crafts Movement with this statement:

> With his sick dream of a primitive pastoral life; with his nostalgia for Homeric cheeses and legendary spinning-wheels; with his hatred of the machine, this maniac for antique simplicity resembles a man who in a full maturity wants to sleep in his cot again and drink at the breasts of a nurse who has now grown old, in order to regain the carefree state of infancy.[4]

How could such an archaic craft as pottery survive in this atmosphere? Partly, I believe, because it has traditionally been made with a machine—the potter's wheel—which produces regular, symmetrical forms, and partly because clay is a cheap industrial medium. This pot was made by Tullio D'Albisola, a Futurist potter who wrote: "The Futurists have created ceramics characterized by the aesthetics of the machine, by geometry and any desire to return to the hybrid and static classicism is cretinous and unpatriotic."[5] Certainly, the rhetoric is more revolutionary than this pitcher trying not to be a pitcher; but this piece with its blue wrench, has been boldly transformed by hard-edge geometry. In this other Futurist piece, the arrangement of forms is certainly more aligned to a piston-rod vocabulary than to traditional pottery, in spite of the lively, crackled surface. The Futurist's love of the machine involved a repudiation of traditional handicraft in favor of the perfection of ready-made industrial forms, but during this same period, the Bauhaus in Germany emphasized handicraft as an important "learning-by-doing" discipline.

The Bauhaus was formed in 1919 by the fusion of two existing art schools in Weimar: one a traditional academy of fine arts, the other a school for educating industrial designers. Walter Gropius, director of the Bauhaus, wrote:

> Architects, painters and sculptors, we must all turn to the crafts. Then there will be no "professional art." There is no essential difference between the artist and the craftsman: the artist is a craftsman raised to a higher power. In rare moments of illumination, unbidden by conscious will, the Grace of Heaven may cause his handicraft to blossom into art. A groundwork of craft-discipline is essential to every artist.[6]

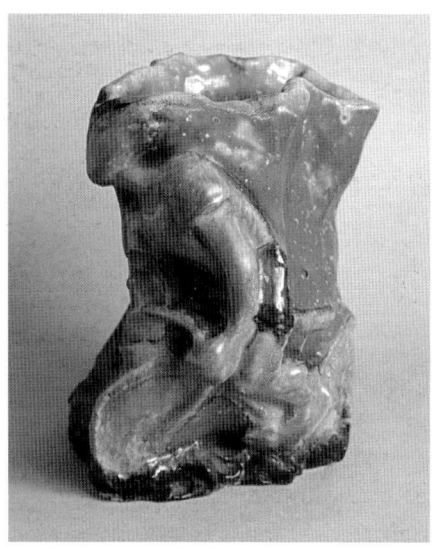

GIUSEPPE MARIO ANSELMO, *VASE IN THE FORM OF A CYCLIST*, C.1937-38. HAND PAINTED EARTHENWARE, 20.3 CM.
PHOTO: JOHN WHITE

In the beginning Gropius sounded very much like a spokesman of the Arts and Crafts Movement; not until 1923, with the arrival of Lissitzky, did Gropius express an interest in designing for industrial production. In the pottery produced at the Bauhaus, we find a mixture of traditional forms drawing from medieval and classical sources as well as modern industrial forms. These pieces by Theodor Bogler were designed in series with interchangeable parts so that several variations could be manufactured from the same individual parts. The Bauhaus and its immigrants to the United States provided the impetus to include craft disciplines within the fine arts curriculum, thus providing a new setting in the university for the education of today's craftsmen.

In Gropius's system of logic, craft operates as an intermediary between artist and industry. Many artists working at that time, especially the Surrealists, would have had reservations about Gropius's statement that craft discipline is essential for every artist. Since craft is associated with skill, training, and tradition, many artists in this century have rejected craftsmanship as interfering with fundamental expression. Whether that expression involved a surfacing of the unconscious, a revelation of the self, or contact with collective primitive origins, traditional techniques were often considered inadequate and even detrimental. Cézanne wrote this to his mother:

> I must go on working, but not in order to attain a finished perfection, which is so much sought after by imbeciles. This quality which is commonly so much admired is nothing but the accomplishment of a craftsman, and makes any work produced in that way inartistic and vulgar.[7]

When the concerns of painting and sculpture were embodied in representing the external world, the craft of attaining a certain type of reality was inseparable from the art. Being able to render "realistic" images became the craft issue for the painter in a similar way that making utilitarian vessels became the issue for the potter. Photography took over part of the painter's craft in a similar way that industry had taken over part of the potter's craft. Painters began to explore spaces beyond or in front of the "Renaissance window," and potters began to explore beyond the format of the functional vessel. Critics were just as outraged by modern twentieth-century painting as they were when potters began to close up their holes and distort their well-thrown forms. Expert handicraft has traditionally been inseparable from art as artists

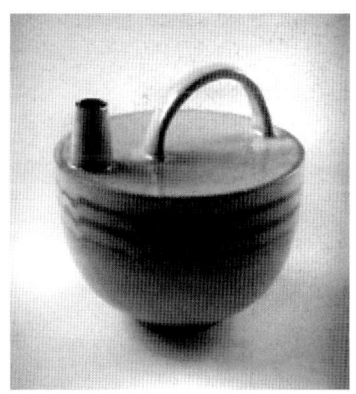

THEODOR BOGLER, *KANNE POT*, C.1925-26. GLAZED FAIENCE WITH BANDED DECORATION, 14 CM.

PHOTO: CERAMIC ARTS FOUNDATION

developed their craft in conjunction with developing technology in their culture. In a highly technological society, we no longer need to prove our technological abilities through our art. What seems to become more important is to be able to express our humanity, our unique sensibilities.

In the early twentieth century scholars as well as artists became interested in access to the unconscious. Of prime importance to this interest was the development of modern psychology. Other major influences included the discovery of prehistoric cave paintings in France and Spain, and an interest in African art. In search of this "primitive" mentality, the Surrealists resorted to automatic writing, closing their eyes and moving the pen in unpremeditated, seemingly random gestures. Critics retorted in shock: "Why even a child could draw this!" That was precisely the point. Adult rational systems were what the artists were trying to penetrate in order to discover more about themselves. The fact that a child could, perhaps, draw as they did would have been important to artists such as Miró and Picasso. They were concerned with primal images and drawing what the mind knows rather than what the eye sees. Both Miró and Picasso worked with clay, using pottery vessels in witty, figurative contexts. The humour, direct freshness, and abstract symbolic language of their work was very exciting for American ceramists in the 1950s and 60s.

In 1967 Robert Arneson wrote a review of the Museum of Modern Art's exhibition of Picasso's sculpture. In admiring the sensibility of Picasso's approach to materials rather than his technical abilities, Arneson speaks for many of his contemporaries:

> So let's look at this phenomenal man and his phenomena from another point of view—not in the technical sense, of course, because it's quite clear he's not a technician or, for that matter, interested in any fashionable techniques. It's his instinctive, catalytic relationship with materials for what they are and what they mean. He talks to them and they talk right back—dead in the eye. The most humble, commonplace material—string, board, nail, paper, tin, etc., manipulated in an almost childlike approach to structure—seem nobly transformed. His intentions are clear and straight, yet each work is permeated with that wit and charm that make it—a Picasso.[8]

It was Picasso's and Miró's approach of incorporating ready-made objects in a new poetic context that provided a method of working for many contemporary ceramists. For many years Richard Shaw has slip-cast bits and pieces of his environment and assembled them into objects of mystery and humour that share many of Miró's and Picasso's sensibilities. Shaw's work, however, adds an ironic twist to the assemblage technique. He uses a high degree of technical expertise to create compositions that appear to be made from found objects but are, in fact, *trompe l'oeil* realism.

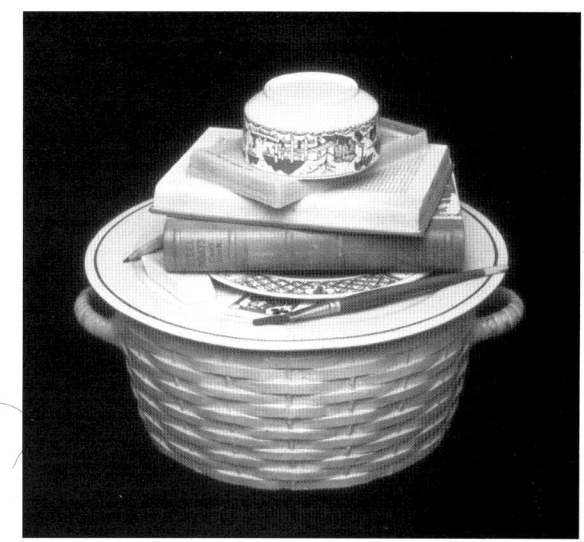

RICHARD SHAW, *CAMDEN PASSAGE #4/5*, 1979-80. PORCELAIN, CHINA PAINT AND DECALS, 26.7 x 36.8 CM.
COLLECTION: DAN JACOBS AND DEREK MASON
PHOTO: RICHARD MEYER

The acceptance of readymades as elements in art challenges the traditional view of craftsmanship. If Miró is interested in the surprise and symbolic content of discovering a figure in the juxtaposition of a jug and a faucet, the most effective way of executing this would be to use an actual jug and faucet. The found objects become the raw materials for the sculpture and require very little physical manipulation. Likewise, Meret Oppenheim's visual metaphor in her fur covered cup of 1936 is powerful because of the simplicity and directness of her incongruous juxtaposition. Many have a difficult time accepting the validity of conceptual manipulation when traditional craft techniques are absent. Nonetheless, these techniques are irrelevant in this type of approach.

Another major influence on modern art and, consequently, on ceramics and issues of craftsmanship was the profound interest throughout this century in Eastern philosophy, particularly in Zen. In the late nineteenth century, trade with

Japan was open again, and Europeans were initially delighted by the fresh new images on Japanese prints and by the elegance of their linear organization. These images influenced painters, appeared as surface painting on art pottery and occasionally affected the forms of the pots themselves. In the 1950s a new wave of Japanese influence hit this country. This time, it was rooted in a pottery rather than a printmaking tradition. Soetsu Yanagi, aesthetician and founder of the Japanese folk craft movement; Shoji Hamada, a mature potter of Zen sensibilities; and Bernard Leach, their friend and colleague made a three-month tour of the United States in 1952. These three greatly admired the unstudied imperfections of folk pottery; their work involved hand-thrown pieces, rugged stoneware clays, spontaneous brushwork, and straightforward utility. These standards were antithetical to the clean, slip-cast art pottery of previous decades, and they gave new direction and commitment to many young American potters.

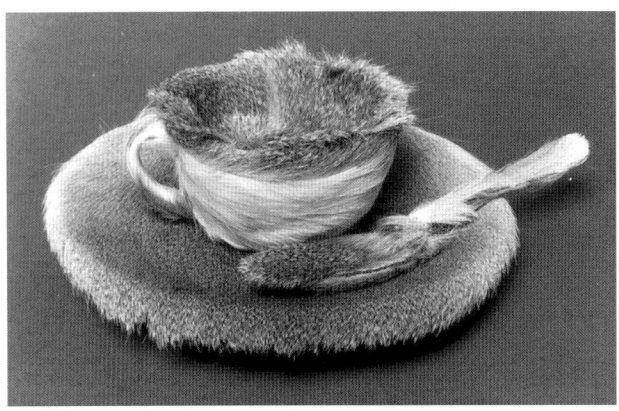

Meret Oppenheim, *Object [Le Dejeuner en fourrure]*, 1936.
Fur covered cup, saucer and spoon, 7.3 cm. (overall)
Collection/Photo: Museum of Modern Art, New York

For many this interest in folk pottery accompanied a longing for a common aesthetic and a vital craft tradition. Leach hoped to revitalize standards evident in Sung Dynasty ceramics and in European medieval pottery. He was an offspring of the Arts and Crafts Movement, romanticizing the medieval handicraft tradition in the face of extensive industrialization. For others, the traditional, utilitarian forms were a constraint and for them, the Zen aesthetic became more important than the folk pottery look. Westerners who turn to Eastern philosophies in search of different values usually bring new meaning and interpretations to these values because of their inescapable cultural conditioning. The interest in Zen Buddhism was adapted to Western concerns with self-expression. In Zen pottery, the distinctive irregularities are evidence of nature and are allowed to surface because of the potter's unassuming restraint and oneness with the universe. In work by American admirers of Zen, the non-symmetry appears to be the result of forces directly operating through the artist's assertive gestures.

Peter Voulkos is the American version of Zen. During the 1950s, Voulkos digested the Japanese Zen aesthetic along with the nourishment provided by Picasso, Miró, and abstract expressionism. Abstract expressionism (as was Surrealist automatic writing) was a gestural attempt to gain access to and express a consciousness below the level of appearances. Voulkos subjected pottery vessels to that type of manipulation. His pots became so punctured, slashed, and conglomerated with additional elements that their integrity as utilitarian vessels was no longer a concern. Yet, on some level, the remnant of the vessel idea was important as a measure of the transformation. The purity of the vessel's function and its abstract symmetry had remained intact throughout the first half of the twentieth century, but its formal and functional content was irreparably altered by the ceramic avant-garde in the fifties. At this point the outraged letters to craft publications began to flow in and still make their appearance expressing righteous indignation and defense of the pottery tradition. Marguerite Wildenhain, an influential potter and teacher who had emigrated to the U.S. from the Bauhaus and who had worked with Peter Voulkos in the early fifties cancelled her subscription to *Craft Horizons* when it began to show Voulkos's new work.[9] If we consider terra cotta pieces by Nakian in the fifties, it is apparent that Voulkos's treatment of clay was

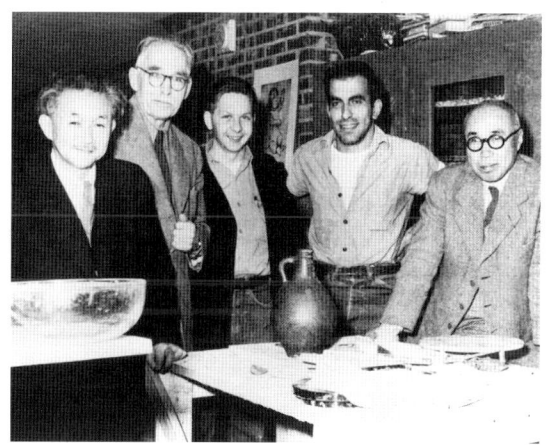

SOETSU YANAGI, BERNARD LEACH, RUDY AUTIO, PETER VOULKOS, AND SHOJI HAMADA AT THE ARCHIE BRAY FOUNDATION IN HELENA, MONTANA, 1952.

PHOTO: ARCHIE BRAY FOUNDATION

COLLECTION/PHOTO: MUSEUM OF MODERN ART, NEW YORK

within a mainstream of avant-garde work at that time; but by responding to abstract expressionism within the context of pottery, Voulkos's work had the peculiar impact of disrupting a recognized craft tradition by challenging its functional as well as its formal values.

The abstract expressionist approach to ceramics involved a very aggressive manipulation of the clay; in an approach which has been labelled process art we find a sensibility which may be closer, in some respects, to Zen aesthetics. An artist such as Larry Shep is involved with exploring the inherent qualities of his raw material in conjunction with time. In order to investigate this, it is necessary to keep manipulative intervention to a minimum and to work out a system of organization so skillfully that it is apparent only as a counterpoint to the clay. This approach does not use traditional methods of craftsmanship; rather, it relies on devising an effective circumscribed situation within which nature can take its course.

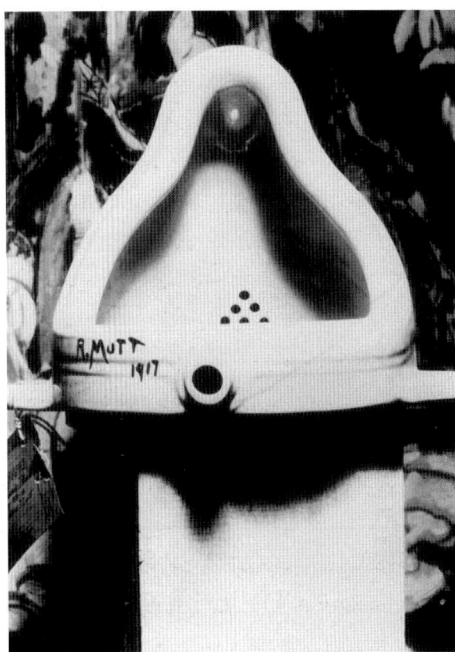

MARCEL DUCHAMP, *FOUNTAIN*, 1917. PORCELAIN, 23.5 x 17.8 CM.

PHOTO: ALFRED STIEGLITZ

A very important aspect of the craftsmanship issue began as an extension of Marxist concerns, which questioned the value and meaning of the bourgeois object. In 1917 Marcel Duchamp took a commercially manufactured ceramic urinal, turned it over on its back and submitted it to the *Independents* show in New York. This piece functions as a Zen koan—dumbfounding, opaque, and provocative—a catalyst for extending beyond the object to consider the nature of art itself. Is art just a precious, tasteful bourgeois object? Does art reside in commonplace objects? Is craft only serving to provide luxuries for the upper classes? This last question is worth considering in reference to a statement (c.1910) by C.R. Ashbee, an active participant in the Arts and Crafts Movement: "We have made of a great social movement, a narrow and tiresome little aristocracy working with great skill for the very rich."[10]

In attempting to avoid making a revered object that relies on the pedestal and an awe-filled public, many artists wish to keep evidence of their technical expertise relatively low key in order to allow more space for the motivated thought process or spiritual aura. For some conceptual and political minds, art should no longer be concerned with making objects at all. From this point of view all object-makers are "mere craftsmen." Other minds are concerned with avoiding the precious object by re-establishing contact with themselves as primary makers and builders. Basic craft operations are essential to their work but are not geared towards creating utilitarian craft objects. Rather, their work may be the contemplation of the essential manipulative operations involved as one might find in a magic ritual. The polished finish that was the mark of quality in a utilitarian context is not relevant in this type of approach.

The issue raised by Marcel Duchamp's urinal did eventually have far-reaching effects on developments in modern art, but in order for them to have a direct influence on ceramics they needed an intermediary emerging from a pottery background. This came several decades later in the form of Robert Arneson. As did Duchamp, Arneson incorporates in his work a lot of self-reflective parody, art-historical references, games and language, and eroticism. Arneson may not have been directly influenced by Duchamp, but he has absorbed part of that sensibility that made Duchamp such an acute and early barometer of many issues in contemporary art. Arneson's work emerged as a West Coast version of Pop Art—tempered and softened by a love of clay, a recent affair with Abstract Expressionism, and the California life-style. As his work continues to develop, his iconoclastic parody is distinguished by its specific, personal subject matter and by the wonderful humour of its puns. Several ceramists are currently trying to identify their work by creating their own witty, historical iconographies; few, if any, share the depth and insight of Arneson's. Arneson is a perfect example of the self-conscious, twentieth-century artist-ceramist who uses history, himself, and his craft as subject matter.

When the craftsman's product is no longer a tool for basic survival, the forming process is considered from a new perspective. This response to a function beyond that of utility operated millennia ago when vessel forms were used symbolically in

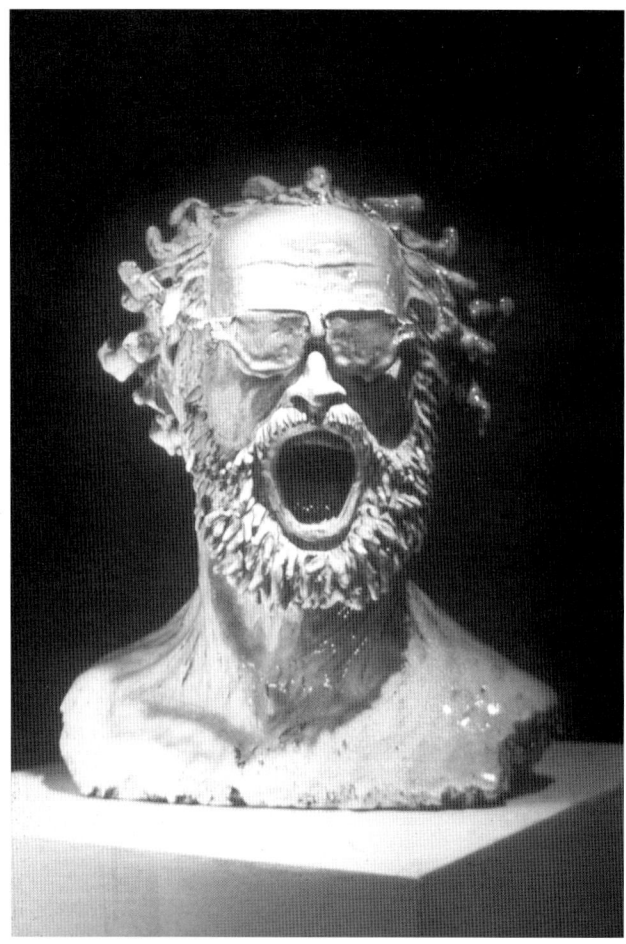

ROBERT ARNESON, *CRAZED*, 1972. STONEWARE, 40.6 CM.

PHOTO: JOE SCHOPPLEIN

various rituals. As the craftsman's options become more varied and complex, so does the maker's perspective. When society is as eclectic as ours, when history has become an accessible cultural sandwich rather than a remote unravelling story, then identity and integrity of our artistic expression becomes very difficult to recognize because of its diverse visual imagery. However, there may be more coherence than is superficially apparent in the great free-for-all of self-expression. This search for meaning in the particular and the personal is, in itself, a unifying cultural expression. In this consideration of craftsmanship, we have found strong developing traditions based on attitudes of approach.

1   Herbert Read, *The Meaning of Art* (London: Faber & Faber, 1931) 41-42.
2   Reynar Banham, *Theory and Design in the First Machine Age* (New York: Praeger, 1960) 102.
3   Banham, 125.
4   Banham, 123.
5   Garth Clark, *Ceramic Art: Comment and Review 1882-1977* (New York: E.P. Dutton, 1978) xiv.
6   Reynar Banham, *Theory and Design* (New York: Praeger, 1960) 277.
7   Herbert Read, *Art and Society* (New York: Schocken Books, 1966) 72.
8   Robert Arneson, "Picasso and Craftsman," *Craft Horizons* (November/December, 1967) 29.
9   Rose Slivka, *Peter Voulkos* (New York: New York Graphic Society, 1978) 18.
10 Gillian Naylor, *The Arts and Crafts Movement* (Cambridge, MA: MIT Press, 1971) 9.

CHAPTER 3

The Transparency of Clay

Doris Shadbolt

To remind ourselves that the work does not carry the value of positive status in all quarters, I repeat the remark which sums it all up, which I first heard from a Montreal artist: "Craft is what you piss in—art is what you piss on!" I appreciate the terms chosen by the symposium, "the vessel" and "the figure," to evoke a wide range of ceramic practice without prejudice, and their intent to relate to a more altruistic level of discussion.

Presented at *Edges: In Thought, In History, In Clay*, 1985, Toronto

There are two notions I would like to bring forward in the few minutes at my disposal. Perhaps it would be more appropriate to say "bring them up from underneath the pile of more immediate concerns which I expect frequently obscures them—though they have been there all the time." I could equally discuss them, switching terms, at a meeting of painters or sculptors; but they are, I think, particularly relevant to ceramists for reasons that have to do with the nature of clay.

I really don't like the way in which the word "art" has become accepted as a status-associated term in the ceramic discussion that I am familiar with, in distinguishing the makers of functional work from, let's say, the others. To remind ourselves that the work does not carry the value of positive status in all quarters, I repeat the remark which sums it all up, which I first heard from a Montreal artist: "Craft is what you piss in—art is what you piss on!" I appreciate the terms chosen by the symposium, "the vessel" and "the figure," to evoke a wide range of ceramic practice without prejudice, and their intent to relate to a more altruistic level of discussion.

Still, since I want to talk about art, I find it impossible to avoid using the word in the various ways it is commonly understood. But eventually I want to get to the point where I can use it in reference to what, as I see it, art essentially does—and that is to give form to human experience; and in reference to its value in the world. This is something not measured in monetary exchange or critical ratings, art is important because it can give us a fresh understanding of who we are and our relation to the world we live in.

So the first thing I want to say is that that high claim for art, the claim I have just made, belongs to ceramists, all ceramists, vessel and figure makers as much as to anyone else; that clay is, no more or less than any other material, one an art worker might use as the medium through which some perception of reality, some intimation of being in the world flows. When that happens, the clay, so to speak, becomes transparent, merely the channel through which something is said. That something comes through, that forms say something, is the condition of vital art.

Why do I imagine that is something worth saying to ceramists? Because I think we have, too much of the time, succumbed to the dictates of pragmatic society and have allowed ourselves to become product minded. I say "we" to include, as well as the ceramists, those in the support structure (including people like myself since I am potentially one of them): that is, the associations and societies where ceramists affiliate for mutual support, information exchange, stimulation, and so on; and the institutions who exhibit and collect the work; the critics who illuminate it; the agencies who fund ceramic programs; and the public who follow ceramics and sometimes purchase it. I believe that to the majority of us, much of the time, ceramics means objects rather than experience, an unconscious attitude that has become habitual and limiting.

I'll use an analogy which I wouldn't try to take too far. To the typographer, the page with its words printed on it has a primary "objectness" which it doesn't have for the person whose object it is to read the words through which the poetry floods its expanded meaning. This is not to deny typography its own limited form of artistry, of course. Even for the proofreader checking for errors, we could say that the words have an objectness of a different kind. Both the typographer's and the proofreader's approaches are necessary in getting the poet's vision out into the objective world (of publication, criticism, and audiences) in its appropriate print form. But only the reader's approach (and the poet's in the act of creation) has to do with what poetry is about in its integral purpose.

In the field of ceramics we have come to settle too often for the typographer's or proofreader's limited vision, and in the process, we have given short change to clay works. We have not demanded of the ceramists enough daring, sustained vision—intensity, big ideas, big enough ambition of an artistic kind—and when they have delivered those qualities, we non-ceramists have often been too insensitive or too prejudiced or too object minded to recognize them.

Contemporary ceramists I know have had to work to justify their existence during a time when the crafts were generally downgraded. And their work, moreover, is by nature so materially insistent, so physical, so demanding of touch attributes that it was regarded suspiciously during the decades of this century, since sculptural forms have received the fallout from an earlier attitude when ceramic sculpture was regarded as something less than work in bronze or marble.

A painting is usually an object that has dimensions, weight, substance, can be picked up and moved around. A work of non-ceramic sculpture is often one too (though not necessarily these days), but this work does not have much "objecthood" for us, partly because the twentieth-century understanding of what art is includes them. That has conditioned a response, at least some of the time, that is appropriate to their purpose—paintings get "read," so to speak, like poetry, for what they say.

The inherent characteristics of clay, which helped place ceramic work at a disadvantage within the critical climate of this century, also made it especially vulnerable to demeaning treatment in the marketplace. Ceramists, like all art workers, face the problem of interfacing in an effective but honourable way within the art market (and its powerful promotional apparatus) which essentially regards art works as objective products that it would like to absorb into its ideology. Ceramic works, for obvious reasons, tend to be relatively small in scale; intimate, apparently domestic in pretension rather than grandiose. Small scale can be a very positive thing, as we know. Miniature objects may acquire an intense psychological presence, compressing, as they may do, qualities and meanings, including that of craftsmanship, into a small form—and they point to grander revelations. But small forms can also lend themselves to an uncritical consumerism which just sees them as covetable, precious little objects comfortably related to the human scale. I am sure that the compulsion, on the part of ceramic sculptors in recent years, to break into a larger format (quite apart from the artist's inner need for a larger scale to handle a changed content) has something to do with this outside pressure—the need to break out of a perception which liked to imprison their work in a category of small, precious objects, and to have it viewed with a fresh seriousness. The presence, too, of a functional component in the vessel side of the practice has been seen as the way of defining an object, of characterizing it, of limiting it, of overwhelming it—if convenient—of dismissing it.

The limiting vision which tends to envelop ceramics can be seen as just part of the broader societal and "art" situation which exists beyond ceramists' particular concerns but with which they have to contend. But perhaps it is something that affects the ceramic community from within as well—that, preoccupied with all the very real problems that they face, they take on some of the materialist colouration of the climate that surrounds them; and they don't often enough remind themselves that their real work is, so to speak, "to write real poetry." If so, this affects how they think and talk about their work, what kind of promotion or accreditation they settle for, and eventually the work itself.

In the old days of open juried exhibitions, as a non-specialist, I often felt I was the only juror not preoccupied with technical things—cones, bodies, glazes, or conformity to some established external standard, to the exclusion of everything else, rather than looking for the hint of life, expressed though a formal cohesion of some kind. That is mostly gone, I trust—both the blinding concentration on narrow technical matters and the old grab-bag exhibition with its competitiveness and exhibitionism and its absence of focus other than a common medium. The exhibition scene is improving (I can only speak of this country), but we still need to push for more, and more seriously curated, exhibitions, one-person or thematic shows with well-developed rationales, where work can be given some edge and can be seen in sufficient depth to grasp its intent, not just because it has special status as clay but because its best products are as interesting and as significant as any other art.

There is an observation which I make with some diffidence. There is something puzzling to an outside observer about an art fraternity held together by its base in a common medium—especially in these days when the medium boundaries in art are so blurred, reflecting a deep compulsion to make art less specialized, more relevant and accessible. (I will have something more positive to say about this later on.) There is no question of the obvious benefits of affiliation. But on the other side are the risks of inbreeding, of limiting vision, of becoming self-protective rather than self-expanding, of feeding off one another rather than letting the world flow through in a constant clearing and refreshing process. The risk is of becoming too centred on the medium itself, as if that has its own status. (Let me say, at once, that I realize this is not the tenor of this symposium.)

In 1983 when Robert Rauschenberg did a large work whose components were made of clay fired in Japan, and Robert Hughes wrote in *Time* that he considered it to be among Rauschenberg's best work, a writer in a ceramics magazine spoke hopefully of the significant influence on the course of ceramic art that this critical acceptance might have. I found that hopefulness a little pathetic because it suggested a longing to be embraced by the promotional machine at a time when many artists have learned to be highly mistrustful of it and some are trying to subvert it. In fact, it made me sad when I thought of the fine work being done by ceramists who had spent years, maybe lives, hoping for a little stardust to fall from the excursions into the medium by an artist like Rauschenberg—and again, because it suggested a medium-bound vision.

It is even more important if medium preoccupation shows in some of the work: as a reliance on tricks and effects and novelty—being new for the sake of being different—the effects that are so accessible and beguiling in a medium as technically layered and as material as clay; or the use of ideas that seem to come from the surface of modern art rather than from the wellsprings that nourish it; or ideas that appear promising but aren't sustained and pushed far enough and deep enough to really mean something; what I call trivia—the things that rely on effects and have no content or relate to no felt experience. Certainly, there is proportionately as much trivia in other areas of art making as there is in ceramics. Partly, it is because the medium consciousness of the clay community tends to call attention to these practices and give protection rather than just letting them disappear and find their own level in a larger art pyramid. And I am not belittling the problems of a community which has had largely, until recently, to rely on its own support system, write its own articles and criticism, organize its own shows, do its own promotion.

So what I am suggesting for the moment, and from time to time, is a shift in focus from any of the various practical facets by which the ceramic world can be examined to the core it has in common with all the arts. I look to the ceramist (as I would look to the painter, the architect, the carver, the poet) who persists through all the necessary concerns—to survive, to improve, to make products interesting to the ceramist and then to others, perhaps to fail, perhaps to succeed—only to find that success is as hard to handle as failure. I look to the ceramist who, through all this, carries dedication, commitment, and openness to life-expanding experience to the point where everything is seen through art. Art becomes a vehicle for apprehending the world, and consequently, art achieves its wonderful clarity and becomes a medium through which some fresh intimation of being in the world radiates. Out of such clarity comes the "newness" in ceramics or any other aspect of art that interests me.

A West Coast traditional potter once told me about the *hakeme*, the coarse-brush technique for slip decorating that he, living a somewhat isolated life, had seen only in Oriental books which he couldn't read. He experimented with various brushes and finally made one of his own out of straws from a broom with which he obtained, he thought, reasonable results. Then one night, he was returning home late from the mainland to the island where he lives and works. His car had broken down, and no one came by to give him a lift. It was dark and wet, and heavy rain was slashing at him. And in the dark, moving one leg after the other, bending his body against the wind and rain, he suddenly had a new understanding of *hakeme*! It was just one of those momentary flashes when things snap together in a way that makes them ours in an internalized sense. He knew *hakeme* not just with his hand as a mechanical technique but with his body and feelings in his mind. This is just the merest and perhaps trivial, literal example having to do with a technique of decoration. But I cite it as a minor instance of the constant interpenetration of art and life that goes on all the time, at all levels and in all the complexity of seeing, thinking, observing, feeling, being sentient and in the world as it changes and goes on around us. And it is out of this continual "equivalencing" that art finds its nourishment and vitality and its authenticity. One assumes the artist is so at ease with his medium and its appropriate and possible forms that it has become a language as natural as speech (perhaps more natural than speech), but it is the constant renewal and fleshing out of those forms through investing them with fresh life experience that keeps them from being imitative or self-repetitive and keeps the clay "transparent."

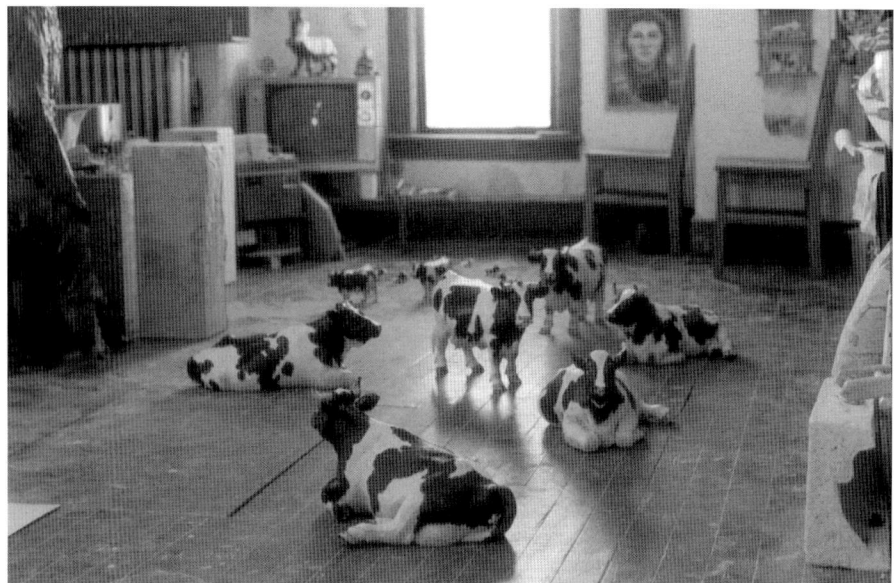

JOE FAFARD, *Cow*, 1978. EARTHENWARE, HAND BUILT WITH PAINTED DECORATION, 30.5 x 45.7 x 11.9 CM. PRIVATE COLLECTION

I think of ceramic sculptors whose work I know well enough to speak firsthand with some knowledge—and you can think of your own examples—of artists for whom clay has been the means of making statements of considerable cumulative power and for whom the medium has been the means by which they go on deepening their own perception and externalizing it in the forms of their art. I think of Gathie Falk and her apparent preoccupation with ordinary objects, which she makes very unordinary. I think you could say they become metaphysical objects—shoes, fruit, shirts—works which, with their dark, murky colours and viscous surfaces, are anything but the merely playful reminiscences that shallow vision might take them for. Instead, they relate to continuing thematic explorations having to do with decay and regeneration and her own experience as a religious person. Or I think also of Joe Fafard (on whom there will be a presentation during the symposium), who similarly sustains a thematic framework which permits him to draw on specific subject material from his own lived experience in the Canadian Midwest, to invest it with cultural and deeply human implications. Such artists (and we could name many others) have achieved their status, not as pickers-up of the latest ideas from the shows or magazines, or because they do or don't work in clay, but because they have dug deeply or sliced sharply into their experience as thinking, feeling, sensing members of the human community who know how to translate that into a medium as art.

For the ceramic sculptor, the life experience that is invested is unlimited in its range because it is freed of the demands of function and traditional methods of construction. All the open possibility of surface or three-dimensional imagery is now available. The vessel maker is limited in range and apt to be seen as the coming out of the past rather than pointing to the future. So the world finds it harder to grant the functionalist the same status as producer of potentially expressive objects, though I think we make a mistake here. Life simply flows through all clay.

I would like to take a special minute to speak up for the vessel maker. Function has been made the convenient dividing line separating craft from art, and that has hardened into the habit of looking at vessels even more pragmatically, less sensitively, less demandingly. Or function is seen as something "hanging out" that must be tucked in or transcended before the art, so to speak, shines through. On the contrary, I would say that function has its own symbolic meaning that may be as integral a dimension of the expressive whole as a function of a great piece of architecture.

Containing, for instance, is an expressive idea as well as a function—that which the vessel does whether holding amply, offering openly, confining tightly, hiding away secretly or whatever—that relates to so many layers of our conscious and subconscious being, our mundane and our symbolic experience. Among the northern Indian peoples of the Northwest Coast of this continent, the "container" was a metaphor for the culture, a concept that permeated all its aspects, including its art. The Tlingit had a single word to convey the meanings of box, coffin, bivalve, shell, womb, outside, opposite moiety—in short, container. We don't have the collective force of a tradition to drive home the meanings of the container, but those meanings are there, at least some of them, perhaps buried in our subconscious but there to be tapped.

The vessel is, in fact, a metaphor for life. Just think for a moment of the potter whose intent is not overtly sculptural and of the possibilities, even within conventional parameters of form and technique. For example, the give and take of pressure—pressure which is energy, as the vessel's volume is pushed out by pressure from within and in turn gives in to the pressure from outside. It is a dialogue of inner and outer forces of which the felt volume and the vessel contour are the witness, the symbol. Or there is the structural symbiosis between the ceramist's concept and the acts of nature to which the creative process is subjected. This potter starts with a vision, a structural concept that can embrace the contributive aspect of improvisation as well as the will of the kiln, the glazes and so on. If the ceramist has been alive to all such life-form equivalences and many others, the object goes way beyond its actuality, its literal objectness, into life implications that are there for us, too, if we are alive to them. And therein lies the art—not in the art effects! (In the midst of such serious talk, I don't want to give the impression that I would exclude humour, or wit, or irony, or play—or, indeed, other art that has been truly received—as part of the life experience that may animate either the vessel or the figure).

In an article in 1961 (much quoted, though more for other statements than the following) Rose Slivka pointed out that "ceramics, more than other crafts, throughout its long history, has produced useful objects that have come to be considered fine art." "Time," she said, "has a way of overwhelming the functional value of an object that outlives the men who made and used it, with the power of its own objective presence, that life-invested quality of being that transcends and energizes it." "When this happens," she said, "such objects are forever honored for their own sakes."[1] Do we have to wait for time to overwhelm the functional value before we can see the life-invested quality? I don't think so. I can recall contemporary vessels that I saw two or three years ago that, because of the intense compression of life they presented, remain so vivid that I could sketch them today. And their function was inseparable from that power.

I know, as we all do, potters who have felt that the inherent limitations of traditional, functional ceramics make their work irrelevant in a society where the artist has increasingly seen his role as that of social reactor or interpreter or commentator. Other than function, they cannot deal with specific content—and I remember Herbert Read's remark of many years ago that "pottery is the most abstract of the arts."[2] Many of these people have either ceased to be active in ceramics or have moved into its sculptural areas. Fortunately, there remain dedicated ceramists of the vessel who know they can make statements of great strength and relevance because they are dealing with values that have to do with the enduring human conditions that underlie the specifics of time and culture. They can retain these values and still create new and fresh forms. I believe these are special people who have achieved a high degree of integration and equipoise, and who have not lost their essential embededness in the natural world—which is our common condition whether we remember it or not. I hope that they will continue to claim the serious purpose that is theirs, despite the failure of so many of us on the outside to recognize their work for the full dimension it may have.

I come to my second point. Having tried to make the "transparency of clay" a useful metaphor to shift the focus of attention from clay as factual object to the life that flows through it, I would turn my coin over and say that at the same time, for me, the effective clay work that I know and that seems to endure accepts and exploits the nature of the medium: its materiality, its conspicuous plasticity, its tactility (touch, let us remind ourselves, is communication), its insistent qualities of surface (that are not just "surface" but express the deep, organic relation to the object—its shape, density and so on), in fact, its literal opacity. The ceramist may be instructed and excited by ideas that animate other mediums, but he or she transforms them into the special terms of his or her own. And (despite the phenomenal extension, during the past thirty or so years, of the range and seriousness of the messages that clay could be employed to deliver) clay has a uniqueness, and that uniqueness is primarily a matter of its materiality and its plasticity.

I notice that many of you who have, in your work, boldly and admirably stuck you heads up to face the winds of change in the bigger art world, still continue to identify with the clay community, though presumably you have the option of being absorbed into that larger world. I conclude that the properties of the medium and its potential for expression have some strong correspondences for you. This is the real reason for the cohesion of the clay community.

I suggest that ceramics, because of those intrinsic qualities, may have particular relevance within the larger art scene and within our present society. The arts, broadly speaking, offer a way to human wholeness; I would say probably the only way, involving as they do the whole human organism in integrated synthesis. This is true both for the maker and the responder in so far as one recreates the work in the act of responding. The recent years of theory-dominated, cerebral art, much of it non-visual, non-sensual, conspicuously disinterested in "hand facture," have attached little value to those special qualities that ceramists are given to exploit.

The conceptual emphasis, like all serious art thrusts, has had its necessary scouring effect, clearing out attitudes and modes that had become tired and empty.

But too many components relating to human wholeness had been left out of the mix. As we now see, they have begun to reassert themselves naturally in ways that are new and unfamiliar. Still, whatever course art takes in the near future, the ceramic arts, both vessel and figure, with their built-in potential for speaking for the whole biological man, I am convinced, will be an important part of it.

1 Rose Slivka, "The New Ceramic Presence" *Crafts Horizons* (No. 4, 1961) 43.
2 Bernard Rackman and Herbert Read, *English Pottery: Its Development from Early Times to the End of the Eighteenth Century* (London: Ernest Benn, 1924) 129.

CHAPTER 4

ANALOGY AND METAPHOR IN CERAMIC ART

PHILIP RAWSON

There may be many areas of reference which we shall never pick up in other people's pots. But that is not a reason for restraining ourselves from picking up any at all. We are duty bound to feel for those levels of symbolic coding which can come across on the basis of our common human experiences. For visual art seems still to rest on a kind of onomatopoeia, the performance of acts that come close to imitation.

Presented at *Ceramics and Modernism*, 1981, New York City

My particular experience with ceramics has induced in me a long view over human history. I shamelessly adopt a perspective which recognizes the likenesses between men and races rather than their differences. Modernism, seen in this perspective, becomes a problem of another kind than when it is seen from much closer to.

In his early work, that great, much misunderstood, and wrongly denigrated philosopher, Friedrich Nietzsche, developed a thought which I believe is very important for us as artists and historians. You will find that it goes much farther than that catchword usage, which Garth Clark criticized yesterday. In *The Birth of Tragedy*, particularly, Nietzsche shed light on the ways in which all kinds of human ideas (he was especially concerned with religious and philosophical ideas) repose at bottom, on complexes of metaphor. This implies that each particular experience gains its meaning by reference to others, like a cross-indexing system. We can only explain one phenomenon in terms of others. But habitually recognized similarities take deep root in our minds; and they become so matted together by our regular thinking and speaking that, gradually, they fossilize. You realize I have just been using them: "matted," "take root," "fossilize"! And because such a procedure is so integral to all our dealings with our life and world, they become invisible to us.

Not only that. When they become invisible, the everyday languages based on them cease to question the roots from which they spring. Only the poets and artists awaken the analogies that lie sleeping in their languages by metaphor. For to bring out the true nature of these metaphors can cast suspicion on the whole upper crust of thought, raising radical doubts as to truth and validity. Certain major, central analogies themselves, when they are dragged out into the light of day, can often seem crudely physical—repugnant even—to the refined intellectual mind, ridiculous to the less refined. And what we now like to call "structures" may actually be abstract reflections of the analogical bonds we take for granted between the highly immediate and physical terms of those mutual metaphors by means of which we establish our reality. Nietzsche, indeed, argued that space, as a concept, embodies a metaphor for metaphor itself. I suggest that what we call aesthetic meaning (as well as intellectual meaning) seems to be a function of that metaphorical complex, and that what constitutes the virtue of good art relates to its success here.

I am afraid I cannot agree with that vein of art criticism which looks on the work of art as simply a new, unclassifiable object, without roots in a language of form. I sympathize with the feeling of disgust with over intellectualizing which that attitude implies. But I do not accept that the major art of the past or of the present actually works at any pure-object level. I think it is probable that the meaning of any art work we make or perceive rests on its own linked series of analogical references. I was delighted to see so many magnificent metaphors shining out in the Bauhaus, Futurist and American modernist ceramics we saw yesterday morning, even though some of the industrial optimism now seems a little misplaced.

The really vital point is that, in a good work, these analogical references will ultimately reach down to rest on and connect up with certain fundamental and immediate experiences. But it is a horrible error to suppose that any one of them alone can ever be a work's whole content. No single metaphor can ever contain the whole meaning of a work or part of a work. Here, I think, Jungians (not Jung himself) may sometimes be at fault. No true symbol ever refers simply to an object—say to a house or to a nude or to an idea, say, energy. This is where Garth's cartoonist showed his own failings. But insofar as it is a symbol, each work of art constellates its own particular field of analogical reference which nothing else at all can constellate.

Its metaphors are mutual, two-way, between what is referred to and the pot. One cannot translate the meaning of a picture, a sculpture, a pot, into simple terms by any obvious device. That would short-circuit and destroy its purpose. At the same time, it may help to bring out into the light of day some of the more deeply hidden metaphorical references into our art. To do this may, I think, broaden the analogical bases onto which modern—not modernist—artists may rest their work.

Of course, no one can deny that in every culture there are layers and levels of symbolic coding which will always be opaque to those who were not brought up on that culture. The words of spoken languages may have to be learned as pure conventions. There may be areas of reference which we shall never pick up in other people's pots. But that is not a reason for restraining ourselves from picking up any at all. We are duty bound to feel for those which can come across on the basis of our common human experiences. For visual art seems still to rest on a kind of onomatopoeia, the performance of acts which lie close to imitation.

I am afraid I don't personally believe in all this talk of new formal orders, new this, that. The general look of things is not the substance of art. I am afraid I am (maybe) going to tax your patience a little by asking you, for a while, to suspend disbelief. To begin with, the slides may seem to hurry, but I want the formal suggestions of each to lie in your minds as its successors pass before your eyes. I hope you will join me in allowing the forms and colours of works of ceramic art to speak to your sympathies on their own account. The works will be familiar. That is part of my point. I intend to speculate freely.

Our first approach to any ceramic work is made, I think, through its body image. We all refer to the "clay body" it is made of. We talk of it having "foot," "belly," "shoulder," "lip." We rarely talk about its "head," though plenty of pots do have heads and faces added, as does this medieval English jug. There are also beautiful Nabatean storage jars, excavated in the Negev, which wear obvious necklaces. We tend to judge the expression of a pot by the way it addresses us, body to body, and by the way we apprehend the posture it takes, as if it were another body. We read a humanoid high-shouldered posture in these two Finnish pots of the fifties. They withdraw from any intimacy with us, but we feel ourselves into the posture they show. A pot, however, is a body we also feel from within.

We still need, I feel, to adhere to the traditional character of ceramics as implying the image of the containing. So our pots lose if they do not have this double aspect: first, of containing and isolating a realm of space, maybe even sanctifying it; and second, of exhibiting outward forms, which define the container as a special kind of presence in the world, no mere inert object. The ceramic image cannot crystallize if the work has only an exterior, as Bill Daley's fine works show.

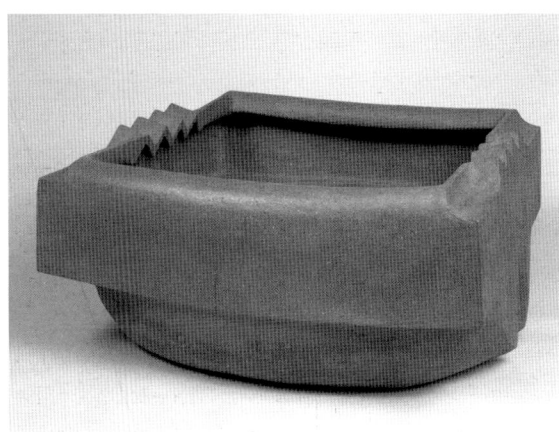

WILLIAM DALEY, *UNTITLED*, 1979. STONEWARE, 27.9 x 55.9 x 58.4 CM.

PHOTO: TONY VINELLA

This T'ang dynasty funeral pot exhibits itself almost like a peacock. But most important, it offers that vital sense of vertical axis which throwing always gives naturally, but which even very early handmade pots virtually always strive towards. That ceramic axis is no mere expedient. It represents the anthropic vertical: the central column both of man and of his sanctified world, the axis mundi, the lighthouse at the centre of reality, the source and focus of creation.

It is this strong axis for the potter's inner space which seems to me to differentiate ceramics from all that straight clay sculpture. We are profoundly aware of inner volume which we understand by an inner sympathy as being centred, as we are centred; we know it to have an affinity with our own sense of being but to be, at the same time, set "over there," over against us, so that we can address it as if it were another. A work like this seventeenth-century tea bowl by Kenzan was deliberately made to provide an outer focus for meditation upon the mutuality of being and not being, of interior and exterior, inner and outer—speaking to us, as body speaks, through our hands as much as though our eyes.

The truth is that pottery, as I am describing it, has actually got an iconography implicit in its very existence. It is no game of open experiment. For one of the great fundamental metaphors in ceramics is the creative female. This little Greek goddess from Tanagra is a piece of potter's work. Her shape tells us so. From the symbols of our artistic language, we recognize the source from which men and animals emerge as a mysterious breeding container, generically female. And pots are one of its type of images. Our own bodies are in some sense our feminine component; our clothing of flesh that continually reweaves itself is a function of the creative principle that presents us as beings to others and to ourselves.

The interesting issue, of course, is what it contains. Greek tradition offers us this figurine of about 6,000 B.C. Later, a thought was expressed by the writer Porphyry that the breeding container of the soul was actually a mixing bowl, a krater. This has an unequivocal formal affinity to the figurine: the kind of large vessel in which the Greeks used to mix wine with many other ingredients to produce their invigorating drink. But then, we can only ask ourselves what on earth this cachepot from the second millennium BC Anatolia was meant to be. We do not know, but with its little opening door in its notional pelvis, it can certainly mean something to us. Maybe it received relics; maybe it was a soul house of some sort. It can clearly "give." Early Western men—and most likely early Oriental men—saw the female's productivity as spontaneous; and they seem to have understood the fertility of the earth, metaphorically, as a colossal transcription of this female productivity.

The famous little Paleolithic relief called the Venus of Laussel, and the great breast-and vulva-filled grotto of Pech-Merle, imply as much. They seem to have passed their heritage down to the famous Eastern Mediterranean mother-goddess known to us from Roman times as Diana of the Ephesians. She was the continually pregnant and propagating mother of all creatures, feeding and nourishing them all with her many breasts. This nourishing function of the pot as mother we find alluded to in many pots when they are shaped as breasts. Here is a very early one, from Iran, of the third millennium BC. It may have had some ceremonial function, as suggested by the great multiplicity of breasts. Here is another from the European Iron Age. You can still buy ordinary coffee mugs molded with pairs of breasts.

The ancient European mother goddess is known to us in many guises. Here is one little-known terra cotta from the Balkans—Romania in fact—dating to about 4,000 BC. The painted striations on its body are thought to be images of some kind of active functioning, maybe connected with water. But it is very interesting to find the motif of striations carried through still, not only in traditional Africa, as on this pot with its deep, wavy ridges, but even on this late nineteenth-century art-nouveau vase. I am not, of course, talking of direct cultural transmission but rather of the continuing underground life of metaphors in human culture, perhaps even via human physiology.

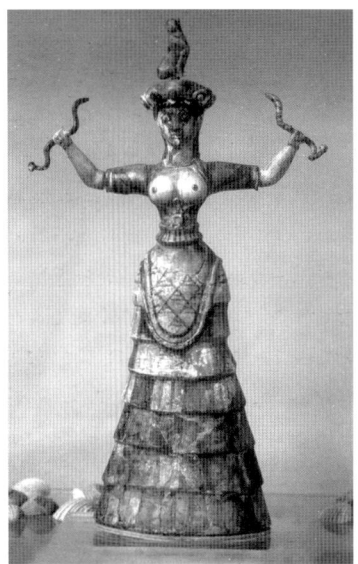

KNOSSOS, CRETE, *SNAKE GODDESS*, C. 1600 BC. FAÏENCE, 34.3 CM. COLLECTION/PHOTO: HERAKLEION MUSEUM, CRETE

For those countries of Western Asia and the Balkans where the ceramic art first flourished were also the home of those mother-goddesses who are still alive as metaphor in modern cultures. This is the course of the river Adonis (or Tammuz, Venus's boyfriend) in modern Syria. The water pours in a torrent from its cave. Once a great temple to the goddess Astarte stood beside it until it was destroyed by the first Roman Christian emperor, Constantine. And also from a site in Syria, of about 1,800 BC, is this goddess holding her vase which overflows with water and fish. We can still find her descendants on the fountains in Western cities, and enlisted to serve as pretty little teapots.

This goddess of ours had another incarnation in one of those cultures that produced one of the greatest ceramic arts of which we know: Crete. Here she is, wearing her flounced skirt, presented in the famous compressed frit sculpture from Knossos, second millennium BC. We can certainly read her as goddess of the waters in this drawing of a Cretan intaglio seal from the same period. In her monster-headed boat she has with her a flowering tree. In personifying her as thoroughly as this, the Cretans did not make the mistake of losing their grasp on her identity as generative principle. The waters were one of her realms—the sea, of course, in Crete. And here we may find her metaphorically incarnated in this gesturing pot with its high, wavy handle, emblazoned with the creatures of her domain.

The pot witnesses her sanctity. It is one of her descriptions, by analogy. No less than the animals, we—her humans—are functionally part of her. She was also goddess of the flowering land and of the mountains. She appears on these other seals in various other guises, as Gertrude Rachel Levy has demonstrated. But as mistress and mother of vegetation, she is embodied in dozens of other Cretan pots now in the Herakleion museum. The way these pots use garlands of the goddess's own flowers to illuminate the sanctity of pot bodies prefigures the floral ornament on tens of thousands of later painted pots; their makers have long since forgotten whose image they were making. The superb floral ornament on this pot shows that the Iznik Turks may have accepted, perhaps, a little more of her than one might imagine, in spite of being Muslims. But the old life-and-death seriousness built into the true mother goddess image is nowadays missing. Of course we make millions of pieces of floral ware without any real concern at all.

Many of us may even feel some slight disgust at the feebleness of our floral imagery. In fact, the boot painters used to keep the goddess very much alive, even in the nineteenth century. The Chiswick press in London was still using this beautiful tailpiece block in the 1860s. I don't think many people would disagree with the proposition that the Chinese were probably the world's greatest masters of the ceramic art as this Ming Cheng-te plate demonstrates. So you will not be surprised if I develop certain notions about the semantics of pottery using chiefly—but not only—their works.

The first point is the basic mode by which ceramics, as I have defined it, spins out from itself an imagery of space. I want to go here beyond the pious generalities of art criticism, e.g. "surface tensions" and "dynamic form relationships" and so on. The great French art historian Henri Focillon developed the idea that space could be incorporated in art according to two chief conceptual poles. They have a variety of possible grades between them. The first implies that the art work contains within itself all the space to which it refers. In fact, when I was looking for a ceramic piece to illustrate this pole alone, I found it extraordinarily difficult. There are a few African examples and Western Asiatic storage jars, but this fine Chaco canyon mug also shows the idea on its surface. Its ornament consists of concentric enclosures which address you frontally when you grasp its handle. You seem to be supposed to focus within them, as symbols of order. They may be meant to represent concentric regions of space.

The other pole is represented by artworks, which generate an undefined and unlimited arena of space around themselves. They do this by reaching around themselves, out into the openness that lies about them. They state it without limiting it. This beautiful Chinese Lung-ch'uan Southern Sung spittoon does exactly that. Its body is, of course, an enclosure; but its flat, conical lip embodies a gesture of reaching. It becomes particularly important in connection with something I mention later that you are able to read this shape and its meaning without being able to see the whole contour at all.

Hear are two of the epitomes of the second of Focillon's poles: two ink paintings by major Chinese masters who were working in the thirteenth century when the Sung potters were potting. They illustrate perfectly the way in which the present objects, which are stated by the ink strokes, send our awareness out into the vastness of that arena of what they do not state, and which they imply they never could. Instead they point towards it.

I am sure you all know that all the arts of China were fundamentally linear. Calligraphy was the mother of the other arts, the highest and most expressive of them all. This is an essay by a T'ang dynasty monk called Huai-su—a very fine work. It embodies beautifully what the Chinese called "the meaning beyond the text." This meaning is conveyed through the formal and kinetic references of the brushwork, its endless inventiveness, its refusal and ever-changing waves of the Tao—or Dharma as Buddhists would call it. The brushstrokes say what the words cannot. In this very famous portrait of the poet Li Po by the thirteenth-century Ch'an monk, Liang K'ai, the strokes do exactly that. Look especially at the rhythms and at the curves. They took time to make. We must take time to re-enact and read them. Hence they embody time. There is no reason why this whole dimension should be omitted, as it is, from much modernist work.

When we come to Far Eastern three-dimensional art, we find that its surfaces are developed out of very skillful lines. In all three-dimensional art, except that made of transparent materials, it is the visible and tangible that conveys rhythms and reveals volume. Well-developed lines like these not only run to and fro across the flat field but also go over and around, into and out of, the depth of the image. Pick any spot to start on, say a fold of the robe under the hands, and then track it as it runs up, across, around, behind, then forward over again. This is a sculpture which most emphatically takes time to follow, like music; and hence it must incorporate reading of the time into its image. It was made in Japan in the epoch of the Chinese T'ang dynasty by an artist who was probably a Korean or Chinese working in high T'ang style. Now it is in the Yakushiji Buddhist Temple, Nara.

I have put in this fifteenth-century Chinese painting of the deity of the sun, simply to make the transition from figurative art to ceramics. The whole expression of this image lies in its graduated, curving lines. I hope the formal point of this comparison will be obvious. The curving contour of the T'ang tombware jar is what generates its form. The vigour of the line which is led in space is what makes it so superb. But of course, that line cannot have been made by an actual gesture as painted lines can be. It can only be a thoroughgoing invention, shaped by the imagination and led with the utmost care through a graded series of inflections. It is not casual in the name of inspiration: the resulting form is the full, inflected image of a mobile body, offered to us as a surface illuminating the receptive and the creative at once.

Exactly the same is true of this beautiful Kuan vase, of the Sung dynasty. This shape, like all thrown and turned pottery shapes, is a function of revolution of its contour line about the fixed axis. And the mobile relationship between that line and the axis of rotation is what gives the pot its specific expression. One can also feel the interaction with the opposite contour. The pacing of the lengths of the inflections of the curves is what gives it the rhythmic quality that enlists our sympathetic responses and exhibits the inner functioning of the fluid creative body. It, too, has its own "meaning beyond the text," beyond the objective facts. In practice, all creation of sculptural form depends upon the generation of a continuous, articulate surface which reveals a variety of implicit structures. Even this modest apple-green eighteenth-century vase has a similar, subtle grading and varying of lengths and qualities of curve. Imagine how banal it could easily become if that little angular inflection at the shoulder were missing. The implications of this for the shaping and our reading of the volumes are enormous. They make it possible for us to read the body as a group of fully intelligible, interpenetrating volumes.

And what about surface decoration? Here a superbly painted overglaze enamel peony swoops around the relatively undeveloped curvature of this bowl. It is undeveloped because, during the Yung-cheng period (1723-1733), such bowls were made as white blanks; we now make our porcelain in the same way. But Chinese artists then used such blanks virtually as canvases on which they painted designs as free and inspired as possible. And since they were true ceramic painters, the better ones laid out their designs in order to express the curvature of the bowl as if it corresponded with the curvature of the painted motif. Here we are again in the presence of a special version of that female ceramic image. And here we need maybe to pick up some of those cultural responses, by using our knowledge. For the early summer peony is a standard emblem in Chinese culture for feminine beauty; it refers directly to the sexual organs, establishing a beautiful visual as well as a notional analogy. And the pot thus conveys a complex and mutual act of metaphorical praise between an image of the female and the rolling year. So the metaphor reaches us in the first place through knowledge as well as through the eye.

In this great Mei-Ping dragon vase, however, we find the interaction of the pot body as spatial presence and surface design carried to an extreme degree. Let us follow through the notional evolution of this pot. First there is the contour, which establishes the surface by its revolving around the axis. This surface moves fully in three dimensions. On it appears a dragon, which represents for the Chinese the celestial and material force permeating the cosmos and its creatures. If an "actual" dragon is coiling among clouds, the shape it naturally takes in space may very well correspond with the three-dimensional curl given to it here by the surface of the pot on which it is depicted. And then we find the image is presented to us by applying the red underglaze to those places where the dragon is not: i.e., it is executed in reverse, and the waves of cloud and water among which this great cosmic energy moves appear to rise in response to the beast's frenetic plunging. Here is a perfect example of the way an image can be extended into several different notional regions by ceramic art alone.

On this Ming plate we have another dragon. He embodies, through a complex of form and cultural knowledge, really very deep feelings. By his greenness, he represents the rising force of the new spring season, circling in and rising from the arena of the dish. He means, in principle, the same as this album painting attributed to Kung Hsien (seventeenth century); but his force is active. The plate was meant, according to Chinese ideas, to be used at that season of the year. It would transmit the appropriate seasonal energies to the person eating from it, for the Chinese and the Japanese recognize that things brought together influence each other.

All things inhabit the stranded weaving of current in the great boiling river of time, the Tao; and the currents that animate one cannot fail to have a powerful effect on another. Good, and hence appropriate, ceramics are therefore good for us in every sense: not because we witness them as external, but because they key in with and co-ordinate the dynamics of our bodily existence.

Here, as a little light relief, is a *famille rose* dish with delicate—no, far from delicate—symbolic allusions. To illustrate how ceramics were woven into life in China, we can read it. To the left is a blue rock, crystallized emblem of that coiling, boiling Tao. Such rocks always have this meaning in China. The two waiting ladies are, of course, imbued with Yin, the dark female essence which forms one polarity of the cosmic movement. They are surrounded by other natural objects, which also burst with Yin essence: the peony, the coiling cloud, the *ling-chi* fungus. And there above them, flying down, is the Phoenix, the sun-bird of noon and high summer, supreme embodiment of brilliant, masculine Yang. They will do each other a lot of good, because the egrets (or cranes) symbolize immortality, or at least the long life which happy and beautifully executed sexual relations naturally produce. How far into semiology and the life order ceramics can reach! This plate if very good for us.

Here I should like to introduce a short digression, just to ride one of my hobby horses, which is relevant to the question of modern ceramics. I have felt, for a long time now, that Western ceramics has been bedevilled by the pseudo-Japanese tea ware which dear Bernard Leach brought over to Britain, and Hamada's example reinforced. Here is a piece of real Chosen Karatsu. But there are thousands of potters who believe that it is possible, by some kind of direct inspiration, to produce superficially similar pots, either "reticent" (that is to say, undeveloped), or wobbly and kinked ones that will somehow express deep insight by those very properties alone. In the absence of the Japanese tradition, complete with its kinetic roots, I do not personally see how this can be so.

This is where the question of art language as convention emerges. For we must remember that the Japanese inherited and developed precisely that Far Eastern linear tradition (here Korean) with which the peach on this Japanese door is incised. Lucy Rie's teapot that Garth showed was a straight Japanese influence—very common then in Vienna. A similar sense of rhythm and variation embodied in this tradition is actually embodied in even the most eccentric raku tea ware. It appears as a refinement upon that superb Chinese linearism I have been discussing—radical certainty. Here is, first, a Chinese prototype: a rhythmic *i-pin* (untrammeled) painting of Zen monks by Shih-ko. And next, its descendant, a Japanese painting by Korin, following its own careful formulae for radical spontaneity.

One must not miss the consciously radicalist revamping of an old tradition of rhythmic expression which actually contributes to the symbol system of this piece of Japanese tea ware. Nor can we forget that a close and intensely cultivated set of qualities codes the piece into its total Japanese environment: an environment, in fact, from which its whole meaning springs, and in which it is consummated—in this case, a work of garden art shows the links. I do not think it is enough simply to claim, as the artists of Beat Zen used to claim, that we should be satisfied with immediate response to the naked object, pointing nowhere beyond itself. Privately, I think this theory sprang from a misreading of D.T. Suzuki, the pioneer of Zen writing in English. It misunderstands the radical sense of "fullness" implicit in Buddhist intuition.

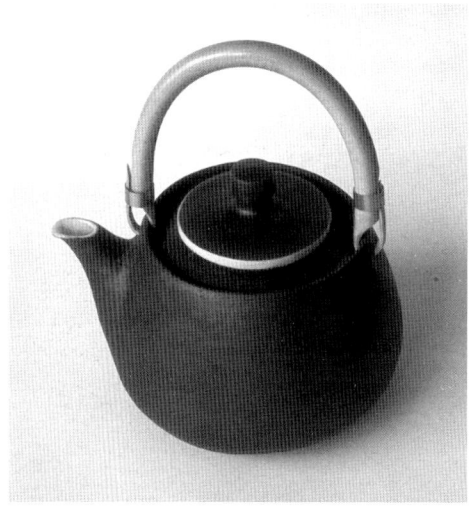

LUCIE RIE, *TEAPOT*, 1965. PORCELAIN, 20.3 CM.
PRIVATE COLLECTION
PHOTO: GARTH CLARK GALLERY

This piece of tea ware relies on what one could call "two-stage" metaphor. It refers to experiences of appearance which are themselves interpreted as indices to the whole of which they are an appearance. The experiences are seasonal and emotional, connected with beloved sanctity and ultimate security, with warmth in the face of change and decline, with the power of modesty in the face of the power of dominion and destruction. For all of these, the pot embodies metaphors, not least by means of the way it was meant to be used, held in the hands at the tea ceremony and gazed deep into.

This question of the more specific fields of metaphoric reference, which pots may embody, I have discussed before in the book. Here, in this tea ware by Koetsu (seventeenth century), we find perhaps an ultimate in subtle statements: Yang white is banded above Yin dark, heaven over earth; they band and part from each other like this in deepest autumn. Yang withdraws upward and Yin fills the abyss; everything is coming to a standstill. Humility, retirement, and autumnal rest are indicated. The striping of the bands is not strict; but it is felt as a shifting adjustment, like the seasonal movement itself. It is the vital key to the meaning. The hands also play a major part in the perception—a tactile image as much as a visual.

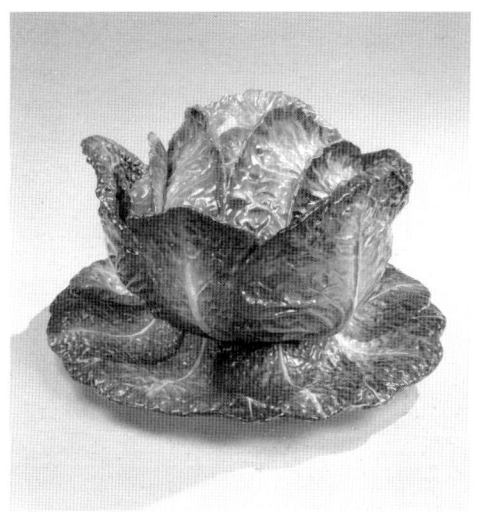

COALPORT, *CABBAGE TUREEN FORM WITH UNDERDISH*, C.1830. PORCELAIN, 23.5 CM.

This kind of "feeling for" rather than "statement of" is precisely what I mean by complexity of metaphor. The pot is dignified by the cosmic metaphor, just as the seasonal phase is by the pot. The clarity and precision of art is a clarity of pointing, not of bald statement. This Tung-yao celadon goes maybe too far in the direction of statement. It verges on conceit. It tells us a little too exactly that the pot is equivalent to leaves and sprigs; though, personally, I can forgive its fancifulness for the sake of its elusive presence and proportions. In a way, I would find it more difficult to accept a Dresden cabbage tureen for its extravagant harshness, or the more extravagant conceits of modernist mannerism, which mimic other objects, like a stand-up comic imitating the president of the United States.

I find the formal allusiveness of this fluted, red Colima (Mexico) tripod vessel infinitely subtle; it does not fall over into conceit, despite its bird-head feet. It claims to turn itself into no actual gourd. Yet the definition of its essence as a pot is pinpointed by strong metaphorical suggestions into our fund of experience; from there, a variety of analogous experiences are awakened to resonate together as we witness

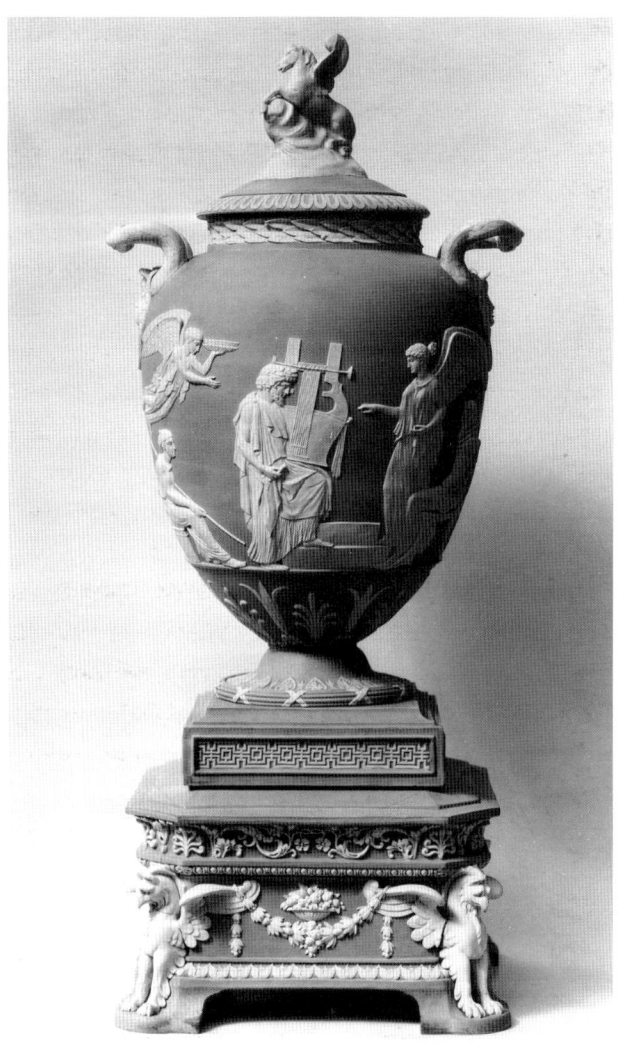

Wedgwood Pottery, *Jasperware Vase with Cover*, 1782.
Jasperware, 47.0 cm.
Collection/Photo: Metropolitan Museum of Art, New York. Gift of Frank K. Sturgis, 1932

it. It and its parts subtend in us a variety of rhythmic acts as we perceive it, appropriate to its status as a pot, body, and container. Its generating contour is superb, counterpointed by the rhythmic flutings; and it has, to the highest degree, that quality of presence I shall be discussing in a moment.

Similarly multi-referential is the glaze on this Sung dynasty Chun-ware dish. This kind of reduced copper flambé seems to have been discovered by the conservative Chun potters by accident. And it was read by the Chinese as a kind of natural cryptography, revealing how the purple energies of heaven—passing through our world from the constellations—penetrate the object and give it quite individual characteristics. My point, in all these last few works, is that the metaphorical image originates in the pot, generating its resonance in us; there was, indeed, a public ready to read the semiotic clues; and we may join that public even before we know we are totally right. There is leeway in the reading for each of us to come up with his or her own valid answers to the question of the object's ultimate meaning. Knowledge can only add to our responses.

How, then, can we look upon this fine piece of eighteenth-century Wedgwood jasperware? It is rigid with signs and symbols, all specified down to the minutest detail. Spontaneity was an irrelevant cultural criterion. The ware relates it to—no, equates it with—the Portland Vase, that great piece of late-classical cameo glass. The design by Flaxman is based on Roman cameos. The lid is crowned by a post-Renaissance, pseudo-Roman, triumphal equestrian monument. One feels that such a meticulous assembling of symbols for the Roman Virtue (supposed to be induced by a classical education) may suggest many things. Among them would be that the people for whom it was made felt happiest living by accepted prescription and learning, rather than by what we would call individual response. There is only one way to read it.

The shape is trimmed and disciplined; one might say lacking in energy. But indeed it satisfies. As the tombstone put it, it is "Pious without enthusiasm." Also, the object seems very self-contained, without interest in its ambience. Probably it would have been virtually an architectural component of the decor of the house in which it sat as an emblem of acquired good manners.

This brings us to a more positive, indeed metaphysical, transcription of the idea of the pot as matrix or material: that is, the notion of presence and presentation. It seems to me to be almost a criterion for judging good ceramics; it goes like this.

When one looks at a fine pottery piece, like this Nazca vessel from Peru, from the normal angle of approach—usually from a little above and to one side—it is the surface that invites one to approach it, not the contours. The part that faces us nearest is what we grasp it by, not the remote edges; this in spite of the fact that the surface is a function of its contours. The point is that there is always that about well-conceived ceramic contours which leads you to the middle of the pot, to apprehend its presence. We perceive a pot not as line but as surface which moves through well-varied and interesting curvatures. Furthermore, any design added to the body will add to the web of its own curvatures—as it does on this Zuni Indian pot—so that the apparently two-dimensional curvatures of the design, which are actually three-dimensional, supplement, in their own way, the complex curves of the actual surface.

Here is where I have some doubts about the Malevich ceramics. I admire his work greatly for the way it generates that extraordinary sci-fi field in two dimensions. This seems to me not to work on the curvatures of rather feeble blanks. For a pot is, above all, a surface offering a variety of rhythmic inflections; and well-painted ornament participates fully in that curvature. This is why merely globular pots, or pots with over-simple or merely busy contours and ornament appear boring. When the metaphors of the shape are carried through by the coded references of the design, which also help to assert the middle of the visual field, we reach a new level of meaning: here blue yin on white yang body. The drawing, as we read it, runs off along different curvatures into the spaces generated by the pot surface.

In this piece of Northern Chinese Sung dynasty celadon—a bowl just the right size to be held in the paired hands. There can be no mistaking the way the design focuses our attention on the body, itself floral. That shape is certainly the consequence of subtle, linear drawing in space. But try, in your mind's eye, to cut diagonal sections through the volume of the pot and see how interesting the curves that process generates are. The volume is by no means a simple one. It is clear, yet it eludes all the obvious categories of analysis.

To illustrate how a ceramic shape can develop its "presence" through our apprehension of surface as an index of subtle volume, take this piece of Southern Chinese Lung-ch'uan celadon. The fluting and facets make us apprehend it—from the middle—as a complex body; but it can be read as a combination of forms. The floral base is crowned by a kind of inverted pericarp. The neck, which is by no means a hard contour, can be inverted as "impaling" the flower calyx. The rings on the neck have a rhythmic, proportional relationship with the optical spacing, horizontally, of the petals. When you look carefully, the contour is by no means simple. But it is not stressed.

I am putting on this more recent ceramic now, not, I am afraid, to praise it. The glaze is splendidly colourful; but this piece, made in Paris in 1896, is a rather good example of a pot that has almost no middle. It lives, it seems to me, by the kinked lift and tuck-over of its outlines—kinked, if feeling, about halfway up. Its interest is accordingly diminished. Its surface curvatures strike me as fairly feebly developed.

Finally, I would like to show you one or two of my favourite pots, because all of them do something extremely interesting. Here, on this hand-formed pot from Mexico, we see the

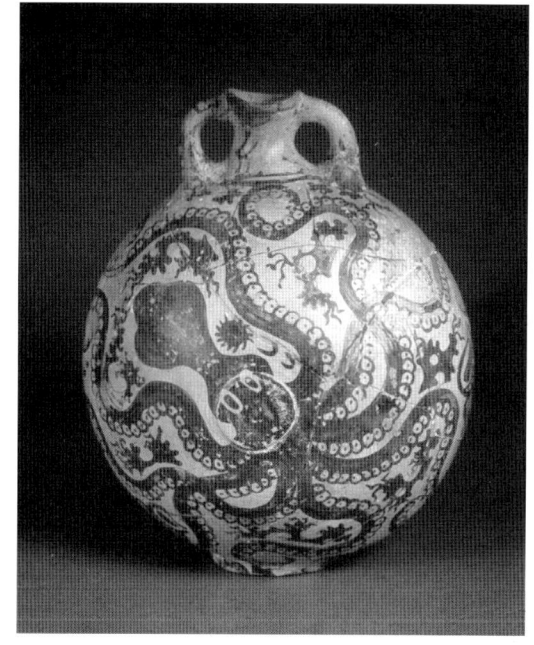

PALAIKASTRO, CRETE, *OCTOPUS VASE*, C. 1500 BC. TERRA COTTA, 27.9 CM.

COLLECTION/PHOTO: HERAKLEION MUSEUM, CRETE

representation of a centipede. Rather as in the Chinese dragon vase, we see that the three-dimensional surface of the pot gives the centipede's body an "actual" curvature, corresponding to that curvature which a centipede's body in our space would have. But he is, emphatically, not in relief. That would spoil it. He is also shown as "climbing up," "reaching for" the lip of the bowl. His movement is thus an active transcription of the shaped surface of the bowl and a presentation of its nature as centred holder and container. There is a similar concordance of design and shape in this Cretan vase, belonging to the Museum of Herakleion. There can be no mistaking the mutuality of the pot form and the upward-growing plant in white. The loops of the petals rehearse and multiply the loops of the lugs. The form itself is by no means as simple as it may look. Do that imaginary cutting of diagonal sections again, and you get some very interesting results. It is more than likely that this vase was meant to support an actual spray of flowers, which would complete its upper form.

The form of this one, the great Cretan octopus jar, is a direct extension of the last. Here we are back again in the realm of the sea goddess, Our Lady of the Sea. The body of the octopus and the movement of its limbs are firmly related to the curvatures of the mobile surface, so we never have the feeling that we are looking into the space of the jar as if we were looking into an aquarium. The body of the octopus remains on the surface and "realizes" the multi-dimensional curvature of the pot itself. So the curvatures of the tentacles can play games with our perception of that surface, which then becomes a subtle image of space; and the apparent "downward" movement of the animal takes place within a definite "upward current" suggested by the shape of the pot. This is, indeed, a valid presentation of that great lady whose creatures are woven of her own substance; they realize it by their presences, embodiments illustrating her creative activity. The pot also refers us back to that dual function of containing and giving, molding and uttering, which I personally feel we need once again to reach for.

Chapter 5

The Mud File

John Bentley Mays

A pre-dynastic Egyptian pot, roughly egg-shaped, the size of my hand: made thousands of years ago, it has survived in more than one sense. A humble, passive, somehow absurd object—yet potent, mysterious, sensuous. It conveys no comment, no self-expression, but seems to contain and reflect its maker and the human world it inhabits, to contribute its minute quantum of energy.
Hans Coper, 1969

Presented at *Edges: In Thought, In History, In Clay*, 1985, Toronto
In memory of Hans Coper

1. In the beginning was the mud. Mama Mud, and that was all, when everything began. But there was this problem, because no people lived yet. And that is why Babymaker went to Mama Mud and why, when he got there, he fashioned a thing out of mud that looked just like her. But the thing didn't have any life; it was just mud. Babymaker then let the sun shine in the mud thing, and he breathed warm breath into it. Presently, the thing that looked just like Mama Mud made a little noise. Then it gave a little sneeze and opened its eyes.[1]

2. My grandmother, a Southern lady of the old school, regularly had her face packed in mud. After the treatments, her cheeks would be pale as fine polished ivory and soft as vellum to the touch. But I liked it best when she still had the clay

preparation tamped down all over her face, with her long gray hair and her tiny frame bound up in wide wraps of sheeting. Then, Grandmother was no longer the genteel old lady in black watered satin, who took me to Sunday School and gave me hot chocolate in an orange Fiesta Ware cup afterwards. Grimacing rigidly, eyes and mouth fixed in an alert expression between astonishment and prayer, she became a mask. She sat quiet as a doll in the beauty parlor, a white-wrapped, plastered devotee in a ritual of stillness and allure. And that is how I remember my grandmother. Our Lady of the Mud Packs. Granny Love and Night. Aphrodite of the Clays.

3. The astrologers at Babylon put the work of potters (along with that of gardeners, undertakers, garbage collectors, and chimney sweeps) under the rulership of Saturn—the Greater Malefic among the seven worlds, author of visions, earthquakes, and the element known as lead. He is the slow, ancient Titan who was turfed out by Jupiter and his brand of young, buckeroo gods, very long ago, in the Cosmic Wars. But he was, nevertheless, allowed to live on and rule in the tomb city, the deep lead mine, the winter dark of the Zodiac: the solstitial House of Capricorn. Saturn, ruler of potters: Old Father Time shuffling along with his scythe at midnight, the strange, grizzled hermit who huddles in the graveyard at the edge of town. Dirty old man mumbling filthy words, some say; others say his words are wisdom from Deep Heaven. Cold, dry, and heavy in disposition, Saturn loves those who handle Earth, the heaviest of the four philosophical elements, the other three being Air, Fire, Water. He enjoys looking over the shoulders of the melancholy workers who create worlds with Mud Mama's mud. Saturn, wondrous patron of the cold spinning paternity of the wheel. (You potters are Babymaker, creating the world over and over again, wonderfully, at Mud Mama's cunt.)

According to Lilly's *Introduction to Astrology* (1647), the members of Saturn's terrestrial tribe, potters included, are inclined to be, "profound in imagination, in act severe in words reserved, in labour patient." They are drawn to the nocturnal: cold, dark, and heavy, earthy and feminine and concave. They will seek solitude in quarries, clay pits, graveyards, cellars. They must guard against becoming "envious, covetous, and mistrustful; timorous, sordid, sluggish, suspicious." They are prone to "all agues proceeding from cold, dry melancholy distempers, palsies, vain fears, fantasies and dropsy."[2]

4. WONDERS OF THE MUD MUSEUM. Our Lady is bald and has no feet. Her butt juts out squarely, more box than bustle, between girlish waist and legs like cannon

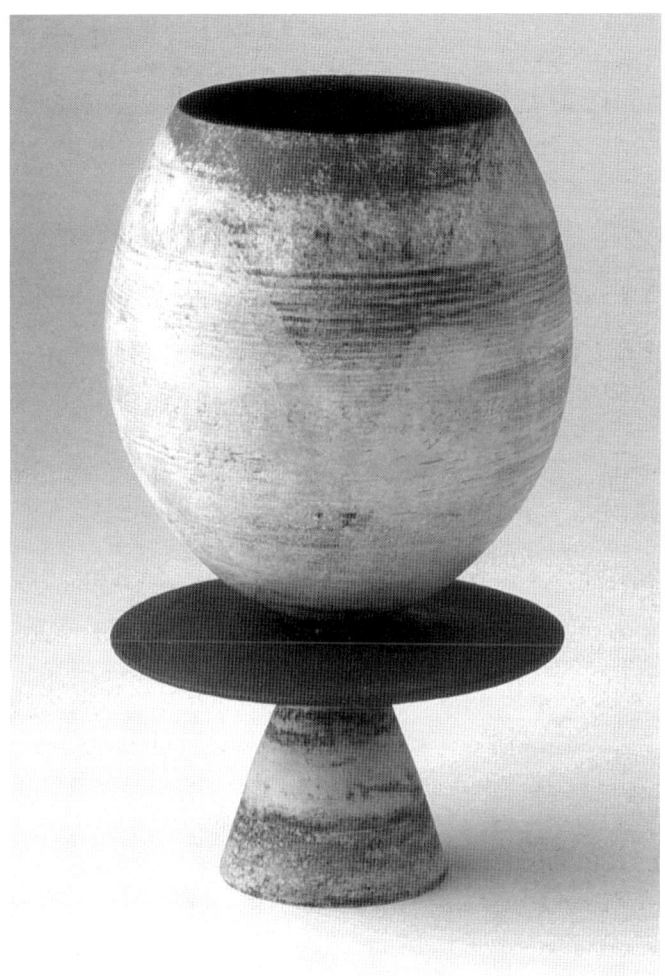

HANS COPER, *CUP FORM*, C. 1970. STONEWARE, 13 CM.

COLLECTION: JOHN PAGLIARO

PHOTO: GARDINER MUSEUM OF CERAMIC ARTS, TORONTO

barrels. The breasts say no more than a middle-aged white man's. Her shoulders are broad as a boxer's, her neck thick. Our Lady's big body is twisted slightly, busily, in nice sex torque. A figure of a young man clamours over the woman's body, simultaneously sucking one of her flattish breasts and penetrating her at the pace and angle she determines. Our Tough Lady of the Matriarchs, calling the shots, keeping her lover a child-man dependent on her whims, wants, lusts. (And that is the way it was in the time before the Revolution of the Men, which is our time now.) When I saw this artifact, I wondered: Is the memory of the Time of the Matriarchs—the mamas on top before the papas got on top—embedded in everything that comes spinning off the wheel? Is everything made of mud always whispering about the old times, when we men worked for the sexy grannies of us all?[3]

5. In the season when I was turning into a man, I kept to myself a lot, haunting the overgrown, rain-cut ravines in the scruffy upcountry woods beyond the graveyard. When not scouting for animal traces or rare plants, I hunted for rocky oddities in the moist, red slit running along the bottom of each ravine. There were brittle knots of clay, the size of walnuts, lying loose in the gully-bottom rubble and muck. Cracked open, each revealed a tiny model of the universe as Ptolemy understood it. At the center was a little Earth, usually a stony nugget. Surrounding that kernel concentrically were the planetary spheres of hardened clay, ranging in colour from yellow and blood-red to black. I pretended these things were the eggs of raw, new universes nestled in the gully like peas in a string-bean pod. I made believe that they would hatch out eventually if kept warm, so I took them home and put them in birds' nests on the mantle over my bedroom's fireplace to get warm. And I guess they are still on that dusty, crowded ledge, my tiny clay cosmologies, years after I laid the last pine-log fire on the red-brick hearth, and left home to be a man.

6. THE MUD SERMON. Understand, O Sariputra, that from age to age, the potters have always pursued their melancholy work. From the beginning, they have clawed the mud from the body of the Earth, from whose round body we all came. From the beginning, they have taken the mud and shaped it into this fragile thing, the tiny, sneezing woman of the old tales, one instant of concave form between chaos and chaos. Know then, O Sariputra, that every pot is the first woman and every potter the first man and that every pot is an image of life itself and the universe, which is but a formal instant between parentheses of chaos. From the beginning, O Sariputra, every pot has been a making real of the eternal Feminine's womb

space, the source of life and Being itself. The emptiness of the pot, opening within Chaos and resisting it, is the Creative itself. The potter, O Sariputra, creates emptiness, not pottery; absence, not form. And in so doing, he creates the unwobbling pivot of the world, the silent centre from which come all love, language, and peace. From the beginning, the pot is the most fragile of made things, O Sariputra, yet the most wonderful. The sword may think himself everlasting, because he is hard, bright, and strong. The diamond may think himself everlasting, because he is able to capture sunlight in his unfathomable depths and blunt a steel point. But alone of all crafted things, the pot alone is everlasting, because it is nothing and peace.

7. Flying from Los Angeles to Vancouver in the summer of 1980, I passed over the most awesome thing I have ever seen. The center of it was the steaming, jagged summit of Mount St. Helens, which had blasted away its cap of ice and stone a month before. But the awesome thing itself was the vast shroud of mud on the land in all directions from the volcano. Trapped under that deadly, leaden coat were the scalded corpses of humans, millions of tree trunks, and countless bodies of animals, all killed by the sudden, hot hail of ash and the torrent of mud. A few weeks ago, in the thick darkness before dawn, a slumbering volcano in South America suddenly awoke and belched forth a river of steaming mud that killed thousands of villagers. Mama Mud as Black Kali, old Mother Night and Nature, calling the lost children back to her terrible bosom.

8. WONDERS OF THE MUD MUSEUM. On one face of it, a clumsy portrait of Frederick the Great being crowned by a putto, and inscribed "King of Prussia," with the date 1757; on the other side, an allegorical figure of Fama and a military trophy bearing the names of the monarch's nine successful military victories. This jug merited the best part of a page in Thomas Carlyle's massive work entitled *Frederick The Great*, published between 1857 and 1865. In this scrap of pottery, the ruthless attacker of Victorian materialism and glorifier of heroes sees a memory of better days. "It is a Mug got up for temporary English enthusiasm, and the accidental instruction of posterity," writes Carlyle.

> It is of tolerable China, holds a good pint; and offers, in little, a curious eyehole into the then England, with its then lights and notions, which is now so deep-hidden from us under volcanic ashes, French Revolutions, and the wrecks of a hundred very decadent years.[4]

Looking for evidence from a time when people had more respect for authorities, Carlyle latches on to a pint mug. Observation No. 1: Pottery is always being used as evidence for something. Observation No. 2: Commemorative pottery usually involves the stamping of an image from male iconography (Frederick as hero-king-saint) on the female form (jug-form, womb-form); hence an attempt at camouflage, an assertion of the dominance of the male over the female. Observation No. 3: The exploitation of this plain beer jug for the purposes of hysterical, anti-modern propaganda is an instance of that most persistent and compulsive modern syndrome: the revenge of mind against matter (the body, especially the body of the woman.)5

9. The mouse-gray topsoil in which my father planted and grew his cotton lies like a thin, torn blanket on the ancient red clays of north Louisiana. At the frayed edge of the fields was a rugged gully, a long red rip in the soil, fun for hiding and climbing in. When we came back up to the house from an hour's play in the gulch, our shoes and jeans would be stained with the gore of red clay. A violent storm came up on the spring morning my grandmother was to be buried, flooding the fresh-dug pit in the cemetery. The undertaker took her little corpse back to town to wait for better weather, leaving me at the open grave, which was filling up with dark water stained red. At the end of the 1960s, a four-lane expressway was pushed straight across the rolling upcountry of north Louisiana. Surveyed from the shaded hilltop graveyard where my father and grandmother lay, the unpaved bed of the new highway nearby looked like a savage gash in the green land, scratch of a huge claw.

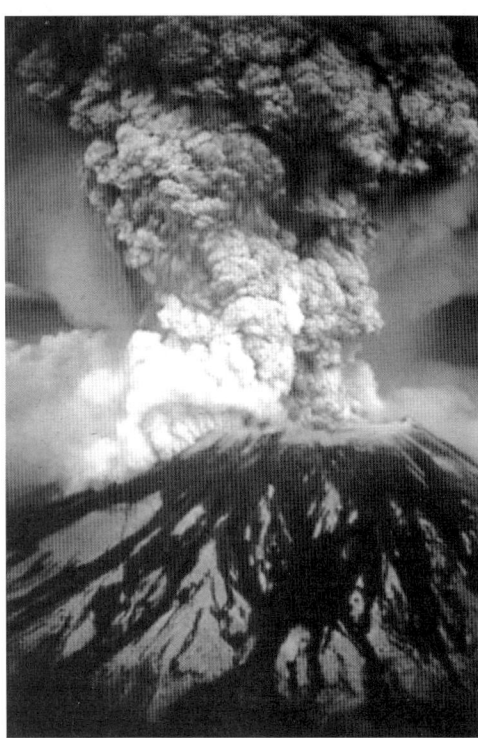

MT. SAINT HELENS VOLCANO ERUPTING, MAY 18, 1980

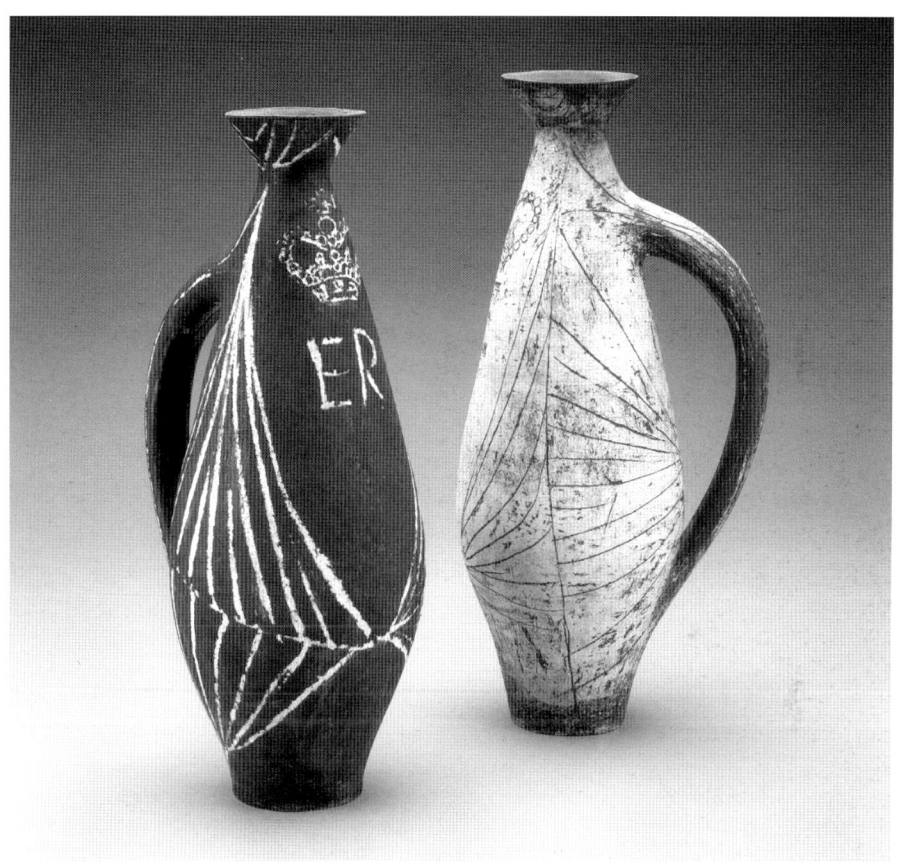

HANS COPER, *PAIR OF CORONATION PITCHERS*, C.1953. STONEWARE AND SLIP, BLACK PITCHER 47.0 CM.; WHITE PITCHER 48.3 CM.
COLLECTION/PHOTO: AARON AND BETTY LEE STERN

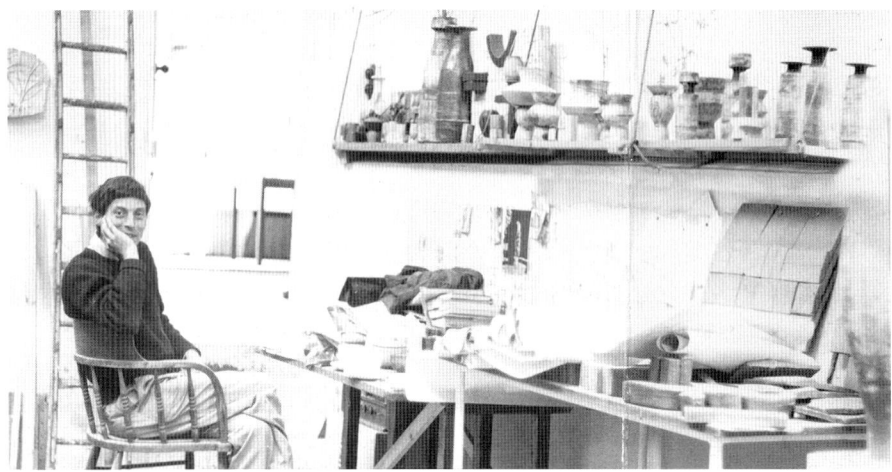

HANS COPER IN HIS STUDIO, FROME, ENGLAND, C.1965.
PHOTO: JANE GATES COPER

10. The mud and the potter. The female Chaos is given intelligible form by the male: an old, old story. The I Ching tells us that

> the Creative is heaven. It is round, it is the prince, the father, jade, metal, cold ice; it is deep red, a good horse, an old horse, a lean horse, a wild horse, tree fruit. The Receptive is the earth, the mother. It is cloth, a kettle, frugality, it is level, it is a cow with a calf, a large wagon, form, the multitude, a shaft. Among the various kinds of soil, it is black.[6]

When the rising, active power of the Creative (*Ch'ien*) meets the sinking, passive power of the Receptive (*K'un*), the result is Peace (*T'ai*), the eleventh hexagram. Peace: image of two lovers perfectly coming together. Peace: image of the potter at the wheel, mind and mud meeting in alert contentment of perfect union.

11. WONDERS OF THE MUD MUSEUM. No blame: "In this way heaven and earth unite, and all beings come into union," says the Confucian commentary. "The light principle is within, the shadowy without; strength is within and devotion without." Solid pleasure, clear purpose, a weighty sureness: the best things a member of Saturn's family can hope for. But the next hexagram (the reversal of the hexagram of Peace) is Stagnation (*P'i*): "Things cannot remain forever united," warns the oracle; "hence

there follows the hexagram of Stagnation." Stagnation: image of the potter tiring of his wheel and honest work, hating the dirt, clutter, and quiet tedium of his studio. Stagnation: image of the potter with clean fingernails, hankering after the bright, metallic chatter of the art world. To whom Confucius says sternly:

> Heaven and earth do not unite: The image of Stagnation. Thus the superior man falls back upon his inner worth in order to escape the difficulties. He does not permit himself to be honored with revenue. The stagnation comes to an end: first stagnation, then good fortune.[7]

A pre-dynastic Egyptian pot, roughly egg-shaped, the size of my hand: made thousands of years ago, it has survived in more than one sense. A humble, passive, somehow absurd object—yet potent, mysterious, sensuous. It conveys no comment, no self-expression, but seems to contain and reflect its maker and the human world it inhabits, to contribute its minute quantum of energy.[8]

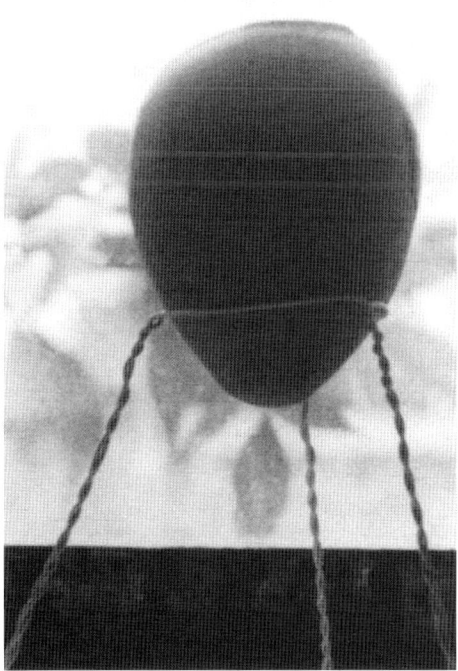

PRE-DYNASTIC: EGYPTIAN, *EGG POT*,
C. 5500 - 3000 BC. FAIENCE, 7.6 CM.
PHOTO: JANE GATES COPER

1 Loosely adapted from a Maori text quoted in E.S. Craighill Handy's *Polynesian Religion* (Honolulu: Bernice Pauahi Bishop Museum, 1927) 39.

2 William Lilly, *An Introduction to Astrology* (London, 1647) 35-37, 64-65.
Claudius Ptolemy, *Tetrabiblos*, in the Leob Classical Library (Cambridge, MA, 1921).

3 Depicted in James Mellaart, *Earliest Civilizations of the Near East* (New York: Mcgraw-Hill, 1965) 108.

4 Thomas Carlyle, *Frederick the Great* (1857-1865) volume vii.

5 Sir Henry de la Beche and Trenham Reeks, *Catalogue of Specimens in the Museum of Practical Geology* (London: George E. Eyre and William Spottiswoode, 1876) 218-220.

6 The summary of the Creative/Receptive doctrine of *The I Ching* appears in Jerome Rothenberg, ed., *Technicians of the Sacred* (Garden City, NY: Doubleday, 1968) 18-19.

7 Quotations from the Oracle are from *The I Ching or Book of Changes*, translated from the Chinese by Richard Wilhelm, rendered in English by Cary F. Baynes (Princeton, NJ: Princeton University Press, 1950) 440-450.

8 Hans Coper quoted in Tony Birks, *Hans Coper* (London: William Collins Sons & Co, 1983) 202.

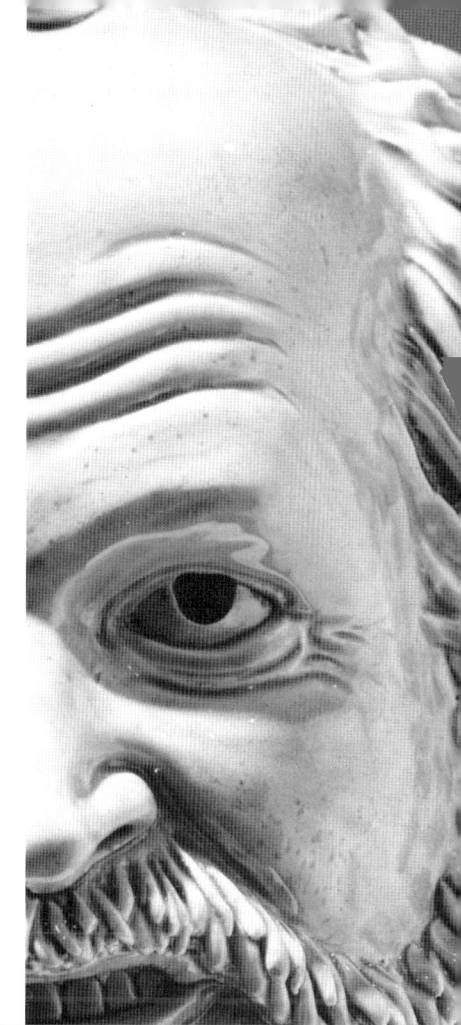

SECTION TWO
CERAMICS AND
MODERNISM

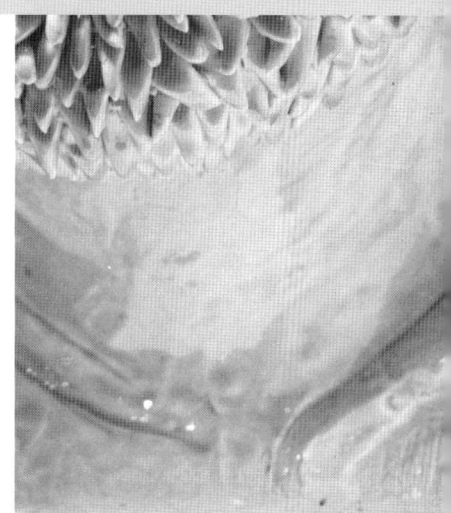

Chapter 6

Radical Ornament:
Ceramics at the *Fin de Siècle*.

Paul Greenhalgh

If one were to look at ceramics as a creative practice in the twentieth century and reduce the entire range of production down to its basic components (a luxury we can afford ourselves at this point in the millennium, I think), an interesting picture emerges. It becomes clear, with regard to vessel and sculptural work, that two central ideological constructs, both developed to their full pitch in the later part of the nineteenth century, have mediated production and characterized its division into types of, and to attitudes toward, practice. I will label these two constructs genre and style.

Presented at *The Ceramic Millennium*, 1999, Amsterdam

At the turn of the last century, a surge of activity in the decorative arts led to the creation of a self-conscious, international modern style: Art Nouveau. A complex, multi-faceted style rather than a single movement or aesthetic approach, the modernity of Art Nouveau was based on an eclecticism that positioned it at the head of the visual arts and allowed it to relate closely to the literary and scientific worlds. It was a golden age of radical ornamentation. Ceramics thrived in this environment. This paper will examine key issues in ceramics, focusing primarily on France, England, and Scandinavia. The idea of modernity will be dragged away from the simplistic notions that privilege the rise of the modern movement in design, notions that necessitate the depiction of the fin de siècle as decadent and transitional in nature, and explore, through the ceramic medium, the intellectual agenda of those who believed themselves to be creating an ornamental modernism.

I want to briefly look at the type of ceramic practice that was deemed to be the most advanced—radical—in the *fin-de-siècle* period, namely, that deemed to be within the parameters of the Art Nouveau style. In April 2000, the Victoria and Albert Museum (V&A) will stage the largest exhibition to be held on Art Nouveau since the style declined toward the opening of the Great War. As lead curator, much of what I have to say to you today occurred to me while worrying about this exhibition. There is a large catalogue with this exhibition, with endless references to ceramics and a chapter dedicated to Art Nouveau ceramics by my V&A colleague Jennifer Opie. So today I don't want to simply repeat the story of Art Nouveau ceramics, as it is to be told elsewhere in some detail. As this is a millennial occasion, and Art Nouveau was a centennial forebear, I thought I would take the opportunity do something else as well. Art Nouveau was the first attempt to generate a modernist style premised on decoration. It was also the last. I will be arguing today that many of the struggles, triumphs, and failings of Art Nouveau relate directly to our current situation.

Indeed, it was only as I finalized this paper for delivery to the *Ceramic Millennium* organizers that I came to realize what it was actually about. Overtly, it is concerned

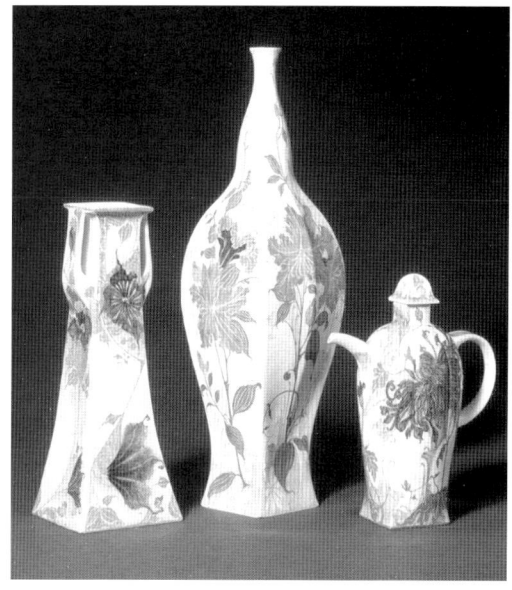

DESIGNED BY J. JURIAAN KOK, PAINTED BY SAMUEL SCHELLINK AND J.M. VAN ROSSUM, TWO VASES AND A COFFEE POT, 1903, 1904, 1909. *EGGSHELL*. MADE BY HAAGSCHE PLATEELBAKKERIJ ROZENBURG.
COLLECTION/PHOTO: VICTORIA & ALBERT MUSEUM, LONDON

with the role of ceramics in the *fin-de-siècle* period generally, and Art Nouveau ceramics specifically; but it is actually about the infrastructure of modernity, about the material and intellectual frameworks that dictate, at any one time, the shape and rules of engagement with the modern.

There are, of course, several frameworks that need to exist for any form of practice to move beyond the arbitrary and subjective into the mainstream of our culture. You need a material infrastructure that provides a machinery to allow things to be made; you need material and technology, facilities for training artists and designers, retail outlets for selling and promoting, publications for debate and dissemination, and entrepreneurs at all points to make the machine as a whole function smoothly. Classically, in our own times, of course, the crafts have lacked such an infrastructure.

For the material infrastructure to function, you also need what I will term an "ideological infrastructure," though this is not an entirely satisfactory label. By it I am implying the ideas, systems of logic, mythologies, symbolism, and—in the widest sense—politics that shape a sphere of practice, that join those practicing within it and that give direction to the whole enterprise: a collectivized, naturalized vision of the meaning of practice. None of you actually *need* to make, curate, sell, or write about the stuff you do. In practical terms, none of your work needs to exist. Utilitarianism does not provide a rationale for studio ceramics. But you do need to do these things, and your audience needs you to do them, from an emotional, intellectual, and psychological point of view. In a higher, idealistic sense, you all have a *why* you do, and it is this *why* that concerns me most at present. These whys need to be better cohered among themselves; they need to be given weight in the form of history, shape in the form of our belief systems, and direction in the form of our coming ambitions for the new century.

And we have to make the material infrastructure synonymous with the ideological infrastructure; that is, we have to reconcile the material and mental realms in practical as well as idealistic ways. As a higher ideal, perhaps, we have to use the arts we are engaged in to struggle with the central issue of modern culture: the unacceptable isolation of the individual from the larger notion of society. We need every technological, artistic, and political device available to us to close up that space, as it is the most destructive space in existence. I raise it here, as it was perceived during the Art Nouveau period to be the central politico-cultural concern of radical thinkers during that period. It continued to be so for modernists in the new century, and it remains, I believe, a major tension as we conclude our own *fin de siècle*, one that postmodernism has not resolved.

One of the key features of practice in Art Nouveau was the attempt to deal with the individual/collective dichotomy, or the space between the individual, his or her consciousness, and the collectivity that was society. In an increasingly global and urbanized world, it began to appear that the individual—the self—could only survive in opposition to the growing omnipresence of mass society. Art Nouveau designers attempted to develop a visual language that might reconcile the two. The chosen means of addressing it was decoration. For these designers, decoration was centrally to do with mediation—with the creation of a vehicle to develop visual language that might collectivize and objectify individual intervention in the object.

This brings me to my subject matter for today. Art Nouveau, with its epicenter in the decorative arts, was a dramatic and flamboyant stylistic development in the visual arts and, after 1893, tore through Europe and North America. It failed in the years running up to the First World War as dramatically as it had triumphed previously. It emerged from the intense activity of a number of entrepreneurs, artists, designers, craftspeople, manufacturers, and writers in the rapidly expanding urban centers. Defined simply, Art Nouveau was the first self-conscious, internationally based attempt to transform visual culture through a commitment to the idea of the modern.[1]

Art Nouveau was deliberately eclectic, a style determined to reinvent the past in order to arrive at a future. The myriad sources used, however, dropped into one of three types, and these are reflected in Art Nouveau ceramics. These types are endlessly explored in the 2000 exhibition and book. Suffice it to say here that they were:

1. NATURE. Nature functioned as a signifier of modernity. Nature itself had undergone dramatic change during the course of the second half of the nineteenth century, leading to a situation in which it was seen as representing a break with the past and a vision of the future.

2. HISTORY. Designers made use of what I will term "alternative histories." New types of historical sources, and especially those from outside the accepted canon, were embraced as a means of radicalizing the subject matter of art and design. The art of the Celts, Vikings, and folk art, for example, were embraced. This also

included the arts of nations from outside of Europe, including North and Central Africa, Indonesia, China, the Islamic nations, and, most importantly, Japan.

3. SYMBOLISM. The intense obsession with psychological and spiritual issues led to an embracing of most forms of *fin de siècle*.

Despite its extraordinary significance for the formation of attitudes to visual culture in the modern period, the *fin de siècle* is rarely cited as a key period for the formation of attitudes to ceramic practice. This is clearly an historical oversight; alongside other genres, ceramics was transformed in the period.

Art Nouveau ceramics fully demonstrated the use of a range of sources. Reoriented history is everywhere; psychologically intense symbolism is a major preoccupation, and nature is omnipresent. Ceramics were produced by four kinds of production units in the *fin-de-siècle* era:

1) Established porcelain factories, often enjoying royal, state or public patronage
2) Smaller, specialist ceramic factories, or "art potteries"
3) Individual studio potters
4) Large scale, factory-based operations

I will deal with these in order.

1) ESTABLISHED PORCELAIN FACTORIES, OFTEN ENJOYING ROYAL, STATE OR PUBLIC PATRONAGE: Concentrated on luxury, these operations would employ high-calibre technicians and import artists and designers of reputation to design their wares. Despite being consumer driven, the more prominent factories also sought to innovate where possible in order to expand the design repertoire of the factory. Most big porcelain factories made things that would count as Art Nouveau, and some developed a whole line. Rosenberg in Holland, Meissen and Nymphenberg in Germany, Royal Copenhagen in Denmark, Rörstrand in Sweden, and Sèvres in France, for example, all produced interesting variations on the Art Nouveau theme.

This type of producer took Art Nouveau up in different ways across Europe. Clever marketers within these luxury-trade producers understood well that Art Nouveau might well have a cachet for certain parts of the market. Too respectable to engage closely with the radical end of artistic practice, the established factories tended to pick up on it as the style revealed its staying power.

The porcelain factories were aware of the implications of a style premised on flux, progress, and change. They understood that there was a class within European society that did not lack funds, that needed to eat off plates and drink from cups, and that was also committed to flux, progress, and change.

2) SPECIALIST CERAMIC FACTORIES, OR "ART POTTERIES": Set up specifically to create unusual or "artistic" wares, usually in a specific style or idiom, these factories, or art potteries as they were known in Britain and the United States, tended to have artistic directors who would have a design vision. Less overtly consumer driven, the smaller factories found their niche within the marketplace by appealing to the artistically inclined middle classes.

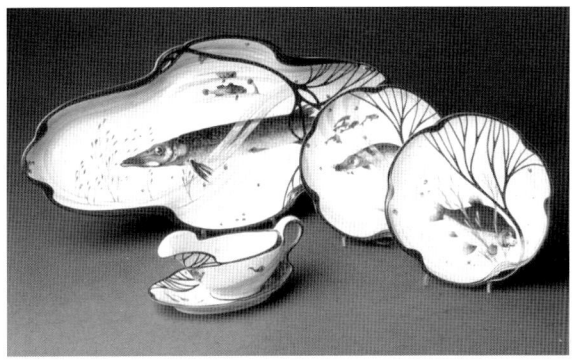

HERMANN GRADL, PART OF A FISH SERVICE, 1899. PORCELAIN. MADE BY KÖNIGLICH-BAYERISCHE PORZELLAN-MANUFAKTUR, NYMPHENBURG.
COLLECTION/PHOTO: VICTORIA & ALBERT MUSEUM, LONDON

These producers were perhaps the most innovative in terms of adventurous ceramics generally, and of Art Nouveau particularly. The art potteries tended to experiment with radical forms far more readily than the larger producers. Occasionally, a large industrial producer set up a small art pottery subsidiary that would function on a quasi-independent basis. Often set up by entrepreneurs who were committed to a radical vision of art, the small, specialized factories operated internationally and saw style, not simply as an historical phenomenon or as a component in the sales procedure, but as a vehicle for the achievement of change. The art potteries in England rarely produced pure Art Nouveau but lived rather in the hinterland between the Arts and Crafts Movement, aestheticism, Morris and Company, and Art Nouveau. Nevertheless William de Morgan, Minton, Doulton, della Robbia, the Martin Brothers, the Ruskin Pottery, and others added texture to the international scene.

Full bloodedly in the Art Nouveau world was the Zsolnay factory in Hungary, which experimented with organic and complex, eclectic forms and brilliant, often lustrous glazes. The Arabia and Iris Potteries in Finland and the Brandjes factory in Holland developed powerful local variations on the Nouveau style. The dramatic rise of the art pottery in America gave that nation one of its few vehicles of expression of the new art. The Teco, Rookwood, Grueby companies and a dozen others in America all produced within the international Art Nouveau milieu. Gallé and Tiffany in France and America respectively, while being centered on glass production, had healthy lines in metalwork, jewellery, furniture, and ceramics.

3) INDIVIDUAL STUDIO POTTERS: In many respects my third category overlaps with my second, in that they clearly practiced as individual makers, but the enterprises they founded often had the scale of small companies. For example, the French potters who were centrally responsible for the explosion of glaze experimentation and the stoneware revival contributed hugely to the naturalist aesthetic of the Art Nouveau canon. Taxile Doat, Ernest Chaplet, Adrien Dalpayrat, Georges Hoentschel, and August Delaherche produced remarkable works. Doat was an important figure as a teacher as well as maker, but perhaps Chaplet was the key figure. Apprenticed to Sèvres before setting up a workshop for Haviland and finally going on his own, he pioneered highly competent, batch-produced and individual wares that hung between an Oriental and European aesthetic. It was he, more than anyone else, who brought Paul Gauguin fully into contact with ceramics. Dalpayrat, Hoentschel, and Delaherche used root and gourd forms in a celebration of natural growth, these vessels being used in Art Nouveau interiors throughout Europe.

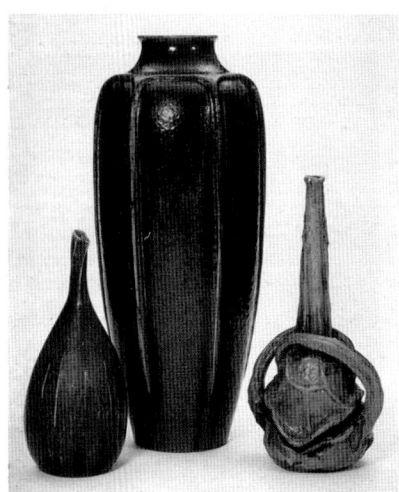

PIERRE-ADRIEN DALPAYRAT (LEFT), AUGUSTE DELACHERCHE (CENTRE), GEORGE HOENTSCHEL (RIGHT), VASES, 1893-1900, C.1890-92, 1895. STONEWARE WITH HIGH TEMPERATURE GLAZES AND GOLD.

COLLECTION/PHOTO: VICTORIA & ALBERT MUSEUM, LONDON

Studio potters are, perhaps, the currency most of us here recognize and identify with most clearly. The studio potter was undoubtedly an invention of the *fin-de-siècle* period, despite the copious literatures that embrace the phenomenon as a quintessentially twentieth-century invention, beginning with—and exemplified by—practitioners like Bernard Leach. The embryonic artist potters were individualist and tended to "bump into" Art Nouveau, as it were, rather than consciously residing at the centre of it. Rather than describing any of them overtly as Art Nouveau practitioners, perhaps it would be best to say that, at certain moments, the work of such potters might easily be included as being within the parameters of the Art Nouveau style. Drifting into their circle, Paul Gauguin became, for a period of a few years, a most interesting ceramic artist, as well as an astute writer on the subject.

More spectacular than any of these, the ceramic sculptor Jean Carries fused Symbolism with the concerns of the Art Nouveau mainstream to produce some of the most gripping works of the *fin de siècle* in any medium. He combined an often brutal realism with mythic elements that lent his work an intensely emotional content.

In Denmark, Theodor Bindesboll's dramatic vessels, heavily painted with expressionist drama, are among the most stunning works in clay of the last hundred years. And in America, Adelaide Robineau and George Ohr, among others, created works that barely sit in the period they belong to.

4) LARGE SCALE, FACTORY-BASED OPERATIONS: Unlike the first three categories, these manufacturers focused on quantity and the broad marketplace. The design of ceramics in such operations was powerfully consumer driven, controlled by decision makers outside of the actual production cycle, and would usually be limited to the reproduction of previously proven designs. In many factories, there might actually be no designer at work, but rather a manager with a pattern book. The mass outlets made little in the way of Art Nouveau during its classic period of 1890-1914. After this it made headway, sub-Art Nouveau borders and patterns appearing in catalogues. The style was used in much the same way as the Rococo, Baroque, or neo-Gothic. It was fodder for the production of a look that might sell in the absence of its symbology and ideological meanings.

The Structure of Modern Ceramic Practice

If one were to look at ceramics as a creative practice in the twentieth century and reduce the entire range of production down to its basic components (a luxury we can afford ourselves at this point in the millennium) an interesting picture emerges. It becomes clear, with regard to vessel and sculptural work, that two central ideological constructs, both developed to their full pitch in the later part of the nineteenth century, have mediated production and characterized its division into types of and attitudes toward practice. I will label these two constructs "genre" and "style."

The tension between genre and style—though not identified in those terms—actually began to develop well before the *fin-de-siècle* period, in debates that can be identified as far back as the 1830s. Style through the nineteenth century was widely accepted to be the visual representation of a culture. A style, such as Ionic Greek, quatrocento Renaissance, or Sarcenic, was held to represent the essence of those cultures. Artist and writer Richard Redgrave, writing in 1853, pointed to the implications of this:

> When these qualities arise out of the purer and nobler of qualities in man's nature, the style they produce will be noble also… the influence of a mean style, founded upon ignoble or sensual qualities, will in like degree tend to degrade not only our taste but our moral intellect also.[2]

The implication is clear. Style was not what individuals made, nor was it to do with practicalities; it was the collective expression of a society, and represented its psychological, intellectual, and moral condition.

In opposition to this vision of style, Gottfried Semper, among others, developed the idea that materials should "have their own say, undisguised, in the shape, the proportions most suited to them,"[3] and he also identified what he termed "tectonics," a system of design based on rationalist approaches to nature. Eugène Emmanuel Viollet-le-Duc similarly attacked the idea of style as emanating out of cultural expression. He tied it powerfully to rationalist-technical approaches to design.

Our aim, then, should not be to know what relative proportions the Ancients or the Moderns have thought proper to give to the Orders.... We should make it our chief endeavor to explain how reason should dictate architectural forms.[4]

Effectively, these thinkers and practitioners focused the idea of creative practice on materials and techniques, and on the logical progression of the tradition of making. So, within debates on the arts, an opposition developed between those who believed the appearance of things to be determined by sociology and anthropology, and those who saw appearance as emanating from the materials and techniques.

During the last quarter of the century, the debate developed markedly, as new intellectual forces came to the fore in visual culture. Style became the subject of evolutionary theory and politics and was increasingly explained in terms of the *Zeitgeist*, or spirit of the age. Within the world of things, style became, for radical designers, a total look capable of transforming the consciousness of the world. It became associated with objective, collective values, and it increasingly came to be perceived to relate to designers working across a range of products.

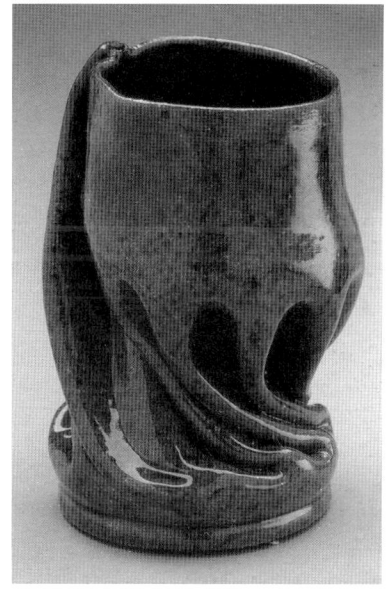

GEORGE OHR, *PITCHER*, 1895-1900. EARTHENWARE.
COLLECTION/PHOTO: PRIVATE COLLECTION, NEW YORK

The genre, on the other hand, became distinctively associated with materials and techniques—the Semperian vision—and also developed a distinctly individualist dimension to it, whereby the artist or craftsperson engaged overtly in a personal struggle with specific materials. Increasingly, it became the terrain of the craftsperson or someone dedicated to a single medium, who would not necessarily engage with the macro idea of style at all.

Design thus became the vehicle for style, and craft became the terrain of craft. An example of two practitioners will serve well here: George Ohr and Henry Van de Velde. Ohr's highly individual exploration of ceramic materials, in order to explore nature, himself, and the world around him, offers an archetypal example of the genre-based artist, working obsessively through a single set of practices and materials to arrive at a highly personal statement. His eccentricities, played up gloriously by the artist himself, masked, of course, an immensely sophisticated understanding of the condition of art in his times. As I implied above, artist-craftspeople like him "bumped into" the notion of style; he drifted through Art Nouveau rather than actively engaging with it. He was a studio craftsman.

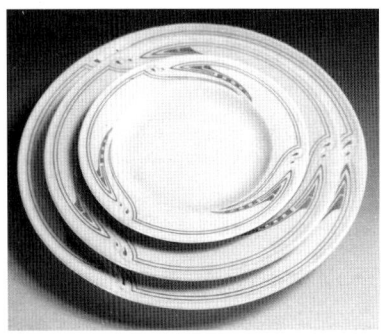

HENRY VAN DE VELDE,
COLLECTION/PHOTO: VICTORIA & ALBERT MUSEUM, LONDON

Van de Velde's vision of style was completely at variance with this. He saw style as a spiritual collective, a phenomenon that could, if it were orchestrated appropriately, transform human consciousness. Having trained as a painter, he came to engage with many materials in his career. He was a designer.

Into the twentieth century proper, style and genre, it seems to me, have become absolutely the domains of the designer and craftsperson respectively. I have very rarely been asked, as someone interested in twentieth-century and contemporary culture, to speak on the issue of craft and style. Alternatively, it is normal for me to be asked to discuss style when the issue is perceived to be design.

Craft and design, as we have them now, were effectively inventions of the *fin-de-siècle* period; they were honed and finished during the new century and brought to their definitive, isolated conditions after the Second World War. Ceramics can be a genre or a material for the expression of design, but—with interesting, exciting exceptions—these two worlds have not been interfacing well. There are reasons for this, I think, which carry me back to my initial points about material and ideological infrastructures.

What many artist-designers within the Art Nouveau milieu struggled with was the relationship of the individual to society. Indeed, their great achievement was to engage with this central issue of the relationship of subjective consciousness to collective society. Ohr and Van de Velde never met, were from different universes, but the issue of private and public language, and the means by which one might deal with this duality through visual culture, was central to them both. Ohr started with the self and attempteding to create a public language to describe it; Van de Velde privileged the idea of society and tried to create art that expressed the collectivity of modern humanity. In this way they were at opposite poles, Ohr playing the ultimate individual to Van de Velde's Utopianism. However, what held them in proximity within the world of Art Nouveau, was a shared concern with the function of the individual in relation to society. This was expressed through the idea of decoration. Decoration held style and genre in proximity.

It is an interesting and instructive exercise to ask ourselves what we feel when we look at Ohr and then at Van de Velde. We realize that the two answer related, but ultimately distinct needs. The first explores questions about an individual being alive in the world; the second pulls us out of ourselves and invites us into discourse with others. The first plays Rembrandt to the second's Poussin.

Whether based in genre or style, Art Nouveau practitioners assumed that the world of decoration, the ornamental arts that had been central to the creation of personal and public environments through the millennia, was the battleground for the achievement of an unalienated modernity. The decline of the concept of decoration as a vehicle for the expression of modernity after Art Nouveau has been, I put it to you, one of the central and debilitating problems of the century for all our professions. The absence of mediation between style and genre, and the absence also of mediation with the larger world, has led to the relative isolation of practice. In ceramics, it can be witnessed in the lack of genuine interface—with famous and notable exceptions—between craftspeople and designers. On a macro-conceptual level, this can be identified as a split between subjective and objective worldviews. The return to strength of decoration in the last two decades is welcome, but the struggle for the decoration of the next century is now afoot, and that implies change and development in the way we all do things. We should remember, also, that while within Art Nouveau decoration reigned as mediator between subjective and objective impulses in the visual arts, those practices within its remit enjoyed a golden age, the like of which we have not experienced since.

Allow me to briefly restate an earlier point. Regarding ceramics specifically and visual culture generally, until the material and ideological infrastructures are effectively brought together and made to work for one another, modern ceramics will always be a partial and alienated creature. Needless to say, ceramics should not operate in isolation from other genres. It should strive, as all modern genres do, to obsessively perfect itself; but the infrastructure, if it is doing its job, will automatically bring it into the arena of the totality of visual culture.

Decoration at the last *fin de siècle* implied collaboration, communication, plurality, contextualization, assimilation, and that much abused component of life, negotiation. It was a process of mediation and absorption. These qualities were not present simply among practitioners but are also witnessed throughout the material and ideological infrastructures among curators, dealers, writers, manufacturers, and patrons. Art Nouveau was Wagnerian—it suggested an orchestration of activity.

I would suggest that the inclusiveness of the Art Nouveau period is a model we might visit again. I am not suggesting that we make things that look like Art Nouveau. Just the opposite. We should reject the look and learn the underlying lesson: collaboration, communication, plurality, contextualization, assimilation, and negotiation. We should be using the best of our political acumen and the sharpest of our new technologies to interface with each other in order that the culture we represent—ceramics—can lock fully into the larger world. This implies development not only in our thinking—the ideological infrastructure—but also a transformation of the material infrastructure. I would suggest that this process has already started: there are companies, galleries, shops, journals, and Web sites that bear witness to this, as indeed does this meeting. We need now to push on I think.

Just as the artists, craftspeople, and designers of the last *fin de siècle* embarked on an adventure to reinvent their world, in the same spirit, we should all hope to reinvent ours.

1 See Paul Greenhalgh, *Art Nouveau 1890-1914* (London: V&A Publications, 2000).
2 Richard Redgrave, *Manual of Design* (London: Chapman & Hall, 1853).
3 Quoted from Paul Greenhalgh, *Quotations and Sources from Design and the Decorative Arts 1800-1990* (Manchester: Manchester University Press, 1993).
4 Quoted from Paul Greenhalgh, *Quotations and Sources from Design and the Decorative Arts 1800-1990* (Manchester: Manchester University Press, 1993).

Chapter 7

Modernism and Ceramics Today: an Overview

Michael McTwigan

When Malevich himself turned his gifts to pottery design, he was only interested in the idea of a cup or teapot, not an actual functioning one. It was left to his followers, such as Nicolai Suetin, Ilia Chasnik and others to apply Suprematist forms to functional objects. A few years, later both Constructivism and Suprematism were out of favor. Nevertheless, Malevich and his followers stand as examples to later ceramists who have similarly tried to rethink traditional pottery forms... as a basis for a kind of meditation on the sculptural and spatial dynamics of ceramics.

Presented at *Ceramics and Modernism*, 1981, New York City

What is modernism? As Erwin Panofsky makes clear in his book Renaissance and Renascences, what is modern to one generation may be ancient to another. Listen to the words of a fifteenth-century architect and sculptor, Antonio Filarete: "I too used to like modern buildings but when I began to appreciate classical ones, I came to be disgusted with the former." [1]

Doesn't that sound like Philip Johnson, our famous postmodern architect? Which buildings do you suppose Filarete meant when he said he was disgusted by *modern* buildings? Gothic cathedrals, of course. I only make the point as a warning. So much has happened in this century, that to trace the influence of modernism on contemporary ceramics would be a lifetime undertaking. But let's explore a few key issues common to both.

Impressionism was the apogee, the furthest frontier, of traditional painting, that is, painting whose aim was to capture the *illusion* of three-dimensional reality on a two-dimensional surface. Artists of the ancient world, of the Renaissance, and of the late nineteenth century were all trying to paint a representation of nature that was so lifelike you could almost touch it.

Picasso changed all that. When he painted the first Cubist painting in 1907, he dispensed with one-point perspective and illusion. This opened the door to a whole new way of thinking about art. For, if painting no longer had to represent something *else*, it could just be *itself*. At the time, this was a scandalous idea. Can a medium that no longer has a function still be valid? It is well to remember that the question of function was debated as heatedly by painters seventy-five years ago as it was by ceramists in the 1950s.

Another aspect of modernism that dates from the mid-nineteenth century is the depiction of ordinary people and everyday objects and themes. Baudelaire urged artists to paint the "heroism of modern life," which Monet and other Impressionists did. The Cubists followed suit, incorporating violins and guitars, glasses, scraps of newspaper, and other objects in their painting. In Italy, the Futurists were enthralled by machinery and the speed of modern life; so they tended to paint bicycles, automobiles, and trains in their compositions. The Russians were hot on the trail, following the various facets of Cubism and its related movements.

Before we go forward, we must go backward a minute. In 1912, Picasso pasted a piece of cloth onto one of his paintings that was printed to look like chair caning. This was the first collage. Collage represented a clear challenge to traditional painting. In effect, Picasso was saying, "If you want to represent a chair seat, just paste one on." Two very important developments in modern art result from this revolutionary step, each of which cut its own separate path in twentieth-century art. First of all, it reinforced the idea I mentioned earlier that painting did not have to represent something else; it was something in itself. It was an *object*, a physical presence, like any other object. The implications of this I'll discuss later. Secondly, for modern painting it was the first step toward the third dimension. Collage introduced just a thin layer of an applied material, whether it be paper, cloth, or whatever. To artists like Vladimir Tatlin of Russia, this signaled the end of the road for painting. He had

had enough of the game of illusion. Why not have the real thing? So, in 1913, Tatlin began making reliefs incorporating pieces of iron, glass, wood, tar, cardboard, and other materials, eventually leading to constructions that did away with the picture frame entirely.

This is a very important precedent for ceramists. Tatlin, professing his "culture of materials," believed that each material generates its own appropriate form. Iron, wood, glass—each has its own unique colour, texture, and method of forming. This is the truth-to-materials doctrine we have heard so much about from modern artists, architects, and craftspeople. For nearly fifty years, this has been regarded as one of the Ten Commandments of modern art. Tatlin argued that color and texture should derive from the materials themselves, and not be artificially applied. I don't think I need tell you how widespread this approach to clay has been in our time.

As if these individual revolutions in art weren't enough, an actual revolution swept through Russia in October of 1917. Tatlin, Kazimir Malevich, and other leftist artists saw this social, political, and economic revolution as the natural companion to their artistic one. They renounced painting as an art form. The poet Vladimir Myakovsky declared in November of that year:

> We do not need a dead mausoleum of art where works are worshipped,
> but a living factory of the human spirit—in the streets, in the tramways,
> in the factories, work-shops, and workers' homes.[2]

And art critic Nikolai Punin urged that art must be available to all people: "The proletariat will create new houses, new streets, new objects of everyday life," he proclaimed and called for the establishment of factories to produce them.[3] Tatlin, Alexander Rodchenko, and their fellow Constructivists wanted to become artist-engineers and to transform life into art, whether it be a house, a teapot, or a pair of shoes. Unfortunately, they were eventually dismissed as impractical romantics.

Malevich, on the other hand, claimed that art was a spiritual activity, and if it became useful, it was no longer art. Since he considered Tatlin's concept of the artist-engineer a mere craftsman, when Malevich himself turned his gifts to pottery design, he was only interested in the *idea* of a cup or teapot, not an actual, functioning one. It was left to his followers, such as Nicolai Suetin, Ilia Chasnik, and others to apply Suprematist forms to functional objects. A few years later, both

Constructivism and Suprematism were out of favour, and two very important modern movements came to a close. Nevertheless, Malevich and his followers stand as examples to later ceramists who have similarly tried to rethink traditional pottery forms, or who have used these forms—the cup, the vase, the teapot, the bowl—as a basis for a kind of meditation on the sculptural and spatial dynamics of ceramics.

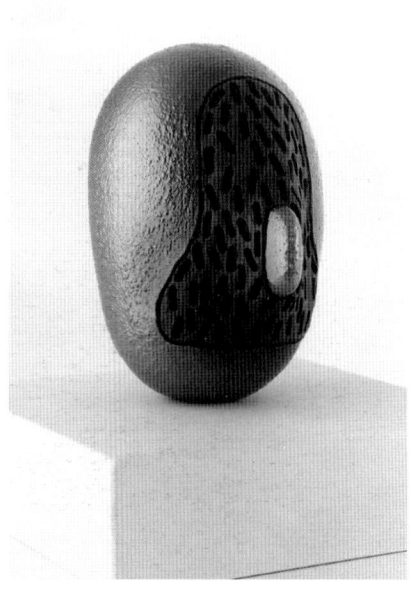

KENNETH PRICE, *M. VIOLET*, 1965.
STONEWARE WITH PAINTED SURFACE, 15.2 CM.
COLLECTION: LORD DUFFERIN, LONDON.

From the beginning of his career, Ken Price approached the ceramic medium in a nontraditional way. His forms of 1965 employ an egg or globe shape that affords the artist an all-over surface—a kind of unending canvas. Approached from any angle, there is something for the viewer to see. Right away, two modernist concerns are apparent: first, the desire to present multiple views of something; second, the importance of colour. Price was one of the first to use colour as an essential element for clay sculpture. His early works also employ the textures of real objects—recalling Tatlin's culture of materials—such as the pebbly surface of an orange or the black layers of slate. Unlike the Constructivists, however, Price did not use the actual materials but mimicked them in clay.

Then began his well-known series of geometric cups, a form he continues to explore to this day. In this series, Price reorganized the spatial dynamic of the cup form to create a new sculptural vocabulary for ceramics. The early examples, made in 1974, adhere closely to the general configuration of a cup: an upright container with a handle. As he continued to work in this format, the so-called cup became more and more abstract, and his current works seem to have completely left the cup rationale behind.

I said before that the egg shapes of the sixties afforded multiple viewing points.

This is just as true of the geometric series. In fact, once you've actually had the opportunity to see Price's cups in the flesh, you realize that to show *any* one view of his work—as I must do here—is very misleading. One might compare it to a postcard of the Rocky Mountains versus an actual hike through those mountains.

There is a major difference between the round shapes of the sixties and the later geometric ones, however. The early works are basically symmetrical in shape and are therefore not very different from the traditional potter's vessel, which means that if you look at it from one viewpoint, you know what to expect from any other viewpoint. But with the geometric cups, Price exercised a truly Cubist perspective. Each viewpoint offers its own laws of perspective that confound our common-sense expectations based on one-point perspective. For example, the rectangular elements that comprise these cups are all slightly askew and end in acuter angles, which creates a false sense of depth that recedes more dramatically in our mind than it does in fact.

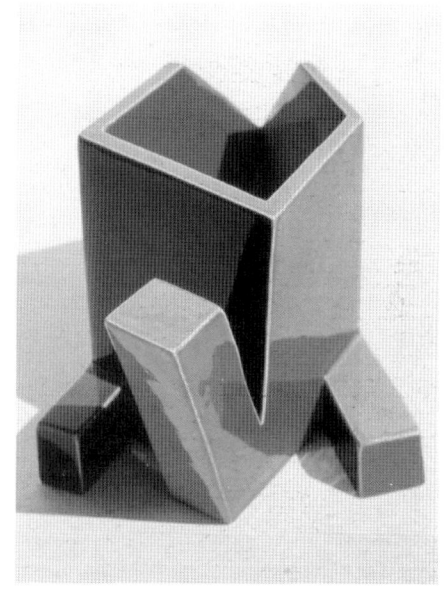

KENNETH PRICE, *UNTITLED CUP FORM*, 1973. WHITEWARE WITH LOW FIRE GLAZES, 9.5 x 14.6 x 10.2 CM.

PHOTO: COURTESY THE ARTIST

Picasso once said that if his paintings were truly successful, one should be able to cut them up and reassemble them into sculptures. This statement immediately made me think of Frank Stella and Ellsworth Kelly, whose canvases have at times resembled two-dimensional sculptures. Ron Davis's paintings on fibreglass come even closer to providing a sculptural experience in only two dimensions. We almost believe we can walk around them to see what's on the other side, to figure out where one plane ends and another begins. But because these spatial illusions are just flat pieces of fibreglass, our journey will have to remain imaginary—which is the point, after all.

Similarly, Ken Price's cups strike me as three-dimensional paintings. And although this might be construed as a criticism, there are several good reasons why these forms are ceramic. First of all, a glazed surface—being glassy and transparent—has a depth and a liveliness unobtainable on canvas. Secondly, the way clay and glaze interact allows Price to have beautifully thin white edges demarcating colour areas. Incidentally, Frank Stella leaves similar borders between colours. Finally, the small scale of his cups enables the viewer to have a very intimate relationship to them. One can't be stand-offish while trying to experience a Ken Price cup.

Perhaps this is an appropriate moment to discuss the painting as an object. As I said before, when Picasso created the first collage, he gave painting some three-dimensional substance. This, coupled with the idea that painting can be an abstract medium, like music, led to the development of "pure painting." The painterly direction led to the Suprematist compositions of Malevich and the linear compositions of Mondrian, who underscored the abstract nature of their paintings by using geometric forms and primary colours. The later colour investigations of Josef Albers were also crucial steps along the way. It's obviously not a very great step from these works to the Minimal art of the sixties and early seventies: Barnett Newman, Ellsworth Kelly, Frank Stella, and Kenneth Noland, to name a few. The emphasis on colour also revealed itself in colour-field painters such as Jules Olitski, Mark Rothko, and Larry Poons.

In the other direction, introducing the third dimension to painting led first of all to reliefs by Picasso, Tatlin, Naum Gabo, and other Constructivists, Max Weber, and Henri Laurens. It also led to paintings that were simply thicker than ever before, as well as to paintings that were literally objects, such as the *Planks* of John McCracken. The effects were much wider than this, however, and its traces can be seen in twentieth-century industrial design and architecture, and in the work of sculptors such as David Smith, Robert Morris, Donald Judd, Carl Andre, Tony Smith, and Guy Dill.

What's all this got to do with ceramics? It affected clay artists in the same way it affected painters and sculptors. It encouraged ceramists to use colour freely for itself, and not as traditionally applied glaze. It spurred bold explorations of form and space, and it offered a precedent for nonfunctional, abstract ceramics.

Peter Shire alludes to ceramic forms—primarily the teapot—which he uses as a springboard for his own particular explorations of colour and form. For example, his zig-zagging slab form is actually a teapot broken down into its components: handle, lid, body, spout. If we compare Shire to Guy Dill, we can see clearly both artists' debt to Constructivism. Of the two, Dill is closer to the spirit of Constructivist principles, for he uses materials in their natural state and allows those materials to speak in their own colour vocabulary, whereas Shire uses only clay, to which he applies colour. Shire's allegiance is to ceramic principles over Constructivist ones. An interesting thing about Shire's forms is that if they were shown to a casual observer, it is doubtful they would be recognized as teapots at all. Rather, they are an artful arrangement of forms painted in a manner reminiscent of postmodern architect Michael Graves.

What other modernist tendencies do we find in ceramics? John Mason gave up expressionist gesture for geometric singularity in 1966, when he fabricated cubes and crosses five feet tall. Glazed in a single though variegated colour, their surfaces were akin to the colour effects of certain contemporary

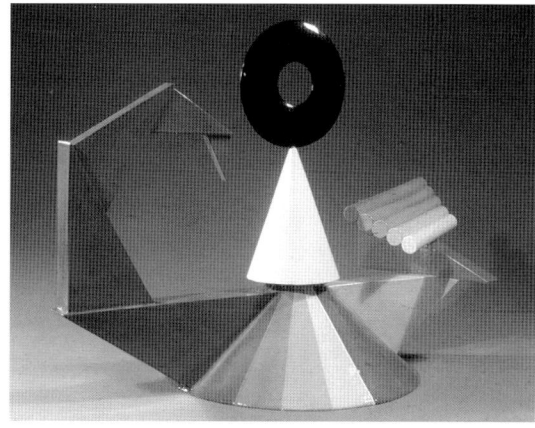

PETER SHIRE, *PAN PIPE SCORPION*, 1984. WHITEWARE, 41.0 × 62.0 × 30.5 CM.

PHOTO: GARY CAPELL

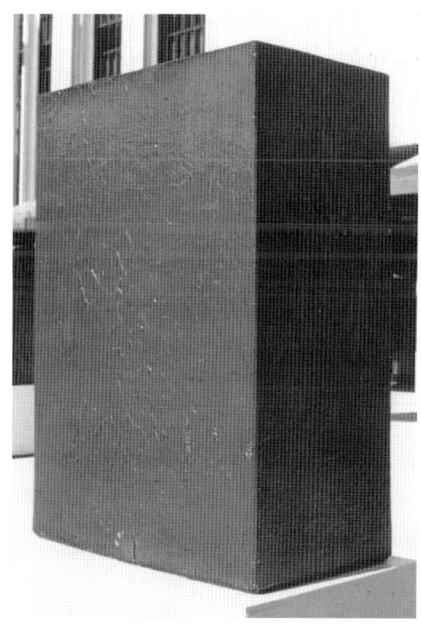

JOHN MASON, *MONOLITH*, 1966. STONEWARE, 152.4 CM.

PHOTO: HANSEN GALLERY, KNOXVILLE, TN

painters, while the forms echoed not only the Suprematist forms of Malevich, but of minimalist sculptors as well. Then Mason did a very Constructivist thing. He abandoned the hand process of craftsmanship to utilize an industrial product—the firebrick—as a module with which to construct sculptural configurations. Gone, too, is applied colour. Like Tatlin, Mason allows the variable hues of the brick to provide any colour effects. Carl Andre also uses firebrick, but in a far different manner. Sounding like a latter-day Constructivist, he said something very revealing about his intentions that are not inappropriate to Mason:

> My work is atheistic, materialistic, and communistic. It's atheistic because it's without transcendent form, with-out spiritual or intellectual quality. Materialistic because it's made out of its own materials without pretension to other materials. And communistic because the form is equally accessible to all men.[4]

Minimalist sculptors tended to play down the element of colour in order to emphasize form. Since ceramists have traditionally been trained to seek after rich glaze effects and to guard their glaze formulas with their lives, it is understandably the rare clay artist who sacrifices colour for the sake of form. Yet several ceramists have done so, for the same reason many sculptors have done so: to impress the viewer with the overall surface, the dynamics of sculptural form, and the mass or volume of the work. To use a word popular in the sixties, artists wanted to present a total gestalt and not dilute the viewer's experience with distracting, high-key colour.

Among the earlier followers of this concept are Peter Voulkos and Robert Turner, both of whom have used single or neutral colours as well as a matt surface in order to emphasize the bodies of their pots. Turner, although he, too, has retained the cylindrical vessel, is much more reductivist than Voulkos; he limits gesture to a stroke or two of the finger. These two artists' relationship to clay is so strong that they could probably never produce the manufactured look of much minimalist sculpture.

By the way, one of the reasons that minimalism may have been difficult for some artists and ceramists to accept is the minimal artist's rejection of craftsmanship. As Gregory Battock points out, the minimal artists "provide just the right surface—

a surface without craft (indeed, without art), in this way rejecting those impulses that claim glory to manual work and nobility in craftsmanship." [5]

William Daley has almost eliminated gesture from his pots so that the viewer can focus on the harmonics of geometric progression. Like Voulkos and Turner, Daley has devoted himself to exploring the dynamics of the vessel. One reason the vessel remains a potent genre, even when no longer functional, is that it is a form more intimate than others; it is inviting. Intimacy is also conferred by its scale and by the fact that it is meant to be a "hands on" experience. Unlike Voulkos and Turner, Daley pays equal attention to both the inside and the outside of his forms.

Jars and vases are primarily convex; we experience them as bodies standing before us, just as we do human bodies. Bowls, on the other hand, are primarily concave; we perceive them as spaces to be filled, which

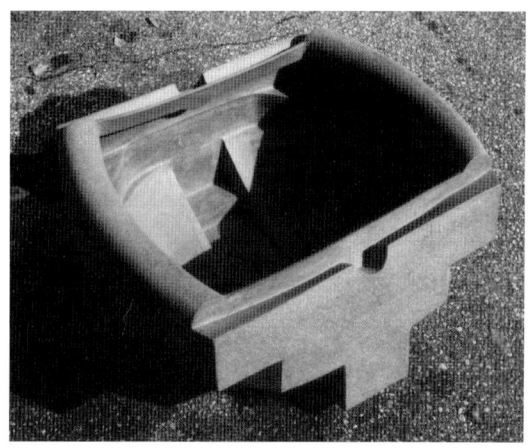

WILLIAM DALEY, *TAOS PROCESSION*, 1980. RED STONEWARE CONE 6 OXIDATION, UNGLAZED, 47.0 × 76.2 × 76.2 CM.
COLLECTION: DR. MARUM SCHIMMEL
PHOTO: JOHN CARLANO

partly explains why they are commonly used as a pictorial field. Daley has balanced these two facets—or faces—of the vessel by making each equally arresting. Looking at *Taos Procession*, the inside surface reads as a negative of the outside; furthermore, the interior space also protrudes, while the exterior mass also recedes. To pursue Daley's art, we've got to look in, duck down, and walk around these vessels. If we look only at their interiors, we miss what's happening outside and vice versa. There is no single, best vantage point.

Even Daley's titles are a clue to this central theme in his work. The carved patterns of *Taos Procession* and *Onegas Passage*, for example, might be viewed as dance notations for a Pueblo Indian ceremony; as we follow their twists and turns with our eye, a kind of performance in conjured up in our imagination. *Our Turn*, which seems to pirouette on toe, is another example of the correspondence between Daley's art and choreography.

Daley himself has likened the vessel to a sonata. Although a Bach sonata and a Daley pot are not one and the same, both forms celebrate rhythm, harmony, movement, and an almost mathematical structure. Philosophers have long recognized, as Sir Thomas Browne ruminated in the seventeenth century, that "there is music wherever there is harmony, order, or proportion," that even the orbiting planets produce what Browne called a "music of the spheres." A like analogy has been made about architecture, which Friedrich von Schiller characterized as "frozen music."

Although founded on mathematical principles, Daley's art is not minimalist, primarily because he takes advantage of the warm colour and sensuous texture of clay. To me, Daley's art is akin to Islamic ornament, of which Henri Focillon observed:

> A sort of fever seems to goad on and to multiply the shapes; some mysterious genius of complication inter-locks, enfolds, disorganizes, and reorganizes the entire labyrinth.... Whether they be read as voids or as solids, as vertical axes or as diagonals, each one of them both withholds the secret and exposes the reality of an immense number of possibilities.[6]

Anne Currier seems to be an out-and-out Cubist whose work owes much to the pioneering efforts of Bill Daley and Ken Price. Like the Cubists, and like Price, Currier has created her own system of perspective, with the result that everything looks askew. Expecting geometric forms to be regular, the diverging lines of Currier's boxes gives us the feeling that we're looking through a wide-angle lens. Like Daley, she minimizes colour in favor of form, and this monochromatic surface tends to accentuate the ambiguity of their shapes. Currier's boxes *are* vessels, but their interiors are concealed, and what may look like an opening will in fact be a dead end.

Now let's look at a few ceramists who *do* use colour. Wayne Higby utilizes the *entire* surface area of the bowl form—inside and outside. He is closely related to modernist painters, and his surfaces are very flat. Although different colours indicate different elements—sea, sand, snow, cliffs and so on—they are painted in either very flat colours or very rich ones, with the result that they look like overlapping papers collaged on top of one another. As with Cubist paintings, it is sometimes difficult to tell what is foreground and what is background. Higby accentuates this by compressing the bowls. They are not perfectly spherical, but oval, so even the depth of the bowl is shallow. Like Daley, Higby plays with the relationship of outside to inside so that the two planes seem to be continuous. This also tends to flatten or confound our sense of depth, and we find ourselves bobbing up and down, peering in and out, to see just how inside and outside fit together. Although dealing with representational subjects—mesas, canyons, and other landscapes—Higby doesn't use colour in a representational way. He seems to want us to enjoy the colours for themselves.

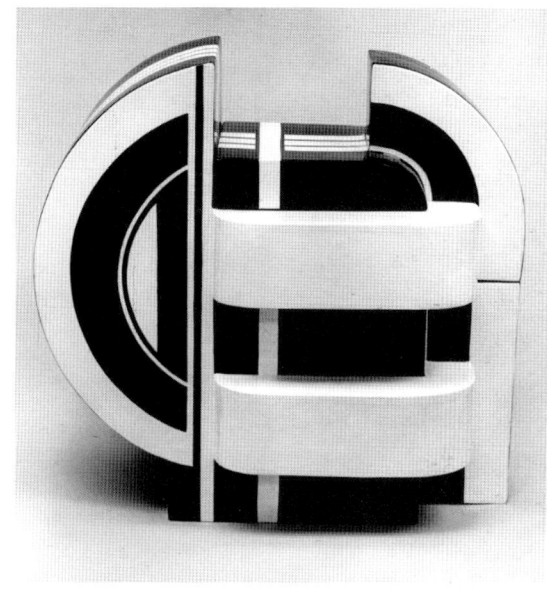

ANNE CURRIER, *Box*, 1975-76. EARTHENWARE, 50.0 x 50.0 x 25.1 CM.

PRIVATE COLLECTION

PHOTO: COURTESY THE ARTIST

Phillip Maberry also uses the bowl form and again takes advantage of its entire surface. His work is in no way illusionistic or representational, but like a colour-field painter, he sets up an overall field within which contrasting colours pulsate, vibrate, advance, and recede. Its effects are very optical; the colour is often sharp and jarring. We are so aware of colour and pattern that the form on which they sit is nearly overlooked at first, which is just what a pure painter would want.

Interestingly enough, Maberry's work relates to the early cups of Ron Nagle, which also employ somewhat violent colour contrasts. Nagle goes for colours like pink and black, peach and gray, peach and green, yellow—colours that were popular in the late fifties. During the mid-sixties, Nagle was representative of the

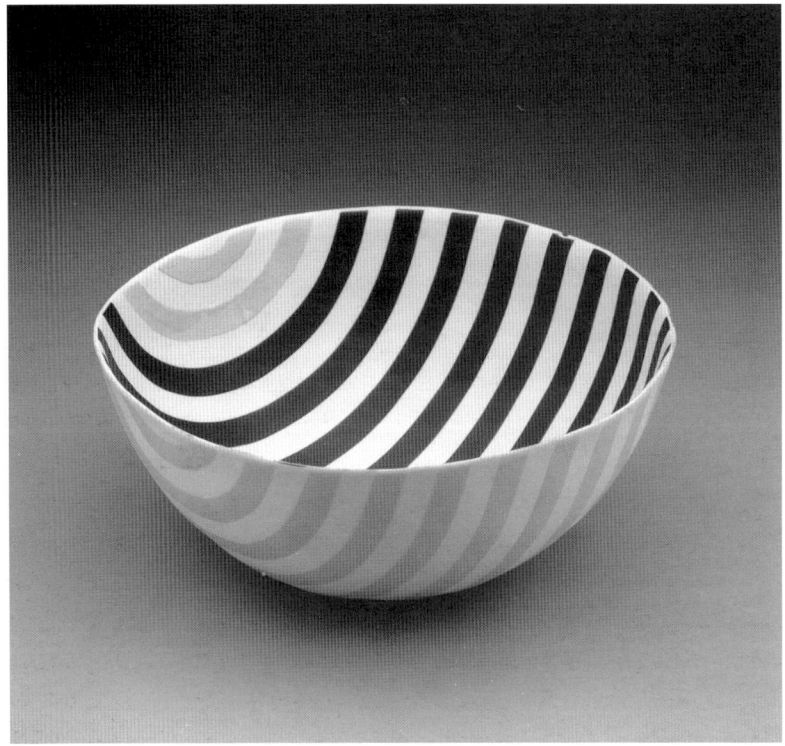

Philip Maberry, *Striped Bowl*, 1979. Porcelain with glaze decoration, 8.9 × 22.9 cm.
Private collection
Photo: John White

California fetish-finish school, whose work seemed to grow directly out of the slick, airbrushed world of hot rods and surfboards. While his early cups stayed fairly close to the cylinder shape of a mug and had container-like openings and handles, Nagle soon developed his own formal vocabulary that is unique. Any remaining trace of their function ceased when Nagle dispensed with the bottom entirely, leaving only a cylinder that you can put your hand right through, providing you have small hands.

The squares of contrasting colour that seem to be tacked on the right-hand side of these forms often remind me of fifties linoleum. Despite the fact that neither the square nor the body are painted bright, in heart-stopping colours, both have enough depth and richness of colour that the longer you look at them, the more awe inspiring they become. And their preciousness and tiny scale force us to take a close look. In recent years, Nagle has given his cups a textural interest that, if you remember, Ken Price used on his early egg forms.

One of the most interesting young clay artists working today is Graham Marks. What is exciting about many of the artists now entering the field is that their way has, in a sense, been paved for them. They don't have to grapple with hard questions like: should I be working on a large scale or a small scale? Should I use bright colours, or is that antithetical to a craft aesthetic? They're not stumbling over these issues; they're just diving right in.

With late twentieth-century sensibilities, Marks constructs what might be termed, in a Euclidian world, "natural" objects. Yet, no matter how much he draws upon nature's inventory of forms, the result is hardly natural. We might best compare him to the painter of still lifes who arranges apples and oranges in dramatic compositions that are rarely encountered outside the studio. Pursued a bit further, this analogy is quite useful, for Marks manages to fuse the still life's usual repertoire of objects – fruit and majolica jug, for example—into one form.

If one was to play God, one might well populate the planet with forms resembling these. Graham Marks has taken the Great Architect's task into his own hands. The result? Nature by design. Of course, the competition between Homo Faber and Mother Nature is long standing. The aim here is not to copy nature, however, but improve on it. Unlike the I-Hsing potter, the Art Nouveau designer, or Le Corbusier, Marks is not designing with nature but against it—much as J.K. Huysman's character created a world of artifice in *A Rebours*.

Consider six works executed in 1979. Examining first the *Heavenly Forms* (my designation), we find three massive sculptures (about 29 inches in diameter) with turquoise-blue skin and earthenware-red flesh. They resemble huge melons or gourds sliced in half. Each is more complex than the next. The first has parallel ridges running along its wrinkled skin and has been sliced cleanly to reveal its inner flesh. Our associations with forms of the vegetable kingdom are strongest in this piece. Except for its central orifice of spiraling coils divided into quadrants, its large size, and its blue glaze (triggering in the memory centuries of Eastern pottery, near and far), we might term this a found object. The second of the three has a thicker skin, a spiraling rind formed by blue coils one and one-half inches thick. This spiral pattern, coupled with the fact that the blue coils retain their skin even along the "sliced" face, leads us to suspect some artificer has had a hand in its making. The last of the *Heavenly Forms* confirms our hunch, for here the blue coils, three layers deep, zigzag over its surface in geometric regularity. The result is sculpture when viewed in the round, painting when viewed face to face. We know we are in the realm of imaginary beings, of make-believe.

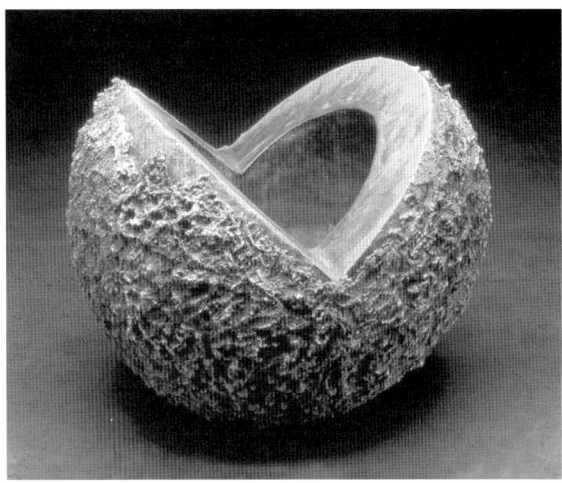

GRAHAM MARKS, *UNTITLED*, 1979. EARTHENWARE AND SLIP, 74.0 CM.
COLLECTION: SHAW FAMILY

We notice other tell-tale evidence. First of all, their enormous size and mass dwarf us so we are made to feel like poor Alice in Wonderland. The artist reinforces this perception by placing them on pedestals, which affects us in two ways. They sit in perfect repose: stable, solid, like boulders at rest. Yet they are round and may roll at any moment. We are impressed by their serene balance, yet somewhat anxious lest this equanimity be only momentary. Earthly gravity, too, is defied, for they tilt up at us in an agile stance that belies their great weight.

By placing them on pedestals, the artist tells us: no matter how familiar, these objects did not fall to earth like apples from a tree. Independent of us and of nature, their uneasy equilibrium, mass, and large scale have the desired effect: we are humbled, even reverent. This is appropriate for the *Heavenly Forms*, with their geometric regularity, their cleanly cut edges, their vibrant blue and red colours, and generally "finished" appearance.

But the three *Earthly Forms* seem out of place in this exalted, white environment. Like Lucio Fontana's clay spheres or Isamu Noguchi's chiseled rocks, these would rest more comfortably outdoors, directly on the ground. If the *Heavenly Forms* are of the vegetable kingdom, the *Earthly Forms* are members of the animal kingdom. They seem to have been broken open, not cut neatly with a knife. Earthly, dark brown, and rough, they looked weathered and old. While the blue forms appeal to our imagination, these fecund bodies stir responses in our own bodies.

1   Erwin Panofsky, *Renaissance and Renascences in Western Art* (New York: Harper & Row Publishers, 1972) 19.
2   As found in Camilla Gray, *The Russian Experiment in Art*, 1863-1922 (London: Thames & Hudson, 1971) 219-20.
3   Gray, 220.
4   As found in Gregory Battock (ed.), *Minimal Art: A Critical Anthology* (New York: Dutton, 1968) 107.
5   Battock, 35.
6   Henri Focillon, *The Life of Forms in Art* (New York: Wittenborn, 1948) 6.

CHAPTER 8

CERAMICS AND MODERNISM:
EUROPE 1910-1940

GARTH CLARK

The Futurists have created ceramics characterized by the aesthetics of the machine and geometry. Any desire to return to hybrid and static classicism is cretinous and unpatriotic. Our aerocermisti have an awareness of the corpus vasorum of all oriental porcelain; of the apothecary's bowls of the indians. They know too the shining classic Italian Majolica and value it as the best in the world. But this is not to imitate. From this knowledge they can forget, overcome and overthrow ideas and techniques of every ceramic secret with the VERY NEW, the VERY ORIGINAL and the never seen.
F .T .Marinetti and T. D' Albisol "Il Manifesto Futurista Ceramica e Aeroceramica." *Gazzetta Del Popolo* 7 September 1938.

Presented at *Ceramics and Modernism*, 1981, New York City

Ceramic art has traditionally played an evolutionary rather than revolutionary role in culture. This conservatism is the product of several factors. The potter is tied to studio, kiln, and reliance upon local materials. The resultant lack of mobility has rendered him somewhat remote from mainstream aesthetics in the arts, frequently promoting regional expression. Other factors that compound the conservative tendency are the protracted craft processes and the ties, if even only symbolical, to functional forms. The potter has therefore not been well placed to participate strongly in volatile, international avant-garde art movements.

Nonetheless, there were several involvements between ceramics and major art movements during the seminal years of modern art in Europe. In this essay, some of the most significant of these experiments will be examined: Suprematist and Constructivist ceramics in Russia and Germany and the Futurist *Aeroceramisti* in Italy.

However, it will be helpful to briefly place Cubism and its influence on ceramics in perspective before examining the other movements. This relationship has been dealt with simplistically. Many writers in the decorative arts label any post-1910 geometric stylization as Cubist. In fact, very little that has been so described actually derives from the style. One of the reasons is that the Cubist painters and sculptors did not themselves work in the ceramic medium because their rigid objectivity was opposed to the facility of this applied art.[1] A notable exception was Albert Gleizes, who collaborated with Anne Dangar in creating superb decoration on vases and plates. But this partnership came in the 1920s, too late to have significant influence.[2] Possibly the most important Cubist influence on pottery was Roger Fry's Omega Pottery, produced between 1913 and 1918, which adapted certain Cubist principles to traditional pottery form. Cubism in its pure form offered little inspiration to those working in clay in the first quarter of the twentieth century. Most of the geometric stylizing popular during the periods of Art Deco and Art Moderne came, not from Cubism, but from the geometric phase of Art Nouveau, from Constructivist influence or from a stylized use of geometric motifs from ancient art, in particular that of South America.

Constructivism and Supermatism

The non-objective art movements called Constructivism and Suprematism continued the innovation of the Sezessionstil movement's experimentation with pure geometric form, although it was not necessarily influenced by this Viennese style. Sezessionstil played an important role in establishing early new form, freeing ceramics from imitating historical styles. Although ceramics was not a major medium within the Russian movements, some important objects were produced, and at least three of the movement's leaders—Vladimir Tatlin, Kasimir Malevich, and Vasily

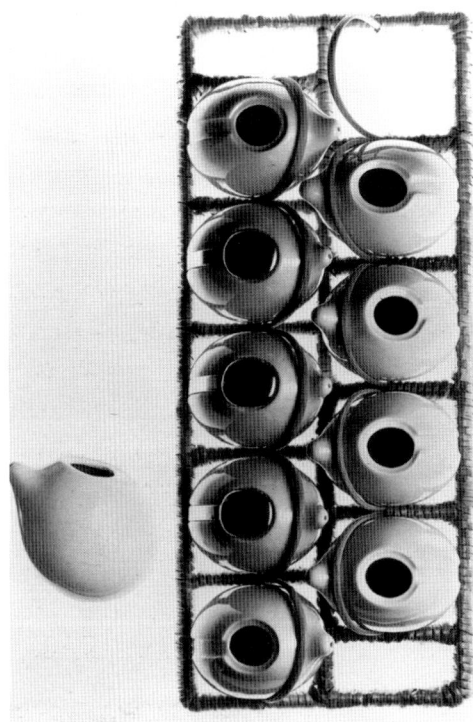

VLADIMIR TATLIN, *PORCELAIN FEEDING BOTTLES WITH RACK*, C. 1930-31. DESIGN BY TATLIN MADE BY ALEXEI SOTNIKOV, DULEVO FACTORY. PORCELAIN WITH WICKER COVERED WIRE RACK.

Kandinsky—involved themselves in creating or decorating ceramics. Kandinsky's work was the most decorative and was concerned with energetic, colourful drawing on tableware and showed little concern for three-dimensional form. The involvement of Tatlin and Malevich was more considered and dealt with new form and function concerns.

Malevich began to design Suprematist ceramics as early as 1915,[3] but his major statement came in 1920 when he was invited to design a teapot and cup for the Leningrad State Porcelain Factory. He demoted function and created the "idea" of a teapot, a brutal assemblage of hard-edged volumes out of which jutted a spout and handle. The cup was cut in half with a complex inner/outer relationship. In converting a utilitarian object into an abstraction, Malevich not only succeeded in creating a Suprematist art object but also suggested an abstract, non-utilitarian role for the potter in the twentieth century. The potter's traditional vessels could be transformed by modern art so that they became form metaphors with the form's shape made all the more ambiguous by the conceptual association with function.[4]

Tatlin's association with ceramics presented a functionalist view. He had become increasingly dissatisfied with the academic concepts of art and considered the art object bourgeois and inconsistent with the ideals of the Revolution. He ceased his work as an easel artist and began work on projects such as the utopian *Monument to the Third International* and utilitarian objects such as a do-it-yourself workman's jacket. In 1927 he was made a member of the ceramics faculty at the Moscow Higher Technical Institute (Vkhutein) where he was able to put some of his "art into life" ideals into practice.

There is only one enticing glimpse of his influence at the Vkhutein: a baby feeder that is double walled to obviate the need for a handle and which would keep the milk warm at the desired temperature. A feature of the design was a wicker rack that held nine bottles. It was designed for the Alexei Sotnikov Dulevo Factory in 1929-30 and had the legend "Culture of Materials" stamped on the base, the title Tatlin gave to his approach to design, which required the artist to "learn to use the tools and materials of modern productions in order to offer his energies directly for the benefit of the proletariat."[5]

The centre for much of the Suprematist ceramic production was the State Porcelain Factory, Leningrad. The factory began its life in the late eighteenth century as the Imperial Porcelain Factory. The factory had the impressive record of surviving the upheavals of the First World War and the Russian Revolution without losing a single day's production. After 1917 its role changed, and during the civil war, it continued to produce small quantities of objects, mainly for propaganda purposes. These were exhibited on Nevsky Prospekt in Petrograd and on Kuznetsky Bridge in Moscow, serving a political and satirical role similar to the posters of Mayakovsky in windows of the Russian Telegraph Agency.

Early Revolutionary works included vigorous portraits on plates of Lenin, soldiers, and peasant farmers. The plates were emblazoned with slogans, such as "Those who do not work do not eat," a somewhat uncompromising message for a dinner plate. Soon a heroic style of illustration emerged based partly upon a stylization of

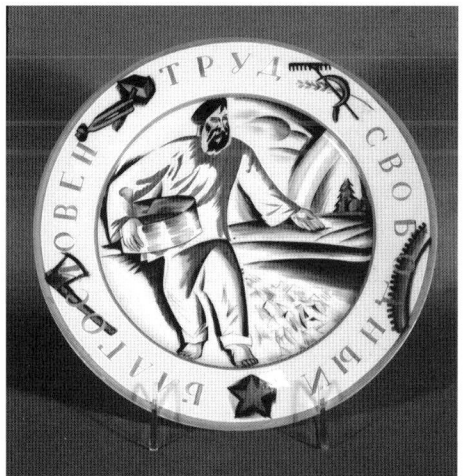

HENRY VAN DE VELDE, *BLESSED BE FREE LABOUR*, 1919. PORCELAIN AND CHINA PAINT, 25.4 CM. COLLECTION: ELVEHJEM ART CENTER, MADISON, WI, DONATED BY LUDMILLA N. SHAPIRO

Futurism. Artists such as Zinaida Kobyletskaya painted tête-à-tête services with landscapes that included hydroelectric stations, factories, electric wires, and fields in process of being harvested. An original style of illustration based on gearwheels was developed by Aleksandra Shchekatikhina-Potoskaya while Natalja Danko and others continued the figurine tradition of the factory, replacing the decadent court figures of the Imperial Factory with portraits of workers and soldiers.

Two of the most radical artists at the factory were Ilia Chasnik and Nicolai Suetin. Disciples of Malevich who worked at the factory from 1922, Chasnik and Suetin designed objects in a Suprematist style, favoring a palette of flat blues, reds, blacks, and grey. Suetin's forms were usually simplifications of the factory's pre-Revolutionary designs. But he did experiment with form to some extent, notably in an ashtray illustrated in a 1927 catalogue of Russian porcelain in which the functional role of the object had been so abstracted that it could only be addressed as a small-scale sculpture.

In 1925 the factory was reorganized and named the Lomonosov Pottery after Mikhail Lomonosov, the renowned eighteenth-century scientist. Few Suprematist pieces seemed to have been made after 1924, and Constructivist repression was introduced under the centralized control of the Union of Artists of the Soviet Union. Modern art became suspect, and so the factory drew its inspiration from folk art.[6]

The Bauhaus

In 1919 Walter Gropius issued the prospectus for Das Staatliches Bauhaus in Weimar. Its yellow cover by Lyonel Feininger was symbolically adorned with the woodcut of a cathedral. It signified the desire of the Bauhaus to provide a pragmatic twentieth-century version of the *Bauhütte*. These were the masons' lodges, where the skilled craftsmen assembled to work on the ideal collective project of art and craft—the medieval cathedral.

Gropius had been profoundly influenced by the writings of William Morris at the time of writing the prospectus, even though he did not share Morris's abhorrence of industry and the machine. In the prospectus, Gropius issued a challenge to break down the "arrogant barrier" between artist and craftsman and went on to argue that art was not a profession: "There are no essential differences between artist and craftsman…the artist is an exalted craftsman."

The school was formed through the merging of Henry van de Velde's Kunstgewerbeschule and the Academy of Fine Art. The Bauhaus was divided into seven workshops, six based on materials and one for colour. Most workshops had two leaders: a *Lehrmeister* who was the technical or craft master, and a *Formmeister*, literally a master of form. Students were obliged to first undergo a *Vorkurs*, or basic course of six months, before choosing a specialty interest. The step was considered a radical one at the time, but the *Vorkurs* has been institutionalized into most European art programs as the "foundation course" or "basic design." The head of the *Vorkurs* from 1919 to 1923 was Johannes Itten, a trained and progressive educator. He saw his role as that of leading the students through a process of self-discovery, defining craft as a spiritual and not a manual skill.

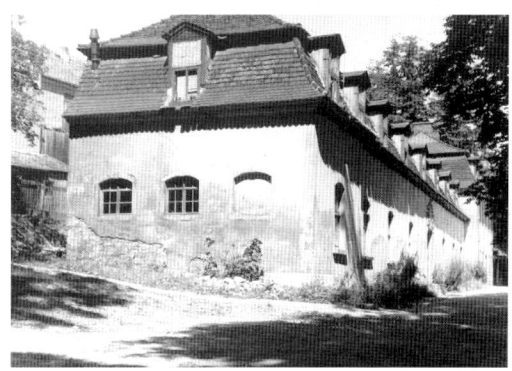

BAUHAUS KERAMIK, *SIDE VIEW OF THE POTTERY WORKSHOP*, DORNBURG, GERMANY.

PHOTO: ROSE KREBS, COURTESY ICH

The first *Formmeister* appointed by Gropius was the sculptor Gerhard Marcks, who was placed in charge of setting up a pottery workshop. Gropius had known Marcks for some time through his membership of the Deutsche Werkbund. In 1914 Marcks had undertaken a commission to produce ceramic sculpture for the Meyer/Gropius buildings at the Cologne Exhibition. However, his knowledge of ceramics was slight, limited mainly to modelling animals for the Schwarzburg Porzellan Manufaktur.

Setting up a pottery in Weimar proved to be problematic. At first, makeshift kilns were set up in a factory "with a ceramist of very mediocre quality."[7] Weimar was close to a centre of traditional pottery, Burgel, but the town shared the Weimarers' hostility to the school and what they termed its "Bolshevik art." It was finally in Dornburg, on the river Saale, some thirty kilometers from Weimar, that Marcks found a suitable site for a workshop—stables in a Rococo castle.

A folk potter, Max Krehan, accepted the post of *Lehrmeister*, and in October

1920, the workshop was opened to students. Walter Scheidig comments that the environment proved ideal. Krehan worked in the traditional, almost folk art manner, supplying the needs of the little rural town and countryside, unaffected by designers or reformers of the late nineteenth and twentieth century. His workshop was an ideal place for getting familiar with ordinary raw materials, the potter's wheel and a simple kiln.[8]

This link with folk art was valuable to the Bauhaus, and the historian Marcel Franciscono contends that the ceramics workshop provided the clearest demonstration of its "renovating" use. Folk art provided an alternative to the elegant geometry of the Werkbund and, as Franciscono comments,

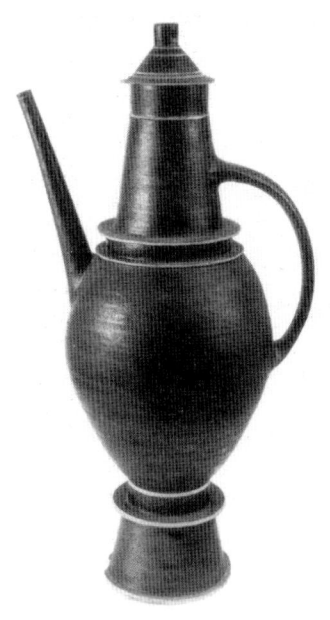

OTTO LINDIG, *HIGH COVER POT*, C.1922. STONEWARE, 68.6 CM.

COLLECTION/PHOTO: BAUHAUS MUSEUM, BERLIN

It [folk art] was not merely a source of expressive strength which had not been extensively exploited in applied arts before then: more importantly it made pure and direct use of those elementary forms and decorative motifs commonly understood to be prior to all more complex manifestations. It was consequently a way of escaping at once from naturalism, the conventional styles of the past and the arbitrariness of merely individual or subjective inspiration.[9]

At the time of the move to Dornburg, twenty students were registered in ceramics, but only five agreed to join Marcks and Krehan for a three-year course at the new workshop: Marguerite Friedlander (Wildenhain), Theo Bogler, Johannes Driesch, Otto Lindig, and Li Foucar. During the course a few dropped out and others joined, including Ellen Mogelin, Eva Overdieck, and finally, in 1924, Frans Wildenhain.

For the first two years the students produced hardly any "independently executed work." The reason for this was that Marcks believed that early students should not have any experimental and theoretical exercises but, rather, should enjoy maximum participation in carrying out the works of the masters. As a result, many of the early pieces carry the signature of both master and students.

The production of cheap, functional earthenware and stoneware continued with the assistance of the pupils, and the sales were a crucial part of the workshop funds. Up until 1923, the Bauhauskeramik reflected the folk pottery influence with its pot-bellied forms and erect protuberant spouts, handles, and necks. A number of pots were decorated, mainly by Marcks, but the students rarely decorated, relying instead on powerful forms, textures, and glazes.

In 1923 changes began to sweep the school. The period up until then is now seen as the romantic phase, dominated by relatively conservative faculty. Kandinsky and Moholy-Nagy were appointed and, together with Van Duesburg, Lissitzky, and others, introduced Constructivism and Suprematism. Gropius held an exhibition entitled *Art and Technics: The New Unity*; and the first *Jungmeister* (young masters) were appointed from the ranks of Bauhaus graduates. The more traditional thinkers who had enlisted under the "Art and Craft" banner felt threatened by the new, tectonic stance. Itten resigned, and others such as Marcks became increasingly suspect of Gropius's motives.

The Pottery Workshop reflected this change by creating a studio for the design of ceramics

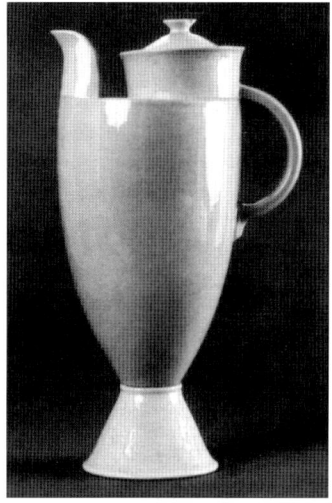

OTTO LINDIG, *COFFEE POT*, C.1923. PORCELAIN, 25.4 CM.
COLLECTION/PHOTO: BAUHAUS MUSEUM, BERLIN

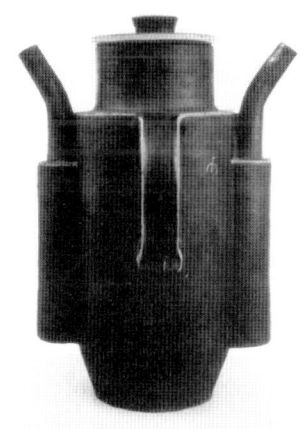

THEODORE BOGLER AND GERHARD MARCKS, *DOUBLE SPOUT COFFEE POT*, C.1924. EARTHENWARE, 24.9 CM.
COLLECTION/PHOTO: NATIONAL MUSEUM, STOCKHOLM

for industry. The two outstanding pupils of the pottery, Theo Bogler and Otto Lindig, were made Jungmeisters under Marcks. The pottery studio became the first Bauhaus workshop to produce successfully and to sell designs to industry. Scheidig attributes this to the workshop's geographic isolation from the fashions and ideological differences that constantly swept the Weimar school.

This began the true Bauhauskeramik as the potters began to rethink all the components of their crafts. They devised their own clay body, a close and vitrified stoneware-earthenware that did not require to be glazed and which was ideal for throwing tense, hard-edged forms. They did not adhere to any traditional school of aesthetics, dispensing with the entrenched maxim that required pottery to have flowing, rhythmic forms that subordinated spout, handle, neck, and foot. They rarely used the formal climax of the pot surmounted by shoulders and capped with a simple lip or concave neck. Where a shoulder was used, it became a plinth on which to mount an elaborate extension or independent spout.

This is in keeping with the modern art tendencies of the time. Constructivism proved to be a liberating catalyst that encouraged the potters to move away from unified compositional rhythms and to give greater attention and focus to the individual components of the vessel. Organic harmony was sacrificed for hard-edged composite volumes, and feet were either merged with the main body or independently developed to counterbalance the neck and spout.

These designs, mainly by Lindig and Bogler, were warmly received by sections of the ceramic industry who recognized the need for design that was free of academic chains. Inspired by the 1923 *Art and Technics* exhibition, Dr. Harkort, owner and manager of a large ceramic factory, wrote the following comment in the periodical *Die Kachel & Töpferkunst* (The Arts of Tile and Pottery):

> The Bauhaus wants to enlist an entire generation of artists in a struggle to solve the creative problems of industrialization. It used to be a more or less chance occurrence for a creative artist to find his way into a factory and to master the problems put to him. Now it should be done consciously and to an extent worthy of the problem. This is of value to the ceramics industry in particular where aesthetic considerations are so imperative and where industrial requirements have had a particularly devastating influence on artistic quality.[11]

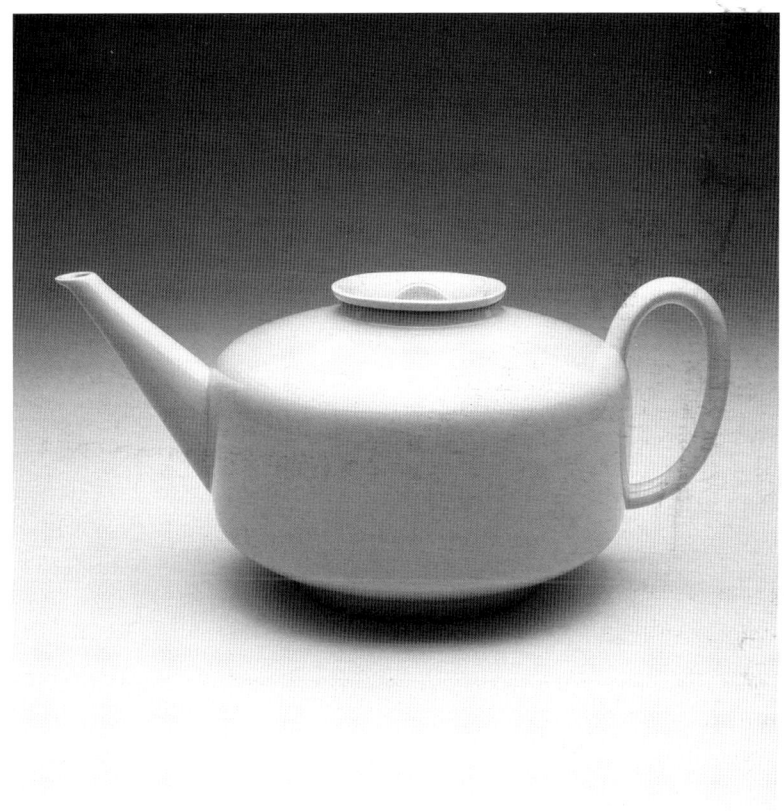

Marguerite Friedlander-Wildenhain, *Teapot*, 1930. Porcelain, 15.3 cm.
Made at the Staatliche Porzellan Manufactur, Berlin.
Photo: John White

However, it must be emphasized that the style of the workshop was by no means homogeneous. Marguerite Friedlander, for example, was more conservative in her approach and concerned with the human rather than mechanistic aspects of the craft. She cites the drift towards technology as the reason for closing the pottery: "Neither Marcks nor any of the potters agreed with the ever more industrialized direction that Bauhaus was taking…it was getting sterile and didactic in working only along abstract and industrial lines."[12]

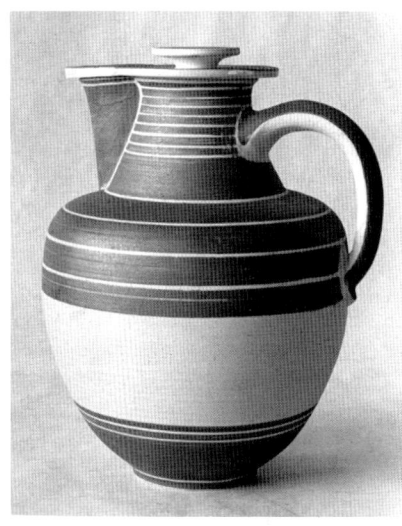

OTTO LINDIG, *STONEWARE PITCHER WITH BANDED DECORATION*, C.1930. STONEWARE, 30.5 CM.

COLLECTION/PHOTO: BAUHAUS MUSEUM, BERLIN

Krehan died just before the workshop closed. Marcks resigned in 1925 rather than move to the new Bauhaus at Dessau, and the experiment came to and end. But its influence continued because of the energy of Bauhauslers, who retained high profiles in the ceramic arts. (Gordon Forsyth's review of modern ceramics, *Twentieth Century Ceramics*, 1936, featured the work of Marcks, Lindig, and both Franz and Marguerite Wildenhain.)

After the workshop closed, Franz and Marguerite moved to Halle, where they married and taught at the local arts and crafts school until 1933. Marguerite produced strong modern designs while at Halle for the Königliche Porzellan Manufaktur in Berlin. After her move to Putten, The Netherlands, she continued to design, working for the Regout factory as well as running a pottery workshop with Franz. Theo Bogler's career was regrettably short. After two years as art director of a stoneware factory in Velten, Dordam, his wife died, and Bogler became a monk. Marcks returned to a distinguished career as a sculptor, although he continued to produce porcelain animals during the thirties.

The most talented of the group, Otto Lindig, remained at Dornburg after the departure of the Bauhaus of Dessau. He arranged for the pottery to be attached to Otto Bartning's Staatliche Bauhochschule Weimar until 1930, when the newly elected Nationalist Socialist provincial government suspended the school's subsidies. It was a severe blow to lose institutional sponsorship during a time of harsh repression. But Lindig decided to continue alone in the face of the state harassment and financial hardship that he endured for more than ten years.

Lindig was a strong influence at the Bauhaus Pottery Workshop and the major architect of the Bauhauskeramik from 1923 onwards. He had studied as a sculptor before the First World War at Henry van de Velde's Kunstgewerbeschule and later transferred to the nearby Academy of Fine Art where he studied under Richard Engelman. When the Bauhaus opened, he decided to join the pottery workshop, a choice that Rose Keebs, an apprentice of Lindig from the thirties and a researcher of Bauhaus pottery, feels he took because "with his skeptical nature [Lindig] felt more at home with the intimate ceramic techniques than in the monumental realm of sculpture."[13]

He did not see the move from sculpture to pottery as a major one, remarking that ceramics had always been a sculptural activity for him, "a continuous search for good, healthy and clear form."[14] Unlike his contemporaries Richard Bampi, Bontjes Von Beek, and Gusso Ruess, Lindig was not seduced by the lure of Oriental glazes. He used only two types of glaze: a crisp, translucent, grey/white glaze with a high gloss and a matte, crystalline glaze. The decoration was Spartan, usually comprising bands of slip or oxide that emphasized the tense, curving line of his forms.

The strength and simplicity of his work can be seen in the Grand Prix vase, the winner of the highest award at the 1937 Paris Exposition. (Marguerite Wildenhain won a medal at that exhibition as well for her Regout designs.) After the war, Marcks invited Lindig to join the faculty of the Kunstgewerbeschule in Hamburg as the professor of ceramics. He remained there until shortly before his death in 1966.

The Wildenhains moved to the United States in the late thirties and shortly thereafter separated. Both became important teachers. Franz taught on the East Coast at the School of the American Craftsman at the Rochester Institute for Technology in New York State, set up through the largess of Eileen Vanderbilt-Webb. Marguerite established one of the most popular summer schools in the country at Pond Farm Pottery, Guerneyville, California. Their interest drifted away from the Bauhaus philosophy (Marguerite actually renounced her Bauhaus roots as cold and meaningless) and with the death of Lindig, the direct lineage of the Bauhauskeramik came to an end.

Its impact was nonetheless considerable. The example of Lindig and the early work of the other Bauhauslers introduced a welcome objectivity to modern functional form at a time when tastes were swinging wildly from a romantic traditionalism to arbitrary decorative excess. They presented a new form logic that grew out of functional needs and not the aesthetic tenets of past ceramic style. The challenge they issued was taken up by potters around the world and found particular favour amongst ceramists in Scandinavia. And their work continues to inspire.

ITALIAN CERAMICS AND THE MODERN MOVEMENT

Italy's participation in the modern ceramic movement was late in coming. It was not until 1925 that this country, with its long ceramic heritage, began to make a major contribution. At the turn of the century, attempts were made to produce ceramics in *Stile Liberty*, as Art Nouveau was termed in Italy. But the objects emerged as a

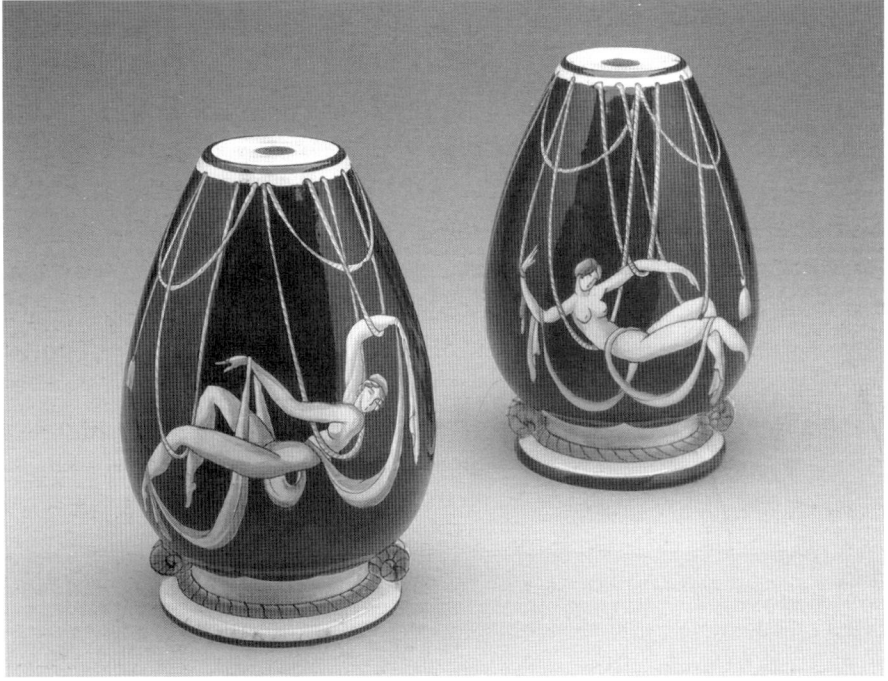

DESIGN BY GIO PONTI: RICHARD–GINORI, *PAIR OF LAMP BASES*, C.1920. HAND PAINTED MAIJOLICA, 21.0 CM.
PHOTO: JOHN WHITE

hopeless muddle of Art Nouveau and Renaissance. Some good work was produced through the Fabbriche Riunite Ceramiche Faentine in Faenza, in particular the designs of Domenico Baccarini. But for the greater part, the Italian ceramists were unable to understand the linear rhythm of the Art Nouveau decoration and its sensual, curvilinear massing and distribution of volume; and the pastiche that emerged—an unhappy marriage between Art Nouveau form and Renaissance painting—was mawkish and unsatisfying.[15]

After the First World War, the Art Deco or *Novacento* movement emerged as a curious mixture of decorative intent and heroic classicism. By 1928, a modernist movement began to emerge, largely through the efforts of a group of Milanese architects led by Gio Ponti. Ponti founded the Architectura Razionale movement and edited the magazine *Domus*, which became the main vehicle for their crusade to bring a modern order out of the neo-Renaissance decorative chaos of the twenties. Ponti was fond of ceramics and encouraged architects to commission ceramic murals from various sculptors, including Rolando Hettner and Fulvio Nardis. His own involvement with ceramics (which continued through his career) began in 1923 when he designed for Manufattura di Doccia della Richard Ginori. He was associated with the factory for several years producing some of the best examples of Italian Art Deco.

The theme he employed was a witty paraphrase of the painted Renaissance majolica, particularly the styles of the late decorative period. The translation into a modern idiom was done without sentiment as he reconstructed visual planes and the deployed space in a Surrealist manner. The flattened images and use of perspective and grid landscapes show the influence of de Chirico and early Surrealist painting.

Another artist working during this time in the Art Deco style was Francesco Nonni (1885-1976), who produced a series of figurative ceramics at Faenza between 1921 and 1925 in the studio of Anselmo Bucci. They show a strong Sezessionstil bias, but as the work developed, it became increasingly original. Nonni's style was to employ balloon-like forms surmounted by the head and shoulders of the figures, characterized by a skillful play of two- and three-dimensional elements.

The work of Nonni and Ponti was unashamedly decorative. They did not attempt to compete with concerns in the fine arts, although Ponti did stylize current influences in modern painting in his pieces for Richard Ginori. The development of an

Italian ceramic art movement, with aspirations towards greater content and a place in the fine arts, emerged through a close relationship between the second generation Futurists and the pottery of Guiseppe Mazzotti at Albisola Mare on the Italian Riviera.

FUTURST CERAMICS

The Futurist movement was Italy's major contribution to early modern art. One of its founders was the Italian aristocrat F. Tommaso Marinetti, who, in 1908, published *The Foundation Manifesto of Futurism* in *Le Figaro*, declaring that "speed is our god, the new canon of beauty…the roaring motor car that seems to run off shrapnel is more beautiful than the victory of Samothrace."

The *Manifesto* was a raw, bellicose document that signalled the arrival of one of the seminal art movements of the twentieth century. It encompassed the sculpture of Boccioni, the painting of Balla, the music of Pratelli, the architecture of Sant' Elia and the free-word poetry (*parolibere*) of Marinetti.

The movement comprised two generations. The first lasted up to the end of the First World War, which claimed the lives of many of the movement's most talented figures including Boccioni and Sant' Elia. The second phase dates from 1919. A number of young, new artists joined and brought Constructivist influences. Furthermore, a link between Futurism and Fascism resulted in a heroic, political content. Overall, the second phase is identified by a stronger decorative intent, as first proposed in Enrico Prampolini's "Manifesto for Futurist Decorative Art in 1919." Prampolini did, however, call for a search for new and unusual materials, which indirectly encouraged involvement with ceramics.

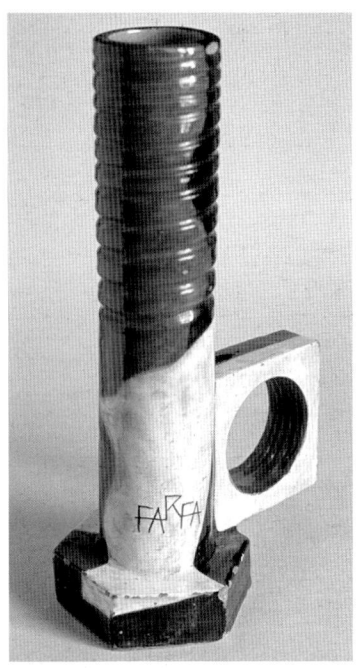

FARFA/GIUSEPPE MAZZOTTI, *BULLONVASO*, 1931-32. GLAZED EARTHENWARE, 27.5 X 15.5 X 10.0 CM.
COLLECTION: ESA MAZZOTTI
PHOTO: CERAMIC ARTS FOUNDATION

The first generation produced only one ceramist of note: Arturo Martini. At the age of thirteen, Martini had been apprenticed to the local potter in his hometown, Treviso. Later his interest in sculpture led him to work for Carlini and Adolfo Hildbrand. After a period of study in various art schools in Europe, he returned to ceramics and, from 1911 to 1915, exhibited polychrome terra cotta busts. The pieces he exhibited with other Futurists at the Galleria Sproviera in Rome and in Milan show a compelling directness, modelling features on his terra cottas with deep, slashing knife cuts. After the War he turned away from the Futurist style, although he retained his friendship with that group.

Martini became involved in the decorative sculpture of the Valori Plastici group and concentrated on biblical and literary themes. He often introduced a tongue-in cheek-humour that parodied sepulchral and museum art, giving his works irreverent titles such as *Fruitcake Nativity*. The scale and vigour of this work recalled the early Renaissance terra cottas of Nicolo di Puglia and Jacopo della Quercia. In addition to the monumental forms which he fired at the Cado kilns, Martini also created smaller works at Albisola which were richly coated with reduction lustre glazes.

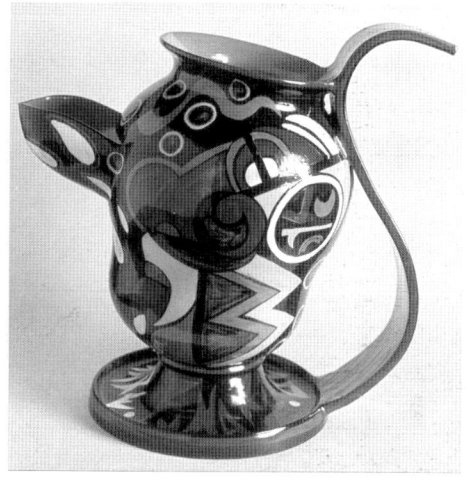

TULLIO D'ALBISOLA, *PITCHER* C. 1929. GLAZED EARTHENWARE, 29.8 × 18.4 × 32.5 CM.
COLLECTION: MUSEUM OF INTERNATIONAL CERAMICS, FAENZA, ITALY
PHOTO: CERAMIC ARTS FOUNDATION

True Futurist ceramics began in 1925 with the work exhibited in that year at the 1925 Paris Exhibition by Tullio D' Albisola (Mazzotti), the son of Guiseppe Mazzotti, operator of a small commercial pottery in Albisola Mare. D'Albisola had created an unusual Cubo-Futurist style, which employed a palette of bright, primary underglaze colours. This work attracted the attention of the Futurist artists around Savona and Turin, and in 1927, Franco Rossi arranged for D'Albisola to meet with Marinetti at the Pesaro Gallery in Milan in order to formulate a direction for Futurist ceramics.

Marinetti and D' Albisola became close friends, and from 1929 on, Marinetti was a frequent visitor at the Mazzotti pottery. Together they created a concept "that would provoke a total artistic renewal going beyond the minor arts."[16] They termed their philosophy *aeroceramica*, literally aerial or spatial ceramics, and began to produce limited-edition Futurist ceramics in Albisola (between 1929 and 1939) of over forty poets, painters, sculptors, and ceramists from the movement's ranks.

The attitude of the Futurist ceramic movement can be gleaned from the following excerpt from the manifesto by Marinetti and D' Albisola *"Il Manifesto Futurista Ceramica e Aeroceramica,"*

> The Futurists have created ceramics characterized by the aesthetics of the machine and geometry. Any desire to return to hybrid and static classicism is cretinous and unpatriotic. Our *aerocermisti* have an awareness of the corpus vasorum of all oriental porcelain; of the apothecary's bowls of the indians. They know too the shining classic Italian Majolica and value it as the best in the world. But this is not to imitate. From this knowledge they can forget, overcome and overthrow ideas and techniques of every ceramic secret with the VERY NEW, the VERY ORIGINAL and the NEVER SEEN which first appeared in the Futurist ceramics of Tullio D' Albisola.[17]

The manifesto did not attempt to set out a visual style, and the *aerocermisti* were free, within broad guidelines, to establish a personal aesthetic. What the document sought was to suggest a spirit and unleash a new energy in ceramics. This was stated in Marinetti's abstract free-word style:

> The *aerocermisti* wish to produce: 1) Multitactile ceramics continuing the thesis on tactilism presented by Marinetti to oppose sandy rough Africa with a velvet and delicate Europe. 2) Simultaneist ceramics to convey emotions both in conflict and in harmony. 3) Streets and squares in gold ceramics, fountains in indigo. 4) Vases of true skies of ceramic, irrigated with pure waters and swelling perfumes, flowers and sun to sell or give to the funereal northern cities. For example to give the skies of Capri to Folkstone.[18]

Many of Futurism's most important figures became involved in the project, including Prampolini, whose group in Rome compromised the most important faction within the movement. But more important to ceramics was the long-standing association of the artists in the Turin school led by Fillia (Luigi Colombo) and the Savona school that included Farfa (Vittorio Osvaldo Tommasini) and Giovanni Acquaviva. Bruno Munari, Umberto Zimelli, and other Milanese painters later became associated with the project as well. The *aerocermisti* acquired a stronger sense of identity from 1930 onwards with the visits of Marinetti and the building of a new pottery by the Futurist architect Nicolay Diulgheroff on the banks of the Sansobbia.

In an article in *Stile Futurista* magazine in 1934, D' Albisola explained the manner in which a style began to emerge from the project:

> Initially we began with simple stylization and later absolute abstraction, taking purposefully useless form and turning it into mechanical compositions of aerial volumes. We used plastic shapes to explore synthetic and constructive planes. Our development seems to be directly stimulated by modern and technical objects and symbols with decoration inspired by Fascist events, aviation and sport. On twisted, meaningless and eccentric shapes—jugs, dishes, vases— under translucent glaze we painted screaming arabesques with the influences coming from DEPERO, or scenes from PRAMPOLINI and even the paintings of the "War Futurists" were reproduced.[19]

The *aerocermisti* produced a wide range of limited-edition objects, but most of the major works dealt with abstracting the vessel format, with the exception of the sculptures of Mario Anselmo, Bruno Munari, and Fontana's figurative sculpture. Essentially, the artists embraced a concept of pottery rather than sculpture. The Futurist vocabulary proved to be sympathetic to this exploration. The wheel and even, sensitively moulded vessels, provided a new interpretation of Boccioni's "spiral architectural dynamism" that rejected classical form in favour of pure, plastic rhythm. The painter Balla's concept of centrifugal force in painting, the thesis (movement and light could destroy the materiality of bodies) transferred well to the kinetic energy of vessel.

While pre-war Futurist theory was a crucial influence, so, too, was Constructivism and a form of neo-Cubism popular in Italy at the time. This can be seen in the work of Fillia, in particular, who created a distinctive style of assembling geometric elements to create small tabletop objects. Although they seem to be sculpture at first it soon becomes apparent that one is dealing with a vessel and its "spatial milieu" as the Futurist referred to the unseen environment of planes and lines that surround an object.

Another unusual approach to the vessel was that adopted by Farfa. Reflecting his interest in Dada and Surrealism, he produced satiric objects, vessels such as the *Nut and Bolt* (1929) and *Shuttered Pot* (1930). Both are interesting pieces and prophetic of the direction that the Surrealist object was to take later in the thirties. *Nut and Bolt* is intriguing because of the manner in which Farfa created the fall of light and shade graphically with underglaze painting, producing a statement similar to Roy Lichtenstein's later ceramics of the 1960s. *The Shuttered Pot* reveals an insouciant humour and a parody of the vessel that has since become a major concern in American contemporary ceramics.

The master of the aeroceramica style, however, was D'Albisola. His direct use of primary underglaze colours established the palette for the *aerocermisti*, and his wit and exploratory use of form created a spirit of healthy irreverence and experiment at the Giuseppe Mazzotti pottery. His work incorporated elements of Futurist painting theory, using lines and planes to create a movement on the surface of his pots and integrating onomatopoeic noises. A device he employed frequently was deliberately to overstate the elements of the vessel, creating absurdly large feet and handles.

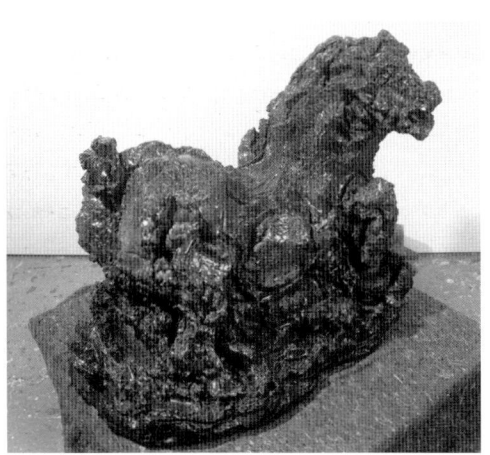

Lucio Fontana, *Cavallo*, 1936. Cat. Rais. No. 35-36 SC4. Glazed earthenware, 68.5 x 58.4 x 43.1 cm.
Photo: Garth Clark Gallery

Some of his volumetric concerns were highly sophisticated. In *Half Pot* (1928) one is confronted with what appears to be simply a pot form cut in half. But on closer inspection it becomes apparent that the pot is double walled. The "real" vessel, therefore, is the sliver of volume trapped in the hollow, concave walls.

Soon a loose specialization developed amongst the artists. Munari was the pottery's animalier, while Giovanni Aquaviva concentrated on Fascist propaganda plates, and Mario Anselmo, the "Sports Futurist" produced what D'Albisola termed "athletic configurations" of cyclists, athletes, and boxers (see page 14). Another artist who concentrated on Fascist themes was the Milanese painter, Ricas, who modelled sinister vases with bayonets as handles, and Ivos Pacetti, whose gas-mask imagery was amongst the most dramatic of the works produced in Albisola.

Amongst the major artists who worked at Albisola was Lucio Fontana. Fontana's work was outside the general aeroceramica style but unified in the spirit of experiment. Most of the artists in Albisola worked towards establishing a precious tabletop, *objet d'art* aesthetic, but Fontana sought to deal with clay in a more radical and non-formalist sense. By the time he arrived at Albisola in 1935, he had already established a reputation as an avant-garde artist and had been working with clay for several years, together with other "unconventional" materials such as bitumen, cement, and plastic.

At Albisola he used the technical capabilities of the pottery to create a series of large-scale, coloured terra cottas, the Leone group, now in the garden of the Mazzotti family in Albisola. Although the pieces were figurative in theme, they were treated as "organic products or variations of the earth itself, merging without any precise line of demarcation."[20] They show a vigour in the clay handling that was prophetic of Fontana's abstract expressionist sensibilities in the fifties. From 1937 he worked at the Sèvres Manufactory for two years, holding his first one-man shows of ceramics at the Galerie Jeanne Boucher in Paris and Galerie del Milione in Milan. His works of this period were too radical to influence the direction of European ceramics, but after the war and his return from Argentina, Fontana emerged as one of the most influential figures in Italian ceramics and continued to work actively in the medium, until his death in 1968, with D'Albisola as his technical facilitator.

Futurist ceramics was also produced in other parts of the country, although the output was sporadic and often uneven. In the 1930s painters and sculptors, including Gino Severini, Nino Strada, and Tato (Sansoni Guglielmo) created large public murals and wall pieces with D'Albisola at the Mazzotti factory and that of Minghetti in Bologna. Sirio Cantatore created elegant porcelain figures, such as *The Monk 919310*, in Milan. The Societa Maioliche Deruta in Perugia also produced Futurist works.21

One of the notable works of this period, in many ways the definitive Futurist ceramic, was *Continuous Profile* (1933) by Renato Guiseppe Bertelli, a portrait in glazed earthenware of Umberto Mussolini. The piece was created by turning a negative template of the profile of Mussolini into a core of clay. The result is an object that resembles an electrical insulator and shows two profiles of the dictator from whichever angle it is viewed. The mechanistic quality of the work that pays homage to machine and industry, the sense of speed and movement that comes from the play of light on the highly glazed surface, and the idealization of Fascist politics, all represent a ceramic paean to Futurist values.22

In addition to the *aerocermisti*, other schools of ceramics were beginning to grow in Italy at this time through the opening of the Institute for Ceramic Studies in Faenza in association with the Museo della Ceramiche Internationale. By 1938 the school had expanded and offered summer courses in the history and techniques of ceramics to foreign and Italian students. A number of ceramists based themselves in Faenza because of its long history as a pottery center (the town gave title to the term faience). Amongst the most renowned of these artists was the master craftsman Pietro Melandri. However, the climate of Faenza tended towards traditionalism, and more original expressions emerged in other parts of the country, coming mostly from two young artists, Guido Gambone in Florence and Enzo Assenza in Rome.

D' Albisola remained the center for the more progressive attitudes in the art. After 1939 it retained this prominence, although the influence of D'Albisola

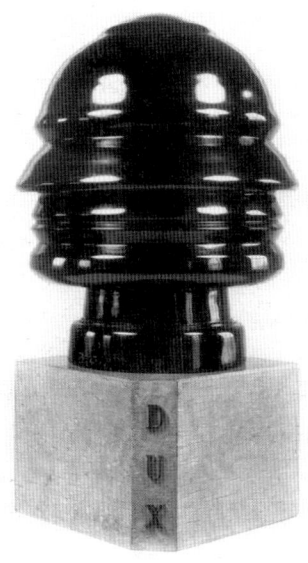

R. BERTELLI, *BLACK POTTERY HEAD OF MUSSOLINI*, 1933. 49 CM.
COLLECTION/PHOTO: IMPERIAL WAR MUSEUM, LONDON

diminished as his attentions moved away from his pivotal role in the Futurist movement and towards the management of the family business. The tradition of visitors to the medium continued, however. Fontana returned in 1947 and soon after, the sculptors Manzu and Garelli worked in Albisola together with artists from the Cobra group: Jorn, Appel, Corneille, and Matta.

Although the ceramists were widely exhibited in the major Italian and European World Fairs and included in most Futurist Movement exhibitions, the activity was not widely documented. No references to the *aerocermisti* or the "Manifesto" appear in any post-war Futurist studies until Carlo De Benedetti's *Il Futurismo in Liguria* (1976). In addition, no accounts prior to this essay have been published in the English language. The work emerges as a significant attempt to ally ceramics to a fine art movement without breaking away from the pottery tradition. The *aerocermisti* saw the enclosure of space as being pottery's central dynamic and explored this in an original and purposeful manner. This body of work also provides a perspective on similar expressions that have taken place after 1960 in the United States, in particular northern California's Bay Area.

Each of the "experiments"—and that is how the activities in this essay are best viewed—added to the growth of a mature contemporary format for the ceramist. Some artists, such as Malevich, showed an undisguised ambivalence in their treatment of the functional roots of pottery. They dealt with the vessel as metaphor and used it as a vehicle to explore formal concerns. Others, such as Tatlin and the Bauhaus potters, sought to create a bridge between art and life by retaining the functional purpose of their vessels. All have the common concern of rejecting dogmatic traditionalism. Constructivism allowed for an informal arrangement of components in the vessel form. The Bauhaus used this freedom to improve functional design, while the Futurists linked painting and pottery to create a broader, more liberal role for the ceramist in the arts. During the twenties and thirties, a mood of change and conceptual growth can be detected springing directly from the influence of modern art that was to completely redefine the ceramic arts after the Second World War.

1. See D.H. Kahnwieler, *Picasso-Keramik,* (Hanover: Fackeltrager-Verlag Schmidt-Kuster, 1957) 15.
2. See Maximillian Gauthier, "Moly-sabata", Art et Decoration (67 September/October 1938) 293-300, for a full account of this collaboration.
3. A plate dated 1915 and signed by Malevich was shown by Galerie Gmurzynska in their exhibition *From Surface to Space: Russia 1916-1924* (18 September-30 September, 1974 Cologne). Until this exhibition, it was assumed by most historians that the ceramic work commenced around 1920.
4. For a detailed study on the debate regarding function and design within the Suprematist/Constructivist camp, see "Utilitarian Art: For and Against" in Camilla Grey's *The Great Experiment* (London: Thames and Hudson, 1982) 243-245.
5. Grey, 244.
6. The main reference source on the work at the Lomonosov Pottery is L. Nikiforova's *Russian Porcelain Hermitage Collection* (Leningrad: Aurora Art Publishers, 1973). The ambivalent position that Constructivist art now occupies in Russia makes the book somewhat suspect, and it seems that ideology has interfered with scholarship. However, the inclusion of Suprematist designs indicates a softening in Soviet attitudes. Further works are illustrated in M.K. Jomohocoba, *Soviet Porcelain: The Artisanry of the Lomonosov Porcelain Factory* (Leningrad 1974). Although it seems that Suprematist designs were discontinued around 1925, occasional examples in this style appear in Soviet design catalogues dated as late as 1934—possibly to show a token involvement in the international Functionalist style. See: USSR, *Le Porcelaine D'Arts: LeCatlogue* (Leningrad, 1938).
7. Marguerite Wildenhain in a letter to the author, June 9, 1976.
8. See Walter Sheidig, *Crafts of the Weimar Bauhaus* (London: Studio Vista, 1967) 40.
9. See Marcel Franciscono *Walter Gropius and the Creation of the Bauhaus in Weimar* (Chicago: University of Illinois Press, 1971).
10. Franciscono, Marcks quoted in letter to Gropius.
11. Source not available.
12. Marguerite Wildenhain, letter to author.
13. See Rose Krebs, "Homage to a Master: Otto Lindig 1895-1966," Unpublished MS (Claremont, CA: Institute for Ceramic History, 1967) 1. The author is indebted to Ms. Krebs for her assistance in the research on the Bauhaus pottery.
14. Quoted in "Otto Lindig" by Johanna Hofman, *Werk und Zeit* (15 December 1966) 2.
15. For an account of this activity see: Gian Carl Bojani's *Ceramica Liberty* Faenza Faentina, 1977.
16. See Tullio D' Albisola, "Dalle 'Tre Grazie' Neoclassiche alle Aeroceramiche Futuriste," *Stile Futurista* (October 1934) 41.
17. See F.T. Marinetti and T. D' Albisola, "Il Manifesto Futurista Ceramica e Aeroceramica," *Gazzetta Del Popolo* (7 September 1938). The manifesto was published as a monograph in the following year by Edizione Ceramiche Futuriste in Albisola Mare. The manifesto is reproduced in the appendix together with the list of "*aerocermisti*" up to 1939.
18. Marinetti and Albisola.
19. See Tullio D' Albisola "Sintesi Storica Della Ceramica Futurista Italiana" in F.T. Marinetti and T. D' Albisola's *La Ceramica Futurista* (Albisola Mare, Edizione Ceramiche Futuriste, 1939) not paginated.
20. See Guido Balla, *Lucio Fontana* (New York: Praeger Publishers, 1971) 67.
21. Aurelio Minghetti's *Ceramisti*, Series XII Encyclopedia Biografica "Italiana," (Milano: Instituto Editoriale Italiano Bernado Carlo Tosi, 1939), provides a survey of the work being produced in Italy during the 1920s and 1930s, both in the Futurist and more conventional styles.
22. Editors Note: Subsequent to this paper, Bertelli's portrait has become something of an icon, intriguing Robert Mapplethorpe, Tony Cragg, and Andrew Lord, among the many artists who have used this image in their work.

Chapter 9

Modernism and Ceramics

Mark Pennings

In modernism, ceramics' aesthetic situation in the realm of cultural production seemed generally limiting. Ceramics could embrace "low" culture by aligning itself with the mass productive potential of industrial capitalism, as Thomas Wedgwood did in England during the late eighteenth and early nineteenth centuries; or at the other extreme, ceramics could reject the realities of industrial capitalism altogether. This was the case with craft practitioners such as William Morris, who saw industrial capitalism as a force which negated individual creativity and produced an alienated psyche.

Presented at *The Ceramic Millennium*, 1999, Amsterdam

In order to illustrate a "modernist" account of ceramics, I will employ an understanding of modernism broadly predicated on Marxist accounts (but only as a broad framework, rather than a strictly political interpretation) in which industrial capitalism is/was conceived of as producing alienation. This concept is important for ceramicists, as for many, ceramics promised to alleviate alienation in modern life.

However, more important than this is the theoretical dialectic imposed by modernist discourse when assessing ceramics. This generated a stark polarization between ideas and practices, especially in relation to art and craft. In this scenario, ceramics found itself as a kind of "other" in the area of cultural production: a negative correlate defined in contrast to the self conscious elitism of the philosophical and utopian aspirations implicit and explicit in avant-garde ideology.

Modernism[1] (generally considered to represent the period 1830-1950) is generally characterized as a pervasive set of ideologies which responded to the conditions of industrial capitalism with accompanying theories or grand (meta) narratives. In understanding modernity, many believed that the industrial age and concomitant faith in progress and science would lead to the attainment of a utopian society. In the realm of cultural and aesthetic theory, there was a general adherence to strictly categorized forms of "high" and "low" culture. "Fine art" held a privileged position in the hierarchies of social practices which would assist in the attainment of a more beneficial social fabric. In this regard, artists considered themselves to be part of an avant-garde in which they saw their role as one of cultural leadership. In contrast, ceramic practitioners were considered to occupy a less significant and marginalized cultural strata.

Generally, modernity, in practice, was characterized by industrial capitalism, and, in theory, by the modernist meta-narrative. High and low art had their place, and if ceramics had any place, it was to ambivalently reside in the shadow of the "high," or to exist in the "low" (seemingly unable to find a comfortable place in the middle). As stated, in art, modernist utopian schemes invariably situated ceramic practice as a marginalized activity (and many craft practitioners conformed to this situation). This meant that ceramics found itself supporting, rather than leading, artistic debates. Modernist society was characterized by its faith in absolutes and the desire to achieve and sustain certainty, but ceramics was never this certain, at least not in the terms defined by fine art.[2]

One can imagine the difficult situation ceramic practitioners were placed in during the nineteenth and early twentieth centuries; for on the one hand, their handmade production of utilitarian objects in a pre-industrial era was rapidly being supplanted by inexpensive mass produced alternatives. In addition, the method of creation, the organic connection between maker and object made, was also being replaced by regimented factory methods. On the other side of the ledger, the ceramist's commitment to the production of objects with a highly refined aesthetic was considered to be either marginal or, at worst, anachronistic.

In modernism, ceramics' aesthetic situation in the realm of cultural production seemed generally limiting. Ceramics could embrace "low" culture by aligning itself with the mass productive potential of industrial capitalism, as Thomas Wedgwood did in England during the late eighteenth and early nineteenth centuries; or at the other extreme, ceramics could reject the realities of industrial capitalism altogether. This was the case with craft practitioners such as William Morris, who saw industrial capitalism as a force which negated individual creativity and produced an alienated psyche. Consequently, William Morris proposed that craft attach itself to the emerging aesthetic of "high" art. Bernard Leach was clearly another important player in the search for an aesthetic that ceramics could claim as its own. Finally, ceramics and craft, whilst aligning themselves with high art aesthetics, could also seek to find a balance between (or to play off) the two positions described above. This was generally the course taken by practitioners in the Bauhaus School.

Industrial Capitalism, Marx, and the Factory

Marxism was a typical modernist meta-narrative and had important repercussions for ceramic practice in the area of cultural interpretation. This was because Karl Marx proposed an all-encompassing theory about industrial capitalism and society, and developed a philosophical system which suggested that he could provide all the answers to political problems from a scientific perspective. Marx made a number of proposals including: this is how capitalism works; this is the effect it has on subjectivity and life; and this will be the teleological and historical developments which will exceed and replace capitalism at some future point in time. In this sense his theories were commensurate with the avant-garde theories of groups like the de Stijl art movement. For they also proposed an all-encompassing theory of the arts in which abstract art (provided by figures such as Mondrian and Van Doesberg) would supply a universal visual code which would logically transform society.

Marx's social theory was predominantly outlined in his *Communist Manifesto* of 1848. Moreover, his major writings over the following decades outlined the basic precepts of the Marxist *Weltenschauung* of industrial capitalism. Marx provided a paradigm of the alienated individual in capitalist society, an individual removed from his or her creative potential in an industrial world. Marxism was also associated with the concept of dialectical materialism. The materialism side of this concept relates to the material facets of existence, which determine the way we think and live our lives. It is *the material* which is the dominant formative determinant of our lives.

The Marxist dialectic was borrowed from Hegel's notion of a dialectic, that is, the opposition of positions which eventually resolves into a synthesis, or higher, middle ground. For Marx, the dialectic was a duality or contradiction in which both sides (the owners of the means of production and those who labour for these owners) were in conflict, and this conflict acted as a driving force of change until a final stage of synthesis was achieved. In capitalist society, Marx believed that conflicts between these groups would be worked through historically until a final synthesis was established which would be the classless society: a utopian endpoint.

The primary effects of the material economic world on individual life was alienation. In capitalism, labour power was transformed into a commodity—the labourer in the factory exchanged his or her work for money and became little more than a thing, an object. People were therefore not a part of what they made; that is, they worked, came home, and rarely saw the outcome of their labours, and became alienated from themselves. No group of "workers" felt this more than ceramists, for they believed that the crafted object was an extension of the self, and with skills developed over a long period of time, ceramists had the potential to create products/objects which were "non-alienating." This was because ceramic objects were supposedly made for their own use value and could be exchanged for other objects. Therefore, the object's use value overrode the abstract/exchange value of the currency evident in the processes of capitalist exchange, another factor in the alienation of life. Because the ceramists could see their product after it had been completed, they could feel a certain pride about its finished appearance and could even use it themselves. Yet, no major ceramic theorist came to the fore during this period, at least not to the extent to which they provided an equivalent to an avant-garde aesthetic through which ceramics could prosper with a fair degree of self-confidence.

Such issues lie at the heart of the ceramist's dilemma during the modern period. Ceramics had enormous advantages over painting. Unlike painting, ceramic objects could be used at close range; they were intimate, practical, and were generally aesthetic. It also seemed that ceramic production had the potential to break the nexus of alienation via an activity in which one was not removed from the product of one's own labour. However, as modernity progressed, it seemed that ceramics' role in this scenario was relegated to playing a bit part to fine art, which had already established itself as the superior cultural practice in this regard. The dilemma for crafts practice during this period was making up its mind and having its mind made up for it. Was it to align itself with fine art, perhaps making products which only emphasized aesthetic value; or was it to concentrate on developing an independent and clearly defined functional and aesthetic identity? Clearly, the situation was much more complex than this, and anomalies persisted; but ceramists continued to wonder about craft's function in an industrial world. What could it be, and what exactly did it have to offer?

Such dilemmas persisted during the modernist period. Was ceramics for industrial capitalism or against it? If it was against it, then it could be purely aesthetic; but fine art had already established cultural hegemony in this instance. On the other hand, if it was for industrial capitalism, then it reinforced fine artists' prejudicial opinion of it as merely functional. Figures such as Thomas Wedgwood had demonstrated as early as the late eighteenth century that craft and capitalism could get along very well. Wedgwood has gone down in history as one of the great leaders of the Industrial Revolution. He utilized industry and scientific research in his approach to the task of manufacturing ceramics, inventing jasperware and a range of new glazes. He also used steam-powered engines for turning lathes which incised decorations on to his pieces. Workers in his factory, "Etruria," serviced a world-wide market for the rising bourgeoisie. He wholeheartedly accepted the benefits of mass production, and his Portland Vase was one of a series of forty-five. Ironically, he also employed the sculptor John Flaxman to create wax portraits and other reliefs for his output, and this represented an ironic reversal of art/craft hierarchies.

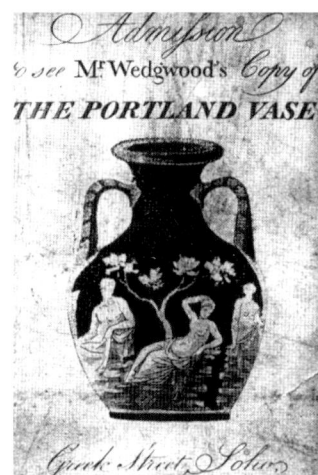

INVITATION TO WEDGWOOD POTTERY
PORTLAND VASE, 1790

COLLECTION: BRITISH MUSEUM, LONDON

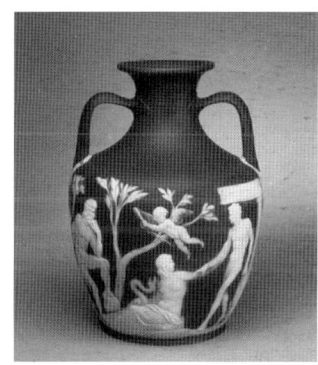

WEDGWOOD POTTERY, *PORTLAND VASE*, 1791. JASPERWARE, 24.8 CM.

COLLECTION: BRITISH MUSEUM, LONDON

Ceramics as High Art

If Marx had alluded to a time before "alienation"; that is, a time before industrial capitalism, when people had a sustaining and fulfilling relationship with the objects they produced, then ceramics was one area of culture which could resuscitate these ideals. In other words, the production of ceramics and other craft objects could provide an antidote to the alienation which seemed so pervasive during the late nineteenth century in particular.

William Morris and the Arts and Craft Movement were important in this regard because they represented the opposite tendency to someone like Wedgwood. Morris proposed a role for craft which was recidivist in the sense that it aspired to the traditions of medieval craft, ostensibly when craft and ceramic producers were not alienated from the manufacture of their goods. Morris posited a fundamentally "reactionary" response to industrial capitalism. In addition, although conceding that craft and art should remain distinct, he, and other of the Arts and Crafts Movement aspired to create objects within the aesthetic parameters of high art. Also, emulating Marx's ideal of a pre-alienated crafts worker, Morris believed that beauty came from the pleasure of the work process itself, and waxed lyrical over the ideals of a socialist rural utopia.

The Arts and Crafts Movement rejected the factory mode of production and the utopian belief that technical progress would improve humanity's lot. Instead, Morris offered a counter utopia of pre-industrial craft-making procedures in order to restore a more "authentic" and sustaining environment that would more adequately serve and express people's needs. He also hoped to avert humanity's enslavement to the machine by saving the home from mechanical anarchy. This would be achieved through the production of finely crafted objects that would restore purpose, balance, and harmony to people's lives. As a result, the Arts and Crafts Movement produced aesthetically beautiful craft and ceramic objects, but who could afford them?

Rather than transforming society and de-alienating the craftsperson, the products produced by Arts and Crafts were often little more than luxury products for a cultural and financial elite. Consequently, the role of craft (including ceramics), in this instance, did not appear to mark out a unique path which would revolutionize cultural life. Instead, it could be argued that craft aligned itself with the high aesthetics of painting and sculpture and lost the opportunity to instigate a broader cultural transformation on its own terms.

In the United States during this period, it seemed that madcap ceramists such as George Ohr instigated a more inventive approach towards getting ceramics to the people. Ohr was considered to be outside any major movement in ceramics, or at least, any movement which was programmatic in a modernist way. Instead, he worked along his own eccentric paths, performing in regional trade fairs and using such opportunities to sell his innovative ceramic pieces. The United States was the fastest developing industrial economy in the world at this time, and Ohr represented a more "homespun" variation of the entrepreneurialism that Wedgwood had taken advantage of earlier in the century.

Ohr's ceramic pieces developed an intense hybridization of forms and provided a mélange of styles more akin to the later work of Adrian Saxe (which Justin will discuss). Much of Ohr's work also offers allusions to postmodern stylistic practice before its time (as did Marcel Duchamp), mainly because of his emphasis on pastiche, rather than a dedicated reworking of older ceramic practices.

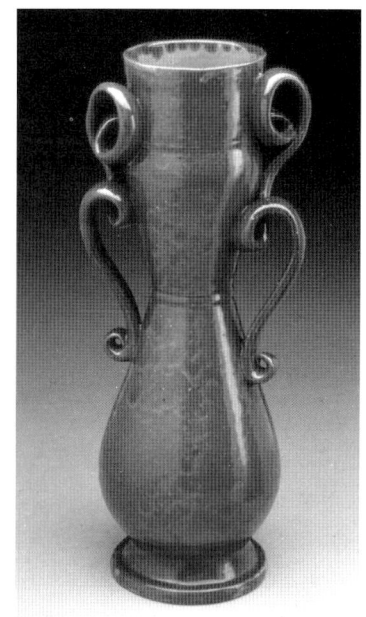

GEORGE OHR, *HANDLED VASE*, C.1895-1900. STONEWARE, 26.7 CM.

PRIVATE COLLECTION, MONTAGUE, NEW JERSEY

PHOTO: JOHN WHITE

THE MACHINE AESTHETIC

The utopian promise of modernity was chiefly dependent on the central role of the machine in transforming people's lives. As I have mentioned, Karl Marx's ideas about the alienating effects of the machine and capitalism was of central concern to figures such as William Morris. However, the role of ceramics in this equation remained equivocal. The contradictions that beset ceramic practitioners meant that ceramists often retreated from dominant avant-garde aesthetic directives and remained on the margins.

The Bauhaus is of interest because it seemingly offered a compromise between the extremes offered by Wedgwood and Morris. Bauhaus design incorporated high art aesthetics, yet simultaneously attempted to create designs which could be mass produced. The Bauhaus saw industrial capitalism as providing new markets and opportunities for craft production as long as craft production aligned itself with the demands of the machine age. On one hand, they accommodated capitalist production methods yet, on the other, produced objects which were often hand made and, in so doing, made a major contribution to industrial and other design principles in the twentieth century.

Although influenced to some degree by Morris's Arts and Crafts Movement and the Deutscher Werkbund/Wiener Werkstätte, the Bauhaus was an interesting combination of the medieval workshop tradition and the desire to accommodate the demands of industrial capitalism. Established during the 1920s by the architect Walter Gropius, the Bauhaus departed from more traditional academy learning environments to create levels of training that responded to times which demanded new forms of architecture and design. Training was predicated on a practical grounding of craft manufacture under factory conditions, combined with sound theoretical instruction in the laws of design. Gropius did not want to make a distinction between "fine" and "applied" art, believing that all could be subsumed under the principles of abstract art, thus creating an "indivisible whole."

He tried to bridge the gap between art and craft by insisting that the artist be experienced as a craftsperson, artist, and designer if there was ever to be an effective coordination between industrial design and machine production. He also proposed that no distinction should be made between "non-functional" artistic expression and the design of practical objects for industrial mass production. Although responsible for producing some astonishing designs, the Bauhaus suffered from disputatious internal factions, as many artists resented having to learn "craft" and argued that specialization was the most effective way to achieve the finest design.

However, implicit in Bauhaus aspirations for design was the modernist faith in the superiority of the machine, and this created some problems for ceramists involved in the movement. This is clear if we consider that earlier in Bauhaus history, figures like Gerhard Marcks and Max Krehan attempted to generate a medieval and classical revival with their ceramic wares, particularly if we consider the "Aegean" character of Marcks's bottle-shaped jug from around 1922.

Many of these objects were difficult to mass produce, so ceramists such as Theodore Bogler, who was willing to adapt the traditional practice to contemporary demands, became more significant in the movement. Bogler concentrated his attention on producing ceramics with component parts that could be assembled under factory-type conditions.

Bogler represented what ceramics could look like when designed as a compromise between high art principles and the demands of industrial mass production. Later figures such as Otto Rittweger became a more notable exponent of this compromise; however, his work already illustrates that metal was becoming the preferred material in creating functional objects for the home, as in his tea set of 1924.

Bernard Leach

Bernard Leach's work and philosophies are indicative of a number of modernist and anti-modernist tendencies. Leach's orientalizing attitude towards Japanese ceramics, such as raku, signaled the desire to merge Eastern and Western aesthetics, which was symptomatically modernist. Moreover, this convergence of ideas would lead to an "international style" which expressed a "truth to materials" idea. This kind of meta-narrative had already been propagated in the international style of modernist architecture which had its own adage of "form follows function." More importantly, Leach also

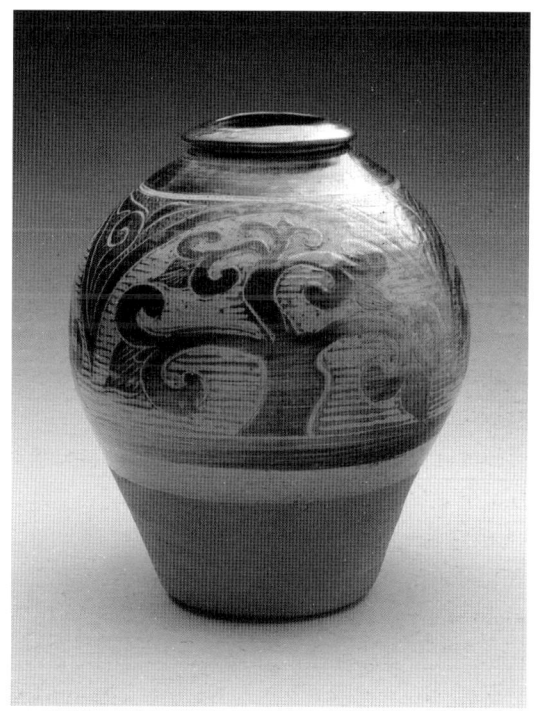

BERNARD LEACH, *VASE*, C. 1957. STONEWARE, 34.3 CM.
COLLECTION: COOPER-HEWITT, NATIONAL DESIGN MUSEUM, NEW YORK
PHOTO: JOHN WHITE

became a kind of all-pervading authority, generating a form of reverence amongst many ceramists, which some would argue worked to the detriment of some ceramics practice in the long term.

Leach's anti-modernist tendencies relate to the manner in which he sought to reinstill a kind of spirituality into the practice of making ceramics. In this sense, there was the desire to return to an organic relationship with the making of pottery, which strongly resisted the alienating effects of a machine dominated age. This was despite the fact that Leach indicated a desire to mass produce his objects. However, he was more concerned with producing ceramics that signaled a crucial balance between utility and decoration. His proposition for a "new balance," was easily connected to the idea of potters working in isolated dedication, spiritually content while adhering to the Leachian maxim that they should also dig their own clay to complete the cosmic cycle. This turn to the spiritual and chiefly, the *romantic*, led to the development of some beautifully crafted ceramic pieces but could also be used as a "cop out" by ceramists who refused to move with the times and retreated from important aesthetic debates during the postwar period.

In other ways, these romantic elements would persist into the 1960s and coalesce with countercultural artistic practices which resisted the instrumental logic of late capitalism and its colonization of consumption in the advertising-dominated world of consumerism.

Consumer Society

As consumer society rose to dominance during the postwar period, its major theorists, such as the Marxist critics Theodor Adorno and Horkheimer of the Frankfurt School, believed that it turned culture into an "industry." They also believed that high art resided beyond the culture industry of cheap mass-produced commodities. By omitting any discussion of ceramics, the Frankfurt School was, by implication, subletting ceramics from art's "superior" preserve. At the very least, ceramics was theoretically marginalized, for anything could only be considered art if it was aligned with the high-art tradition. Although it is true that some ceramics did align itself with this position, the Frankfurt School did not believe that ceramics had enough aesthetic content to transcend the conditions of the culture industry.

Despite these theoretical barriers, ceramics became more self-confident as a practice but was still plagued by its duplicitous identity. Firstly, the distinction between design and craft became blurred. In addition, ceramics, like other craft areas, continued to be caught between two modes of thinking (high/low art) and attempted to satisfy both while searching for some kind of identity in the midst of conflicting ideological and aesthetic propositions. Ultimately, much ceramics production continued to adhere to the high/low distinction between art and craft emphasized by formalist critics such as Clement Greenberg. In such cases, form, function, decoration, style, media, technique, and skill were linked to the idea of self as origin, self-expression as subjective intention, and aesthetic evaluation predicated on formal analysis.

In the ceramic field, figures such as Peter Voulkos and, later, Paul Soldner aligned themselves with an abstract expressionist aesthetic. This entailed: 1) Faith in individual creativity as "unique" 2) this uniqueness could be expressed and represented in artistic forms 3) by inference, the psychological make up of the individual remained beyond the grasp of the uniform tendencies of mass cultural forms and expression, and 4) consequently, one's "authenticity" and "integrity" could be expressed as a form of "resistance" to the colonizing tendencies of mass culture.

THE 1950S AND 1960S: THE WORLD OF POP

During the postwar period, the rise of mass consumerism seemingly broke down the hierarchies of high/low because "lifestyle" became crucial in relation to new notions of identity: i.e., how one looked, what objects one carried around and surrounded oneself with. Lifestyle thus became a central social and economic signifier of notions about self. What mass consumption offered was the opportunity for everyone to accumulate a certain cultural capital, not just the very rich. The notion of elite "taste" persisted, but the opportunities to display one's taste were broadened as the products selected could say a lot about the individual in a society which valued symbols of cultural capital. This so-called "aestheticization of everyday life" meant that consumers applied aesthetic discrimination to a broader range of goods, not just to fine-art painting but to many consumer items available in society. Culture began to assume a "social" definition where it was understood in a broader fashion, and rather than being "high" and "low," began to be regarded as a "whole way of life."

This in part explained the rise to popularity of industrial design during the 1950s. Products such as typewriters and other implements became sought after (fetish/fashion objects) items for a mass audience. Industrial design, with its alignment to mass production, met this demand. As Mike Featherstone has suggested:

> The different elements—design, consumerism and the image making of consumerism created through advertising—[became] fluidly related, including: 1) consumer durables—such as hairdryers, electric kettles, vacuum cleaners; 2) Craft—handmade pots, furniture, textiles, jewellery; 3) High-design artifacts—artifacts that [could] include a lot of workmanship (expensive cars, watches and tea services are included).[3]

Ceramics was clearly caught up in this realignment of aesthetic judgments. In addition, art had less claim to its exalted status as the luxury item *par excellence* at a time when people possessed a diverse range of consumer choices through which to express notions of taste and discrimination.

Developments in Pop Art during the post-war period had already indicated to the savvy ceramics practitioner that by drawing on mass and popular culture for ideas, Pop was challenging the elitist and polarizing tendencies of high aesthetics. Consequently, the status of the avant-garde came under question, and many claimed that it had ceased to have any relevance in a post-modern culture. In the art of Lichtenstein, Warhol, and others, it was clear that originality in the old sense was no longer important, and art was seen as a commodity and as a fashion item, like any other form of cultural production. In this movement, art abrogated its responsibility to forge a link to cultural leadership in society. Therefore, if art was foregoing the high/low art distinction, then the ramifications for ceramics were very promising indeed.

Robert Arneson, with his American "funk" approach, was a ceramist from this period who produced work which swung wildly between what was conventionally considered to be high and low aesthetics. He represented a consummate engagement with the fluidity and breadth of Pop aesthetics with works that were playfully anarchic and reliant on humorous puns and self-deprecating commentaries. By the early 1970s, ceramists such as Adrian Saxe followed such work with a more disciplined and semiotically charged investigation of historical and stylistic references symptomatic of postmodern aesthetics.

If Pop art was jumping out of the sinking ship, then it also meant that a craft practice such as ceramics was left to fend for itself and, in so doing, was released from the restrictive categorization of its practice which was central to the modernist perspective. However, it seemed as if many ceramists (especially those still under the sway of Bernard Leach) felt that this was a threat rather than a challenge. However, ceramics' very mobility was its strength; and its ability to move between shifting categories of taste in a postmodern consumer world with a product that was more intimate and accessible while being "handcrafted," provided it with a freedom which was, and continues to be, significant. As objects, ceramics can constantly shift aesthetic allegiances. This is because they are objects which are "closer" to

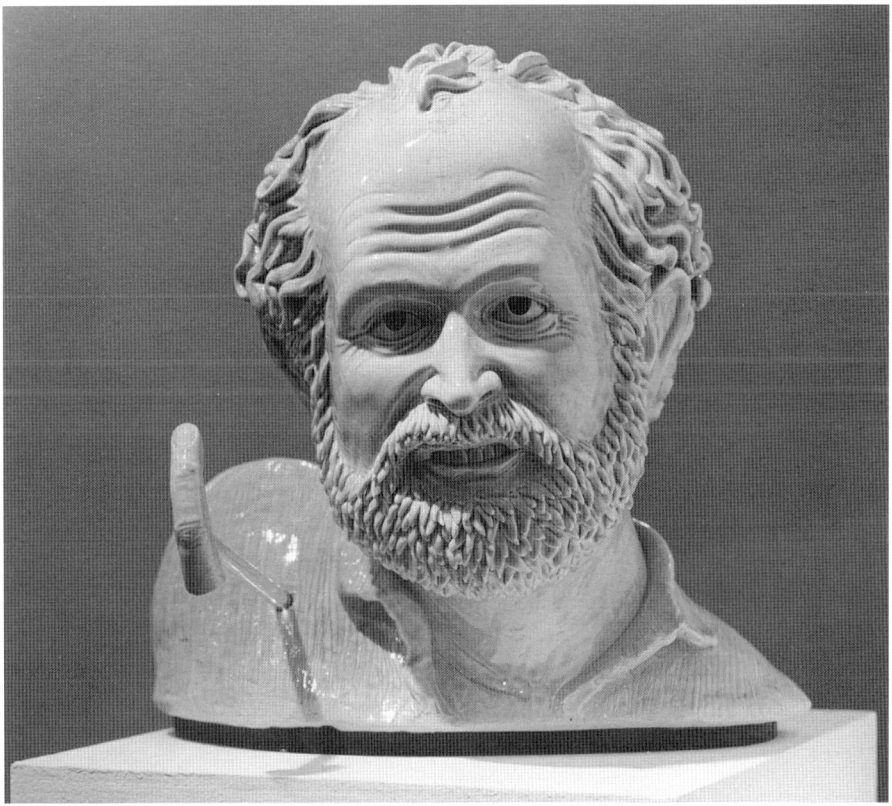

ROBERT ARNESON, *BIRD*, C.1972. STONEWARE WITH ACRYLIC ROD, 40.6 CM.
PHOTO: JOE SCHOPPLEIN

hand, so they have a more direct relationship with familiar consumer items. In this sense, ceramics can successfully respond to the consumer's desire to be attached to intimate objects in a fetishized manner.

The rise of consumerism, the emphasis on pleasure, and the seeming breakdown of aesthetic hierarchies promised a new world; but what was this new world to be after the failure of the New Left, the Paris riots of 1968, and the dissipation of the counterculture and other radical youth movements by the early 1970s? Postmodernism now emerged as a dominant cultural sensibility, and this had important ramifications for the ceramics practitioners, especially in relation to fine art practice, but this is something Justin Clemens will discuss in more detail in his talk.

CODA

I wanted to end this lecture by referring to the contemporary situation in which it is becoming apparent that what has been traditionally known as fine-art discourse is being increasingly applied to the evaluation and interpretation of ceramics.

Does one conceive of this situation as a hegemonic invasion or infiltration of ceramics practice, or does it mean that ceramic production is now being given due credit? This kind of question leads us back to the beginning of the lecture; for the broader idea in the ideology of modernism was that ceramics had be either art or craft, and this meant that it was evaluated according to a criteria of either/or: either one or the "other." However, in the postmodern, global era, ceramics can be either *and* or: both infiltrated and resistant; both defined and having the fluidity and freedom to move beyond such discursive boundaries.

Importantly, this freedom may enable it to move from an "ideology of embarrassment" to an "ideology of flexibility," providing the practice with a position of great strength in relation to other areas of cultural production.

1   There were many "modernisms" (i.e., Cubism, Futurism, Surrealism, etc.) and clearly, a broad range of ceramic styles and practices, but the modernism I'll use is a broadly applied programmatic modernism which represented a dominant set of attitudes during the nineteenth and twentieth centuries.
2   I mean a strongly oppositional set of values including clear demarcations between dominant/marginal, central/peripheral, authentic/inauthentic, professional/amateur, conceptual/artisanal, etc.
3   Mike Featherstone, *Consumer Culture & Postmodernism* (London: Sage 1991) 16.

Chapter 10

Postmodernity or "The Breaking of the Vessels"

Justin Clemens

The invention and development of modern aesthetics in the eighteenth century parallels the establishment of what might be called the relatively autonomous spheres of "art" and "life." This is the moment at which the aesthetic is directly and explicitly linked to the destiny of humanity. The aesthetic becomes at once act, fact, and capacity; it is integrally linked to the potentialities of the human psyche. Art becomes the place where ideas become sensible. Art images utopian possibilities. The crafts, on the other hand, do nothing of the kind.

Presented at *The Ceramic Millennium*, 1999, Amsterdam

Ill-communication. I compose this thesis as a stranger, at least quadruply displaced. First of all, I am not a specialist in ceramics, although I have certainly written on ceramics and so-called "craft-practice" more generally. Secondly, I speak and write in English, a language that is certainly not the first language of the country in which this conference is taking place (Holland) nor of many of the participants. Furthermore, I express myself in a vernacular and with an accent that is itself a minor variant of an old imperial tongue. Thirdly, I am a citizen of Australia, a country whose destiny and importance apparently lies very far from the determining global events of the present New Ceramic Order or Disorder. Finally, I have been invited here to speak on something called "postmodernism"—itself a term that has, to my knowledge, only relatively recently acquired a certain ambiguous pertinence in craft discourse.

What makes my irremediable foreignness paradoxically appropriate in this context is the fact that postmodernity is exemplarily an epoch of dislocation, marginality, translation—and, of course, absolute commodification. As Jean-François Lyotard has put it, parodying Marx's dream of social life after the revolution, postmodern man "listens to reggae, watches a western, eats McDonald's food for lunch and local cuisine for dinner, wears Paris perfume in Tokyo and 'retro' clothes in Hong Kong."[1] Global, mobile, technophiliac, erratic, eclectic: postmodernity is witness to the proliferation of heterogeneous worlds, centers, choices, customs, languages, commodities. Hence, as Zygmunt Bauman writes, "the problem of the postmodern world is not how to globalize superior culture, but how to secure communication and mutual understanding between cultures."[2] Which is also why, in the postmodern world, communication has become at once impossible and necessary. It is, as the Beastie Boys have put it, "ill-communication."

This paper can only provide the briefest of introductions to recent developments in contemporary theory. What is called "theory" is drawn from a number of quite different academic disciplines, e.g., philosophy, literary and cultural studies, social theory, anthropology, art theory, etc. This lecture, furthermore, will necessarily unfold on the basis of my own disciplinary interests and training. However, when researching for this lecture, it soon became apparent just how much recent philosophy and fine art in fact owes to its often anxious and antagonistic relationship to a craft which it wants to disinherit or denounce. Even more interestingly, it seems that the most sophisticated recent thought constantly turns to craft as a practice that exemplifies its philosophical arguments. It is this situation which I will attempt to ill-communicate.

FROM LIFE TO LIFESTYLE; FROM WORK TO NETWORK; FROM SPACE TO SPACE-LESS-NESS. Whether fortuitously or not, these problems of ill-communication are intensified when one turns to the authoritative texts on and of postmodernity. Not only are the dates, places, and nature of postmodernity in dispute, but there are those who continue to doubt its existence at all. If commentators such as Zygmunt Bauman, Jean-François Lyotard, and Fredric Jameson have proselytized for its existence, for writers such as Jürgen Habermas and Niklas Luhmann, "postmodernity" is merely a misapprehension or abdication of the conditions of our accelerated modernity.[3] In an attempt to render this intractable debate less obscure, I have divided this paper into two major sections. The first is a broadly historical account of postmodernity "in general"; the second examines in more detail the consequences that postmodernity has had on ceramics.

Now, some terminological clarifications: I take "modernity" and "postmodernity" to designate epochs of the broadest social and historical significance, whereas "modernism" and "postmodernism" will be used as names for more restrictively cultural phenomena. Recently, there has also been much talk of "globalization." On the one hand, it is possible to argue that "postmodernity" and "globalization" are effectively synonymous; many phenomena that appear under this latter heading have been similarly treated in the debate over postmodernity. On the other hand—and this is more important than it may seem at first glance—whereas the term "globalization" refers quite directly to an ongoing process, "modernity" and "postmodernity" obviously and primarily refer to some sort of temporal sequencing. Modernity is most often understood as dating from the late eighteenth century; post-modernity begins—if indeed it begins at all—sometime following World War II.

I will isolate five major headings around which the postmodern debate has typically circulated. It is necessary to add that these headings are only analytically distinct and are inextricably knotted together in practice. They are: 1) Economic; 2) Techno-scientific; 3) Informational; 4) Subjective; 5) Aesthetic. I will go through these one by one.

1. ECONOMIC. Various influential accounts of postmodernity have been concerned to mark its economic specificity in the very names and slogans that they give to it: "consumer society," "late capitalism," "disorganized capitalism," "postindustrial society," "post-Fordist flexible accumulation," etc. In such accounts, postmodernity is integrally linked to new economic developments—and therefore tends to be opposed to the modernity that antedates it, and which is still held to condition it in a number of different ways. As Scott Lash and John Urry have put it:

> At the end of the twentieth century circuits of commodities, productive capital and money qualitatively stretch to become international in terms of increases in global trade, foreign direct investment and global movements of finance.[4]

If such a globalization of capitalism entails a mutation in the relationships between capital and labour, a reorganization of class structures, the growth of multinational corporations, and a concomitant shift from a productivist to a consumer ethic, it therefore also entails a mutation in the powers and limits of the classical European nation-state, itself historically indissociable from European imperialism.

Postmodernity is thus also the era in which these historical limits are exposed as such: the liberal nation-state, upon which the very notion of a modern representative democracy was founded, is no longer the major site of policy formation and governmental decision making. Such decisions are now primarily subjected to the vicissitudes of global capital. Bauman, again:

> No longer capable of balancing the books while guided solely by the politically articulated interests of the population within their realm of political sovereignty, the nation-states turn more and more into the executors and plenipotentiaries of forces which they have no hope of controlling politically.[5]

It is thus no accident that the recent war in Europe was prosecuted by vast multinational military blocs and newly reformed "ethnic" groups—and not simply by single states and dissident populations. It is also no accident that questions as to possible financial motivations for the conflict have, for the most part, gone unasked.

2. TECHNO-SCIENCE. An understanding of the consequences that new technologies—most crucially, information and biotechnologies—have had on all aspects of life is central to postmodern theory. As Peter Schwarz, a Shell economist, once noted "it's this electronic money sloshing around the world in vast quantities. Trade is only about ten percent [of Gross World Product]; it's trivial. Movement of money itself is the game."[6] But one should also mark the essential military-corporate investment and development of such technologies as the internet: the Pentagon is, naturally, obsessed with C3I and C4I systems (Command, Control, Communications, Computers and Intelligence), as are corporations concerned to functionally simplify, cheapen, and accelerate their processes of production and distribution.

If such nineteenth-century technologies as the telegraph, telephone, typewriter, photography, gramophone, and film had already begun to displace the monopoly of writing with respect to the recording, storage, and transmission of information following the invention of the television, video, and computer, the "informatic effects" of technoscience are intensified and globalized. Control of the environment, medium, or network through and by which information can pass becomes more important than the content of particular information. Or, as Marshall McCluhan famously put it, "the medium is the message."

3. INFORMATICS. Communication technologies crucially affect the scope and status of knowledge in the postmodern era. Knowledge becomes data; ideology is subordinated to performance and efficiency; "facts" are either military-commercial secrets or already obsolete. As Lyotard puts it, "the games of scientific language become the games of the rich, in which whoever is wealthiest has the best chance of being right."[7] In this transformation, all the traditional foundations for knowledge—"God," "Reason," "Humanity," etc.— are stripped bare as illusions. Whatever modernity had considered universally "true," "beautiful" or "good" are revealed to be contingent, culturally limited fantasies, riven by duplicities and inequalities, founded on and supported by violence of every kind. No longer immutable, every purported "truth" now comes with a use-by date stamped on its face. As Jean-Luc Nancy writes:

> History can no longer be presented as…a "grand narrative," the narrative of some grand, collective destiny of mankind (of Humanity, of Liberty, etc.), a narrative that was grand because it was great, and that was great because its ultimate destination was considered good. Our time is the time, or a time, when this history at least has been suspended: total war, genocide, the challenge of nuclear powers, implacable technology, hunger, and absolute misery, all these are, at the least, evident signs of self-destroying mankind, of self-annihilating history, without any possibility of the dialectic work of the negative.[8]

Modernity began as both the beginning and the end of history: it was the beginning of history as a discipline, and of an understanding of universal history as a rational and rationalizing development of the world. But modernity was also its (own) end. Modernity began by already being over, an incessantly repeated "year zero of reason." Postmodernity, however, no longer believes nor trusts in history, nor in any universal ends; its realm is that of incommensurable, impossible, disjunctive histories that are as virtual as they are real. Nothing can ensure or verify that communication between or within different worlds has in fact been successful. Marketing, hype, and publicity become the primary elements of communication; a product without publicity is no product at all. Indeed, cultural products can now only circulate successfully if they are constructed in advance with a view to their marketability. A book, for instance, is no longer a "book": "it" should also be a film and interviews and tape recordings and Websites and a video game and a sequel and a prequel and a T-shirt and....Hence the situation of ill-communication that I invoked at the beginning of this paper.

4. THE SUBJECT. All of the aforementioned factors fundamentally affect the nature and constitution of the human subject itself. If modernity often presumed that humans were essentially rational beings capable of reflecting upon themselves and their actions, and able to make informed and intelligent decisions on that basis, postmodern theorists emphasize that individuals are now nothing more than mere aggregates of various drives, desires, tensions, fashions, body parts in constant movement and mutation. New models of subjectivity are constantly proposed: a number of writers, Fredric Jameson and Gilles Deleuze and Felix Guattari, for instance, have come to think of the schizophrenic as the very emblem of the human under post-modernity. This is not a clinical conclusion—these theorists do not simply mean that we are all in some way medically psychotic—but rather that, in postmodernity, all humans, like the way in which schizophrenics experience the world, find themselves dispersed and divided within the divergent spaces of their lives by vast impersonal forces which cannot be satisfactorily controlled or explained. We are now living the effects, as David Harvey would have it, of a "space-time compression."[9]

5. Aesthetics. If subjects are not, then, truly individual, then modern or romantic notions of the author as someone who creates something new and absolutely unique find themselves breaking down. Hence the notion of a "personal style," which depended absolutely on 1) notions of individuality that could be expressed in a work of art, and 2) a constraining normality from which individuals took their individual difference, also breaks down. For Fredric Jameson, then, the postmodern world celebrates, in place of the parodic aesthetic of modernity, what he famously calls "pastiche":

> Pastiche is, like parody, the imitation of a peculiar or unique style, the

wearing of a stylistic mask, speech in a dead language: but it is a neutral practice of such mimicry, without parody's ulterior motive, without the satirical impulse, without laughter, without that still latent feeling that there exists something normal compared to which what is being imitated is rather comic.[10]

Jameson's famous distinction indicates just how thoroughgoing the transformation in the nature of the work of art (and, indeed, of "work" in general) has been in postmodernity: no longer the expression of an individual genius or the representation of immutable truths, but the piecemeal reorganization of disparate materials that exceed the control of their makers. But what Jameson neglects to mention here is the political intensity newly generated by the problem of fictional representations. As the postmodern economy is effectively depoliticized, the regime of politics is abandoned to cultural representations, which now compel the intense partisanship and dissension once directed towards state political formations. At this point, the question might arise: What on earth does this have to do with ceramics?

POSTMODERNITY AS THE EX-POSITION OF THE MODERN.

Modernity and modernism ensured that rather strict hierarchies—between, for instance, "Art" and "craft"—pertained within the more general sphere of culture itself. Yet if culture (in the broadest sense) was certainly considered a zone essentially foreign to the exploitative exigencies of capitalist life, it was not, strictly speaking, a generic concept for various species or types of culture. If anything, such terms as "culture" functioned in an anti- or non-generic sense, that is, as a name for ambiguous practices to which value could not easily or clearly be assigned. Hence "Art," although supposedly one of the highest expressions of culture, could also be figured as precisely in opposition to culture—and as an anti-generic name in its own right. This is, in sum, the problem of the avant-garde in modernity. As Thierry de Duve has succinctly put it: "The notion of artistic quality, which previously had been linked to technical mastery, to talent, and to relatively unchanging notions of style, now finds itself irrevocably connected to the notion of innovation."[11] I will come back to this point; for the moment, I want simply to mark the problems posed to craft artisans and manufacturers (including ceramists) by such a situation. For modernity is also the moment at which "craft" becomes "craft" and "Art" becomes "Art," by way of an institutionally ratified division.[12]

Indeed, in modernity, particular economic, class, and symbolic benefits came to be rather strictly identified with various types of aesthetic practice. Certain materials became, in and of themselves, more valuable than others; certain forms of cultural production became inherently superior to their rivals. Those who worked with paint and canvas were certainly more elevated than those who worked with ceramics. Furthermore, this vast opposition of "Art" versus "craft" served to isolate and confuse practices that were, in fact, radically different, but which were thereafter treated as if their ontological freighting and social value were consonant (jewellery, ceramics, weaving, etc.). These hierarchies were installed, maintained, and enforced by a variety of state and (at least nominally) extra-state institutions, such as journals, salons, galleries, museums, academies, and associated educational apparatuses. Different conditions and locations were available for production, display, and distribution of these differing works. Although there were obviously national differences that permitted some play between the zones—as Peter Dormer has noted "France has continued the tradition of accepting that its painters and sculptors will make forays into the applied arts—a flexibility that is seldom found in the Anglo-American world"[13] The possibility of such forays only underlines the different status accorded "Art" and "crafts."

A battery of ideological equipment was developed to police and to naturalize these internal cultural divisions. The invention and development of modern aesthetics in the eighteenth century parallels the establishment of what might be called the relatively autonomous spheres of "Art" and "life." This is the moment at which the aesthetic is directly and explicitly linked to the destiny of humanity. The aesthetic becomes at once act, fact, and capacity; it is integrally linked to the potentialities of the human psyche. "Art" becomes the place where ideas become sensible; "Art" images utopian possibilities. The "crafts," on the other hand, do nothing of the kind.

If the major aestheticians of modernity are to be believed, craftspeople—unlike artists—can only ever be talented and thus without genius; craftspeople work with multiples or limited editions rather than with true originals; craft is too prosaic to be the object of genuine good taste; craft is to do with everyday life rather than with the exalted realm of ethics; craft smacks too much of business and industry to be truly free.[14] Unlike the hand of the painter, which is connected to ideas and ideals, the hand of the craftsperson is at once too much a hand (or several hands) and too little a hand (it is not linked to ideas; it is not a unique hand). The modern anathema towards decoration and the ornament—both essential to craft—is also revealing. As Rae Beth Gordon has put it,

> Virtually every definition of ornament connotes the inessential, the superfluous, or the superficial, the 'merely' decorative. Ornament, as commonly understood, is an accessory designed simply to please and is therefore fundamentally without meaning, if not morally reprehensible.[15]

Yet craft—precisely because of its degraded status—remains an insistent problem and an affront to high aesthetics. Indeed, the modern discourse on taste is also fractured in its origins by the definitional problems created by the very artificiality of the art/craft and art/manufacture distinctions. As John Guillory has pointed out:

> Such a sharp distinction was troubled by the production at its border of objects which shared some features of both categories: On the one side, for example, novels and prints, which could mimic aspects of manufacture for the general population; and on the other, commodities of manifest utility which yet incorporated elements of design borrowed from the Fine Arts (Wedgwood china, or Chippendale furniture).[16]

Nonetheless, my central point remains: throughout modernity, the value of those practices designated "Art" (painting, sculpture, poetry, etc.) is incomparably higher than those designated "craft" (ceramics, weaving, glass, etc.).

One might even cite here the direct links between these determinations and European colonialism. As Sandor Gilman has pointed out:

> Once the secret of manufacturing porcelain was uncovered in Europe in the late eighteenth century, the value of [Chinese] porcelain as an aesthetic object produced by an alien but higher culture was diminished. With the decline of the porcelain trade, the association of Chinese art and science in the West became a negative one....[17]

Again, aesthetic theory was mobilized to explain the respective differences in practice, technique, materials, audiences—differences that are meant to justify the concomitant evaluations that the terms "Art" and "craft" imply. The reciprocity between art practice and art theory was necessarily extremely close in modernity.

Given such a situation, craft can only ever enter such a system as either something essentially inferior to or something to be reintegrated or subsumed under art production in general. In the most general terms, the relationships that ceramics could entertain with the high arts in modernity were therefore restricted to:

1) EXCLUSION. For the philosopher Georg Wilhelm Friedrich Hegel, smell, taste, and touch were definitionally excluded from the realm of true aesthetic appreciation. It would be easy to cite a variety of (logically incompatible) adjectives typically invoked to support such an exclusion. Ceramics practice—at least compared to "high art"—was too industrial, domestic, feminine, etc.

2) SUBSUMPTION. Ceramics could enter the realm of art as one of the latter's regional disciplines, inferior to but nonetheless a genuine part of art practice. If the Bauhaus and Pablo Picasso share anything at all, it is the conviction that ceramics can be a legitimate material for art, without, for all that, disrupting the characteristic logics, operations, or value of art itself. Craft is only acceptable on terms of its regional domiciliation under governing principles ultimately superior to its own.

3) FUSION. Ceramics is already genuine art. William Morris is perhaps the most famous figure to have attempted such a transvaluation. This version nonetheless remains thoroughly marginal in the dialectic of aesthetic modernity; it, furthermore, seems only able to have been expressed in the most nostalgic and sentimentalized of terms (e.g., neo-medievalism).[18]

4) EXPLOITATION. The division between "crafts" and "Art" also opens up the possibility of disavowed exploitation of the one by the other. This is not to suggest that ceramics practice (or craft more generally) has not had a crucial role to play in aesthetic modernity. On the contrary, throughout modernity, ceramics have been globally produced and distributed; the forms and functions of ceramics radically increased and diversified; new techniques were invented for its fashioning and expression; ceramics provided hitherto unforeseen economic opportunities for skilled artisans and labourers. The central roles played in modernity by such manufacturers as Thomas Wedgwood—who at one time was a patron of such major romantic poets as Samuel Taylor Coleridge—ought not be overlooked. Paradoxically

enough, this situation also entailed that art and craft continually drew on each other as resources, responding to and pilfering from each other in all sorts of covert and disavowed ways.

In the era of postmodernity, however, the strong distinctions between "Art" and "crafts" are widely held to have broken down: these distinctions are no longer politically, economically, aesthetically, or philosophically justifiable. I would say that postmodernity is the moment at which these relations are ex-posed as such. Or, in other words, the internal contradictions already working within such evaluations now become apparent. This new patency is bound up with the exhaustion of the traditional avant-garde movements insofar as they were cultures of politico-aesthetic negation and innovation, with universal ambitions. Confronted by the injunction to innovate, the avant-garde often responded by turning towards hitherto unheeded or undepicted subjects (e.g., to the rural proletariat, to Parisian lowlife, to non-Western art and cultures), and towards new materials, techniques, and loci of reproduction. Hence also the disavowed necessity of avant-garde artists to at some point return to craft materials and techniques in their attempts to create new differences within "Art" itself. It is thus no accident that the most influential artists of the twentieth century turn to ceramics and to glass. Marcel Duchamp's urinal and his *Large Glass* are a case in point. More recently, we have Warhol's Factory, and Jeff Koons's consistent and explicit exploitation of ceramicists and ceramics throughout his work.

What postmodernity perhaps exposes is that "Art" was always more dependent on "craft" than the other way around; "craft" was a fundamental condition for "Art" and not simply its aesthetically degraded shadow. In postmodernity, both "Art" and "crafts" suffer a dislocation. "Art" is decapitalized and dispersed, i.e., new arts (such as "video art" and "sound art") proliferate, whereas the old "Arts" lose their traditional centrality and legitimization. The "crafts," however, if also unleashed from the strictures of modernity, find themselves on the verge of a historic opportunity. There is now the chance for a ceramic art (and new practices and poetics) that is not simply submitted to the regimes of technologies of reproduction, nor identified in its essence with the logics of the hand, nor opposed nor subordinated to the dictates of the other arts. Ceramics is in a singular situation: at once perhaps the most archaic and genuinely universal of the arts, it now finds itself at the cutting edge of aesthetic-technical innovation. But, as the sociologist Niklas Luhmann has put it, "the only certain thing about tomorrow is that it will be different from today."

1   J-F. Lyotard, "Answering the Question: What is Postmodernism?" in *The Postmodern Condition: A Report on Knowledge*, trans. G. Bennington and B. Massumi (Minneapolis: University of Minnesota Press, 1993) 76.

2   Z. Bauman, *Intimations of Postmodernity* (London: Routledge, 1992), 102.

3   A very truncated selection of the relevant pronouncements on the subject would have to include, in addition to the afore-cited works by Lyotard and Bauman, Fredric Jameson's, *Postmodernism, or, The Cultural Logic of Late Capitalism* (Durham: Duke University Press, 1991) and *The Seeds of Time* (New York: Columbia University Press, 1994); N. Luhmann, *Observations on Modernity*, trans. W. Whobrey (Stanford: Stanford University Press, 1998); J. Habermas, "Modernity—An Incomplete Project" in H. Foster (ed.), *The Anti-Aesthetic: Essays on Postmodern Culture* (Seattle: Bay Press, 1983), 3-15. Diverse recent work in a number of disciplines (e.g., art-, social- and literary-theory, philosophy and history) tends to see the contemporary period as still "modern," i.e., as beginning some time in the late eighteenth century in Europe.

4   S. Lash and J. Urry, *Economies of Signs and Space* (London: Sage, 1994) 2.

5   Z. Bauman, *Globalization: The Human Consequences* (Cambridge: Polity Press, 1998) 65.

6   Source not available.

7   Lyotard, *The Postmodern Condition* (Manchester: Manchester University Press, 1984) 45.

8   J-L. Nancy, *The Birth of Presence*, trans. B. Holmes *et al.* (Stanford: Stanford University Press, 1993) 144-145.

9   D. Harvey, *The Condition of Postmodernity* (Oxford: Basil Blackwell, 1989).

10 F. Jameson, "Postmodernism and Consumer Society," in *The Anti-Aesthetic* (Seattle: Bay Press, 1983) 114.

11 T. de Duve, *Pictorial Nominalism* (Minneapolis: University of Minnesota Press, 1991) 26.

12 As J-L. Nancy has remarked, "We have been saying 'art' in the singular and without any other specification only recently, only since the romantic period," *The Muses*, trans. P. Kamuf (Stanford: Stanford University Press, 1996) 4. Nancy, however, fails to note that art's singularization and capitalization is directly effected at the expense of the crafts (lower-case, plural).

13 P. Dormer, *The New Ceramics: Trends and Traditions* (London: Thames and Hudson, 1986) 14.

14 As Susan Cohn has expressed this state of affairs, "In the Western world, at least since the Renaissance, craft has also been forced into the minor league by its associations with utility." "The Crafts: on their own terms," in P. Timms (ed.), *The Nature of the Beast* (Melbourne: Craft Victoria, 1993), 23. This domination was integrally linked to class distinctions: the avant-garde of modernity was invariably bourgeois and masculine. Hence the associations of craft with petit-bourgeois artisans and femininity; hence also the continuing investment of the residual *aristocracy* in craft-type products.

15 R.B. Gordon, *Ornament, Fantasy, and Desire in Nineteenth-Century French Literature* (Princeton: Princeton University Press, 1992) 4.

16 J. Guillory, *Cultural Capital: The Problem of Literary Canon Formation* (Chicago: University of Chicago Press, 1993), 307-308. The relationships between the crafts and written literature are of especial interest in modernity. For example, literature itself acquires artisanal qualities (writing as a "craft"), and writers as different as William Morris and Stephane Mallarmé turn to craft for their privileged metaphors and physical vehicles.

17 S. Gilman, *Disease and Representation: Images of Illness from Madness to AIDS* (Ithaca: Cornell University Press, 1988) 141.

18 The most terrifying attempt to transvalue "craft" in modern philosophy is that of Martin Heidegger — also one of the greatest philosophers of the century. In Heidegger's work, clay jugs can become the privileged topics for ontological meditation and, indeed, "thinking" itself ultimately becomes a handicraft. See M. Heidegger, *Poetry, Language, Thought*, trans. and intro. A. Hofstadter (New York: Harper and Row, 1971). As already noted, however, this revaluation suffers from a dangerous nostalgia. As James Ward has remarked, "The apparent priority of 'simple craft conditions' suggests that for Heidegger handiwork and handicraft production occupy a position superior to that of mass or machine production. If this is the case, it is argued, I think correctly, that Heidegger stands with the *völkisch* anti-industrial and antimodern supporters of National Socialism and shares with them a radically mistaken understanding of it which he later corrects when he comes to recognize that the Nazis had not set out to repeal modernity," J. Ward, *Heidegger's Political Thinking*.

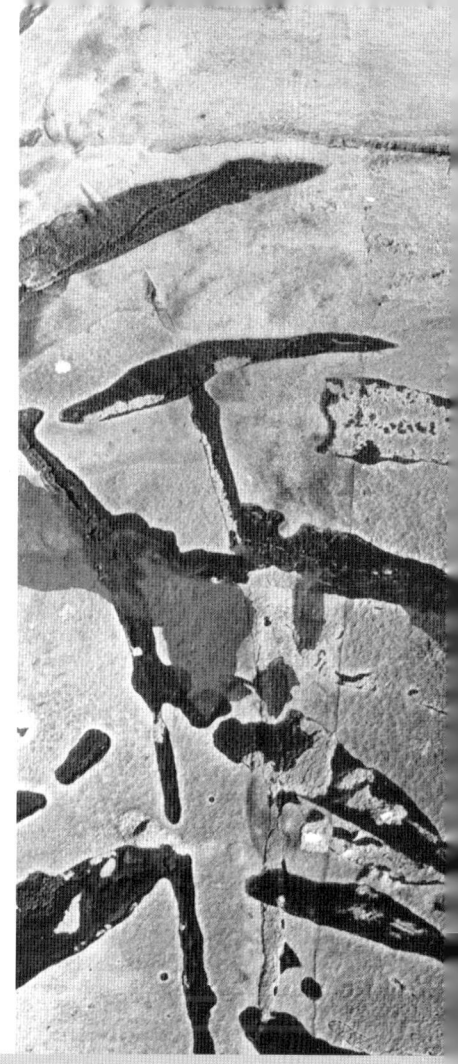

SECTION THREE
THE DECORATIVE

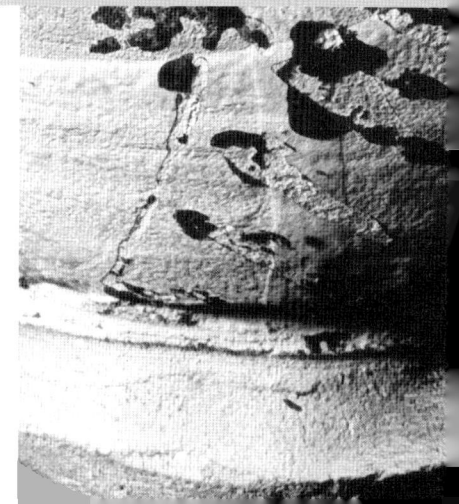

CHAPTER 11

CERAMIC DECORATION AND THE CONCEPT OF CERAMICS AS DECORATIVE ART

GEORGE WOODMAN

There are many artists in clay who are constantly walking a very fine line between the permissiveness of the decorative and making the claims of sculpture or painting. Much of this imagery revolves around issues of taste. Bad taste has been a rich source for ceramics. It is necessary to understand what sleight of hand is going on here. Decorative art, by definition, aspires to good taste; therefore, to produce ceramic imagery in bad taste attempts to transform the object into art because art is not concerned with taste. Issues of taste do not matter in art.

Presented at *The Ceramics Symposium*, 1979, Syracuse

Decoration, unlike most notions in art, is clear and unambiguous. We don't have to misuse it. When we refer to most painting, marks, or other applied forms on ceramics as decoration, we are frequently making a mistake. Usually it is not decoration; it is something quite different, and I hope to indicate what it is. Furthermore, it should be added that decoration is bound up with the gentle notion of the decorative and that ceramics has long been tied to the concept of a decorative art. There are issues here which are important to the directions in which ceramics is going today and will be taking in the next decade.

Decoration is a relational concept. One thing decorates another. One thing serves to adorn, to beautify, or to embellish another thing. What, then, is the relationship between marks on pots and decoration as opposed to the relationship between ceramic decoration and ceramics as a decorative art? Most people do not look at paintings and call them decorated canvases, although some canvases can be considered decorative painting. A look at the tradition in ceramics indicated that most painting, most application of painting to pots is not decoration. The pot in relationship to its painting is parallel to the canvas's relationship to painting, as in the case of a Frank Stella. Consider the Greek "vase." It is a very generalized object, produced in quantities, with no really distinguishing characteristics other than being prepared to be their field for a painting. It is by no quirk of history that the name of the artist who did the painting on the pot is known to us and that of the person who fashioned the pot is lost in oblivion. A great deal of modern work in clay is equally tied to painting, and the thinking of many artists working in clay is to essentially produce some kind of situation in which clay and painting come together.

Contrast what I would call the generalized ceramic vessel. The material rules of ceramics produce an expanded envelope of an elastic material, and that is all there is to see. In the "undecorated" pot, the only specific thing to see is a contour or silhouette; it really has no particular identity except in its edges. This at once separates vessel ceramics from sculpture. A sculpture is constantly being articulated so that we look into it and see more than its silhouette. Ceramics, on the other hand, has an enormously long and significant tradition of painting into that interior surface so that we have information about the shape of the pot, its character, its form, its degree of vitality somewhere besides simply at its contour.

It is a mistake, however, to call this decoration. This would be to assume that the function of the painting is to embellish or adorn an object which has an identity otherwise. In fact, the clay object really is often generalized and unspecific until it is painted. Europeans, thanks to the gifts of language, don't fall into this trap. In Italy such a painted design would not be called a decoration, but rather a *motivo* or motif. The relationship of that form to the painted motif is not incidental or unimportant; it may be a powerful, subtle, and beautiful relationship between object profile and motif. Other materials can also be applied to ceramics to achieve the same ends. The reason we prize the exaggerated effects of fire on certain Japanese glazes is that they perform essentially a painting function. The result is an elaboration of surface and texture which makes it possible to read something inside of the contour.

Ceramics is an artistic expression which involves a unity between a clay form and its surface treatment which cannot be separated out, and it cannot be said that one is more important than the other.

I think that the understanding of this connection between pots and the marks applied to them has partly been obscured by the notion that ceramics is somehow connected to sculpture. There are even schools which suggest you study sculpture or have sculptural experience before you take ceramics. This is, in my mind, erroneous. The natural handmaiden of ceramics is not sculpture but painting, because a sensibility to the organization of surfaces in relationship to their contours is not really the province of construction and space but of visual organization of fields. It is true that ceramics is a rather dirty occupation involving heavy materials, perspiration, and machinery, which makes it resemble sculpture as an activity. Ceramics has an almost intellectual dimension involving a perceptual finesse which we seldom find among sculptors. A *decorated* pot is usually a very simple pot, not all that interesting, and has been embellished, has been adorned, so it has painting on it which we can truly call decoration. By the line of thinking which I am presenting, perhaps one pot in a thousand is really decorated. With a *decorative* pot, on the other hand, what is put onto it has a different function. In a decorated pot you paint on the pot to embellish the pot. With a decorative pot the pot is embellished to decorate something else. To be decorative is to play a role. A decorative pot enters a room under rules for its admission. It performs a function there. It is something like the guest you might invite to your salon. It may be a very important person in the room. I didn't used to understand these kinds of grown-up notions but now that I can look back and reflect, they become clearer to me. When I was a child, one did not put the pickle bottle on the dining room table. There was a glass container into which the pickles were placed, and it went into a silver filigree object, and that was placed upon the table, and that is what decoration is all about. It is about something called civilization, which is rapidly disappearing but not to be despised.

Decoration has a force and clarity that represent an artistic position which is forthright, interesting, and which I think I will have an increasing impact. Decoration involves objects playing a different role than in "art." One of the problems of contemporary ceramics is the attempt to make an object into which is poured everything. That is impossible. In decoration, however, a thing is made which comes out into everything. Decoration is founded upon the orchestration of the arts. As a word, it derives from the Latin word for "decorous," and there is another word derived from decorous in English called "decorum." Decorum refers to what is proper, suitable, and seemly; and I think decorum in the arts is something worth reflecting upon. Decoration is seldom ambiguous. It speaks a coherent and consistent language which is shared among many objects. That is one reason why decoration is seldom highly personal. This may seem paradoxical; but if you think of an elaborate room at Versailles, for example, the work of a hundred people may have gone into it, but their identities have all been submerged to a single decorative effect. Decoration is not self-expressive; and for that reason, since the romantic period, decoration has fallen like a chill on people who want to be self-expressive. Amy Goldin, who had great insight into decoration, used to say that decoration is intellectually empty, but it doesn't have to be stupid.

It is hard to imagine any decorative tradition without its language, and this is expressed in ceramics as well as all the other arts. For instance, in eighteenth-century ceramics we find reverse curves, shells, perforated forms, lattice forms, broken contours, feathery forms, the colour white, unclear symmetry divisions, and a rather theatrical character. And, of course, these characteristics, this lexicon of common language, appears in many different guises and has many kinds of inflection in architecture, painting, and sculpture as well. And it is fascinating how, from the rather hothouse warmth of Bavaria, we can arrive at the Arctic chill of English plaster work within the same principles of language. There are many decorative traditions. The period I am using to define the decorative tradition is also the period of the theater, and the theater with its notion of many roles, many ways of acting, many types of appearance, has its visual analogies. Architecture can involve itself with ceramics: European architecture involves unending quantities of stone ceramic forms, which can sometimes achieve rather imposing scale. In all of this, ceramics plays its own unique role, a role which is fascinating to observe in its contrast to contemporary art. The typical drawing room of the late eighteenth-century had a cabinet of ceramics. Not in the kitchen but in the drawing room are plates and teacups correctly and appropriately framed in cabinetry—the decoration speaks of scale and character which relates to the wallpaper and drapes and all the rest.

Modern ceramics follows a crisis in decoration and a crisis in the theory of the role of decoration in the fine arts, and that is certainly well enough known to all of us. We all know about the arts and crafts movement and the fulmination of someone like Morris against a poor little innocent, factory-made pitcher, which doesn't happen to have fingerprints all over it. The early twentieth century was a period both of rejection of ornament, and rich and lush achievements in decorative art. To quote Tolstoy, "Real art, like the wife of an affectionate husband, needs no ornament. But counterfeit art, like a prostitute must always be decked out." It is not surprising that, in the thirties and forties, decoration was to be rejected absolutely; and we had the dawning consciousness of something called "good design." People who were really into aesthetic chic were taking laboratory porcelain and glassware into the kitchen. I can remember many years ago bright young things in their kitchens being so pleased that, somehow, domestic life and industrial life had been brought together, and they were participating in it.

This brings us somewhere close to the present and to a series of attitudes and responses in ceramics which have dominated recent experience. We need to consider a variety of ceramic objects under several categories. The first category is what I call the "natural pot." Many of us have hungered after some kind of a vision of objects, free of the past, free of style, free of chic, free of sophistication, which somehow, like bread and homemade soup, brings us to a natural and restorative life. It's a longing that one can easily understand and perhaps find difficult to resist, and many people working with clay have found a very honourable and meaningful career in producing what we would call the "natural pot." The natural pot aspires to the character of a fresh-baked loaf of bread more than it aspires to any particular kind of ceramic object that we have encountered in recent history. The natural pot, when it looks for artistic inspiration, tends to look for the most quiet and understated and thoughtful examples of ceramics which we have known in the twentieth century. They tend to come from that school nurtured and fostered under the care of Bernard Leach. Decoration on the work is often absent and, if present, is usually understated, and aspires to be decoration only in that sense of painting completing the pot. When its aspirations move elsewhere, towards some more vibrant form of decoration, we find in this movement a kind of uncertainty, a faltering quality which marks many of the ceramics from the late forties and early fifties. It is a tradition which still presents life and opportunity today.

The next kind of pot I would like to talk about is the "art pot," which should not be confused with the "art pottery" movement of the turn of the century. The art pot represents a non-decorative stance, and it does this by taking as its point of inspiration serious works of art rather than decorative traditions. The examples most well known to us are those ceramics which are the outgrowth of abstract expressionism. It is a large body of work of tremendous importance, of which the most well known exponent is Peter Voulkos. These are ceramics which insist that you take them seriously in the way that you would take seriously a painting by de Kooning. It is a movement which is rich with successes, and at the same time, has almost built into it the problem of almost always trailing a little bit behind movements in other worlds of art. In the recent works of Voulkos, for example, he treats the plate, in a sense, as a format for painting.

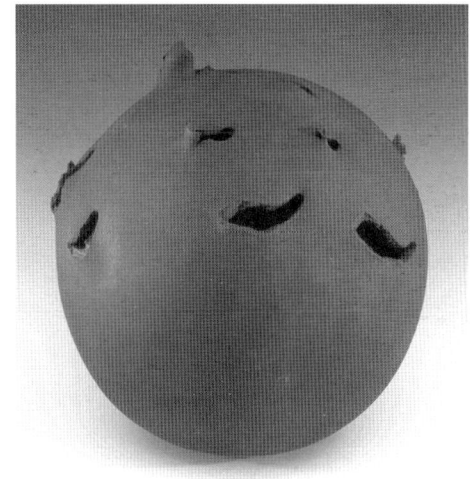

LUCIO FONTANA, *CONCETTO SPAZIALE*, C.1964.
EARTHENWARE, 31.1 CM.
COLLECTION: MAXINE AND STUART FRANKEL ART FOUNDATION
PHOTO: NOEL ALLUM

One of the challenges to painting in the twentieth century has been the work of Lucio Fontana, who, in the early 1950s, decided to slash and perforate the canvas; so we have, some fifteen years later, the decision to slice and perforate the plate.

The list of artists who worked in the vein of ceramics which is painted but not decorated, who have made the art pot, is a long one. Paul Soldner is a very important artist. Betty Woodman and myself collaborated on a number of raku pieces in which the ideology is clearly the same. Wayne Higby's or below landscape pots are pots which certainly are not decorated, and they insist that we take them seriously as some kind of an image. Rick Dillingham's pots ask that we take the same kind of serious attitude towards them by making reference, not to contemporary art, but to archaic modes of art, with the particularly solicitous and imaginative concept of essentially echoing the character of reconstituted pots of other times and cultures. The kind of seriousness an art pot has can come from any other kind of seriousness in art, and I find Richard DeVore's and William Daley's work fascinating because, to

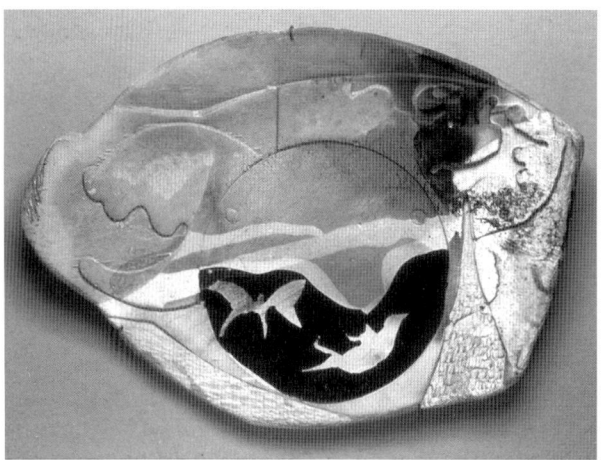

PAUL SOLDNER, *PLAQUE*, 1979. RAKU WITH STAINS, 43.2 × 61.0 CM.
PHOTO: TERRY A. COLLINS

my mind, they are the conceptualists of the vessel, raising issues about what is an edge: Can you take an edge and add it to an edge? Can the inside be on the outside, and can the rim exist somewhere besides and at the edge? These are the kinds of issues which an essentially conceptual art raises.

The third category is a group of works which I have put under the rather awkward rubric of "the old decoration and the new image." Consider a decorative plate from the eighteenth century bearing a simulacra of contents modelled in clay. Such a plate is decorative, partly by the conceptual transfer of its function into the object itself. A real plate holds leaves, if you wish. This decorative plate is not a real plate because it is an image of a plate performing its function. The decorative function of ceramics is often connected to the suppression of actual function and is combined with an exaggerated manner in appearance. Decorative ceramics are focused outwards. They make external references. They are always looking out into the world, not into themselves, and they have an overtness which is often very abrupt and very frank. Decorative art gets away with this by the sense of tone and grace which is implied in the object. Today, many pieces of decorative art seem outrageous to us. They seem outrageous only because we look at them as pieces isolated from the context in which their decorative character is realized.

The types of artists who are now working out of the decorative tradition are very varied. There is a tremendous amount of painting on clay which comes down to what I call illusionism and extended reference. The desire of the object to reach out and grab and connect with many other kinds of things and situations, as we have seen, is characteristic of the decorative. I don't know if Richard Shaw had ever seen

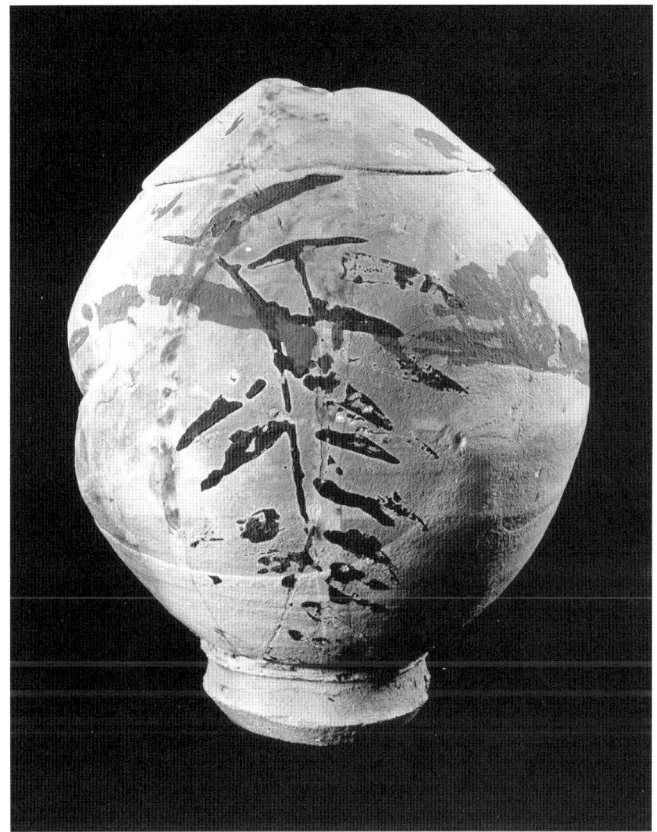

Paul Soldner, *Bottle*, 1964. Earthenware thrown and altered, 22.9 × 17.8 cm.
Collection: Everson Museum of Art, Syracuse, NY
Photo: Jane Courtney Frisse, Salt City Imageworks

them, but in the late eighteenth century, there appeared porcelain plates painted with little illusions of engravings stuck under splinters in the illusory wood of which the plate was apparently constituted. Illusionism has passed through American art and craft like a prairie fire. Illusion is what people of uneducated sensibilities always look for, and some artists deliver it with a degree of satisfaction guaranteed that is quite extraordinary. What separates this kind of illusionism from illusionism of great ceramic traditions is that it is not bound by any frame of reference which gives focus to it.

Many of these artists realize that the identification of an object as clay places it in a certain perceptual context. I was sufficiently stupid to wonder why Patty Warashina bothered to make things out of clay. It seemed so difficult to produce objects so fragile, but finally I realized that the whole point of making these objects in clay is that we see them as belonging to a certain world which they would not belong to if they were made out of wood or plastic or something else. And that is the world of a minor art, and a minor art enjoyed certain privileges which major arts

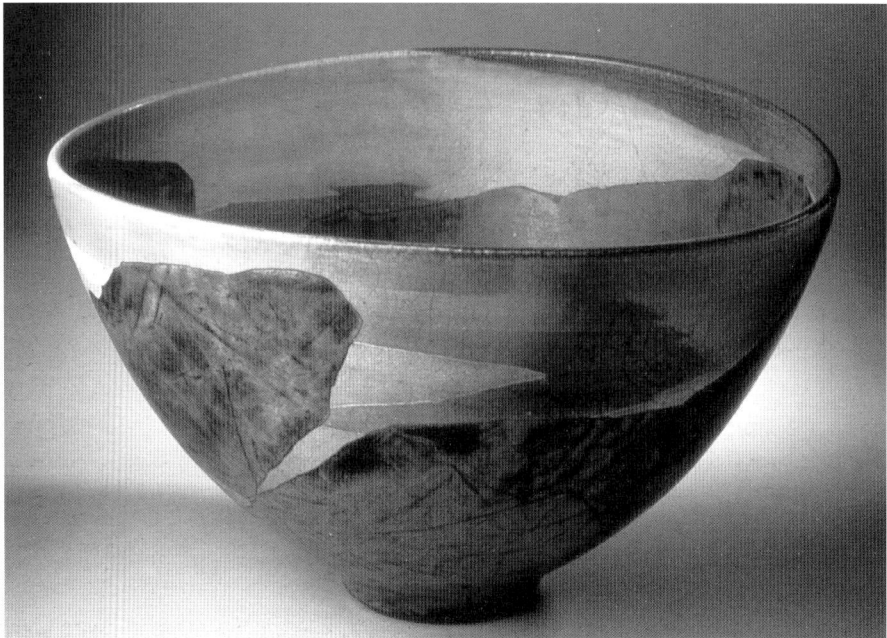

WAYNE HIGBY, *IMAGINARY BAY*, 1979. RAKU, 26.7 × 45.7 CM.
PHOTO: JOHN WHITE

do not. Decorative ceramics is a minor art that enjoys an extraordinary permissiveness. You can do anything in clay and get away with it. What I would call the indulgently permissive object has really only existed in clay.

I.A. Richards in his book, *Practical Criticism*, identified four kinds of meaning in poetry: sense, feeling, tone, and intention. Tone is one aspect of poetry that I think is very important in ceramics. Richards defines tone as an attitude towards the listener, a sense of how the poet stands to him. In the decorative arts, tone is critical, and the success or failure of the decorative is often bound up by that sense of how the artist, with what tone, is speaking to us. The tone of much new imagism derived from the old decoration can be very varied. It can be humourous, cajoling, dissimulative, didactic, threatening, chic-chic, ironic, mystifying, aloof, or overbearing—just to name a few tones popular since the sixties. It is an enormous contrast to the tone in which Bernard Leach asked ceramics to speak. He asked for sincerity, while Voulkos asked for seriousness. We live in a time of fascination with different kinds of tone and complexity of tone.

What might be called the "collaging synthesis," which Rauschenburg and others (a generation after its invention by the Cubists) brought to American art, has permeated ceramics also. If we are to correctly assess the new imagism based on the old decoration, we have to realize that added to it is the collage mentality. Some of the problems in the new imagism were to put into focus by the *Soup Tureen* show. The objects were clear as to what they were but fuzzy as to intention and what decorative context to which they could be referred. We find, at times, in much contemporary ceramics, a confusion between the decorated object and the imagism of the decorative object. The decorative tradition is very open and permissive, but open and permissive only because we know that decoration is neither serious nor expressive. Much work now being done in clay out of the decorative tradition, at the same time, attempts to be expressive.

I find it difficult to accept the emotional tone of seriousness suggested to make clay images which are expressive. The master of tone manipulation is, of course, Robert Arneson. The tone of contempt for the viewer has become, essentially, the foundation of a career and a mode of expression. It's a game which I find not always easy to play, because it seems to be trying to cut both ways. If we are involved with a decorative object, then everything is permitted. The decorative object is a little bit like the child or the idiot: everything is permitted to it. The work of art, on the other hand, is expected to behave responsibly, like a grownup.

There are many artists in clay who are constantly walking a very fine line between the permissiveness of the decorative and making the claims of sculpture or painting. Much of this imagery revolves around issues of taste. Bad taste has been a rich source for ceramics. It is necessary to understand what sleight of hand is going on here. Decorative art, by definition, aspires to good taste; therefore, to produce ceramic imagery in bad taste attempts to transform the object into art because art is not concerned with taste. Issues of taste do not matter in art. They did not concern Goya or Pollock. But to work in something which presents itself as in a decorative mode and then to make the transformation to art through the manipulation of taste is a very complex and perhaps perilous undertaking.

The last kind of pot to concern us is the "new decorative vessel," and we consider it at a moment when attitudes towards decoration in the fine arts are becoming rapidly transformed. There have recently emerged an articulate group of artists who reject a great deal of recent avant-garde art as elitist, sexist, racist, and capitalistic, and who find the whole possibility of decoration exhilarating and broadening. I tend to be very sympathetic with these artists and find much of the art which we have seen in the last fifteen years drab and boring. There is an influential and subversive movement in American art today ready to reconsider the whole relationship of decorative art and so-called "fine" art or serious art. The future we hope for ceramics may not consist in finally bubbling up through the aesthetic soup to the top little bit of scum where the "fine" arts are, but in fact the whole thing may be about to turn over. There are artists all over the country who are interested in and concerned about the decorative stance. For people in clay to jump out of that ship after having staunchly stayed by it for so long would be probably the worst timing that could ever occur.

There are artists for whom the decorative spirit has never disappeared. Wayne Higby, or above with a prescience seldom granted to the young, in the mid 1960s produced a body of work which represented a frankly decorative quality which I think is going to be seen very much in the future. Andrea Gill is making pots animated by a sense of the decorative tone, a sense of an object which does not have the seriousness, the kind of boring pompousness in terms of expressive intent that we have been treated to in recent times. Betty Woodman's recent pots represent a frankly decorative outlook, playing a kind of sneaky game with function. They are to be used, and used with a sense of decorative ebullience and not some mean notion of the "function" of eating and life at table. John Gill, among others, is producing objects which are vessels without function. Yet they are not expressive images; their tone is clearly and simply decorative. John Glick seems to be joyfully wheeling along a similar road. Among younger, sensitive potters there appears to be a dawning awareness that the decorative stance is one of the strongest and most appropriately taken in ceramics. Attempts to avoid, disguise, or transform the "minor" arts into "real" art are the result of a misconception of the nature of decoration, in part brought about by the critical assumptions underlying an increasingly attenuated and artificial framework of cultural values.

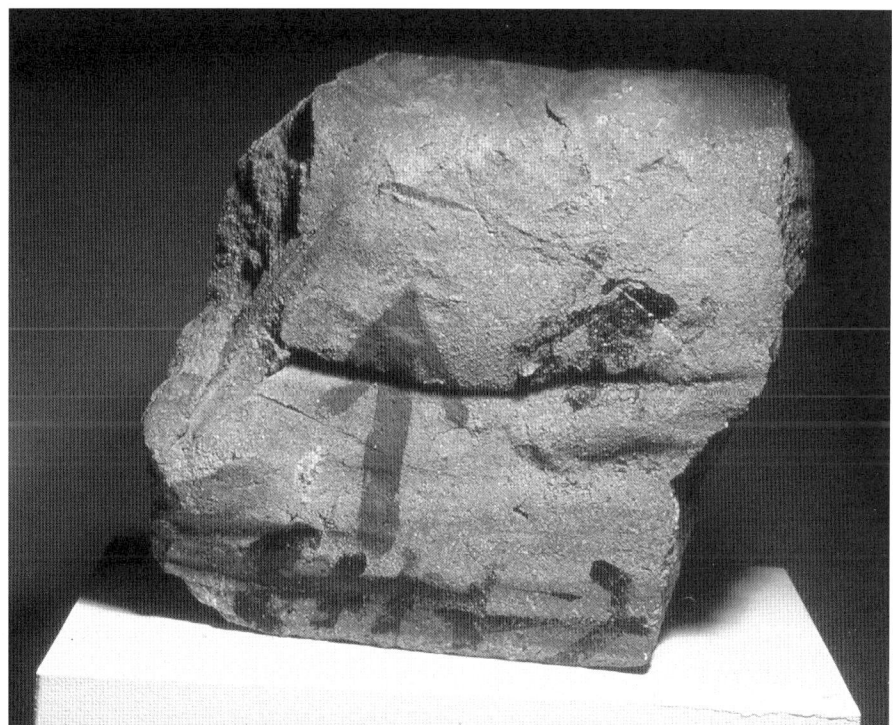

ANTONI TAPIES, *ARCHEOLOGIE II*, 1986. STONEWARE, 36.2 × 40.0 CM.
PHOTO: GALLERY LELONG, PARIS

CHAPTER 12

THE DECORATIVE VESSEL

GEORGE WOODMAN

The surprising juxtapositions of Echoes may initially invite one to raise questions of sources, influences, or appropriation on the part of the modern potter; but it should be recognized that to do so is to slip back into the procedures of traditional criticism, with its preoccupation with unravelling influences, clarifying intent, and otherwise looking beyond art. Worse yet would be to yield to the temptation to judge the work of the contemporary artists by that of their predecessors as a standard.

Presented at *Echoes: Historical References in Contemporary Ceramics*, 1983, Kansas City

Some shows exist simply as an opportunity to view works of art, much like the visual equivalent of a gourmet meal. Others are concerned with affecting our perceptions of and challenging our ideas about some class of objects. I suppose that *Art Treasures from the Vatican* would exemplify the first kind of exhibit, whereas Barbara Rose's painting in the eighties represents the latter, a type of exhibit which could be called critical, if not polemical. *Echoes* is certainly a critical exhibition. It has a point to make; in fact it raises so many points that it is exercising to try to grasp them all. *Echoes* raises a host of questions about how we look at contemporary ceramics, indeed, any ceramics, finally making us realize that the exhibition, in itself, is a critical act.

Criticism is often thought of as dealing with intention, trying to grasp what the artist was trying to do and asking if he was successful in achieving it. In crafts, "intent" is often displaced in the thoughts of the critic, to be replaced by the notion of function. We ask what an object is "for," seeing if it "functions" successfully. Criticism has recently shifted increasingly away from the issue of intent toward that of context, toward determining the situation in which things are properly to be viewed. Discussions of post-painterly abstraction insist that Stella's work of the late sixties be seen, not in the context of "picture," but of "thing." Such an argument, based on the shapes of the paintings, can be extended to ceramics. Is a teapot an object (à la Stella), of a format (as the rectangle is to painting), or is it an image (can a teapot be "of" a teapot)? The objects brought together here invite us to ask these questions, although they hardly answer them.

What things should be shown with what? The Museo Nazionale degli Abruzzi, with charming naiveté, exhibits a fossilized mastodon along with ancient Etruscan sculpture. After all, aren't they both of the class "old object dug up from the ground"? What governs our assumptions of context with respect to time, nationality, medium, subject matter and craft versus "fine" art? Much of recent art has itself brought up issues of context. Warhol's soup cans, like Nagle's cups, have a relationship to the kitchen, but what is that relationship? Does Scott Burton make "furniture"? The answer can only be a contextual proposition. The work of artists associated with "pattern and decoration," such as Kushner and Carlson, raise complex issues of context. The minor art status of ceramics is itself dependent upon assumptions of context. If the appreciation of Nagle required getting the "cup" out of a context as a kind of "thing" (in a kitchen) to one of a kind of "image," then Ken Price has taken the even bolder step of taking along the context of ceramics (curio cabinet, kitchen) and making it, in turn, an object in yet another context: the gallery or museum. Thus the mug remains in its original context (curio) but is translated with that context into another.

The "Decorated Object" section of *Echoes* brings together old and new pots to create a context of formal similarities among objects. The premise of apparent "likeness" is unsettling as a context when we are used to the grouping of objects by period, nationality, material (clay), etc. What would it be like to see an exhibition of "green" paintings? Should Picasso's early cubist paintings be shown together with African masks? How would we feel seeing Kenneth Noland's stripe paintings

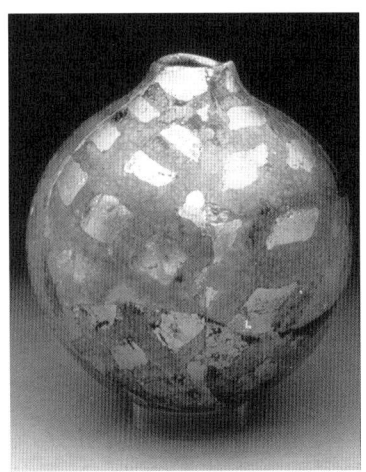

Rick Dillingham, *Globe*, 1979.
Earthenware, 13.9 × 12.7 cm.
Collection: Barbara Rozenthal
Photo: Tony Vinella

shown with other stripes, classic awning materials? Should these latter be presented as awnings, chairs, covers, or could we stretch them with Noland-like formats? These issues are delicate, ranging from the artist's "right" to include the context of viewing in his intent, to the almost universal insecurity about the impact of context felt in all art today. A few years ago the *New Yorker* had a cartoon showing a perplexed viewer wondering if the fire extinguisher in the corner of a gallery full of modernist sculpture was part of the exhibition. In candor, most of us would have to confess to having had similar experiences.

The echoes among these pieces exist on many levels. Shapes, colours, designs, formats, and images are all in reverberation. Materials and their associations also have their dimension of echo. And then there are echoes of taste, of mood, of entire predilections for certain effects. The criss-crossing of reverberations, the overtones, to extend the acoustical metaphor, are particularly interesting. Ferguson echoes the traditional theme of an "Adam and Eve" plate; but the echo of the spirit of his piece, lies some where else, probably not in ceramics but in French painting five years ago. It is not hard to see a reverberation between Ralph Bacerra and Imari or Kutani ware, but aren't we also reminded of 1960s oilcloth with its own echoes of "modern" European decorative art?

The surprising juxtapositions of *Echoes* may initially invite one to raise questions of sources, influences, or appropriation on the part of the modern potter; but it should be recognized that to do so is to slip back into the procedures of traditional criticism, with its preoccupation with unravelling influences, clarifying intent and otherwise looking beyond art. Worse yet would be to yield to the temptation to judge the work of the contemporary artists by that of their predecessors as a standard.

At this juncture it seems immaterial to inquire how Rick Dillingham came to the rather unusual techniques by which he makes pots. Of greater interest is the opportunity to see his work in the context of early Pueblo pottery (and, more specifically, those pieces which we have encountered in the context of archeological museums as reassembled shards) and sensing the precise quality of that echo. It seems difficult to imagine that an appropriately comprehensive grasp of his work should not include echoes (mental, if not actually present) of these ancient pots. Equally interesting is whether or not, after sensing the Dillingham reverberation, we can again see reconstructed pots in a museum, without having to consciously acknowledge the accidental but entirely evident beauty conferred upon ceramics by the vicissitudes of destruction and reconstruction. It goes without saying that these echoes are part of the response of any experienced and sensitive connoisseur of art, and that the polemic force of this exhibition is to take a class of intended relationships and present them as actual, thereby forcing us to acknowledge the determination of context as a primary critical gesture.

It would be naive to suppose that the echoes here are primarily between contemporary and historical pieces. In the historical group we cannot fail to be struck by the relationship between Japanese I-Hsing and British imitations thereof; or between the Spanish Hare bowl and the English slipware version of the same subject, or, for that matter, the different stances toward realism on the part of Higby. Shaw and Saxe remind us that the echoes are as much among the modern pieces as between them and the historical.

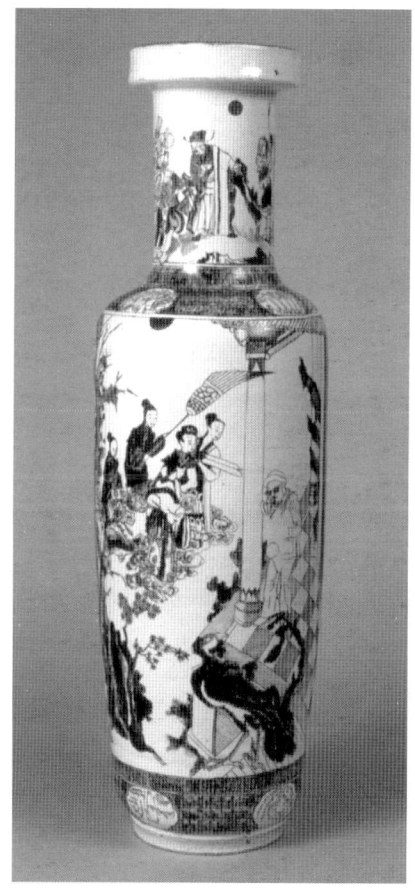

MICHAEL FRIMKESS, *CASA GLORIA*, C.1977-78.
PORCELAIN WITH COBALT DECORATION, 72.4 CM.
PHOTO: TONY VINELLA

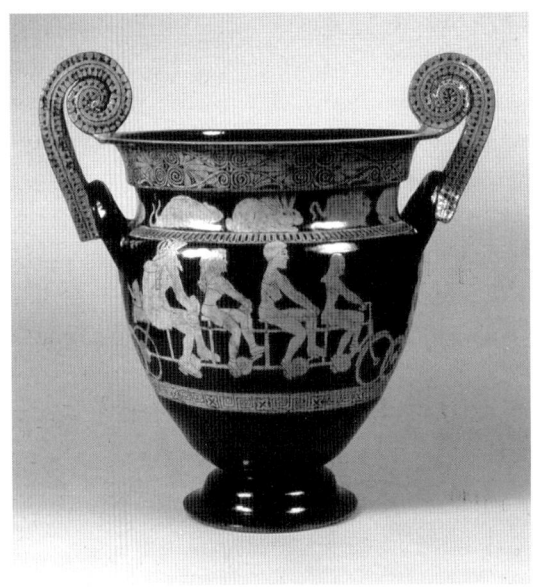

MICHAEL FRIMKESS, *ECOLOGY KRATER II*, C. 1976.
EARTHENWARE WITH BLACK SLIP, 66.0 CM.
COLLECTION: RENWICH GALLERY, SMITHSONIAN AMERICAN ART MUSEUM, WASHINGTON
PHOTO: TONY VINELLA

The concept of "echo" suggests a reproduced, a secondary likeness between one thing and another. Yet the interest of these echoes lies somewhere beyond similarity. The fascination of the Frimkess's shapes and decorations lies in the clarity with which we see them in a clear context of other art, yet are vividly aware of their difference. This is distinctly opposed to imitation which seeks only to blur that distinction. The artists in this group seem almost consciously to espouse an aesthetic in which objects are placed in correspondence without permitting us to confuse the new pieces from the types that they are about. This distinguishes them from, say, those American and English pieces, common in the fifties and sixties, which aspired to inclusion in the form world of their Chinese and Japanese models but finally fail, and pathetically, because they tended to resemble photographs of those models rather than the originals.

The juxtaposition of pieces presenting apparent similarities among pieces usually perceived in separate contexts raises two types of question. The first seeks an explanation: How did these similarities come to be? This leads to a consideration of causality in art, invoking such concepts as influence, borrowing, imitation, etc. This may also require a consideration of what Aristotle referred to as "material cause." Is it not possible that given certain glaze materials, clay bodies, firing techniques that certain effects are likely to occur, regardless of variations in culture or temperament? Or are there not certain determinants in format? After all, on a certain level, is not a pitcher a pitcher with certain possibilities of design, regardless of historical or cultural context? Looming behind the question of causality and similarity remain the larger general questions of originality and creativity. *Echoes* certainly has created a situation which requires us to take a steady look at originality and all of the mystique which surrounds it. Modern criticism has increasingly identified quality and achievement in art with originality. However disquieting it may be, it must be salutary for us to have a situation in which this issue is brought forward in such uncompromising terms. My feeling is, that considering both the historical and contemporary works in this show, that the most arresting and satisfying pieces are not necessarily the most original.

Interesting as it may be, I find the question of how similarities come to be, their causality, less interesting than that of what is a similarity. How do we recognize it? What varieties may it present? On this level *Echoes* stands as a fascinating invitation to take seriously the phenomenology of perceived similarities. It is not appropriate to attempt to develop such a theme in this essay, but I am left with the conviction that, beyond the question of causality, increased clarification and analysis of the experience of echo and reverberation would enrich our experience of art and advance the efforts of thoughtful criticism.

The exhibit would seem to be based on the assumption that echoes exist primarily among objects. This should not blind us to the fact that they may also be present within the experience of a single piece. The Meissen pseudo-Imari tray is a tantalizing example of such a piece in which Japanese and Rococo elements have an amazing dialogue.

Echoes might have been a show of painting or sculpture with great effect;

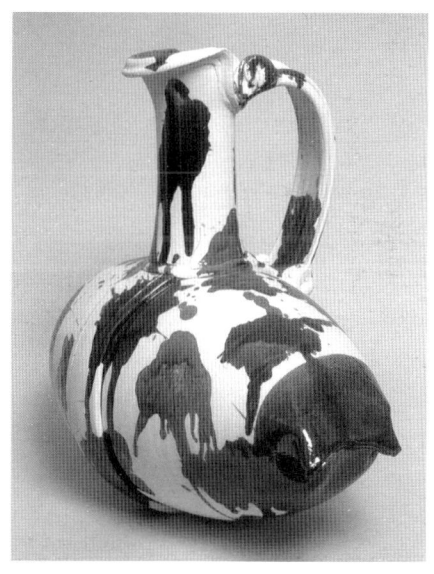

BETTY WOODMAN, *TANG PILLOW PITCHER*, 1981.
EARTHENWARE, 50.8 × 71.1 CM.
COLLECTION: METROPOLITAN MUSEUM OF ART, NEW YORK
PHOTO: TONY VINELLA

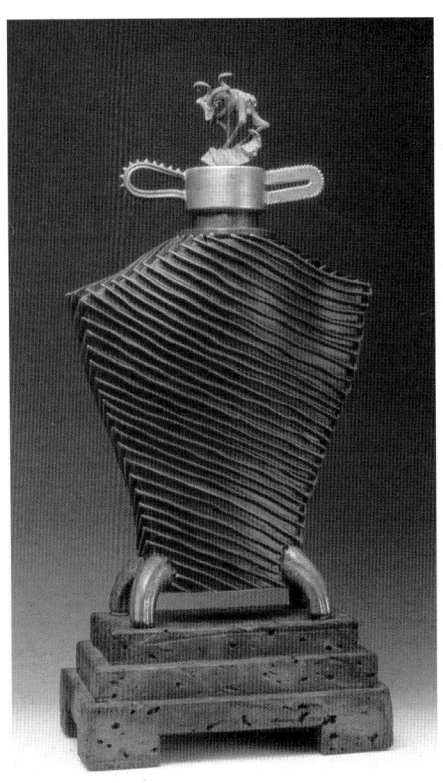

ADRIANE SAXE, *PARISIENNE CHAINSAW MASSACRE*, 1982. STONEWARE, 63.5 x 30.48 CM.

COLLECTION: GARTH CLARK AND MARK DEL VECCHIO

PHOTO: TONY CUNHA

but it is particularly appropriate that it should be of ceramic objects, because ceramics has a particularly strong tradition of borrowing and adoption throughout its history. "Modern" art, particularly painting and sculpture, has made a dogma of eschewing reference to earlier styles and types. It has forced itself into a straightjacket from which ceramic artists have been refreshingly free. In current criticism, eclecticism has become a term of opprobrium, whereas this has by no means always been the case as, for example, in the late-sixteenth century, when it was understood as a specific and valid methodology of making art.

Internal echoes seem particularly present in the work of several of these artists. Higby's juxtaposition of a pictorial space—not at all characteristic of ceramics—with the real space contained in his bowls leaves us with a haunting sense of the unfamiliar in the familiar. But it is perhaps in the far-reaching eclecticism of Woodman and Saxe that the internal echoes are the most complex. The contrast between these artists underscores that an echo is not merely the fact of a perceived similarity, but that it can, and should, have a flavour, a colouring which is highly personal. Saxe's echoes are permeated by a didactic virtuosity in which contrasting styles and motifs are brought together in a kaleidoscope of surprises that are truly heir to the intrigue of Sèvres. In Woodman, on the other hand, diverse elements of form, colouring, and format are appropriated by some impulse of love for the originals and filtered through a very specific sensibility to ceramic values.

THE DECORATIVE VESSEL 161

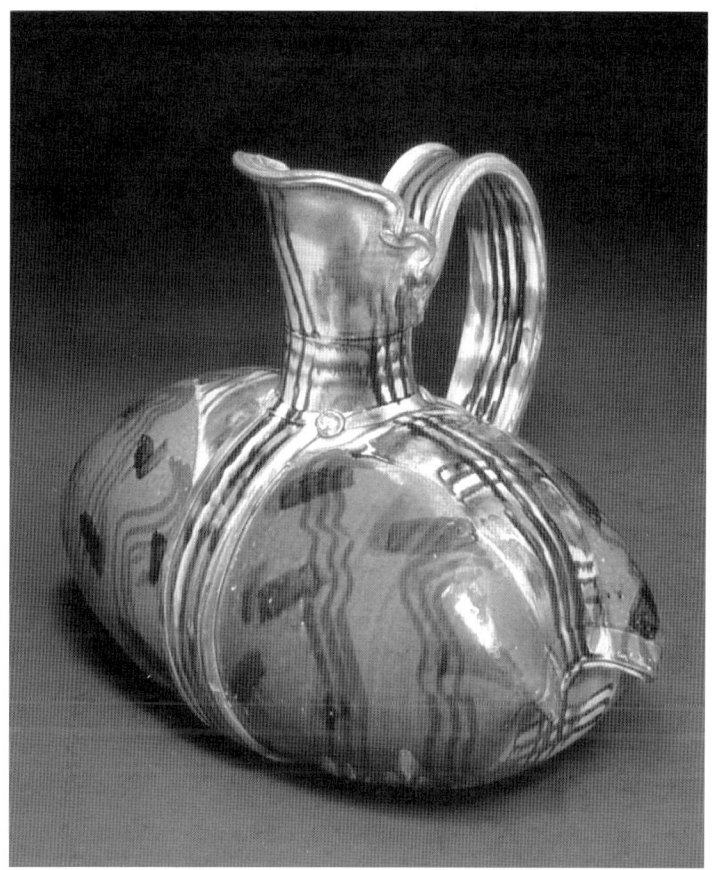

BETTY WOODMAN, *PILLOW PITCHER*, 1981. EARTHENWARE, 55.9 × 33.0 CM.

COLLECTION: MR. AND MRS. JOHN L. HOFFMAN

PHOTO: GARY SUTTON

One can only conclude that echoes, single or manifold, of past or present form, internal or external are a constant possibility in all arts and most especially in ceramics. Furthermore, it is apparent that, beyond identifying or explaining the presence of an echo, it is even more important to be sensitive to the unique flavor or quality which it gives to an artist's work and our response to it. The recognition that a ceramic object is often imbued with a presence pictorial, decorative, or expressive—beyond its mere existence as a thing—should be further enlarged by the realization that it also may have a poetic life. The key to poetry is metaphor and the vast power of association within language. The key to metaphor in ceramics is in the experience of echo possible within the act of seeing a clay object. The poetry of ceramics rests in the power of a single piece to summon the values of objects not present, thereby metaphorically participating in some larger dimension of ideal values extending beyond that which is now before us.

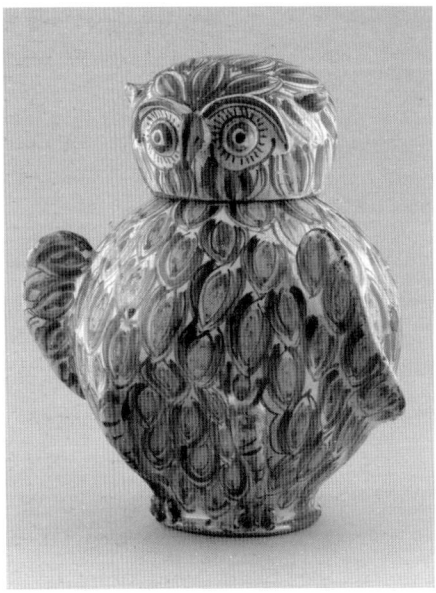

Owl Wine Jar and Cover, Italian (Siclian), 18th century. Earthenware, tin-glazed, 34.3 cm. Collection: The Nelson-Atkins Museum of Art, Kansas City, MO. Gift of Mr. Frank P. Burnap, F76-41
Photo: Jamison Miller

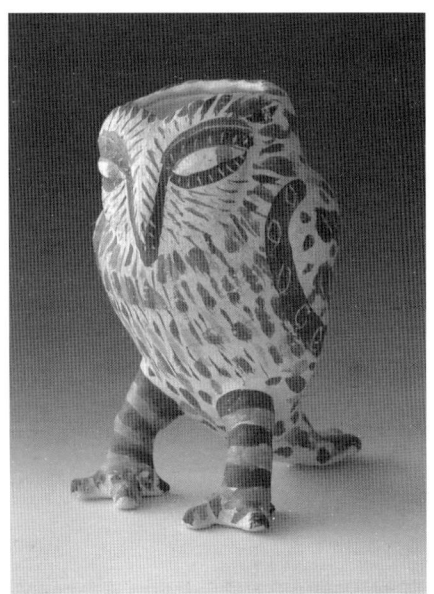

Akio Takamori, *Owl*, 1982. Earthenware with oxides, 27.6 x 16.5 x 23.5 cm. Collection: Kurt Weiser
Photo: Gary Sutton

Chapter 13

Discourse and Decoration:
The Struggle for Historical Space

Paul Greenhalgh

Accepting continual crossovers and correspondences between ceramics and other media, and the interdisciplinary nature of much clay activity, there are core practices and usages within the ceramics heritage that give it meaning and guarantee its continued existence and prosperity. I don't just mean the vessel or the wheel; I also mean the wide range of sculptural activity that has always been associated with ceramics, and the myriad of architectural and domestic decorations and fittings that have continuously been produced.

Presented at *History and Its Role in Contemporary Ceramic Art*, 1993, Syracuse

Ceramics is occasionally the subject of art history, but more often it is its victim. I am speaking here, of course, not of art history simply in the sense of the art of the past, but of art history as a profession; as a vast collection of scholars, books, journals, archives and collections; as a series of institutions and other repositories of knowledge. In short, I am suggesting that, to date, that large and powerful industry, art history, has not dealt with ceramic as it might have done.

This is not to say that there have not been scholars of immense stature who have dealt with ceramics. There are, as it were, many beautiful beads in the form of individual contributions to ceramic history; but there is little in the way of a thread. And the provision of this thread is not to do with the creation of works of general overview (although this would do no harm at all), but with the clarification of the historiographic and ideological position of ceramics. What has this broad, amorphous, collective culture of clay meant? How does it recognize itself? How is it differentiated from other media, and how exactly are we, the contemporary audience, supposed to respond to it? Before I take up these questions, I will note the consequences of the negation of ceramics by the art history industry.

Theory without history gives you tyranny. If you attempt to theorize about a thing in its absence and in the absence of its past, you run the inevitable risk of misrepresenting it. Theorists of race in the nineteenth and twentieth centuries, for example, studiously avoided the real peoples they categorized. "Model" Greeks, Jews, Africans, and, eventually, Americans were invented, then described and classified, without the troublesome, empirical data that might have confused the picture. We are still picking up the pieces of these particular theories.

In a less tragic, though no less marked fashion, theories that were created in the absence of ceramics are constantly being used to criticize and marginalize it. An interesting instance of this is the idea of the avant-garde. Apparently, ceramics has become moribund because it isn't avant-garde anymore. Indeed, in the broader arena of visual culture, avant-gardism is widely perceived as being an important, even permanent, fixture at the fountainhead of creativity: a measure against which culture is tested. But what exactly do we mean when we use this term? It is worth pondering its usage in contemporary fine art circles.

We can assert immediately that "avant-garde" does not, in the proper historical sense, simply mean experimental, original, or innovative, though these things might be features of avant-garde practice. The term is closely connected with the rise of European modernism in the period 1870-1940, and is used most accurately to describe the activities of various groups in Europe in that period. The central aim of these groups was to subvert normative values in order to achieve the transformation of society through the radical use of the arts. The avant-garde in the military sense is that force that goes in advance to check the terrain before the rest of the army follows on. In the cultural sense then, avant-garde movements did not wish to change art, they wished to change the world. Cubism, Futurism, de Stijl, Constructivism, Purism, the Bauhaus, Dadaism, and Surrealism were all part of the broad movement collectively identifiable as modernism. Many historians have seen the Second World War as a decisive, terminal point for much of this activity.

What am I trying to say? Two things, I suppose. First, it is by no means clear that America or Europe has had significant quantities of avant-garde practice of any kind for some considerable time. Indeed, most of the forms, strategies, and idioms used in contemporary fine-art practice were learned in art school, which in turn inherited them from previous generations of artists. In other words, strictly speaking, these forms are no longer avant-garde; they are academic (i.e., historical strategies legitimized through public institutions). At the end of the day, avant-garde strategies were geared to the destruction of institutional life in the broadest metaphorical meaning of the term; but contemporary practice tends to bolster, not subvert, the cultural institutions of America and Europe. Few normative values are being challenged; rather, the norm is constantly being consolidated. Does all this change, radicalize, or even threaten society? Hardly. My assertions are contentious, generalized, and not new; but they do highlight the possibility that much contemporary fine-art practice is not avant-garde at all, but rather a mélange of tired establishment formulas.

The second, and most important, idea I am trying to express is the lack of relevance of all this to ceramics. However it is defined, avant-gardism was not invented or developed with ceramics in mind. Ceramics has rarely functioned in movements or been accorded the institutional clout that would render significant an anti-establishment radicalization. To accuse ceramists of not being avant-garde is to criticize them for something they don't do, and rarely ever did. As I have said, experimentation and innovation are not the same as avant-gardism.

There are many other instances of theoretical structures that ignore the historical record. The endless art/craft debate (i.e., Am I a craftsperson? Am I an artist?) and other related diatribes are absurdly ahistorical in their premises and assumptions, so much so that we can say with depressing confidence that we have wasted twenty years in meaningless discussion of the topic.

Accepting continual crossovers and correspondences between ceramics and other media, and the interdisciplinary nature of much clay activity, there are core practices and usages within the ceramics heritage that give it meaning and guarantee its continued existence and prosperity. I don't just mean the vessel or the wheel; I also mean the wide range of sculptural activity that has always been associated with ceramics and the myriad architectural and domestic decorations and fittings that have continuously been produced.

Theory has to grow; but it has to do so around the historical reality of the medium. To use my earlier analogy, if there is anything more useless than beads without a thread, it is a thread without beads. So we must go down two roads simultaneously. We have to continue on with the empirical project of researching, collating, and presenting information; and we have to develop (and borrow) relevant theoretical models.

Let's dump, temporarily at least, the entire package of theory as it relates to fine-art history—all these formalist, anti-formalist, realist, phenomenologist, minimalist, situationist, installationist, etc., etc., etc., debates, which were designed in admirable fashion for painters, sculptors, photographers, installation and video artists—and let's move on. I must reiterate. I am not suggesting that any of this is false or uninteresting. I am simply saying that it is misapplied to most of ceramics, even if aspects of it may eventually prove relevant. Some ceramists may wish to have one or more of these models applied to them, and this is perfectly acceptable if that is their chosen milieu.

Perhaps the starting point for ceramic theory is to be found in the way that ceramic objects are perceived rather than conceived. I suppose I am saying that we should look carefully at the relationship between people and objects, since it is at the site of this interaction that ceramics is most interesting.

Art objects of all kinds can make us think simultaneously in five distinct areas: 1) the process of manufacture and the methods by which the item came into physical existence; 2) the person (or people) who made the object; 3) the subject matter it represents, depicts, or symbolizes; 4) the other objects to which it might relate, both from the present and the past; 5) the object's relation to ourselves, our life experiences, and the knowledge we bring to the object. The successful object provokes interest in all five areas, aggregating into a single, total experience that is more than simple addition of the five areas. Inevitably, different genres within the visual arts have developed strategies that satisfy us more immediately in some areas than others.

Let's imagine, for example, a nineteenth-century Staffordshire figurine. The poetry an object like this might impart to us is to be found in places that are not necessarily the same as, say, in a painting of the same date; and it was never intended to be. As with many ceramic objects, we probably don't know the maker (or makers), and even if we did, his or her personality and individual history would be unlikely to advance our understanding of the object beyond a certain point. The emphasis lies elsewhere.

The size, colour, form, and subject matter of the object were determined and modified by a web of sources and aspirations, which lend the object a certain aesthetic tension. The scale, for example, was dictated by kiln size, the needs of the retailer, and by the interior space it finally inhabited. Scale also relates to the hand size of both maker and consumer, and the intimacy of touch that both experience through the object. The level of detail also relates to the domestic interior; the back might be bare; the glazes on the front chosen to pick up the light. The modelling would probably allude, through mimicry and even irony, to earlier, more illustrious predecessors in Meissen or Chelsea. A deeper set of references would carry us back to the ancient Greeks, who fully developed this scale and form of work in the absence of glaze. The subject would most likely be intended to charm, instruct or titillate through the medium of contemporary Victorian life—a posed snapshot in coloured stone, invariably containing a poignant melancholy.

The aspirations of such an object were not great. It was intended to decorate someone's home and, via this, the owners life. But the process of history is a peculiar one; by working upon the object in two directions at once, it can make it far more significant than its maker intended. The first way it works, as I have already suggested, is through the genre itself. Over a period of time, ceramics has accumulated complex and unavoidable iconographies, forms, and processes. As soon as one uses them, one participates in a heritage that outstrips the aspirations of both object and maker. The second way is concerned with what we might call the "afterlife" of objects. Ceramic objects can survive the millennia, and by doing so, they come to have meanings that have little to do with their makers. Because of ceramics's physical durability, the whole genre comes to collectively participate in what I would call a conceptual longevity, whereby the form and language of the objects seem to keep a certain distance from the personality of the maker, even when that personality is a strong one. This is as true for ceramists now as it was for our Victorian Staffordshire figurine maker. Both participate in a game far larger than themselves.

To sum up this rather metaphysical meander, the historical space I refer to in my title might well be achieved by paying attention, not only to the process of making, including the views and personalities of the makers, but also, through a larger analysis of the meanings of ceramic objects in the world, to the finished work of art: a history of roles, of emotional responses related to the environment an object was used and enjoyed in. This could, and should, lead to more ambitious theoretical projects, such as the testing of physiological responses to objects, the deeper analysis of the specific languages of ceramics, and the analysis of class and society through the medium of ceramics.

Ceramics does not change the world with gestural sweeps by large individuals; it is absorbed into the world and transforms it by being deeply assimilated into it. Theory should therefore be engaged with these processes of assimilation: how they occur, how they change things, and what kinds of poetry they produce. Design historians, museologists, and theorists of mass culture have already produced significant work in this area, especially over the past two decades. The project begun, we can look forward to developments in ceramic history with more than hope.

The next move will not come from the makers; they are too busy making. It must come from the historians. The most important thing for makers to do is to resist that particular urge of the modernist ethos: to be embarrassed about the cultural heritage of ceramics—all those figurines, pots, ornaments, decorations, etc. Whether one is engaged at this time in large-scale sculptures, design for industry, vessels, figure modelling, centerpieces, or whatever, this previous life is one to be celebrated, not replaced with inappropriate ideologies from elsewhere. Ceramics is a plural activity and has always enjoyed stealing from anywhere and everywhere within visual culture. But there is an internal core of meaning—the thread—that makes it what it is. It is this thread we must expose to the light in order to gain our historical space.

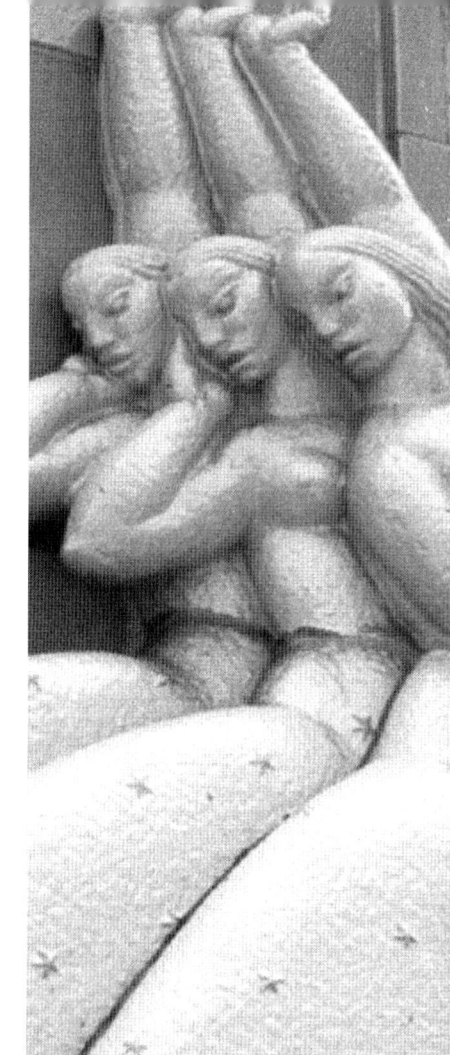

Section Four
Architecture

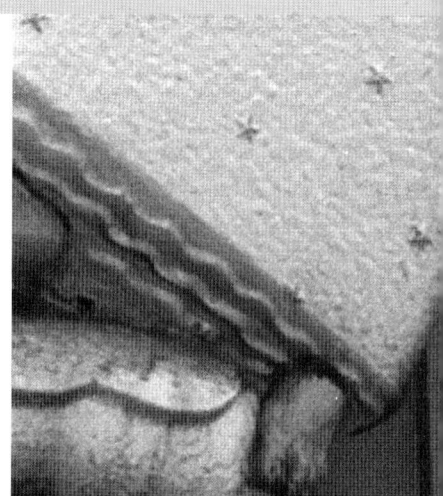

Chapter 14

Licence to Decorate

David Hamilton

The pendulum swings. Now, you can just hear the sounds (mostly off-stage) of a possible revival of decoration in architecture. If this movement were to find real expression, which materials would best suit such a style? Did I hear terra cotta, faience and stoneware? However, the skills of fabricating terra cotta are almost extinct. The designing of facades and the technique of translating the design into sections for pressing might just be capable of resurrection but unless this happens soon—within ten years—the whole art of terra cotta manufacture will have to be reinvented....

Presented at *Ceramics and Modernism*, 1981, New York City

If you like your architecture penny plain and simple; if you think that the style of architecture in our redeveloped city centers has created a joyous environment; if, for you, a house is above all a machine in which to live, then read no further. You are well adjusted and this article can only cause you unnecessary pain. But if the idea of a decorative architecture does not fill you with horror, you may be interested to hear that a seminar on terra cotta was held last November at the Gladstone Pottery Museum, Stoke-on-Trent, initiated by the director, Francis Celoria. The Museum has a collection of bricks, tiles, chimney-pots, and architectural details, together with some of the moulds from which these items were made; and all of them are decorative. They contribute to the structure a little richness above and beyond the call of duty.

Terra cotta, literally "fired earth," is any clay which is fired but not glazed or vitrified; glazed terra cotta is often called faience. Stoneware (clay fired until vitrified, and glazed or unglazed), put to architectural use, was sold under commercial names, such as Carrara Ware, by Doulton, which was designed to look like marble. Some of the finest architectural terra cotta is found in Renaissance architecture, which influenced English architecture in the eighteenth century. During this period, there were several attempts to recreate a mythical "material of the Ancients," believed to have been an artificial stone used in antiquity to cast sculpture. Terra cotta in general, and Coade stone in particular, came close to this ideal. From 1769 until 1840, Mrs. Coade's Manufactory, situated on the South Bank of the Thames in London, supplied statuary and architectural details in artificial stone, which was, in fact, terra cotta. The high reputation this company enjoyed lay, not only in the refinement of technique and material, but also in the excellence of the artists employed.

It is difficult to recognize the work which came from the Coade factory as being terra cotta, because much of it has been painted. Coade stone set a standard. As late as the 1940s, when the Terra Cotta Society of Great Britain made a last desperate effort to ensure the survival of an already small industry, the then Minister of Works stated that, were they able to demonstrate their ability to produce a terra cotta of the quality of Coade stone, he would then consider the post-war reconstruction of London in terra cotta rather than Portland stone. The analysis which Dr. Hamilton undertook between 1951 and 1954 at the Building Research Centre revealed no magic ingredient, and he could only conclude that the secret, such as it was, lay in the skill and care shown during manufacture.

Terra cotta lends itself to a decorative style of architecture: it is easy to model, and it can be pressed in plaster moulds to reproduce an original model many times. Victorian architects, who designed elaborate facades for their buildings, found aesthetic as well as practical satisfaction in the fabrication of details in clay, alongside the brick structure, as opposed to a combination of stone and brick. This, in turn, led to the development of the terra cotta hollow block, which was load-bearing and much larger than a normal brick, reducing the number and frequency of joints and future maintenance of the facade.

Victorian manufacturers were interested in the monumental uses of terra cotta, but principally as a by-product of their primary concern: the manufacture of bricks, tiles, or other building materials. Architects who included decorative elements in their designs would offer the contract for the supply of building materials to those who could tender for a whole contract; terra cotta was never really profit making for the manufacturers. It was what we would now call a "loss leader," but unlike soap or cereal sold at below cost in order to gain profit from the rest of the grocery bill, terra cotta was used to gain a reputation—for skill, artistry, invention, and refinement—much as Rolls-Royce sells cars with clocks which don't tick, on the understanding that the rest of the car does.

Faience blocks were a natural development from terra cotta and found their place in Victorian dream palaces—public houses, whose etched glass, mahogany woodwork, and gaslight, and their glazed exteriors and interiors, could create a sense of luxury and richness which seduced clients from the squalor of the real world, until alcohol induced a totally rose-tinted vision. A little over seventy years later, the same material was adopted for the pre-Second World War picture palaces, particularly the Odeon cinemas and helped produce a similar effect without recourse to alcohol.

Not only great public buildings were thought to require ceramic details. Alongside the elegance and grandeur of areas like Kensington in London, speculative builders of late Victorian and Edwardian London had access to a wide range of catalogues of details (tessellating tiles, sometimes encaustic or tube-line, modelled brick string-courses, ridge tiles and finials, as well as stained glass and marble and wood fireplaces) to produce a rich variety of housing. Almost all buildings, no matter how modest, included a range of details juxtaposed to produce a specific character for each house. In the road in which I live in West London, out of thirty houses built by the same builder within a few years of each other circa 1907, no two have ceilings, fireplaces, or tiled floors of identical pattern. No doubt this was a profitable trade for the manufacturers in a way in which large one-off facades were not. Nevertheless, the quality of these mass-produced details was underwritten by the reputation of the supplier, established by major architectural commissions and international exhibitions.

The decline of the use of terra cotta and faience, except as a thin cladding in the form of tiles, came about for two reasons: the economics of building construction and the stylistic attitudes of the modern movement in architecture. If L.T.C. Rolt is correct in saying, in his book *Victorian Engineering*, that Britain has been in

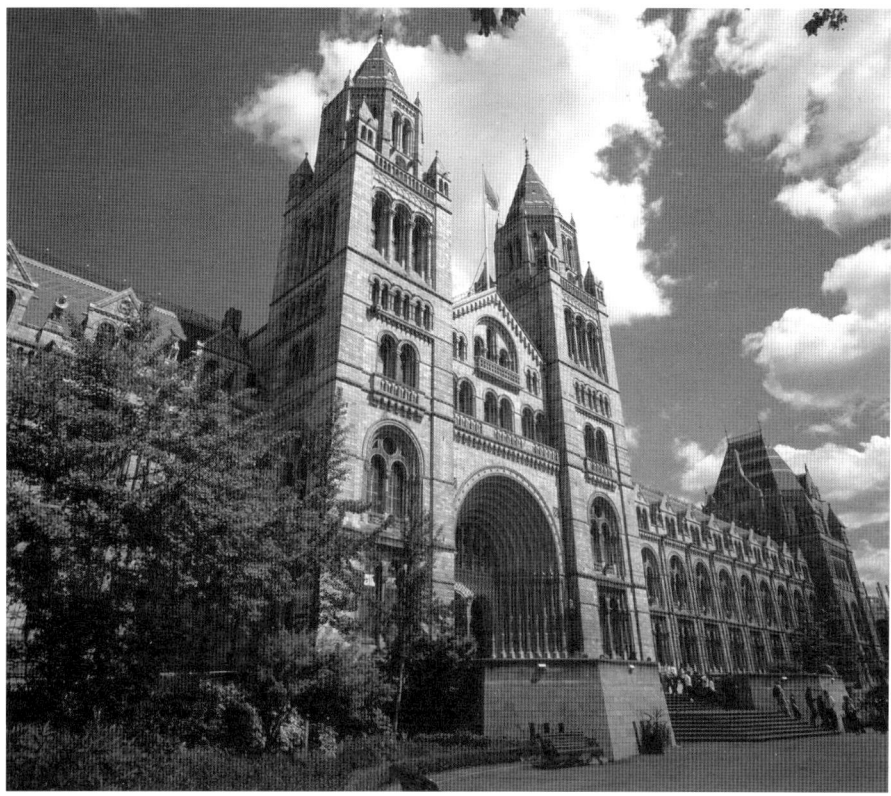

NATURAL HISTORY MUSEUM, TERRA COTTA FACADE, LONDON
DESIGNED BY ALFRED WATERHOUSE, OPENED IN 1881.

economic decline since 1851 and that the dominance of American, Swiss, and German engineers after the middle of the nineteenth century led to the creation of economic wealth in those countries, while the gradual demise of the Empire as a source of cheap raw materials worsened Britain's plight, it is not surprising that public buildings in Britain are down in price, rather than up in quality. Add to this the puritan notion that a building is a machine, and any richness, decoration, or superfluous detail becomes economically, socially, and aesthetically unacceptable.

The pendulum swings. Now, you can just hear the sounds (mostly off-stage) of a possible revival of decoration in architecture. If this movement were to find real expression, which materials would best suit such a style? Did I hear terra cotta, faience, and stoneware? However, the skills of fabricating terra cotta are almost extinct. The designing of facades and the technique of translating the design into sections for pressing might just be capable of resurrection; but unless this happens soon—within ten years—the whole art of terra cotta manufacture will have to be reinvented: not only the recipes for materials and the methods of installation but also the skills of manufacture and modelling.

Traditionally, an architect would design the terra cotta building. This design was then handed over to the factory design team, who would produce half- or full-scale drawings of the facade and divide it into units to provide the quality of detail required with the minimum number of moulds. Few architects today are capable of designing this type of facade, let alone a complete building (the Natural History Museum of London is an excellent example). Neither is it really a field in which potters can be expected to excel, although some have done so. In general, their talents and experience do not concur with the sensitivity of working on a large scale. It is more likely that a painter or sculptor could be encouraged to acquire this capability.

A hundred years ago, a sculptor commissioned for a terra cotta or faience relief panel could visit several factories, model in clay or wax his prototype designs, take them to a factory for their modelers to scale up, detail the panel himself, and see it installed. Today, he would be hard put to find in himself the modelling skills which are necessary, let alone a factory with the ability and skills to undertake the work.

All this reinforces the argument for the establishment of a skills preservation center—not a museum of lifeless artifacts, but a center where technical innovation and artistic skills can be preserved by subsidized application. Recently, there have been moves to preserve building skills, for example by the establishment of the Crafts Council's Conservation Register; but less is being done to train young craftsmen in these skills. Time is running out, and soon there will be no one in the factories and workshops who can pass on the techniques. Today, only one company—Shaws of Darwen—is capable of making hand-pressed terra cotta; and they have only one skilled craftsman to do this (photographs of over seventy years ago show over two dozen pressers in their pressing shop). In due course, some of these skills will be required. We cannot tell in advance which these will be, but their preservation is not only a matter of historical interest or curiosity. These skills represent a valuable resource which is being disregarded because of their apparent irrelevance.

What form should this establishment take? What work would it do? Answers to these questions may be revealed if we consider the nature of public and private art.

For decades, young artists have been encouraged to see their future as potential leaders, as the avant-garde. Given that only a miniscule proportion will ever achieve a quality of work which warrants this status, art education has moved on to the principle that the study of art through practice is in itself worthwhile. This should be carried a step further. Self-expression should not be seen as the exclusive purpose in educating potential artists. In other places and periods, painters and sculptors have seen their main activity as the creation of public art, often in the form of architectural details. If you put together the idea of a center concerned with the preservation and development of skills and the possibility of public art, you have a scheme which serves two purposes: the revelation of art in public places and the consistent application of skills which would otherwise die out.

How is such a creation to be funded? In certain states in America, in Canada, and parts of Europe, there is a scheme called "a half percent for art." The exact percentage varies from scheme to scheme, but the principle remains the same. On each publicly financed building, some proportion of the overall budget must be spent on art to delight, excite, or stimulate those who see or enter the environment. The quality of art obtained in this way varies, but so does the architecture. These are quite separate problems. The sums of money released to the arts could be substantial and, in this country, would provide an excellent basis for the existing Arts Council and Crafts Council to collaborate and use their contacts with artists and craftsmen by channeling funds towards those who would provide the finest art realized through the skills and materials most appropriate for the commission. A positive policy for public art and craft.

If our economic position prohibits funding in this way, the advertising budgets of major companies would find a more creative raison d'être if five percent were diverted into the arts, design, or craft to achieve similar public artistry. It has been said that half of any advertising budget is wasted, but you can't tell which half. Five percent for art may be a saving of ten percent of otherwise wasted money.

In this way, a whole range of arts and crafts could be nourished. Use could be made not only of terra cotta and faience but also of encaustic tiling, domestic stained glass, stone cutting and carving, wood carving, fireplaces, plasterwork, and metal casting to enrich public and domestic architecture as well as acting as a center for the creation and manufacture of public art, which is different from private art in public places.

CHAPTER 15

Architectural Terra Cotta: Preserving the Inheritance

Susan Tunick

One of the unique qualities of clay, namely its ability to mimic other materials, has ironically resulted in the fact that terra cotta has frequently gone unrecognized. More than fifty percent of the architectural terra cotta made in the United States was intended to imitate various stones, such as granite, marble, or limestone. In rare instances it even mimicked wood or iron. Clay did such an excellent job of disguising itself that, in many cases, careful scrutiny is required to identify terra cotta.

Presented at *The Ceramic Millennium*, 1999, Amsterdam

Architectural terra cotta became an integral part of the American cityscape well over one hundred years ago. During much of the last century, however, this exceptional material has received little attention, escaping the notice of most city dwellers. New York, our largest and densest metropolis, is filled with structures which use terra cotta. A startling statistic reported in the *New York Times*, May 14, 1911, confirms this:

> The New York skyline—which, without exaggeration, is the most wonderful building district in the world—is more than one-half architectural terra cotta.... And yet, not more than one lay mind in a thousand appre-

ciates the fact, and even to some architects and builders, this truth will come as a surprise.... Brick and stone the average man would say.[1]

I find the idea tantalizing that New York is a "clay jungle" rather than the more familiar image of a "concrete jungle." Throughout my years of training in art, there was a pervasive attitude that the fine arts of painting and sculpture were really paramount, while the decorative arts, including the crafts of ceramics and pottery, were considered to be less significant. It therefore amazed me to discover that a monumental clay legacy existed. This heritage of vast ceramic skyscrapers stood in stark contrast to the belittling treatment that the crafts received from the world of fine arts.

Clay is never part of the picture when artists described the personal impact of New York's buildings. Even Peter Voulkos, one of America's most important ceramic artists, seems to have been unaware of the role terra cotta played in shaping architecture. His vivid description of New York's buildings lacks any reference to clay:

> My scale comes out of what I see. I always liked large things. Take New York skyscrapers. Those are more awesome to me than mountains. You take a mountain for granted, but a skyscraper just blows my mind.... Manmade is a different trip—like even those spaces between buildings in New York—they're fantastic.[2]

One of the unique qualities of clay, namely its ability to mimic other materials, has ironically resulted in the fact that terra cotta has frequently gone unrecognized. More than fifty percent of the architectural terra cotta made in the United States was intended to imitate various stones, such as granite, marble, or limestone. In rare instances, it even mimicked wood or iron. Clay did such an excellent job of disguising itself that, in many cases, careful scrutiny is required to identify terra cotta.

In the *Story of Terra Cotta*, Walter Geer wrote that terra cotta, more than any other building material, offered a true reflection of the personality of the architect. Frank Lloyd Wright agreed, commenting that terra cotta was "as sensitive to a creative brain as a dry plate is to the lens of the camera. A marvelous simplifier, this material, rightly used."[3] Since architectural terra was not kept in stock, every job was individually executed, with special attention paid to each set of requirements. More so than any other architectural product, terra cotta was "hand-tailored" to the highest degree.

The process of terra cotta production, from the architect's blueprint to the final installation, was a complex and fascinating one. Before the actual manufacture could begin, the preliminary stages involving shop drawings, models, mold production, and the selection and preparation of clay and glazes had to be completed. The architect supplied the terra cotta company with a set of scale drawing and plans for steel framing. The company's drafting department then made shop drawings showing full-size details as well as the joints and construction of the terra cotta. These were enlarged to allow for the special ruler, which was thirteen inches long but divided into twelve "inches," to ensure that the finished pieces would be the correct size.

Once the drawings were accepted by the architect, they were sent to the modelling room where they served as a guide for the creation of full-size clay or plaster models. This step was of vital importance, since a successful outcome depended on the skilled and expert execution of the clay models. Modellers brought a variety of backgrounds and experience to this important task. This was one of the highest-paying jobs within the factory, and records from the mid-1920s indicate that modellers received two dollars per hour, while other workers were paid only about sixty cents.[4] Photographs of the finished models were usually sent to architects for approval so that the process could continue and the plaster moulds could be prepared. Once all the approvals had been submitted, eight to ten weeks were needed for actual manufacture.

The plaster moulds were made, allowed to dry out, and then sent to the pressing department, ready for the first actual step of manufacture. The simplest plaster moulds, usually consisting of four separate sides and a bottom which fit together very snugly, were tightly bound with wire bands. When the moulds arrived in the pressing department, clay would be packed into them carefully so that all of the ornamental details would be fully realized on each unit. Holes were usually put in the webbed partition walls, making it easier to handle the pieces while in the factory and also providing a place where metal anchors could be inserted during installation.

Following the pressing, the clay was left to stiffen in the mould. This usually occurred rapidly, since the plaster walls absorbed moisture from the clay. The mould would then be disassembled by unfastening the wire bands, and the clay piece would be left to harden until it was ready to be finished. Additional drying time was required before the piece could be glazed or fired.

Although there are several ways to make terra cotta, the method explained thus far describes the oldest type, "molded terra cotta block," which is very deep and has a hollow back with webbed clay walls to provide additional strength. These are inset into the wall of the building using metal anchors, and the partitioned back is partially filled with bricks and mortar.

Two alternative methods to hand pressing developed. Once process, extrusion, became widely used in the late 1920s, as a desire for simpler, flat pieces of terra cotta increased. A steel die is cut to match the specific profile form, and clay is squeezed through the die using an extruder. (The general technique is easiest to envision if one thinks of squeezing toothpaste from a tube.) Successful extrusion relied on very minimal ornament, and only one-directional designs can be used. The resulting "extruded terra cotta block" is hollow, with an approximate depth of four inches. These are attached to a building using the same method as the moulded blocks. Machine extrusion also allowed for the production of "ceramic veneer," which is backless and thus even shallower, with about a two-inch depth. This material is typically not decorated and can be installed with either thin metal tie rods or by directly adhering it to the building's facade. An additional forming method, used in many jobs today, is ram pressing. Shallow moulds can be produced that are suitable for pressing by machine. This speeds the process of production and helps to reduce the cost per unit.

The thoroughly dry terra cotta, whether hand-pressed, ram-pressed or extruded, was moved to the glaze room where the spraying department, equipped with compressed air apparatus, applied the appropriate number and types of glazes or slips. A glaze, whether glossy or matte, combined chemicals that included large amounts of silica (glass) and oxides, which could produce a wide range of brilliant colours.

Glazed terra cotta units were carefully lifted into the kiln and set on benches formed by blocks of fireproof material. The actual firing process took from ten to twelve days, typically reaching 2300 degrees Fahrenheit. The most difficult part of firing was maintaining even heat in all parts of the kiln. This required great skill, since the largest kilns were forty-eight feet high and twenty-four feet in diameter.

After the cooling process, finished terra cotta was sent to the fitting department. Here all the pieces were laid out on the floor, checked for proper fit, and numbered according to the setting plan so that installation at the building site could proceed smoothly.

The final step was packing the pieces in hay to protect them during the journey to their destination. This was a crucial procedure, since breakage could halt the progress of a building and greatly increase the cost of a project. The more fragile pieces were carefully crated, but still concern remained about how the ware was unloaded and transported to the building site. Edward H. Putnam states, "Here is a material carefully made by hand, perhaps rich with expensive modelling and executed in a number of colors—and it is frequently thrown into a cart and actually dumped upon the ground as if it were common brick! Consider the result!"[5]

When terra cotta was first introduced into the United States, it was used in its unglazed form. The colour, which resulted from the clay body, was typically reddish-brown or buff. Terra cotta provided ornamentation and helped make the load-bearing structures of the late-nineteenth century more fire resistant. Because the architecture of this period was constructed with walls that carried the entire weight of the building, heights usually did not exceed eight stories.

Remarkable technological innovations changed the face of architecture at the turn of the century, and terra cotta played a key role in this transformation. The refinement of the passenger elevation and the development of the metal skeleton frame led to the design of much taller buildings. For architects, the "cloudscraper," later the "skyscraper," created a new series of structural and stylistic challenges. Aesthetic concerns included the desire to express the building's framing structures and the need to unify the facade through a careful balance of proportion and scale. Terra cotta and metal framing provided greater possibilities for new architectural styles at considerably less cost (terra cotta was roughly one-tenth the cost of an equivalent piece of ornamental stone) and weight (terra cotta cladding on metal framing was one third the weight of masonry walls) than those of traditional building materials.

The curtain wall, an essential element in skyscrapers, consisted of panels that extended horizontally from column to column and vertically from girder to girder. Terra cotta served as an excellent material for curtain walls: it was fire resistant, lighter than stone, could provide repeating motifs through the use of moulds, and offered varied decorative possibilities. The use of terra cotta as cladding helped to free the material from its earlier role of imitating stone or iron.

An outstanding early example of a terra cotta clad facade is Louis Sullivan's only New York design, the Bayard Building, constructed in 1897-99. This striking facade reflects its method of construction, producing an unusual and lyrical composition. It combines intertwined geometric motifs and natural organic forms. Extensive undercutting of these designs (which was done by hand, after the pieces were removed from the moulds) helps to create a wonderful play of light and shadow across the building's surface. The facade terminates in a deep cornice, with an enormous series of winged figures placed just beneath.

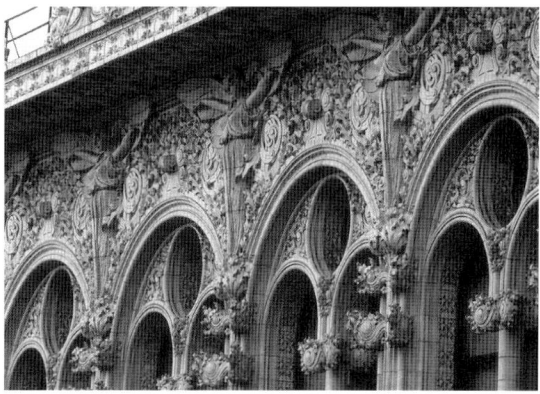

BAYARD-CONDICT BUILDING, 655 BLEEKER STREET, NYC, 1897-99. DESIGNED BY LOUIS SULLIVAN. CERAMIC CLADDING BY PERTH AMBOY TERRA COTTA COMPANY.

PHOTO: PETER MAUSS/ESTO

As stated by James Taylor, "When architects found that their ideas could be so thoroughly expressed in form by the clay-worker, they, like the Athenians of old, began 'to look for something new.' Having obtained form, why not ask for color?"[6] Until the late 1890s, architectural ceramics with coloured glazes was usually limited to tiled walls and floors. White glazed brick was used in courtyards and airshafts, applications that took advantage of the reflective property of glaze. It was generally assumed that glazes could not be used without a second firing, which was prohibitively expensive and time consuming. But, as the twentieth century neared, several companies undertook experiments to develop suitable once-fired glazes.

In 1898 the Perth Amboy Terra Cotta Company manufactured terra cotta that used coloured glazes developed through the efforts of T.C. Booth, an employee trained in England. Shades of pink, yellow, green, blue, and beige were used on the Broadway-Chambers Building, designed by Cass Gilbert in 1899-1900. Located at 227 Broadway, this New York City Landmark provides a rare opportunity to view

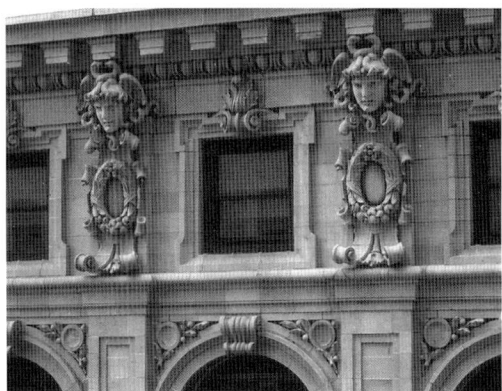

BROADWAY-CHAMBERS BUILDING, 277 BROADWAY, NYC, 1899-1900. DESIGNED BY CASS GILBERT. CERAMIC DETAILS BY PERTH AMBOY TERRA COTTA COMPANY.

PHOTO: PETER MAUSS/ESTO

early polychrome terra cotta.

An interesting contrast to this building is the very colorful polychrome ornament produced four decades later (1938-42) for Parkchester, a massive housing complex in the Bronx, New York. It contained apartment buildings and appropriate amenities intended to serve the needs of more than twelve thousand families. Federal Seaboard Terra Cotta Company, the last surviving East Coast manufacturer of the era, produced simple terra cotta units as well as brightly glazed statues and plaques that help provide some considerable charm and whimsy to this vast residential community of brick apartment buildings.

One of terra cotta's most significant contributions to architecture was the ability to provide permanent, vivid, eye-catching colour. This is ironic, since it was frequently used to simulate other materials and thus hide its true identity. The use of strong colours on the exterior of buildings highlighted rather than hid the terra cotta, drawing the viewers' attention to it. Leon Solon, renowned architectural colourist, succinctly described this experience: "Color is a terrific force when introduced into an architectural combination, and is capable of producing an effect upon the observer equaled only by the fascination which firearms possess for small boys."[7]

The long-recognized durability of terra cotta is graphically described by Sir Charles Lyell in *The Antiquity of Man*. He states: "Granite disintegrates and crumbles into particles of mica, quartz, and feldspar. Marble soon molders into dust of carbonate of lime, but hard, well-burnt clay endures forever in the ancient landmarks of mankind."[8] Although clay can survive the elements, and its crisp modelling is unaffected by acid rain and pollution, our terra cotta heritage faces many challenges. New York (and all our cities) certainly has suffered serious losses—most commonly through long-term, deferred maintenance; financial motivation, which leads to the replacement of historic structures with new, bigger buildings; willful destruction of buildings through demolition or neglect. One particularly serious example of demolition by neglect is the group of structures in the Seaview Hospital and Farm Colony Historic District.

The Seaview Hospital complex was designated a New York City Landmark in 1985. Built between 1905-1938, it was the largest and most costly municipal facility for the treatment of tuberculosis of its kind in the country. The first successful trials of the drugs, which finally led to a cure for tuberculosis, were conducted at Seaview. Four surviving Women's Ward Pavilions (originally there were eight), designed in 1905 by Raymond Almiral, are ornamented with architectural ceramics and superb cut-tile murals manufactured in Delft, Holland. They were made by the Joost Thooft & Labouchere Company, which was founded in 1672 and is still in operation under the name De Porceleyne Fles (the Porcelain Bottle).

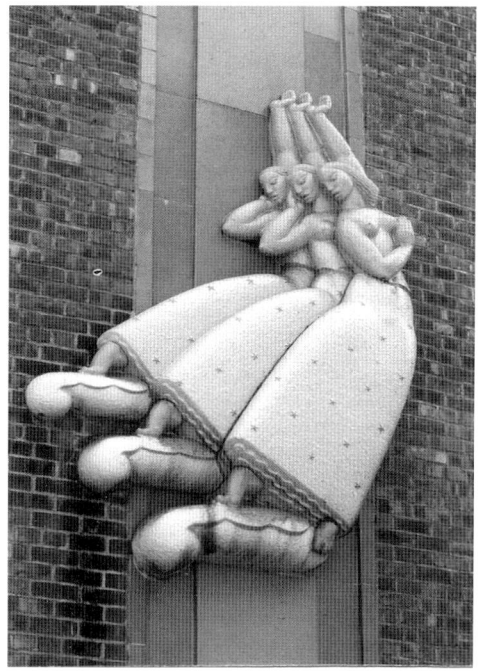

PARKCHESTER, EAST TREMONT AVENUE, PURDY STREET, MCGRAW AVENUE, HUGH GRANT CIRCLE, WHITE PLAINS ROAD, BRONX, NY, 1938-42. RICHARD H. SHREVE (CHAIR OF BOARD OF DESIGN). CERAMIC FACADE FEDERAL SEABOARD TERRA COTTA CORPORATION.
PHOTO: PETER MAUSS/ESTO

These are the only exterior works by the company that are known to exist in the United States. The six-inch high ceramic friezes encircle the upper story of the pavilions and run the entire length of each building perimeter, approximately three hundred and fifty feet. These buildings, along with some of the other historic structures, are in serious disrepair. It has been impossible, thus far, to get the owner (New York City's Health & Hospitals Corporation) to seriously consider adaptive reuse or even to seal these buildings from the elements. Wonderful images of doctors, nurses,

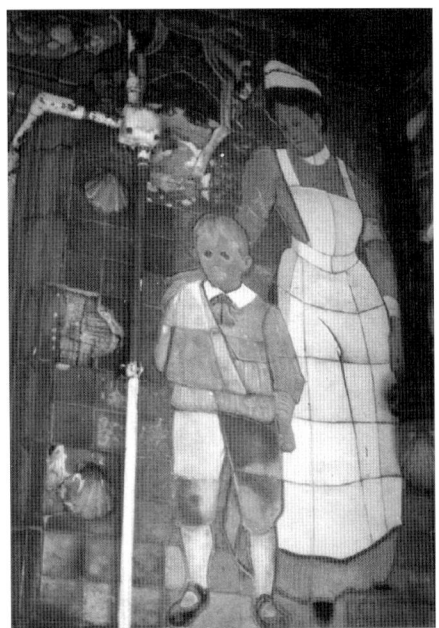

SEAVIEW HOSPITAL, (WOMEN'S PAVILLION), MANOR ROAD AND ROCKLAND AVENUE, STATEN ISLAND, NY. 1905. DESIGNED BY RAYMOND F. ALMIRALL. CERAMIC DETAILS BY JOOST THOOFT AND LABOUCHERE OF THE DE PORCELEYNE FLES COMPANY, HOLLAND.

PHOTO: PAUL TUNICK

and children (sixteen different scenes in all) are deteriorating through lack of maintenance and, in some cases, through vandalism.

This is especially distressing when so many New York buildings are being carefully restored with new terra cotta manufactured by both Gladding McBean & Company and Boston Valley Terra Cotta. Not only are these companies (and two in England: Ibstock Hathernware, Ltd. and Shaws of Darwen, Ltd.) working on restoration of historic terra cotta buildings, but in recent years, terra cotta has begun to be incorporated into contemporary architecture. The reintroduction of ornament, colour, and surface pattern into new buildings has helped contribute to a growing interest in terra cotta.

After many years of steel and glass structures, architects are now using a wider range of materials and incorporating more rich and varied elements into their designs. One architect, Robert Venturi, has taken a bold stand in favor of ceramic ornament in several buildings. He has made insightful comments about the potential contributions of terra cotta:

> Opportunities abound for using terra cotta for the sensual enrichment of architecture. It is a surface material…that promotes ornament—ornament involving color, pattern and relief. Because of its easy repetitiveness and inherent refinement, terra cotta can be a means of our building's today. It is a way to bring back "human scale" to our cities as well as color and ornament.[9]

Contemporary terra cotta manufacturers have been receptive to developing original designs and are helping to re-establish a feeling of collaboration among craftsmen, artists, and architects. This type of interaction was once commonplace in the industry. Positive signs such as these suggest that a prophecy published in the *Real Estate Record and Builders Guide.*

1   "Architectural Terra Cotta: A Big Factor in New Building" *New York Times*, May 14, 1911.
2   Rose Slivka and Karen Tsujimoto, *The Art of Peter Voulkos* (Japan: Kodansha International, 1995), 60.
3   Frank Lloyd Wright, quotation from the inside cover of the publication of the *Atlantic Terra Cotta Company* II (June 1932).
4   Sharon S. Darling, *Chicago Ceramics & Glass* (Chicago: Chicago Historical Society, 1979), 200.
5   Edward H. Putnam, "Architectural Terra Cotta Its Physical and Structural Properties," *The Brickbuilder* February 1911: 32.
6   James Taylor, "Front Brick, Their relation To Architectural Design." Proceedings of the 7th Annual National Brick Manufacturers Association (1893): 165.
7   Leon V Solon, "The Philadelphia Museum of Art," the publication of the *Atlantic Terra Cotta Company* VIII (February 1927).
8   Sir Charles Lyell, *The Antiquity of Man* (Philadelphia: G.W. Childs, 1863).
9   Robert Venturi, "Introduction," in *Impressions of Imagination: Terra cotta Seattle* (Allied Arts of Seattle, Inc., 1986), vi.

CHAPTER 16

Architectural Ceramics

Edward Lebow

At one time or another, anyone who has stood within the walls of a Gothic structure has probably thought it seems impossible that the middle ages have passed away. Essentially, we are struck by the fact that the building remains poised to serve people and purposes that have long since expired or changed. So we see it as an objective symbol of once vital lives and values, feelings, and sensibilities, freighted with associations of its old function and history.

Presented at *Echoes: Historical References in Contemporary Ceramics*, 1983, Kansas City

Virtually every civilization that has raised a wall and capped a roof has produced objects that reflect the character of its buildings. The array of materials out of which they've been made is enormous. And their indigenous functions are so diverse, even quarrelsome, that they elude the description of any single category. Given that they manifest architectural motifs, we want to know what else they have in common. If buildings themselves embody our inner relation to our environment, for instance, then what do these architectural images portray, and what compels us to view them as one?

    The difficulty with "architectural ceramics" is that it offers such a parochial glimpse of the answer. Consequently, it forces us to try to visualize the whole. While that entails looking outside the medium, it also requires that we see these objects "not as consecrated by time," in T.S. Eliot's words, "but beyond time." And to do that, we must soften our scrutiny with generality and ignorance. Only then can we remove the pieces from date and place and see how memory has absorbed and contemplated architecture throughout the centuries, thus giving particular expression to the urge to come to terms with the world, with life, and with death.

Much of what we know about life in the distant past has been conveyed through the kind offices of the dead. Their undisturbed sanctuaries often appear to encapsulate the nature of existence in their respective eras. In addition to providing clues to what life was like, mortuary objects evince the blessings of the living. And throughout time, their purpose has remained constant: to focus the survivor's sense of pain and loss and to prepare the soul of the dead for departure.

This ritual of providing for the safekeeping of the ghost accounts for the architectural models from the Mexican Nayarit and the Han and T'ang Dynasties of China. The Nayarit dwelling seems to suggest more about the occurrence of death than do the Chinese models, with both the arrangement of its figures within the structure and its form indicating a death vigil.

It shelters a vigilant dog, staring out from a ground-floor opening beneath a set of stairs. Sealed in by three walls, the dog is flanked by two persons. Between them sits a plate of food. On the upper floor of the house, a man lies with his head propped against a wall. A woman watches him from across the room, while two skirted figures, their legs dangling down the side of the dwelling, look out the open rear wall

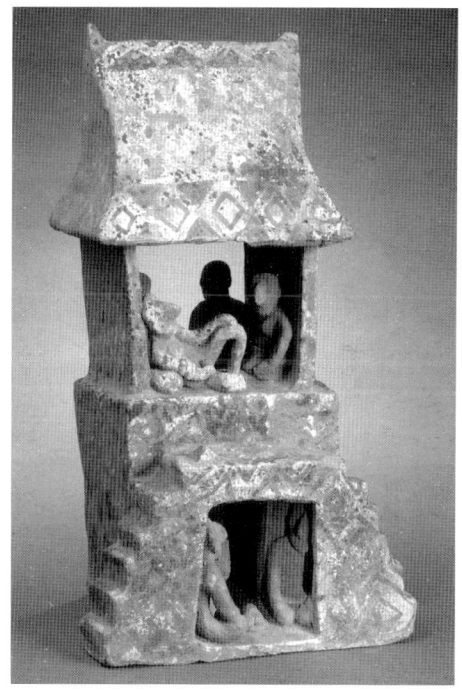

MEXICAN NAYARIT, *TWO-LEVEL HOUSE MODEL*, LATE PRECLASSIC 200 BC-300 AD. EARTHENWARE WITH CREAM SLIP AND RED AND BLACK PAINT REMNANTS, 36.0 × 20.0 × 15.6 CM.
COLLECTION/PHOTO: SAINT LOUIS ART MUSEUM, MO

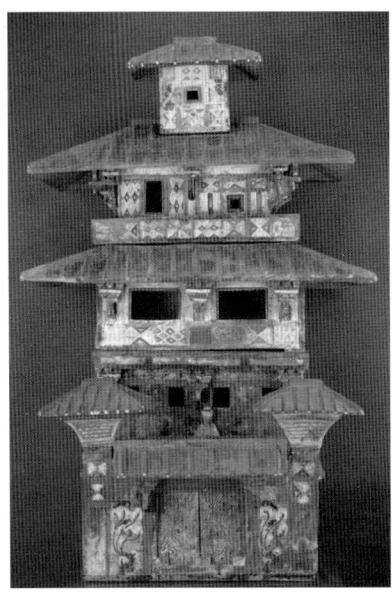

TOMB MODEL OF A HOUSE, CHINESE, EASTERN HAN DYNASTY (25-220). EARTHENWARE WITH UNFIRED PIGMENTS, 132.1 X 85.1 X 68.6 CM.
COLLECTION: THE NELSON-ATKINS MUSEUM OF ART, KANSAS CITY, MO. PURCHASE: NELSON TRUST, 33-521
PHOTO: ROBERT NEWCOMBE

of the gabled portico. Seen together, they seem to convey that the animal and his attendants await the arrival of the newly dead, while the figures overhead view the passage of life.

The Chinese structures give us a more elaborate picture of beliefs surrounding the exchanges between living and dead. The multi-storied house from the Eastern Han Dynasty is thought to be one of the most complete of its kind. Its details indicate that the dwelling after which it was modeled comprised post-and-lintel wood construction, tiled roofs, and a fairly complicated system of brackets supporting the eaves.

Since the customary practice was to surround the corpse with practical and symbolic items from life, the house was probably interred with a variety of *ming ch'i* (spirit objects). The smaller T'ang dwelling, for example, was one of about twenty tomb furnishings recovered from a site in the Honan Province. In addition to houses, these may have included models of animal yards, complete with a menagerie of livestock and miniature wells. Granaries, such as the one in the exhibition, contained food, the stench of which must have preceded the soul's arrival in the realm of the immortals. And small stoves were outfitted with utensils, food vessels, cooking pots and storage jars. Some of these were made of iron, bronze, and stone. And the clay examples were usually worked to imitate the structural details appropriate to these other materials, showing rivets and hinges, for instance.

From the variety of such objects, it is clear that the needs of the dead were imagined to be similar to those of the living, and that the contented spirit journeyed form this life into the next in the style to which it had grown accustomed. Thus well provisioned and secured in its surroundings, the ghost would find no cause to return malevolently or without warning to haunt the living.

Thus, these mortuary objects were valued for their power to evoke not only a kind of place but also a specific one, a place where the released soul could find the eternal comfort of familiar surroundings, persons, and activities; in short, a place which housed the memory of mortal being.

This association of memory and life everlasting goes beyond the notion that our afterlife exists in the remembrances of those who survive us. As the organizing force in the life of our

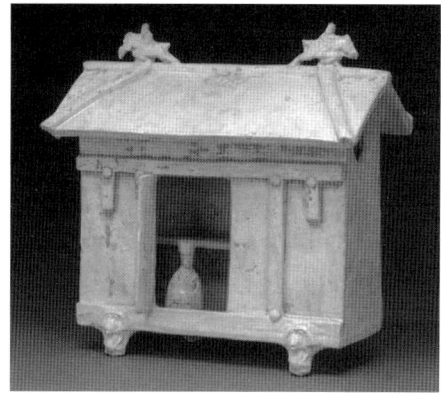

STOREHOUSE, CHINESE, EASTERN HAN DYNASTY (25-220). EARTHENWARE WITH IRIDESCENT GREEN GLAZE, 40.6 x 21.0 x 41.3 CM.
COLLECTION: THE NELSON-ATKINS MUSEUM OF ART, KANSAS CITY, MO. PURCHASE: NELSON TRUST, 34-204
PHOTO: JAMISON MILLER

minds, memory encompasses all. Therein, wrote St. Augustine, "meet I with myself, and recall myself, and when and where, and what I have done and under what feelings." Combining and refreshing old experiences with new, it brings sentiments and beliefs to recognition. And from those we "infer future actions, events and hopes," all of which, he said, we "reflect on as present."[1]

This sense of the continuous present is one of the vital traits of memories. Their constant revision of our past modifies and enlarges our sense of being. And through the continuity of evolving self-awareness, we acquire an intimate understanding of time as it affects us, rather than as it exists in an external sequence of events. So while our past guides our future, our future reveals what the past has meant. In a remarkable passage written shortly before his death, Leo Tolstoy described the steady point from which we are able to apprehend this flux of life:

> I have keenly experienced consciousness of myself today, at 81 years, exactly as I was conscious of myself at 5 or 6 years. Consciousness is motionless. And it is only because of its motionlessness that we are able to see the motion of that which we call time. If time passes, it is

> necessary that there should be something which remains static. And it is consciousness of self which is static.[2]

Thus, by removing the events of life from their strict chronology, memory brings timelessness—the stillness Tolstoy described—to each moment of self-reflection. That is why memory has always been treated as the path to life everlasting and to the source of the spirit memorialized in tombs and their furnishings.

Of course we find this same sense of timelessness embodied in buildings. At one time or another, anyone who has stood within the walls of a Gothic structure has probably thought it seems impossible that the middle ages have passed away. Essentially, we are struck by the fact that the building remains poised to serve people and purposes that have long since expired or changed. So we see it as an objective symbol of once vital lives and values, feelings, and sensibilities, freighted with associations of its old function and history. Invariably, we realize that "what the people are within," in Louis Sullivan's words, "the buildings are without." And the manner of that inwardness seems much clearer once we are no longer living the lives that express it directly, once memory has had the chance to place it in perspective. In this way we come to think of buildings as landmarks. Whether personal or communal, they arouse our full repertoire of sentiments, ranging from fond remembrance to religious fervour.

That is what we find in the commemorative vistas decorating the Meissen ecuelle, the Austrian cup and saucer, and the German porcelain cup. The Meissen piece carries a view of Venice, the Austrian a view of Vienna's Josephsplatz, and the German cup shows us where Rudolph D'Oench last housed his family in Reichenbach, Silesia. In all likelihood, the scenes gave these objects an heirloom or souvenir status. Their quick sentimental appeal was probably not much different from that which we find in contemporary souvenir plates, cups, or pitchers bearing view of favourite tourist sites. Each time we see or use the objects they enhance, these images spark the "what," "where" and "when" of the scenes they show. In their weak way, they suggest a leap from now to then, or from our current place to the one they represent. However narrowly, they embody a sense of journey. And here we begin to feel the limits of our category, for outside ceramics we can find objects that are more vividly architectural and that better express not only the idea of physical travel but also that of spiritual journey.

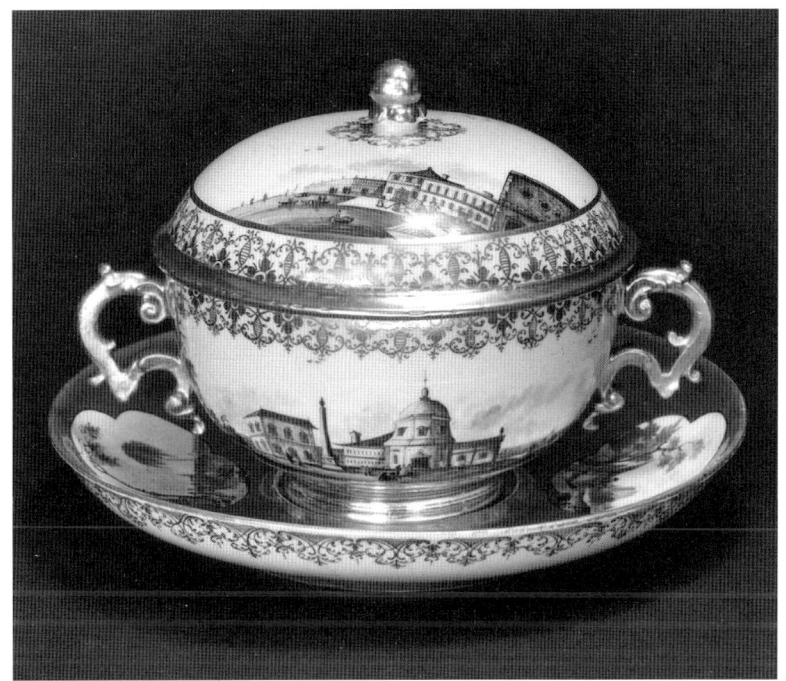

Meissen Porcelain Manufactory, Germany; *Ecuelle with Cover and Stand*, c. 1735-1740. Porcelain, 12.7 cm.

Collection/Photo: Saint Louis Art Museum, Friends Fund

The reliquaries that appeared throughout Europe during the middle ages are a particularly good example. Made of precious metals and adorned with gilt and enamels, they took the form of miniature cathedrals. Such shoebox shrines often housed the bonier tissue of deceased saints or mementos brought by pilgrims from the Holy Land. Their church-like appearance identified them immediately as objects of spiritual concentration. And they were given appropriate sanctuary within the Romanesque and Gothic churches of their day, where they were worshipped as symbols of the journey by which man reached the realm of God, a course outward across the Mediterranean to the Levant and inward to the seat of spiritual consciousness. Like the crossing from life to death of the Chinese and Nayarit souls, this religious venture was expressed in the symbolic language of its adhering community. So it spoke with the force of a unified tradition, which bound the experience of its participants from womb to grave.

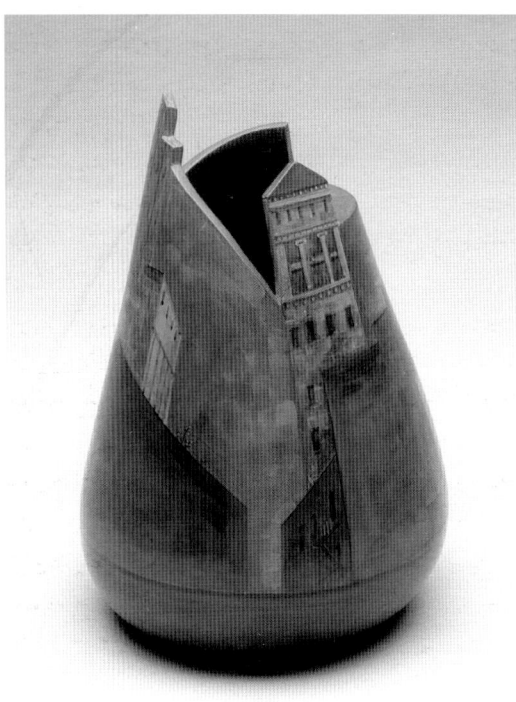

LYDIA BUZIO, *SKYLINE POT*, 1982. BURNISHED EARTHENWARE, 34.3 CM.

COLLECTION: BETTY ASHER

PHOTO: LAUGHMILLER ©1982

Since the range of modern architectural objects permits only general thoughts, we should keep in mind that even a crab, as William James remarked, would be outraged to hear itself classed as a crustacean. Admittedly, the works are individual and various, and need to be seen as such. In that alone we see the striking change brought by the modern era. Rather than expressing the uniform values of a homogenous group, the objects stand as landmarks of the inward journey undertaken by individual artists. Speculation about the impetus behind Raymon Elozua's ruins or Lydia Buzio's cityscapes leads invariably to the realization that each was shaped by the synthesis of personal memories. They are not recreations of specific scenes or settings; rather, they are creations which use the associative powers of architectural motifs to summon our outward senses to the inward one of their makers.

What's more, they reveal that the realm of God and collective beliefs has become synonymous with that of individual consciousness—the two encompassing the same inward experience.[3] Consequently, the Almighty for whom St. Augustine scoured his memory and could find "no place" is now equated with the innermost states of mind that Tolstoy described as having no identifiable time. So we find the dwelling of God shaped according to the framework of the individual psyche, with each room symbolically accommodating a separate stage in the development of self-awareness.

In fact, those are the terms used by Carl Jung to describe the construction, over the course of thirty-five years, of his own house in Bollingen, Switzerland. Begun in 1923, it was initially planned as a single-story house, embodying the idea of familial wholeness. By 1927, however, he had come to feel that something was lacking, so he added a central tower and annex. Another four years passed, and the building again seemed incomplete. He wanted a room in the tower where he could exist for himself alone, "a place of spiritual concentration." In 1935 he added a courtyard and a loggia, and after his wife's death in 1955, he felt impelled to build again. Putting it in the language of the house:

> I suddenly realized that the small central section which crouched so low, so hidden, was myself! I could no longer hide behind the "maternal" and "spiritual" towers.... I added an upper story to this section which represents myself.... Earlier, I would have regarded it as presumptuous self-emphasis. Now it signified an extension of consciousness achieved in old age.[4]

Reflecting on his completed dwelling, Jung saw the tower as a place of maturation where he could become who he was. "Only afterward," he wrote, "did I see how the parts fitted together... [in] a symbol of psychic wholeness.

Of course, such an awareness belongs as much to the past as to the present. For between mother and tomb, we have always moved among shelters. And although the use of their encompassing symbol is everywhere varied, it remains for contemporary artists, as it was for the dead of the centuries, an evocative link to what is foremost in the life of their minds.

1   *The Confessions of St. Augustine*, translated by Edward B Pusey (New York: Collier & Sons, 1909), 174.
2   Quoted from Roger Shattuck, *The Banquet Years* (New York: Vintage Books, 1955), 352.
3   For an exhaustive treatment, see Joseph Campbell *The Masks of God: Creative Mythology* (New York: Viking Press, 1970).
4   C.G. Jung, edited by Aniela Jaffé, translated by Richard and Clara Winston, *Memories, Dreams, Reflections* (New York: Vintage Books, 1965), 225.

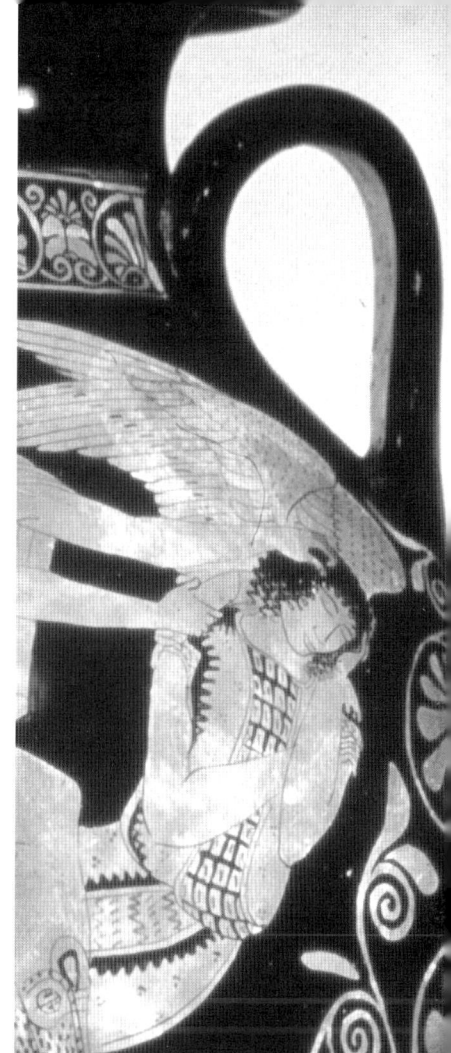

SECTION FIVE
HISTORY AND
TRADITION

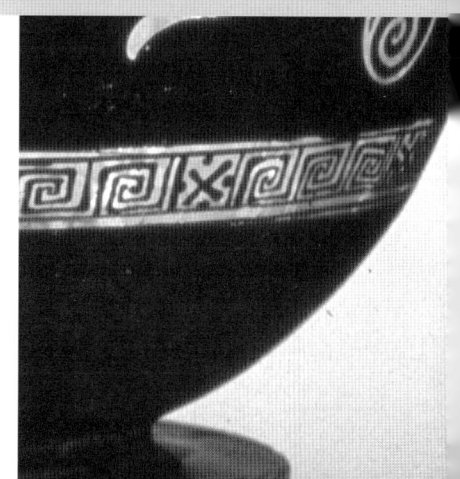

CHAPTER 17

THE ROLE OF THE TRADITIONAL POTTER IN CONTEMPORARY SOCIETY

GERRY WILLIAMS

Juanita tells me why she makes pottery. "It's just a happy feeling," she says. "We don't judge our potteries with others, just ourselves. We just want to do it and be alone." She then talks about the ceremonial bowls she has made for the kiva and some of the Indian customs concerning their use. Afterwards, she tells me she regrets having spoken of these secrets to me. When I return, home I find that this passage is inexplicably missing on the tape recorder.

Presented at *The Ceramics Symposium*, 1979, Syracuse

I have been given the task of defining the role of the traditional potter in our society. Considering the enormous scope of the subject, I have decided to confine my remarks to those aspects which relate primarily to the situation in the United States and to a quite personal interpretation of the meaning and purpose of tradition.

There is a fondness in America for regarding the growth of our society as a development unhampered by tradition. Leading thinkers in the crafts have also pointed with pride to the extraordinary level of aesthetic and technical sophistication as an asset directly resulting from the lack of tradition. This is not necessarily so. I believe there is a mainstream in which American potters work. I believe that aberrant aesthetic schools are merely tangential to that mainstream. I believe there is a universal life force with which we potters can identify and from which comes the source of our vitality.

In this paper I would like to briefly identify four types of traditional American potters, try to define tradition and re-examine it in a more meaningful context, put that meaning into social and historical perspective, and conclude with some personal insights into what it means to be a potter.

1. TRADITIONAL POTTERS: HELEN CORDERO AND JUANITA ARQUERO. The road to Cochiti leads up the dry desert valley of the Rio Grande in New Mexico, past the Sandia Mountains, and not quite to Sante Fe. A sudden rise in the road reveals the village of Cochiti, an ancient habitation of low, brown houses. Several hundred Pueblo Indians live in the village. They are mostly farmers and raise cattle. The old people always have known Cochiti by its Tewa name, but they seldom speak it. There are many things the old people know and are reluctant to speak of. Helen Cordero is in the yard beside her house making pottery. She is using sandpaper to smooth down the surface of a half-completed effigy called *The Story Teller*, a seated figure, fourteen inches high, aswarm with little clay children. The figure represents her recreation of the role that her grandfather, Santiago Quintana, played as the oral historian of his tribe.

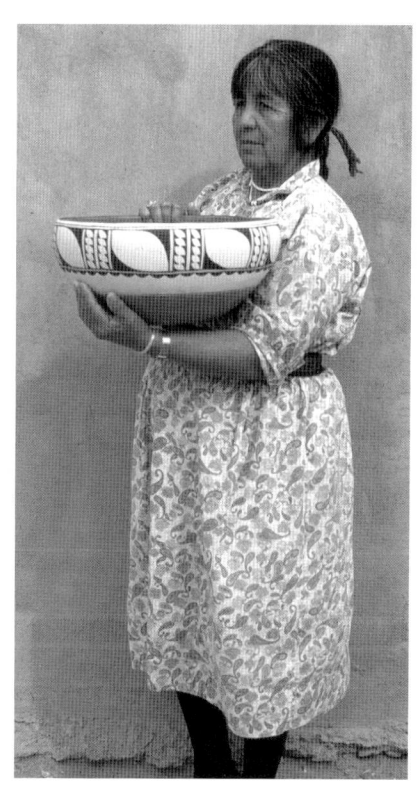

JUANITA ARQUERO WITH HER WORK

As Helen works on the effigy, she tells me: "Our old people, the Na'wa'ya'thitse, used these traditional methods when they were here. I'm pretty sure they would like us to do what they did. People will treasure it more because it came from our old people."

Helen's friend and neighbor, Juanita Arquero, is visiting. Juanita has brought over a large bowl she has made to show me. I admire its elegant shape and generous enclosure of space. She tells me it is a bread bowl and explains how it is made in the old Indian manner, with coils of clay shaped by a little piece of curved gourd and decorated in the Cochiti style with the black liquor of the bee weed.

Juanita tells me why she makes pottery. "It's just a happy feeling," she says. "We don't judge our potteries with others, just ourselves. We just want to do it and be alone." She then talks about the ceremonial bowls she has made for the kiva, and some of the Indian customs concerning their use. Afterwards, she tells me she regrets having spoken of these secrets to me. When I return home, I find that this passage is inexplicably missing on the tape recorder.

2. ZEDITH TEAGUE. Zedith Teague, a traditional Appalachian potter, lived in the small town of Rollins, North Carolina. Until her death three years ago, she made pots for over forty-four years on the same site as her father, "Duck" Teague, did before her. Her pots were burnt in a 200 cubic-foot oil-fired kiln. She turned most of the ware herself, with the help of her husband and an occasional apprentice.

Zedith once said: "In order to be a good potter, you got to be just as ornery as the dickens. If you ain't, and ain't as cantankerous as they come, someone is going to come and change you, and you're going to be turnin' out stuff that, inside, you don't want to make."

A perceptive observer recently noticed that there are potters by the same name in England, around the area of Stoke-on-Trent. There were, he also noticed, similarities between the types of ware produced by the Teagues of North Carolina and the Teagues of England. If so, this represents an admirable case of cultural continuity.

3. CLARY ILLIAN. Clary Illian lives in a very small town called Garrison, in the classic corn-yellow middle of Iowa. Clary was born and brought up in Cedar Rapids, Iowa, studied pottery at the University of Iowa, then went to England to apprentice at the Leach pottery in Cornwall. While there, she learned disciplined throwing in an atmosphere of intensive production.

The pottery she now makes in her Iowa workshop is graceful, understated, and utilitarian. She and her apprentice, Liz Kraus, produce casseroles, plates, pitchers, soup bowls, and beer mugs—the whole range of kitchen ware—which they sell inexpensively from the premises of their workshop.

"My philosophy about utilitarian ware," Clary says, "is what keeps me honest. It's important to be in the service of something greater than oneself. Utility is the peg upon which I hang my whole spiritual search." She goes on to say: "For years the most important thing for me to say was that I am a potter. That was synonymous with saying, I am Clary. It is still a source of great strength for me."

4. TOM COLEMAN. Tom Coleman and his wife Elaine are self-supporting production potters in Canby, Oregon. They live with their children in a traditional farmhouse, in a green sea of wheat that stands astride the track of the old Oregon Trail. Their studio is a reconditioned barn. He studied painting at the Portland Museum School of Art, then switched to clay and apprenticed himself to several production workshops in the Portland area. Today he is a widely respected master potter in the northwest area. His pots are to be seen in sell-out, one-man shows, and at art gallery exhibitions and fairs. He specializes in porcelain and is fond of throwing spectacularly large porcelain pots with very thin walls and decorated vigorously in a classical Chinese manner. He produces some of the best copper reds in America.

I have chosen these five potters, out of at least 12,000 professional potters now working in America, because they are representative of some basic categories extant among potters in America today. These categories are:

> 1. The Native American who works within a distinctly identifiable cultural heritage.
> 2. The production potter living in a cultural enclave linked directly to our colonial heritage, and who is also closely identifiable with comparable European tradition.
> 3. The contemporary production potter whose experience, training, and aesthetic values largely come from abroad, either, Europe or Japan.
> 4. The contemporary studio potter, trained either in an American school or through an apprenticeship, working in one-of-a-kind production.

DEFINITIONS. We potters are not unique in the use of language to describe our special points of view. There are hidden meanings, but these are often the key to new understanding. We tend, for instance, to use words like plate, jar, and bowl to describe the perspective of form rather than use. The closer we get to process, the more we use words such as stoneware, salt glaze, or earthenware to describe the clay and its surface, rather than form and use. We are almost always object oriented and do not use words connected with the purpose for which any object is made. Basically speaking, our language has the peculiarities of any special-interest group, interpreting prejudices and values, and filtering our undesirable elements. It is, as usual, understood best by its own members.

In studying the variety of subcultures in the American craft world, it is useful to learn the language or at least to become aware of its subtlety. Since a lexicographer has yet to publish a dictionary of craft language—exclusive of technical terms—I have the privilege of making up definitions without serious challenge.

The word "tradition" is as loaded a word as any in the potter's language. The dictionary definition is: "A cultural continuity in social attitudes and institutions; the handing down of information, beliefs, and customs by word of mouth or by example from one generation to another without written instruction." This definition is slightly ludicrous, as on those terms, there may be only two such traditional cultures left in the world: one a New Guinea tribe on the upper Sypek, and the other the Trique enclave in southern Mexico, neither of whom can read or write! This definition is a little too tight for me, and I would like to modify it slightly for my purposes.

The contemporary American craft community actually has associated the word "traditional" with the potter who works in the utilitarian mode. Such a potter is usually production oriented, not university based, and is considered to be a professional in that most of his income is earned from the sale of his pots.

Now, there are a number of words linked to this traditional or utilitarian mode which have, for us craftspeople, rather emotionally charged meanings. The first and generic word in this general category is "crafts,"

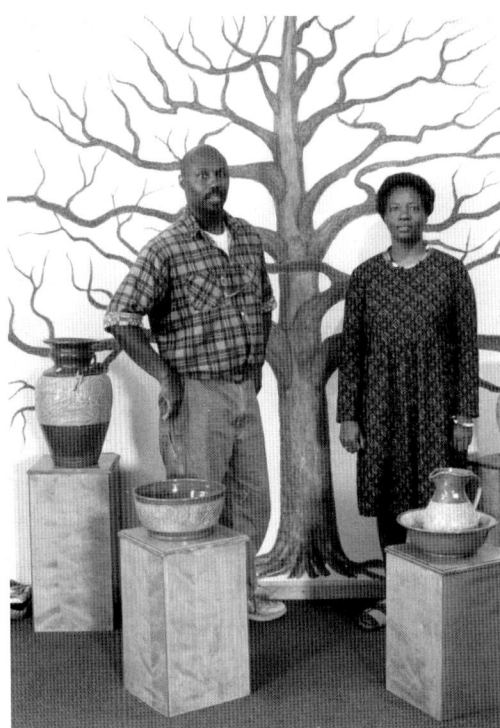

WINTON AND ROSA EUGENE, COW PENS STUDIO, SOUTH CAROLINA.

meaning useful objects made by hand and heart. The gender for this word is "craftsman," "craftsperson," and includes anyone not considered an artist, although some claim to be both, and no one can be the latter without also being the former. The next words in line are "pottery" and "potter," denoting the person and his product, as universal as common clay, who produces pottery in the utilitarian mode. The terms "utilitarian ware" and "functional pottery" refer to pottery made for use in the home, and specifically in the kitchen, though sometimes in the bathroom. The words "studio potter" generally have agreeable connotations (excepting lost subscriptions) as the role model of the functional potter who gains in prestige. (In New Zealand it is badmouthed for being dilettantish.) A "professional potter," however, is a really serious person whose skill and dedication enable him to earn a living from his work, and who enjoys peer acceptance. It is the key word in this whole mode of pots—not as in pots and pans—but as in the end product of a fascinating but elusive process which combines the mastery of technology with the spirituality of the ideal. A talismanic word, it links potters together as surely as a secret handshake.

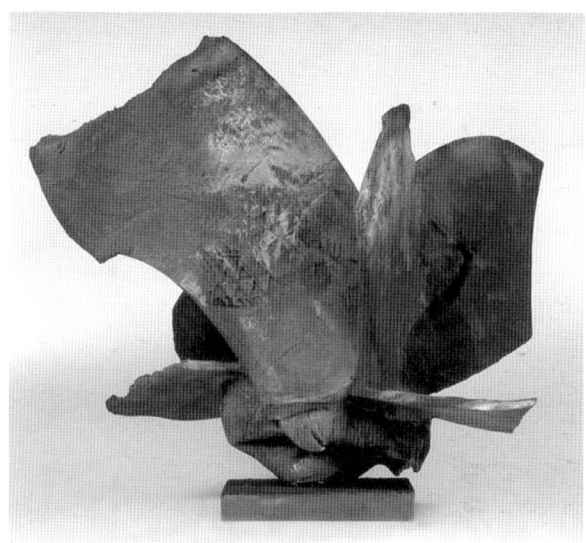

PAUL SOLDNER, *VASE*, 1975. RAKU FIRED STONEWARE. 60.9 × 106.7 × 45.7 CM.

PRIVATE COLLECTION

There is another grouping of words essentially identified with the concept of art. The subculture has its own language, and the generic word is "ceramics." While this word has several meanings, including that of cast figurines and toilet bowls, it has come to be associated specifically with non-functional work, and is thought to be *de rigueur* in academia. In this context the potter becomes a "ceramist," or

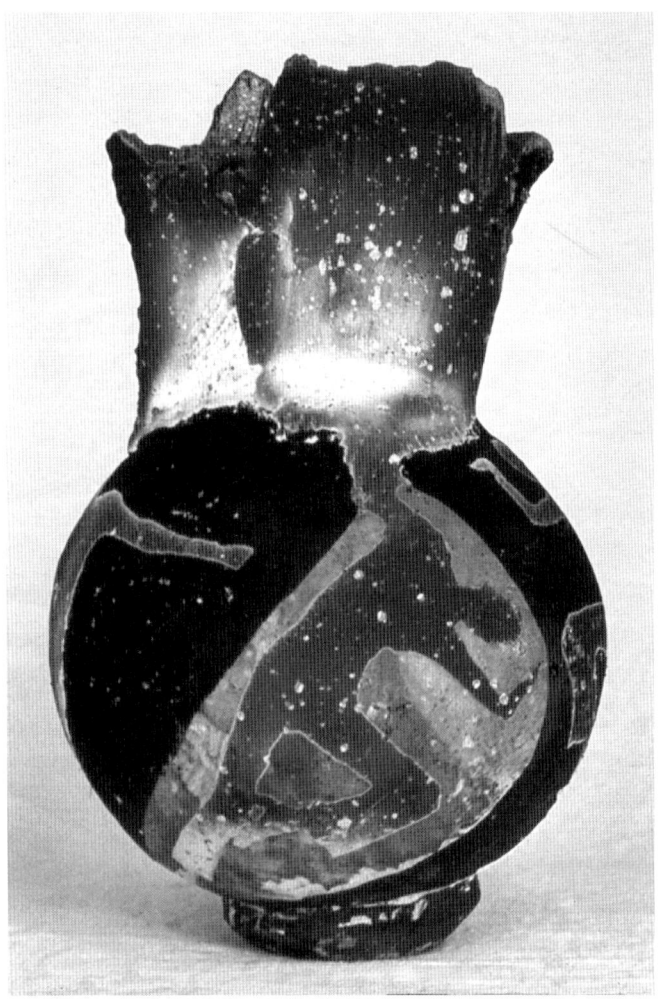

PAUL SOLDNER, *VASE*, 1972. RAKU FIRED STONEWARE, 35.6 × 22.9 CM.
PRIVATE COLLECTION

"ceramic sculptor." (The name "designer-craftsman" is mercifully obsolete.) Work in this mode is affirmatively negative: "non-functional," "nonrepresentational," "non-utilitarian." Ceramists use language spilled from the table of the fine arts: "environmental," "conceptual," "sculptural," "abstract expressionist." Ceramists often work on an "object" (those made in America are referred to *Objects: USA*[1]), though lately there has been a quasi-religious and tentatively conciliatory association with something called the "vessel," as in ritual. "The New Ceramic Presence"[2] of the middle 1950s had, in fact, the stunning conceit to consider its mission the freeing of the traditional potter from dogma and convention, which it promptly did. Now known as the period of the "Great Freeing of the Traditional Potter," this resulted in a new aesthetic, permeating crafts in America and carrying its influence abroad. The language of this aesthetic has dominated our teaching and criticism for the past decade.

HISTORY. The most famous potter in America is a traditional potter. Busloads of tourists from afar daily drive up to see Maria Martinez in San Idelfonso. With brittle bones and anecdotes about presidents, she shuffles her walker forward and greets them with the radiance of an angel beating wings.

Maria Martinez is at the present end of a history of pottery in America that goes back at least four thousand years. Earthenware found in Georgia and Florida has been radiocarbon dated at about two thousand BC. It is reasonable to suppose, therefore, that tradition has existed in this country for this length of time. Whether for the Indian or white man, the mainstream of this great cultural current has flowed for many years, now here, now there, sometimes underground, sometimes above, always present.

Yet there exists today in America a lover's quarrel between art and craft. Potters or ceramic artists, we play a duet on an ill-tempered clavichord. In a perceptive essay called "An Historical Review of Art, Commerce and Craftsmanship," the New Zealand potter Harry Davis puts the origin of this conflict into perspective. He first points out distinctions that exist in the English language regarding the origin of the words "art" and "craft." "Art" and "artist" derive from the Latin word meaning skill. "Craft" derives from the Teutonic word also meaning skill. But when the Norman invasion of Saxon England took place, social attitudes became linguistic distinctions. In the visual arts, what was aristocratic became associated with the ruling Norman class, and what was menial became associated with the subservient Saxon class.

David then goes on to show how this distinction was crystallized during the Renaissance, when the rise of a commercial class in Europe began to curry Church patronage, resulting in the open quest by merchant princes for kudos and prestige through commissions. He points particularly to an event that took place in 1563 that has had its effect on the visual arts ever since. That was the founding by Cosimo Medici II of an academy for his artist friends to absolve them from obligations previously imposed on them by their guilds. It was at this point in history, says David, that fine arts became a status and power symbol, a division that has remained a feature of western society ever since.

It is always safe to blame people who are dead for such events. Certainly Cosimo cannot reply. Neither can Albert Einstein. While the world before 1905 was complacently safe in the bosom of Newtonian mathematics, confident that the universe was being governed by a practical if inscrutable machinery, Einstein came along and tilted the table. His theory of relativity not only provided a brilliant new perception of our physical world but jolted the rigidity of the art world as well. It is fair to surmise that this new perspective influenced—or may have given rise—to Constructivism, Dadaism, Abstract Expressionism, even Voulkoism. We craftsmen are the direct legatees of this new consciousness.

Whatever the cosmic nudge, the single most salient factor as regards the development of pottery in America in the last forty years has been the role of the university after World War II. It undeniably developed into the prime training ground for craftspeople. New aesthetics were imported by veterans returning under the G.I. Bill. The alma mater became Ohio State, Alfred University, Cranbrook Academy, the University of California, Berkeley. The super teachers were superstars and daily dealt us delicious blows of funk, pop, and porn.

Academia presently dominates pottery in America. It is pervasive in craft training, aesthetics, role models, and the dispensation of power and prestige. Academia, looking into a mirror, has modelled pottery into an intellectualized art form called ceramics. Thus the only organization with widespread membership in the ceramic community is the National Council for Education in the Ceramic Arts, whose professed mandate is involvement with "teaching or educational aspects of the ceramic or glass arts." While generally benign and tutorial, the university has occasionally assumed the arrogance of power. Some graduate ceramic departments have refused acceptance of "vessel-oriented" applicants, an attitude reflected in the pre-

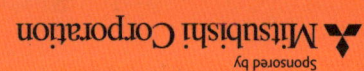

Sponsored by
Mitsubishi Corporation

Co-organised with Agency for Cultural Affairs of Japan
In collaboration with Tokyo National Museum
A Japan-UK 150 Event

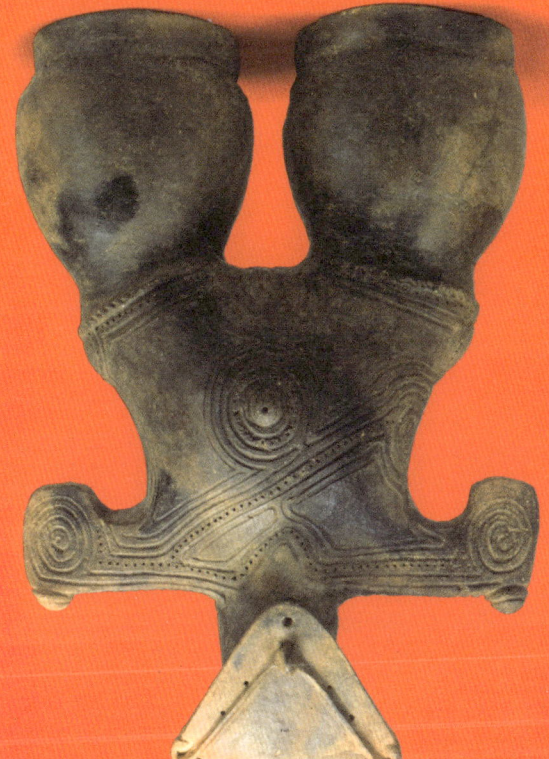

10 September – 22 November 2009
Admission free
Daily 10.00–17.30
www.britishmuseum.org

THE POWER OF DOGU
CERAMIC FIGURES FROM ANCIENT JAPAN

THE BRITISH MUSEUM

THE POWER OF DOGU
CERAMIC FIGURES FROM ANCIENT JAPAN

10 September – 22 November 2009

This exhibition highlights the beauty and power of remarkable ceramic figures known as dogu, mysterious masterpieces that were produced in great numbers in prehistoric Japan.

Dogu are from the earliest-dated tradition of pottery manufacture in the world, dating to the prehistoric Jomon period, which began 16,000 years ago. Many of the objects on display are designated Japanese National Treasures or Important Cultural Properties and all are on loan from public and private collections in Japan. Most have never been seen outside Japan before. The exhibition will also explain the origins, development and disappearance of dogu, and demonstrate how they shed light on the archaeology of prehistoric Japan.

Admission free

The exhibition catalogue (£19.99) is available from the Museum shops or www.britishmuseum.org/shop

Manga by Hoshino Yukinobu at the British Museum

Visit Room 94 to view a free display of original artwork by Hoshino Yukinobu, a leading artist of *manga* (Japanese comic book art). The imaginative work brings the world of dogu and the Jomon period to life through the adventures of the fictional Professor Munakata.

Enjoy a free display of a new exclusive manga by Hoshino Yukinobu in Room 3 between 5 November 2009 and 3 January 2010. Join Professor Munakata for an adventure around the British Museum's collection. *The Asahi Shimbun Displays*

Free related events include gallery talks in English and Japanese, a family workshop and a symposium. For more information and to view a selection of the figures from the exhibition, visit www.britishmuseum.org

Masked dogu from Nakappara, Nagano Prefecture, Japan. 1500–1000 BC. On loan from the Chino City Board of Education. Designated 'Important Cultural Property' by the Japanese Government.

THE BRITISH MUSEUM

Great Russell Street, London WC1B 3DG
⊖ Holborn, Russell Square, Tottenham Court Road
Telephone +44 (0)20 7323 8000
information@britishmuseum.org
www.britishmuseum.org

© The Trustees of the British Museum 08/2009.

occupation with conceptual art by university students and their exhibitions.

University of Chicago sociologist Edward Shills has recently argued that the true function of the university is its quasi-religious mission to pursue truths about man and nature, but, it is fearful that governmental and technological encroachments might cripple that function. The one who pays the piper calls more and more of the tune. Professor Shills may be right. I believe the politicizing of education will eventually take place, due to pressures of energy and high technology. Down the long road, I see that the crafts will have to search for an alternative to intellectual development. As the hand withered and became obsolete during the Industrial Revolution, so can the brain through automation and signalling. Yet this can mean a new direction for us.

This is the age of transition, says Michael Cardew, that ancient marinator. We move on because we must. Yet, in the midst of negative signs and fears, in the midst of concern for the worldwide shortage of firewood and concern for the bad writing in the craft field, there are hopeful signals. One of these is surely the rise, within the past fifteen years, of the professional craftsmen in America. Their grace, energy, and versatility is astonishing. Their alignment with the traditional mainstream is one of the most hopeful of all signs and an affirmation of the continuity in crafts that will persist across boundaries and space and time.

VISIONS. I believe the traditional potter is the mainstream. The varieties of aesthetic adventurism we are now experiencing are its branches. This great, deep stream has always been present, never absent; always catholic, never exclusive; always creative, never destructive. This is the reason why I have been a potter for thirty years; the energy of this great source has sustained me. There are five features that make up my vision of the ideal studio potter:

> 1. THE STUDIO POTTER CREATES A HUMANIST ROOT. The potter seeks not to diminish his cultural heritage but to nourish and expand it, believes that a continuity exists between the past and the present and searches to ensure its projection into the future, and strives to work in ways to contribute to the welfare of mankind.
>
> 2. THE STUDIO POTTER DEALS WITH FUNCTION. The potter sees function, form, meaning, and use as principles underlying all work. These unifying elements are what the Chinese call social consciousness. The best

work, they believe, is the result of a completely unified human endeavor, rather that the product of a solo genius. The principle of function, therefore, results in pottery that is a truly genuine expression of life.

3. THE STUDIO POTTER EMBRACES THE CONCEPT OF APPRENTICESHIP. The potter sees apprenticeship as a means of nurturing intrinsic values of love and spirit for the craft, as well as transmitting professional information to the young craftsman. Apprenticeship is a living, growing relationship, with its own special place in the creative environment. The elements of apprenticeship are: experiential learning, dedication to one's life work, authority with free will, synergy, and a positive forward-thrusting relationship. The apprentice's experience is thus a learning helix, which spirals around the central core of the master's knowledge.

4. THE STUDIO POTTER IS A FUTURIST. Decisions concerning work values and aesthetics are made within a future time frame. The potter stands in the present, uses past data, and synthesizes the future, is continually dealing with scenarios for the future in his concern with form, function, and meaning. A potter responds vigorously to the commonsense desirability of appropriate intermediate technology and projects future alternatives and designs innovations for the potter's work and life.

5. THE STUDIO POTTER IS DEEPLY IDENTIFIED WITH LIFE FORCE. Known by many traditional cultures, including the American Indian, life force is the universal soul that begins with the spirit of mankind and works up through the laws of the universe. Life force exists in all forms of consciousness and is the medium through which the process of creating, sustaining, and recreating is carried out. Life force is breath as well as spirit, and is, to the beholder of truth, the only mystery worth investigating. Truth through tradition is one important aspect of the continuum.

---

1 This is a reference to the influential traveling exhibition and book by Lee Nordness, *Objects USA: Works by Artists-Craftsmen in Ceramic, Enamel, Glass, Metal, Mosaic Wood, and Fiber.* (New York: Viking Press, 1970).

2 See: Rose Slivka, "New Ceramic Presence," *Crafts Horizons* No.4, 1961.

CHAPTER 18

ECHOES: AN INTRODUCTION

PHILIP RAWSON

What is an echo? It is a sound that comes back to its source from some reflecting surface. If you call towards the cliffs, what returns is the echo of your own voice and of what you called. In the famous story of Echo's love for Narcissus, the girl Echo was condemned only to be able to repeat the last words of what she heard. Narcissus was absorbed in the reflection of himself in the water of a pool. This contains a profound image that can point to what we might mean by ceramic echoes.

Presented at *Echoes: Historical References in Contemporary Ceramics*, 1983, Kansas City

Some pots, especially porcelains, are in fact resonant, like glass. It is part of many great wares to be audible. Their sound is a function of their shape. One could reverse that proposition, even to say that the shapes may be designed as generators of specific sounds, like music's "resonant structures." They can literally resound to frequencies aimed at them—another kind of echo. It implies that the object itself has the potential for providing special qualities of echo. This, too, is important as a metaphor for what a ceramic echo might be.

The potter shapes a pot to make it resonate visually. But in itself, it waits dumb. It is only matter, shaped clays, and glazes. It waits for a person to approach it who can call to it with imagination and awaken its latent echoes. This is a critical and

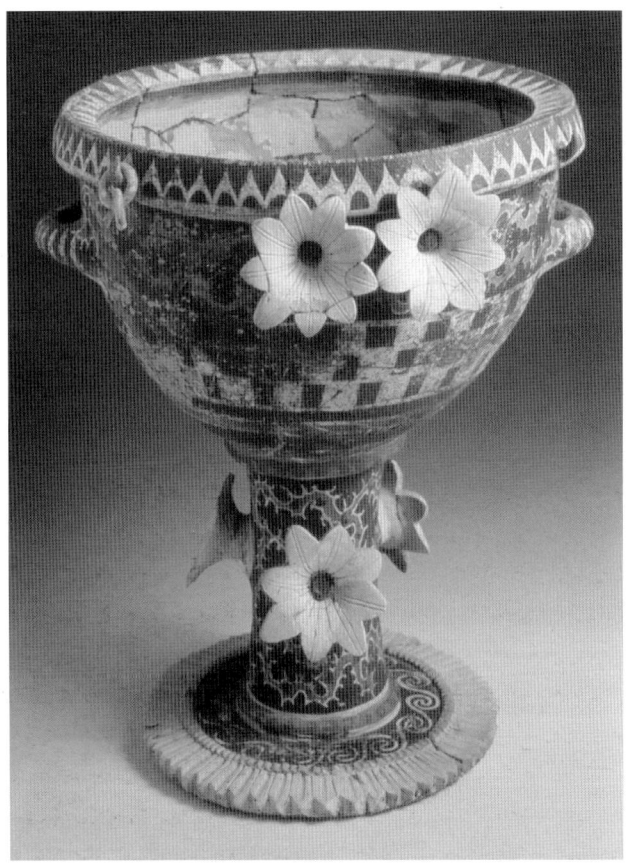

CRETE: PHAISTOS, *KAMARES KRATER WITH WHITE RELIEF LILIES,* OLD PALACE PERIOD c.1900-1700 BC.

COLLECTION/PHOTO: HERAKLEION MUSEUM, CRETE

fundamental fact in all art. It implies that you get from a work an experience of what you actually have it within you to experience, something you already own, but which you may not have known before was part of you. The work uncovers what lies there waiting to be uncovered, and, most important, shapes and unifies it. You read the work actively.

The paradigm, of course, is reading—a novel, say. You sit in a chair at home, in a train or aircraft; and as you trace those little black marks on the paper, you become both Echo and Narcissus. Your open and active imagination is focused to receive returns and these awaken resonances and memories within. You know what patterns of phrase and gestures implying feeling "mean." You recognize character traits, the inevitability of people's acts, the kinds of physical consequences of what you "see" must be collision courses. The book itself shapes out and coordinates your inner references, responses, and expectations.

References, responses, and expectations: these are what ceramics also evoke, in their own terms. And among those references are echoes of other ceramics and other art. In the sphere of words and reading, we know very well that a word or phrase does not only refer to facts of life, the immediate here and now, the body and its parts; all its usages, the places you heard it and met it before, constitute vital elements of its meaning. George Steiner and John Livingstone Lowes are two of the people who devoted their lives to raking through the nature of verbal meanings in literature. Words and phrases can never mean anything without implicating other words, other conversations where they appeared, other books. Their meaning is a cultural phenomenon. This is how literature embodies living culture.

There are vital differences, of course; but generally speaking, we can accept that pots also refer not only to our immediate experiences but also to other pots and other art. They, too, embody a living culture. The echoes they can send back to us refer not only to our sensuous world but also to the cultural world of similarities and contexts which the pots themselves inhabit. Pots thus echo the echoes of pots. Indeed; our ceramic culture is filled with echoes and we have to be pretty alert to pick them up. This is where ceramic history, museums, and books come into it. They can supply some of the references and contexts to which potters—especially modern potters—may be referring, and so actually feed the meanings we can get from actual pots.

To give an example: the shape of a sophisticated eighteenth-century Chinese

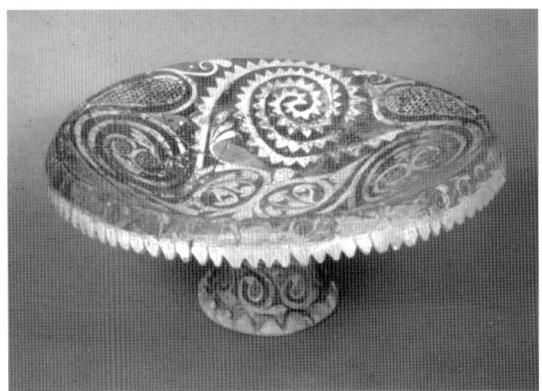

CRETE: PHAISTOS, *KAMARES FRUIT STAND DECORATED WITH SPIRALS* OLD PALACE PERIOD C.1900-1700 BC.

COLLECTION/PHOTO: HERAKLEION MUSEUM, CRETE

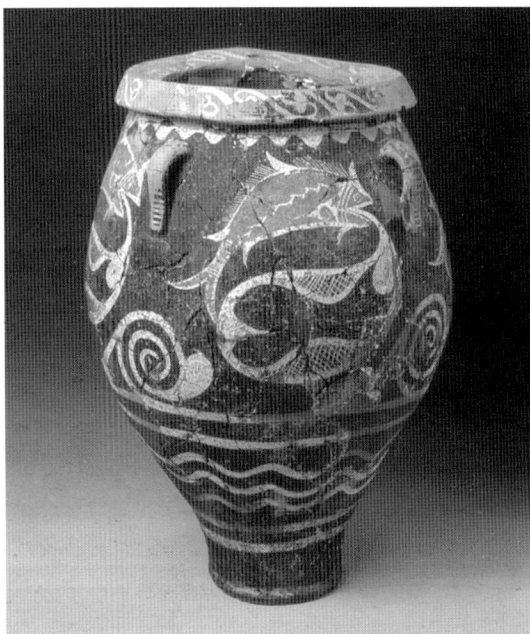

CRETE: PHAISTOS, *KAMARES PITHOS (STORAGE JAR) DECORATED WITH FISH AND SPIRALS*, OLD PALACE PERIOD C.1900-1700 BC.

COLLECTION/PHOTO: HERAKLEION MUSEUM, CRETE

porcelain may refer to the shape of a Sung stoneware bottle—a cultural reference—which itself referred to a peasant bottle shape of earlier centuries, which referred to a leather bottle used by nomads from Inner Asia. The first may not look very much like the last, but the sum total of the first's meaning may have had quite strong undertones of Buddhist history and feeling. We might prefer to say we would rather not bother with all that stuff, the shape of the first is great, anyway. But then we would lose and miss the point. If we cannot hear all the utterances of beautiful Echo, we lose a chance to know something of what we ourselves own and might become.

As I am writing this, I have on my desk two postcards from the Herakleion Museum in Crete, showing pots I remember very well. One is a huge stem bowl with white, modeled flowers standing far out from its body. Another is a pedestal dish, with its entire rim pinked downwards, and great coiling shapes painted on it in blue. A third is a large storage jar with a curving, tapered foot painted with a design of ochre fish, white coiling shapes, and undulating lines on a green-blue ground. The echoes they send back to my questing imagination are of the vegetable world and sea. The fish and flowers are the only "things." The rest are forms of motion and activity for which I must search in my own memory for references. And what I find fills me with awe and respect; for, incidentally, the people who made these were usually less than five feet tall!

A fourth, and later, Cretan pot has decoration that quotes the designs on other pots of its own ceramic culture, reaching through the quotations to an original experience of the kind I just described but adding new dimensions of its own. For those designs are laid onto a pot shaped like a cave-house containing a little figure, with other figures surmounting it. The meaning of this pot is an accumulation in which the quotation plays a vital part. I should also say that its references are all well aimed, socially and culturally precise. They are not vague, general, and casual.

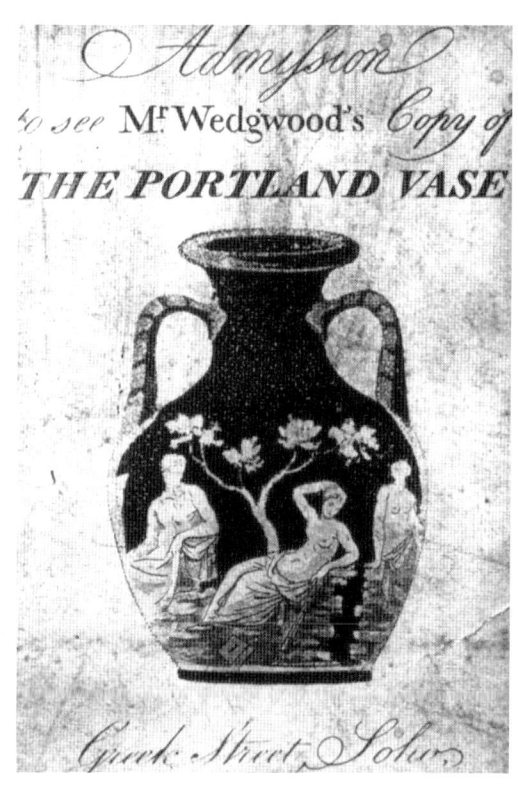

INVITATION TO WEDGWOOD POTTERY, *PORTLAND VASE*, 1790

COLLECTION: BRITISH MUSEUM, LONDON

To shift far on in time to the fringes of our own culture, we all know the vast numbers of quotations of classical art on Wedgwood's jasperware. The basic reference of the white-on-blue figures is to the famous Roman Portland Vase (now in the British Museum) made of white on blue glass cut in cameo. But there are, of course, many far more detailed references among the relief figures both to genuine classical imagery, such as cameos and seals, and to the vast quantities of fakes and reworkings, claiming to be classical, that passed current in the latter decades of the eighteenth century. Such ceramics were made virtually for the sole purpose of evoking echoes, though most did retain some basic utility as tablewares.

It is with this type of echo that we enter our epoch, with its dialectic of society and its discontents, of conformity and utopian rejection of societal norm, and individualism. Our own ceramic practices are probably infused with echoes of other pots and other art as deeply as the Wedgwood wares. The interesting questions are: What are those specific echoes, and why those in particular?

Our answers can only be speculative at this stage. But there seems to be one overwhelmingly powerful reason for using quotations to evoke cultural echoes. They lift the spirit. For various reasons, they add a dimension to the pot that enhances the life of the user, by expanding the world's sphere of meaning. If we examine a number of cases, a set of interesting questions present themselves, most of them having to do with the relationship of the individual to society. For one of the basic facts about pottery is that, until a couple of decades ago, it was basically a social art. Potters paid their way and lived by providing wares for a public of some kind—only rarely a public of connoisseurs. Many still do, either through the big industrial companies or as studio potters. The notion of the potter as a heavy, individual artist is quite recent with us. And in such cases, the question of echoes may be especially important.

Generally speaking, deliberate echoes embody references to values cherished by societies and/or individual potters and their patrons. Such values lie at the hub of complexes of feelings. The vital question is how deep rooted, serious and honest these values are. There is a distinction (one that is very difficult to draw but which it is the job of criticism to assess) between solid values and catchpenny styling. I do not think there are any easy answers. Each case comes up on its own merits, and each will have its own halo of problems.

There are several categories of echo which ceramics can embody. I offer a few suggestions here. First are references outside ceramics itself to kinds of things which embody values and meaning, often as symbols. Second are qualities of the work which refer to other works of ceramic art and related forms. Third are references to other materials and media, and to works made in them. Specific echoes may be conveyed by shape and texture, by speeds and spacing, by decoration and qualities of glaze, by some or all of these combined.

The first category of echoes is an enormous one. It obviously includes straightforward figurative references but at a subtler level, its manifestations range from invocations of recognizable objects and what they mean as symbols to forms of change in time not confined to single objects. The objects evoked include, for example, those breasts with nipples shown by some Iron Age European pot shapes, and those opening lotus-bud fruitshapes exhibited by Sung Chinese bowls and vases in several types of ware. Such references are truly metaphorical in that they combine both factors—the echo and the identity of the ceramic object—in a single reflex of the imagination. These kinds of echo are often given to the pot shape by what you can too easily dismiss as mere decoration: the added, functionally inessential nipples; the incised indications of petals; the stem leaves painted or incised at the base. Those references to flowers and the sea on Cretan pots I mentioned above belong to this group. So, too, does Picasso's interpretation by linear drawing of a joined pair of pots as horse and rider.

When we come to consider the reasons behind the adding of such echoes, we need both speculation and critical judgment. We know enough about Chinese art to recognize that Sung ceramics were part of a culture which would accept echoes of flowers and fruit, with a mixture of direct and acculturated responses. Those objects of nature were admired and valued, both as objects and as symbols for value systems. The "object" aspect poses few problems. The symbolic certainly includes the broad imagery of the lotus in the realm of profound feeling—attitudes belonging to the Buddhism of faith—cosmic visions of total compassion and purity in the face of actual despair and vileness.

About the Iron Age nipples we can only speculate. We have no texts. We can guess something of the food-creation-feeling complex involved from the survival in northwest Europe of great names such as The Paps of Anu by which a pair of Irish hills are still called. This, too, we can access as a complex of echoes related to both the actual and the cultural. But what about the Picasso? Sheer wit seems to be the answer.

The pleasure of wit seems to be the place where, nowadays, we locate a good deal of poetic talent. Some wit, especially if it is imbued with irony, can conceal serious value judgments and intuitions. Some of Picasso's wit was of this order.

So, too, was Duchamp's. But wit may also be no more than the joke of a moment, equivalent to one of the many wisecracks of daily conversation. Very many modern potters aim at wit. I think of one assemblage that suggests dinner plates hung out to dry, like washing on a line; another shows little frog-like figures growing indifferently out of straight pots and pots that "are" cabbages; another is a solid, tall rectangular vase, fashionably rough, with a simple bottleneck that is adorned with a row of buttons down its front and a pseudo-cloth belt. Real wit! Our questions can only be: How deep does such wit go? How much is it worth, in terms of effort, money, and attention? Is it as valuable as a pot that evokes more complex echoes, and echoes which may seem, somehow, more ontologically serious; that is to say, reaching deeper into issues that matter more?

My second category of echoes consists of echoes of other ceramics and objects that already have close affinities with pots. Pots easily refer to pots. No one could miss the reference if, say, a potter used the Greek terra cotta and black combination. Countless versions of Greek shapes were made in the latter eighteenth century; in the nineteenth, even pictures of Greek vases were printed on blue-and-white wares, such as Spode. Since Bernard Leach, our potters have been overwhelmed by the feeling that all true ceramics must be imbued with echoes of Japanese Zen raku tea wares, with their enlisting of hazard and the accidents of process: not only direct echoes, but echoes of echoes incorporated by earlier Western potters. Only when they have made their bow in that direction do many potters feel entitled to refer to their own direct experience.

This might now be called sheer sentimentality. But so, too, might the equally common references to components of machinery. Industrial ceramics are machined; even throwing and turning on the wheel are machining of a kind. But what the wheel produces is not meant to function as a machine. The mechanical resemblances may be echoes of a sentiment of optimism about the machine's benefit to humanity, which we may want to interrogate pretty closely.

It seems often to happen that pots' references to other pots are to exotic wares, to originals that have arrived in the potter's consciousness garbed in romance. Certainly we know that the great seventeenth-eighteenth century vogue for things Chinese in Europe was imbued with a quite mistaken vision of China as a paradisal Cathay, ruled by philosopher-kings totally unlike the grim feudal monarchs of the West. And things Japanese arrived in Europe imbued with a revamped version of that vision. Van Gogh's declaration in one of his letters to his brother is revealing. On the verge of his departure from the gloomy north to the colour and light of the south, he wrote: "I am going to my Japan." How many artists and potters have sought to follow him and fill their pots with echoes of that mythical landscape of the imagination! Even the Bauhaus and Vienna schools read the combination of space, brilliance, and serenity in Japanese ceramics and lacquerware as some kind of glorious relief from the clutter of current bourgeois taste, some of which was itself full of echoes of Islam! And Leach completed the process. So what are we looking to do if we fill our pots with echoes of indigenous American art? And how deep can a real assimilation go?

Knowing more, and being more cynical about, cultures which once charmed us by their exotic romance, many potters have turned to irony: quotation and the use of negation or parody are one highly modern way of implying positive notions without being obliged to define and so to limit them. Chinese *famille verte* and Japanese raku have certainly been subjects of irony. And irony itself can only, it seems to me, be picked up as a kind of echo. The blatant quotes of native arts made, for example, in northwestern Canada, or of Dyak work by Borneo Chinese cannot be called irony, though they may be the subject of ironic distancing.

The third category of echoes refers to human art works in other media. The most obvious ones are also the most familiar. Many "primitive" pots retain features of baskets whose shapes they imitated; others of stitched leather prototypes, such as English medieval jugs. The basket echoes can be especially interesting once again to us today, partly because there are certain characteristic kinds of pattern that basketwork—especially using fine fibers—can generate. These are based, like weaving patterns, on counting and numerical parameters. Some Pueblo pottery designs do seem to echo such textile thinking. And nowadays many potters are developing parametric "musical" designs in surface treatments based on horizontals and verticals. The echoes here may resound from the processes embodied in the original media rather than from the objects themselves.

One important set of ceramic echoes in this category derives from other works valued far more highly than pottery. Usually pottery has been relatively cheap. (A major exception was fine porcelain in seventeenth- and eighteenth-century Europe.) So ritual vessels and tablewares, especially, have often echoed the forms and chased decoration natural to gold and silver wares—often with some technical difficulty. In T'ang and Sung China this was beautifully done, but the ceramic substance remained itself, keeping its own meaning. It did not try to look like gold; though it is possible that some of the finest white wares, like the Ting (Ding), did try for the appearance of silver.

Here we reach another region of echoes of other work, one we are not so aware of nowadays as other epochs have been: the meaning of substances. The idea that celadon resembles jade—with all its cultural meanings in China—was familiar in the East. But in the West, we are powerfully aware of the depth and subtlety of reference that ceramic textures and glaze colours and qualities can attain. It is easy for a modern potter to become wrapped up in technology as pure process and lose contact with the meaning-as-echoes—going far beyond the mere stimulus of appetites—that technology may put within reach. An older time may have read echoes of colour and substance as reflections of the cosmic-alchemical complex expressed in gems, glass, and enamels. Today we may be watching for other allusions. And one extreme kind of case—meant possibly as another form of irony, maybe the modern conceit—whereby some non-ceramic object, such as a briefcase, is translated into glazed ceramic with a skill so consummate that it deceives the eye, if not the hand.

By far the commonest type in the category of echo—framing—involves building into ceramic work references to other arts of the culture which society rates more highly. The aim is usually to attach some of the value, both cultural and financial, to the ceramic version, and so bring it up to the required symbolic level for the user's idea of his own status. One could say, with some reason, that today this has become standard procedure.

To begin again with remoter examples, the calligraphy, flower, and landscape compositions painted on their porcelains by the Chinese and Japanese reflected their immense cultural emphasis upon the original brush arts. Something similar was done when engravings of classical ruins and topography were transfer-printed onto Spode blue-and-white wares of the early nineteenth century. A less superficial, more deeply entrenched echoing is involved when ceramics are given shapes originally invented for architectural decor, to fit them to play roles in interior decors of grand style. This happened a great deal in the seventeenth and eighteenth centuries in feudal Europe. Humbler ceramic wares could then bring something of courtly magnificence into the homes of burghers.

As method, this must now seem so familiar! We live in the shadows of industrial-political-aesthetic complexes, fortified by the publicity and museum industries, which have laid down for us certain aesthetic value-norms based, for the most part, on painting. Our ceramic studios produce shoals of work which modify and adapt the publicized images of "major" arts to the ceramic media. Rosenthals commissioned designs from well-known major artists (like Eduardo Paolozzi) which are mechanically applied to mass-produce, if up-market, wares. This could be seen as a way of spreading abroad into a society a sense of the values established in the "major" complex.

But it is only one aspect of a wider phenomenon. Art-publication, air travel and magazines have offered to the eyes of our potters a vast range of formal images from the exotic art of the world. Many of the images derived from photography, especially, have a very powerful impact; and potters everywhere have set out deliberately to assimilate something of that impact into their own work. The idea behind adding to your pots' flanges, derived from photos of Maya ornament, or laying out their interiors as Pueblo ground plans, may be, in the first instance, a result of wishing to attach to your pots the sense of awe and wonder the other art produced in you. But it does have at least one other very important function.

This is to lead the potter's mind into new realms of form, to lead him to invent things ceramics has not done before and that artists in other media have not done. Our ransacking of the "Imaginary Museum" has changed the nature of ceramic art. There are purist potters who stubbornly persist in making those ceramic things that people use. But how many more are really making pieces of interior decor based on other work they saw in magazines that give casual fissions by means of echoes that have no roots and affect nobody's lives? And who would put a set of $8,000 pieces into a dishwasher anyway? Are "artists in ceramic" still potters? Do the categories still match? Are there any intellectual or moral reasons why they should?

There is, of course, one important issue in all this. In the complex phenomenon that is modern art, it is clear that certain strands of development in formal-visual thinking continually define themselves. There are architectures of formal ideas which cross the boundaries of media, just as they did, say, in the days of Cubism. And there may very well be older stands of thinking which ceased developing not from exhaustion but for historical or personal reasons, and which are capable of further development. It is probable that potters/ceramists may very well make their own totally characteristic contributions to these developments via clay, glaze, and furnace. One reason for this may well be that they are able to evoke and compound echoes which are available only within the tradition and field of ceramic languages. It is of course vital that the potter do more than recapitulate the processes of sculpture, or imitate its "look."

Echoes are echoes. But works of visual art are more than echoes, or even bundles of echoes. However many echoes a work may evoke, it exists to make them real and to unify them by its own presence. The ceramic presence is not, like words, a "here," which points by convention to a "there"; its meaning and its presence cannot be separated. It arouses echoes by every aspect of its presence if the work is good. It is possible for a pot to succeed in evoking a cultural echo, say the grim majesty of Chinese Shang Dynasty bronzes, purely by a general resemblance, while, apart from that general look, its ceramic substance may offer no forms that cohere and make sense.

On the other hand, a triumphant pot may combine such a cultural echo with other resonances of reality, and maybe of other cultural phenomena, by means of the variety and coherence of its forms. It seems to me that one of the great bonuses of taking ceramics still to be congruent with pottery is that the basic pot concept can establish a kind of a priori unity for any ceramic work. And, in practice, a "purely sculptural" piece made of clays and glazes will carry with it echoes of its own substances and their traditional meanings.

Chapter 19

The Primal Vessel:
Explorations in History, Tradition, and Time

Garth Clark

Even in the most primitive of cultures one finds pots so exotic and stylized in their embellishment that we must accept that the idea of connoisseurship, of emphasizing the "art" of a pot, not only existed for thousands of years but existed in a manner of some sophistication. Such particular expression was no doubt codified through ritual use of pots into "academies" of taste as elaborate as our own. It is this desire to assume aesthetic responsibility (by both maker and viewer) and to refine a visual language that gives man one of his most direct and unconscious forms of communication.

Presented at *Echoes: Historical References in Contemporary Ceramics*, 1983, Kansas City

"Pottery" said Sir Herbert Read, "is the most indestructible of the arts." It is also one of the most elemental, traditionally a marriage of creative expression and our demands for human survival. Pottery form originally developed out of the human need to store and serve food; these two functions, one concerning access (open), the other an issue of protection (closed), resulted in the full range of pottery form. Even Peter Voulkos's most radical plates and stacked pots derive from this utilitarian root. Yet today, Voulkos, like most contemporary potters, works outside the

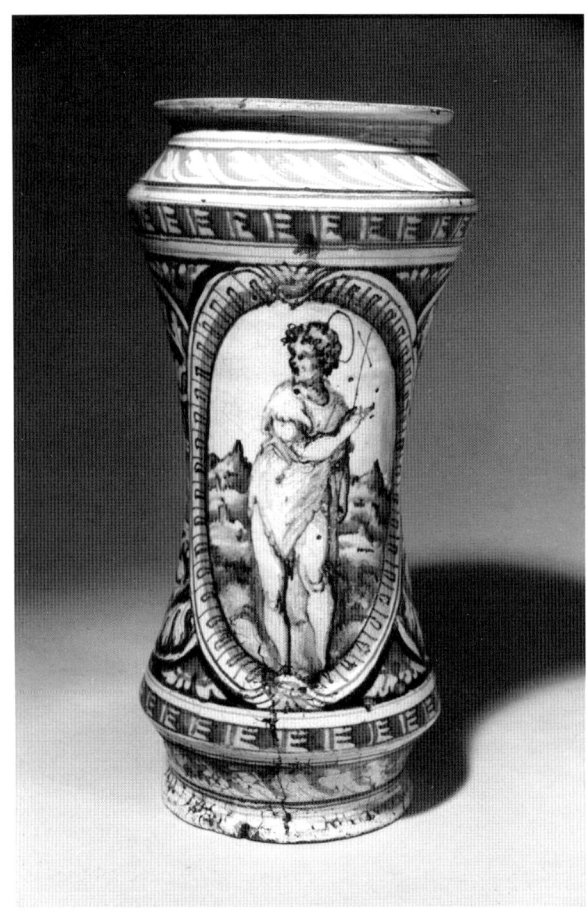

ITALIAN, *ALBARELLO FORM*, C. 1550-1570. EARTHENWARE (MAIJOLICA), 29.2 x 14.3 CM.

COLLECTION: SAN FRANSISCO MUSEUM OF ART. GIFT OF JAKOB GOLDSCHMIDT

actual constraints of functionalism. The issue of containment that primarily concerns potters is tied to the aesthetic notion of pure form expressed in the manipulation of volume.

While we acknowledge differences in intent between the makers of the historical and contemporary works shown here, there is nonetheless a strong commonality that binds them. Moreover, when placed together, a symbiosis takes place between the works, which offers greater access to the mystery of the vessel than if one were viewing either the historical or the contemporary as discrete groups. This is not to suggest that all the pots in this grouping covering the primal vessel were created under the same conditions or with the same goals. Indeed, there is a decided difference in the societal role between contemporary and ancient ceramists.

Contemporary potters are primarily university-educated artists working in a fine-art milieu. The ceramic works of the past, however, were made by individuals whose place in society varied from common artisan to slave. Young boys, undoubtedly under harsh conditions of forced labour, for instance, decorated Tzu Chou pottery. Farmers, brewers, or innkeepers, all of whom pursued the craft as a source of summer income, often produced early English pottery. Still other pieces from the nascent Industrial Revolution were created by what I term "corporate potters," a production line comprised of highly skilled artisans, each limited to the practice of one limited skill. It is unlikely that early potters produced their wares primarily for art's sake. In most cases the objects had to function effectively in daily use and were created in styles that were strictly prescribed by religious ritual or by the tastes of a ruling elite.

The works in the exhibition are further divided by periods ranging from two hundred to two thousand years of time and the attendant barriers of differing cultures. One may then ask, what is this commonality that binds this expansive chronology of works together? The common denominator is what I prefer to call "aesthetic responsibility." In the most utilitarian of works, we find certain touches of elaboration or refinement that instruct us that the potter was attempting to satisfy more than brute utility. In these often complex works, the potter was making aesthetic decisions, and thereby had the responsibility for beauty. The logical extension of this assumption is that there must also have been an audience for these visual statements.

Even in the most primitive of cultures, one finds pots so exotic and stylized in their embellishment that we must accept that the idea of connoisseurship, of emphasizing the "art" of a pot, not only existed for thousands of years but existed in a manner of some sophistication. Such particular expression was no doubt codified through ritual use of pots into "academies" of taste as elaborate as our own. It is this desire to assume aesthetic responsibility (by both maker and viewer) and to refine a visual language that gives man one of his most direct and unconscious forms of communication.

The premise of *Echoes* is that we can reach back thousands of years and touch a common response between a ceramist working then and one working today. However, it is obvious that only the most elemental aspects of the pot's creation reach us through the barriers of history. As Philip Rawson points out, in every culture there are layers and levels of symbolic coding that will always be opaque to those who were not brought up within that culture.

While there may be areas of reference that we will never pick up in other people's pots, "that is no reason for restraining ourselves from picking up any at all.... We are duty bound," says Rawson, "to feel for those [references] that can come across on the basis of our common human experience since visual art seems still to rest on a kind of onomatopoeia, the performance of acts that lie close to imitation."[1]

The next question is to ask exactly how we might begin to "pick up" on the works of the past, or for that matter, even those of today. Rawson suggests that, "our first approach to any ceramic work is made, I think, through body image." This view is reinforced by the fact that, in nearly every culture in which we have record of language, the pot is known by common anthropomorphic metaphors—neck, lip, mouth, belly, shoulder, and foot. "We tend," Rawson continues, "to judge the expression of a pot by the way it addresses us, body for body, and by the way we apprehend the posture it takes, as if it were another body."

But this should not be read too literally. One would not expect the virtue of each pot to rest on its imitation of human form; however, this pervasive suggestibility is always present in pottery as an underlying metaphor that brings a unique intimacy of contact between viewer and object. This "anatomical cartography" that connects the human body to the clay container has been one of our most universal, persistent forms of symbolic language.

In Nepal, when villagers reach the day before their hundredth birthday, they are placed in a vessel, which is then broken in a ritual, signifying rebirth. A thousand years ago the Mimbres Indians in the American Southwest buried their dead seated upright in a grave dug into the floor of their home with a bowl placed over the face of the deceased. A hole was knocked out of the bottom of the bowl so that the person's soul could escape from the corporeal world through that aperture into the realm of the spirits. Literature, from the Bible to *The Rubaiyat of Omar Khayyam*, is filled with the metaphor of the pot as man and the potter as God. The shaping of the vessel on the wheel in modern writings has taken different metaphors, according to Robert Browning, John Keats, and others. In their renditions, the spinning sphere or cylinder on the potter's wheel stands in as the rotating earth itself and signifies the destiny of all mankind.

Bernard Leach wrestled with "equivalency" in metaphor when he wrote in 1961 that the particular quality, which is fundamental in all convincing pots, is life in one or another of its modes: inner harmony, nobility, purity, strength, breadth,

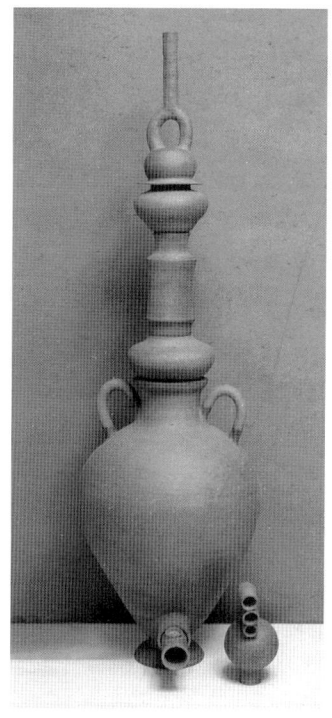

MICHAEL FRIMKESS, *MELTING POT*, 1975. STONEWARE, 134.6 × 45.7 × 40.6 CM.

COLLECTION: MR. AND MRS. JEROME NERMAN

PHOTO: GARY SUTTON

and generosity, or even exquisiteness or charm. "But it is one thing to make a list of the virtues of man and pot and another to interpret them in the counterpoint of convex and concave, hard and soft, growth and rest, for this is the breathing of the Universal in the particular."[2]

While all these metaphoric notions of the vessel expand our understanding and sensibilities, the visual quality of a pot is finally about one main issue, what Michael Cardew described so succinctly as "the majesty of form."[3] This concept is, of course, not new to art criticism. Cardew's notion of "absolute form" is similar to that which Clive Bell called "significant form." In his 1917 essay, Bell wrote:

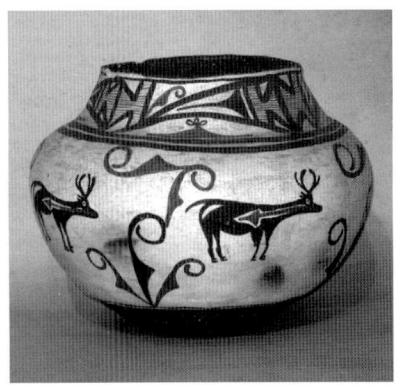

ZUNI INDIAN POT

That there is a particular kind of emotion provoked by works of visual art, and that this emotion is provoked by every kind of visual art, pictures, sculptures, buildings, pots, etc., etc., is not disputed, I think, by anyone capable of feeling it.... There must be some one quality without which a work of art cannot exist; possession of which, to the least degree, no work is altogether worthless.... In each, lines and colors combined in a particular way, certain forms and relations of forms, stir our aesthetic emotions. These relations and combinations...I call "Significant Form," the one common quality to all works of visual art.[4]

Another member of the Bloomsbury group, the influential art critic Roger Fry, also contributed to this debate by bringing another perspective to the discourse. His remarks seem all the more apropos because Fry worked as a self-taught potter for the Omega Workshops, which he directed in London from 1913 to 1918, and so he had a special love and respect for the medium. Fry suggests that just as the primal vessels of past and present are united by the absolute of form, so, too, are they connected by another abstract, aesthetic vision:

> Suppose for example, that we are looking at a Sung bowl; we apprehend gradually the shape of outside contour, the perfect sequence of the curves, and the subtle modifications of a certain type of curve; we also feel the relation of the concave surfaces of the inside to the outside contour; we realize that the precise thickness of the walls is consistent with the particular kind of matter of which it is made, its appearance of density and resistance; and finally we recognize, perhaps, how satisfactorily for the display of all these plastic qualities are the color and dull lustre of the glaze. We feel that all these sensually logical conformities are the outcome of a particular feeling, or of what, for want of a

better word, we call an idea; and we may even say that the pot is the expression of an idea in the artist's mind. Whether we are right or not in making this deduction, I believe that it nearly always occurs in such aesthetic appreciation. But in all, this no element of curiosity, no reference to actual life, comes in; our apprehension is unconditioned by considerations of space or time; it is irrelevant to us to know whether the bowl was made several hundred years ago in China or in New York yesterday. Such, then is the nature of the aesthetic vision...with which we contemplate works of art.

Fry admits that we may, at any point, switch from this aesthetic and become involved in "all sorts of quasi-biological feelings":

We may inquire whether it is genuine or not, whether it is worth the sum given for it, and so forth; but in proportion as we do this we change the focus of our vision; we are more likely to examine the bottom of the bowl for traces of [authenticity] than to look at the bowl itself.[5]

The difficulty with history, as it is currently taught, is that it would generally direct us to first establish authenticity. If the bowl then produces a surprise, a clay body used earlier than previously recorded or some other chronological phenomena, history would give that object inordinate importance. Fry's "aesthetic vision" would at best be a descriptive subnote. In a different manner, modern art criticism has the same pedantic considerations of "authenticity" in which novelty can be given greater significance than more substantial achievement.

For this reason, *Echoes* is not an exhibition of a conventional historical nature. Indeed, it is critical of the manner that history—and in particular, art history—has manipulated and rationalized time. Too often in art, we are caught up in Fry's "quasi-biological" interests, all held neatly in place by the picket fences of time and the rhythm of historic equations of decades, centuries, and millennia.

The rationalizing of time has an impact upon our perceptual mechanisms, because time is the matter of our consciousness. The more we accept the logical, ordered arrangement of traditional history, the less we ourselves are free to perceive and question. In many cases, art history suggests in words the answers to things that can, in fact, only be seen and felt. As a result, in the mistaken belief that we now have the answer, we neglect to look as closely as we should.

The most pointed criticism of this form of didactic history comes from scholar Jose Arguelles, who sees history as being what he terms "the playground of our forgetfulness"[6] in which the senses are decapitated, and the right-hemisphere functions of the psyche are banished. Arguelles argues that, through the combination of history, rationalism, and the printed word, art becomes "the by-product of criticism in which verbal wrangles [confirm] the emergence of the critic as the foreign minister of the sense organs."[7]

Echoes does not take as radical a stance as that of Arguelles, but there are areas of accord. The ceramist has a particularly acute understanding of what Arguelles means when he remarks that "to make history is to exert power." Until recently—ceramics and, more pointedly, the vessel maker—were denied a place in fine arts based upon modernist pedagogy. Frustrated by this rejection, "ceramic culture" set about trying to deny its past, by insistence upon an acceptance based on new (and misunderstood) modernist terms. In the process, traditional associations became immediately suspect (as they did in painting and sculpture as well, for other reasons). And yet, despite all these protestations by artists to disconnect from the past, tradition remains the sustaining force in all art, without which art is without context or basis of quality. Indeed, without tradition there cannot be innovation.

Acknowledging tradition does not mean, as some might automatically assume, an abdication of avant-garde progressiveness. Nor does it suggest an alliance with an anachronistic craft ghetto. After all, one of the supreme traditionalists was Pablo Picasso. Few artists have drawn more successfully or with greater innovation from the past than this master. In the same sense, Voulkos, Viola Frey, and others of the great innovators in ceramic art, are also traditionalists.

The problem is not with tradition but with semantics. Tradition is understood by many contemporary artists and writers to be synonymous with anachronism. Yet Michael Cardew asserts, on a point of definition, that only an innovative artist can be viewed as a traditionalist. The others, who mimic art of the past, "are really the traitors of tradition.... They murder it in order to be able to take measurements of the corpse."[8]

Artists have at various times written about this issue and insisted upon its inevitability and importance. In the words of William Blake, an artist "must drive horse and cart over the bones of the dead," while T. S. Eliot said that no artist or poet has his significance alone but that his appreciation is based upon all the dead artists and poets who preceded him. What both Blake and Eliot suggest is not that artists should be historians, but that they should be ready to absorb and then grow from that which they inherit. As such, tradition is a natural cycle wherein death facilitates the continuity of life.

The Zen view of tradition is even more emphatic: without a golden cord of connection with the collective past, all actions are random and meaningless. This is explained by the Japanese crafts philosopher, Soetsu Yanagi, who sees tradition in the Buddhist sense of a "given power," an aggregate power that transcends the individual, "the accumulation of all the experiences and wisdom of generations."[9] Yanagi notes that tradition never asks who is enlisting its help. Nor, by implication, would it then question what the individual seeks to do with this resource.

Tradition does not dictate the next step the artist may take. What it usually does dictate is that point from which the artist steps forward. Nor does it inhibit avant-garde expression. The conventions and moribund academies that we wrongly associate with traditionalism are not reflections of this "given power," they represent man's imprisonment of it.

If *Echoes* has been successful, it will be resonant with tradition, and so with growth and renewal. In these primal vessels, unconcerned as they are with literal imagery or intellectual symbolism, we can see this tradition vibrating with life, from the rugged Shigaraki storage vessels to the plates and pots of Voulkos, with which they correspond. We see the same refinement and articulation of formal elements in the vessel of Sung pottery as in those by Bob Turner and Richard DeVore, even though a difference in culture is apparent. The drama and color of Elsa Rady's bowls are echoed in the regal Kang Hsi monochromes. In the process of recognizing these echoes, our eye and mind play games with time and our concept of the contemporary. Rick Hirsch's tripod vessels seem to carry more of a sense of antiquity than their counterparts from western Mexico circa 200 BC. Ancient pots seem startlingly modern; contemporary works seem stridently ancient.

In this context, George Kubler, writing in *The Shape of Time*, remarks that a pleasure shared by artists, collectors, and historians alike is the discovery that "an old and interesting work of art is not unique, but that its type exists in a variety of examples spread early and late in time, in versions that are antetypes and derivatives, originals and copies, transformations and variants." Kubler sees the common thread in these works as being different solutions to a common problem and "as linked solutions accumulate, the contours of a quest by several persons are disclosed, a quest in search of forms enlarging the domain of aesthetic discourse."[10] This view was enlarged upon in his writings on formal sequences and the concept of linked solutions:

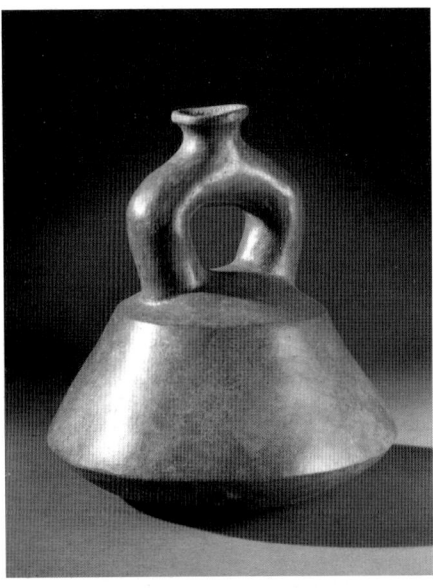

MEXICAN; TLATILCO, *STIRRUP SPOUT FORM*, C. 1000-500 BC. PAINTED EARTHENWARE. COLLECTION/PHOTO: SAINT LOUIS ART MUSEUM. GIFT OF MORTON D. MAY

Every important work of art can be regarded both as a historical event and as a hard won solution to some problem. It is irrelevant now whether the event was original or conventional, accidental or willed, awkward or skillful. The important clue is that any solution points to the existence of some problem to which there have been other solutions, and that other solutions to this same problem will most likely be invented to follow the one now in view. As solutions accumulate the problem alters. The chain of solutions nevertheless discloses the problem.[11]

This grouping comprised of the primal vessel (and indeed the other three divisions in the exhibition) should be viewed as a specific visual "problem," and the works themselves as chains of linked "solutions." Time does not matter in the conventional sense of a material culture. Time now takes on a more immediate presence in a history of like things. The works are not separated by years, by value, or by rarity, but simply by the differences in visual solutions. This does not mean that time has no place in this context; the echoes of the primal vessel are partly movements in time and space. But more importantly, these pots are echoes of content and meaning, rebounding against the same walls of tradition that have inspired the potter for over seven thousand years.

These walls of tradition are tangible in every aspect of the arts and not just pottery. Without them there would be nothing to bounce back against, no measure of time, space, or quality, no foundation for innovation. Although writing about modern painting, Clement Greenberg makes the same point: "I cannot insist enough that Modernism has never meant anything like a break with the past.... It may mean a devolution, an unraveling of anterior tradition, but it also means continuity.... Nothing could be further from the authentic art of our time than the idea of a rupture of continuity."[12] Art, Greenberg argues, is continuity, and it is to this notion that the primal vessel and the exhibition *Ceramic Echoes* is dedicated.[13]

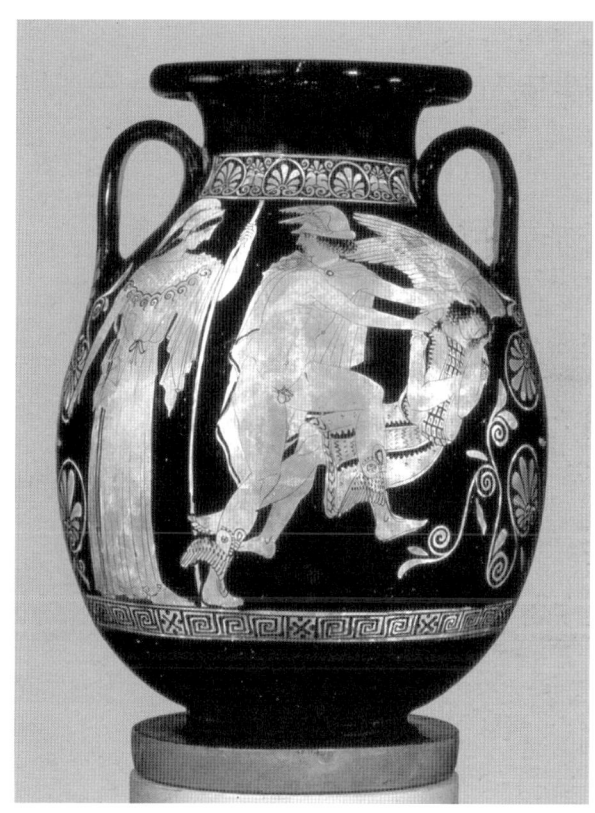

GREEK, ATTR. TO POLYGNOTOS, *ATTIC, RED FIGURE STORAGE JAR (PELIKE): PERSEUS ABOUT TO KILL THE SLEEPING MEDUSA,* C.450-440 BC. EARTHENWARE WITH SLIP, 46.0 CM.

PHOTO: ROSENTHAL ART SLIDES

1. Philip Rawson, "Analogy and Metaphor in Ceramic Art" in Garth Clark, ed., *Ceramics and Modernism: The Response of Artist, Craftsman, Designer and Architect* (New York: Institute for Ceramic History, 1982), 37.

2. Bernard Leach, "Belief and Hope," in Garth Clark, ed., *Ceramic Art: Comment and Review 1882-1977* (New York: E.P. Dutton, 1978), 88. (This essay was originally published in, *Bernard Leach: 50 Years of Pottery* [London: British Arts Council, 1961], and subsequently in a pamphlet issued by the St. Ives Town Council.)

3. Michael Cardew, "Why Make Pots in the Last Quarter of the 20th Century?" *Studio Potter* 7 No.1 (1978): 47-48.

4. Clive Bell, *Art* (New York: P. Smith, 1947), 17-18.

5. Roger Fry, *Vision and Design* (London: Chatto and Winders, 1920), 34-35.

6. Jose A. Arguelles, *The Transformative Vision* (Berkeley, CA: Shambhala, 1975), 54.

7. Arguelles, 61.

8. Michael Cardew in "Cardew at 75," *Tactile* (Spring 1975), 5.

9. Soetsu Yanagi, "The Buddhist Ideas of Beauty," in Garth Clark, ed., *Ceramic Art: Comment and Review 1882-1977* (New York: E. P. Dutton, 1978), 127. Originally published in *The Unknown Craftsman* (Tokyo: Kodansha, 1972), this is an adaptation by Bernard Leach of Yanagi's writings.

10. George Kubler, *The Shape of Time: Remarks on the History of Things* (London and New Haven, CT: Yale University Press, 1962), 45.

11. Kubler, 33.

12. Clement Greenberg, "Modernist Painting," *Art and Literature* 4 (Spring 1965): 75, 77.

13. I would like to thank Ed Lebow for assistance in this essay, Charles Fiske for being an unseen but constant presence and Walter Ostrom for directing me to Heather Dawkins's unpublished manuscript, "From the Ground of Daily Experience," which I found very helpful in organizing early thoughts for the essay. My special thanks to a tireless Sherry Cromwell-Lacy for assistance in the proofing and assembly of this catalogue, and to Ken Ferguson for his role as consultant to *Echoes*. Lastly, I dedicate this essay to John Hoffman for his crucial role in putting *Ceramic Echoes* on the road, and his patient and constant encouragement.

CHAPTER 20

THE USE OF CERAMICS HISTORY IN CONTEMPORARY CERAMICS

LÉOPOLD L. FOULEM

Ceramics has valid, specific, significant idiosyncrasies. There is no universal art vocabulary. Not only is there no universal language for discourse about art, but also, some concepts and words are non-existent or even mean something entirely different in either group. Is Paul Mathieu's recent Garniture *site specific, or is it an installation? Some late-modernist concepts such as allover, drip, site specific, and installation, to name but a few, have been a part of the ceramic tradition long before becoming mainstream, avant-garde concepts.*

Presented at *History and Its Role in Contemporary Ceramic Art Criticism, Scholarship, Education*, 1993, Syracuse

When I was asked to speak at the Seventh International Ceramics Symposium, I was informed that the theme for this year's event was the use of ceramic history in contemporary ceramic art. Tom Piché mentioned to me that my role was to present this theme from an artist's view.

There are many venues I could have chosen to discuss this pertinent topic. The difficulty was not, I must say, the scarcity of material to debate such a theme but to decide which path I would pursue. Since the given time was short, extensive research was impossible. Considering the point of view I was to address, I felt that it would be appropriate to focus on some ceramic pieces by four Montreal artists now exhibiting in the galleries of the Everson Museum of Art: Jeannot Blackburn, Paul Mathieu, Richard Milette, and myself. I hope that you will have no objection to the showing of a few examples of my own work in this context.

As awkward as this may sound as a preamble, I must say at once that I believe that most vessels are about history or about tradition and that tradition, also deals with history. Therefore, any ceramic container could have been selected for inclusion in this presentation. However, I intend to concentrate, in the short time that is allotted, on ceramics that are overtly concerned with historical precedents within the generic group. These borrowings could be either at the formal or conceptual levels. Thus, in the selected vessels I have chosen to present, ceramic history is used as concept or as content.

Ceramics has valid, specific, significant idiosyncrasies. There is no universal art vocabulary. Not only is there no universal language for discourse about art, but also, some concepts and words are non-existent, or even mean something entirely different in either group. Is Paul Mathieu's recent *Garniture* site specific or is it an installation? Some late-modernist concepts, such as allover, drip, site-specific, and installation, to name but a few, have been a part of the ceramic tradition long before becoming mainstream, avant-garde concepts. A place setting or *garniture* is literally site specific; and a druggist's cabinet full of Majolica jars, like that of the Fombeure Collection in the Sèvres Museum is, at first glance, an installation.

Perhaps one may think that such allegations are farfetched because traditional linear backgrounds in art history have prepared one to think in linear, lateral terms. Nonetheless, I postulate that the holistic knowledge of cultural history within each specific group is crucial to the evaluation of an art object, and that formal or conceptual breakthroughs can then only be recognized and acknowledged within that genre. Otherwise there is simply "no avant-garde in sight."

The four Québécois ceramists at the Everson Museum share more than simply a city or a Canadian province to link them as a group. At one time or another, they were associated with the now-defunct ceramic department of the Cégep du Vieux Montréal.

However the most important factors which group our works together are the pervasive use of the vessel as format for artistic expression and the unfaltering conviction that ceramics per se is a valid generic group. Richard Milette's 1993 *Blue and White Teapot* acknowledges not only the long-standing tradition of this type of

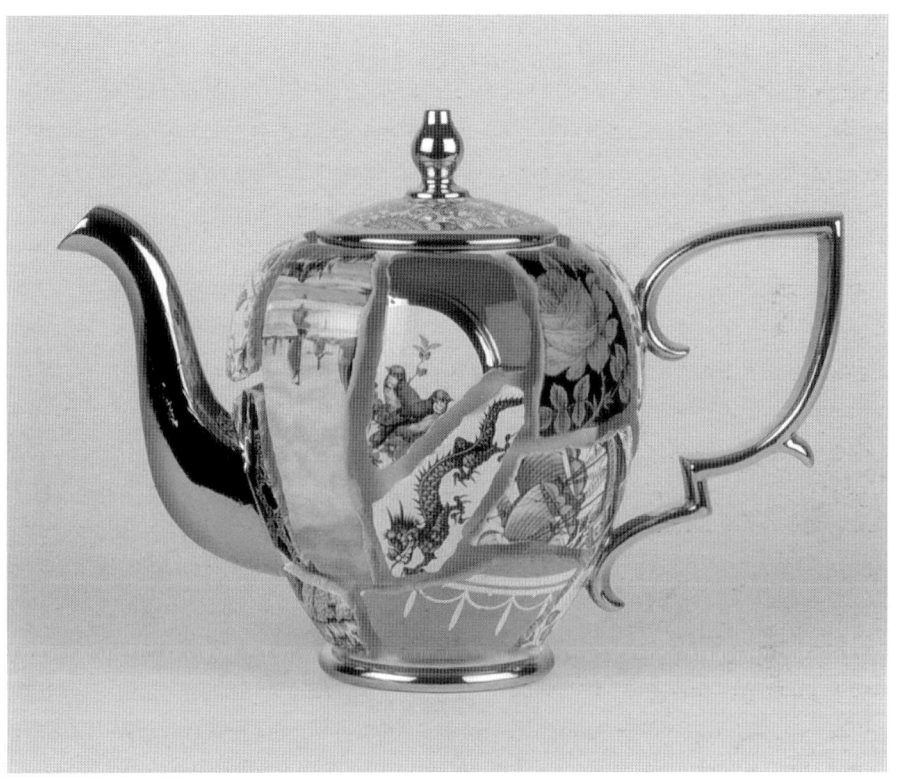

RICHARD MILETTE, *TEAPOT*, 1993. CERAMIC, 22.0 × 32.0 × 17 CM.

PHOTO: RAYMONDE BERGERON

decorative surface throughout the history of ceramics but also contextualizes mnemonic shards as independent time sequences and artifacts. His use of a stereotypical teapot of English origin becomes a silhouette for the history of styles and, by extension, an homage to man's ingenuity. The tangible segregation between the white ground and the polychrome surfaces can be seen as an affirmation of the separation between form and surface, or the volumetric and the pictorial within this generic group. With this teapot, Milette does not reinterpret, nor even mock, the blue-and-white tradition, as was the case with southern California artists Michael and Magdalena Frimkess, in their undated blue-and-white pseudo-Chinese vase *Rouleau*.

Here the teapot is made up of historical ceramic surfaces, the blue-and-white vase is essentially dealing with the narrative of the surface, contextualized by a specific Chinese shape. The major conceptual differences between the teapot and the vase is that the latter is about artistic input and the significance of the narrative in the interpretation of the object; Milette's teapot is about ceramic as concept and content.

There are innumerable ways for artists to draw upon the huge historical and archeological pool offered by ceramics. Take, for example, New York City ceramic artist Matt Nolen's *Apothecary Jar*, a porcelain vessel of 1992. Here the artist uses a stereotypical vase, an apothecary urn, modifies slightly the type, and uses the surface as a billboard for a political narrative about the futility of the pursuit of stereotypical physical beauty. On one side of the lidded container is the image of a woman who has had breast surgery, and on the opposite side, the image of a man who has had muscle implants. The narrative is expanded outside the regular pictorial format by the addition of surgical scalpels on both sides of the jar. On top of the lid there are wonderful collagen lips showing off dental implants. Another type of borrowing at the narrative level can be illustrated by using Jeannot Blackburn's 1980 teapot depicting a fifties beauty queen. Other prototypes could have been used as examples, such as the old-lady-in-the-shoe teapot (now on the screen) by the English manufacturer Sadler. From this theme Blackburn has made, throughout the years, a few series of teapots. In 1987 there was his bride teapot series, where the figural element underwent a prenuptial sex change. In this series, there is not only a drastic change of imagery but also a pledge for a shift in cultural values.

The figural lid, once a fifties prom queen, is now a postmodern drag queen

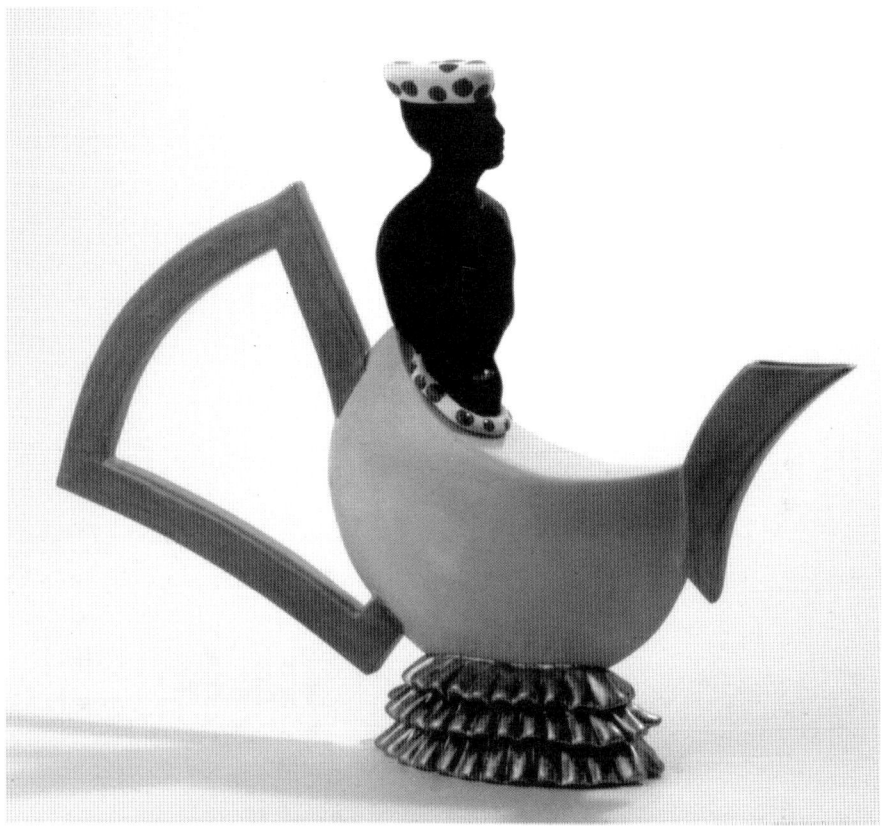

JEANNOT BLACKBURN, *BRIDE TEAPOT*, 1987. EARTHENWARE.
PHOTO: HUNO

coming out. The skinny black silhouette of an emasculated male-Venus torso replaces those stereotypical woman-Venus cherub finials of countless ceramic vases. The male in this situation becomes a domestic accessory, an object of contemplation and manipulation in a tactile sense. Yes, there is recurring homosexual imagery in the works of these four artists. Richard Milette, too, appropriates a prototypical vessel. Here the artist has combined a pre-Columbian stirrup vase with a twentieth-century popular icon, Mickey Mouse, to achieve a highly potent politically charged image. This vessel was part of a series made for five-person exhibition called *Gayramics* held at Lieu Ouest Gallery in Montreal last June. Four of these ceramists are featured in the *Quebecers* exhibition now at the museum. In this group of pouring vessels, Milette has transformed Mickey Mouse, a symbol of innocence, into an aggressive drag queen. In so doing, the artist alludes to the highly commercial aspect of mass culture. He also pays homage to Jeff Koons's famous, sexless, stainless-steel *Rabbit* of 1986.

In the same category of politically incorrect works, I should include my own *Rhyton* from *The Tropics*, a 1983 ceramic and found-object drinking vessel. This ceramic vessel was inspired by the ancient container form the *rhyton*. The work is taken from a one-person exhibition entitled *Are They Laughing at My Rhytons?* In this series of objects, concepts take precedence over the anecdotal, and the trivial becomes sublime by the disengagement of all sentimental or vernacular relationships. The utilization of an idealized penis as the main formal element has no other reason than to render more unusual the situation of the object.

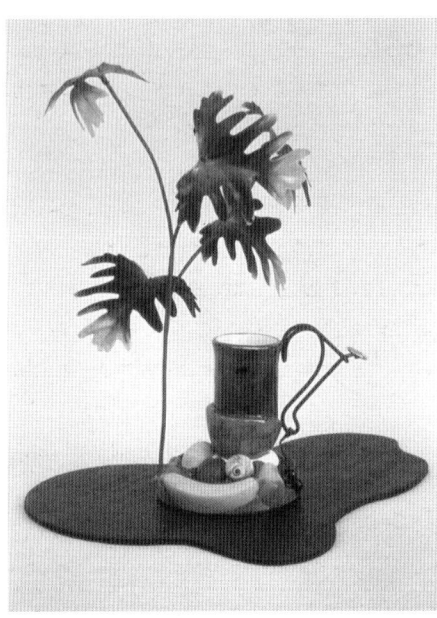

LÉOPOLD L. FOULEM, *RHYTON FROM THE TROPICS*, 1983. CERAMIC, FOUND OBJECTS, 35.5 × 28.0 × 34.5 CM.

PHOTO: RICHARD MILETTE

In using an image so full of prejudices, the penis was not meant to deal more with matters of sexuality, any more than, say, an image of a house is about architecture. The signifier is not equal to the signified. In this other view, you can see that the *rhyton* can most definitely be used as a functional drinking vessel. However, to do so, the user has to experience a tactile relationship with this idealized penis.

The settings for this series of works are parodies of the European fetish of mounting precious oriental porcelain in metal contraptions. As an example of this fashion, I will juxtapose the image of an undated porcelain potpourri vessel in ormoulu mount. Notice the elaborate composite decor for setting off the rare, *sang de boeuf* covered porcelain vessel. Found Oriental celadon birds are used as tripod;

porcelain flowers (probably Vincennes) are added to the eccentric, flamboyant set, with the definite intention of enhancing the preciousness of the object.

In *L'égnime de l'être*, a 1990 monochromatic porcelain covered tureen with platter, Paul Mathieu demonstrates his knowledge of ceramic history. Numerous historical references span many centuries and continents. The artist borrows from eighteenth-century French pottery, such as the well-known, *trompe l'oeil* Niderviller surfaces as shown on the porringer and tray from the collection of Musée de Cluny. He also borrows from the black-and-white pictorial traditions of China and America, and the painterly floral surfaces of Japanese potter, Ogata Kenzan, and also from photography as process and genre.

Mathieu's *Tureen* is a most complex object. A knowledge of ceramic history adds a major dimension to the complete understanding of its significance.

The black-and-white pictorial field acknowledges the two-dimensional vessel surface (the term vessel, in this case, to be understood as an all-inclusive term). By equating black and white with photography, and photography with flatness, the artist questions the veracity of a pictorial representation of volumetric form. Also inferred is the common practice of publishing black-and-white illustrations of polychromatic art objects.

If one looks closely at the Niderviller porringer and tray, one notices, pinned on the surface, three monochromatic landscapes. On the contemporary porcelain vessel, Mathieu has substituted these landscapes for black-and-white photographs of a male nude, rendered in *trompe l'oeil*. He thus shifts the focus of the narrative surface to imply a reverse reading of the object. By replacing the monochromatic landscapes by a series of stereotypically flat images and by painting the vessel as a continuous panoramic landscape, Mathieu suggests a literal transposition of the inside/outside relationships either at the narrative or formal levels, the final result being a nude in a landscape to be interpreted as a metaphor for high art. This male nude is a sexually explicit image; and the photography, by being hand painted, reveals the subversive nature of this innocent tureen.

It is a very different political statement that New York artist Cindy Sherman makes with her original *Madame de Pompadour Soup Tureen with Accompanying Platter*, edited in 1990 by Artes Magnus. Very few twentieth-century high art artists have made such significant contributions to the history of ceramics. Sherman's tureen is a notable exception. Most painters and sculptors who have dabbled in clay in this century did not understand the conceptual aspect of ceramics nor use the specificity of a generic group as formal premise. Sherman does not utilize the volumetric vessel as an anonymous black background for decoration, as so many of her predecessors have done. She respectfully appropriates the concept, borrows heavily upon historical precedent while commenting on the history of taste.

What is so intellectually exciting about her vessel is the effective desynchronization of concepts. As in the case of Paul Mathieu's *L'énigme de l'être*, the full extent of the formal relevance of the objects resides in the correct contextualization and the adequate knowledge of the idiosyncrasies proper to ceramics.

Cindy Sherman's decision to add a photographic transfer of herself as Madame de Pompadour on a rose Pompadour vessel is most fitting and yet, at the same time, both sacreligious and satirical. The negation of the uniqueness of painted vignettes adorning original Sèvres vessels, the use of a clichéd Sèvres prototype as a ready-made, the acknowledgement of mechanical production in decorative processes, the commodification of the rare and precious object, all make this remarkable *Soup Tureen with Accompanying Platter* a truly significant postmodern artifact.

As if this dynamic mélange was not enough, consider the linear, decorative elements employed. They are not the traditional, gilded sprays of flowers but, instead, are made up of countless little fish, little *poissons*. As we know, Madame de Pompadour's maiden name was Poisson. Jeanne Antoinette Poisson, marquise de Pompadour was Louis XV's mistress. She was a patron of the arts, and it is her influence which was decisive in getting the King of France interested in the Sèvres porcelain factory.

My *Shallow Tureen with Metal Stand*, a ceramic and found object piece, illustrates another conceptual approach to the type. More analytical and cerebral than my polychrome *Rhyton* discussed earlier, this covered vessel again uses, with irony, one of the same major historical citations, which is the European practice of mounting oriental porcelain in precious or semiprecious metals. Whereas the *Rhyton* series had a flamboyant and quirky allure, the series from which this tureen is taken is more austere and minimal.

The usual way in which precious ceramics were mounted was to bring the vessel to a *marchand-mercier*, who was responsible for having the mount fabricated by a bronze caster and then gilded by a *doreur*. In this *Shallow Tureen with Metal*

Stand, there is a shift of intent and a change in focus. In this case, I found the readymade, recycled the found objects, and made a ceramic form to fit the metal armature. The metal frames became domestic sites. The volumetric vessel not only turned into an image of itself—because the normal function of the container was annihilated—but also became a visual, generic stereotype of that other vessel that is now lost. The black and pitted surface covering the fictional covered container allude to vestigial remains of charred objects.

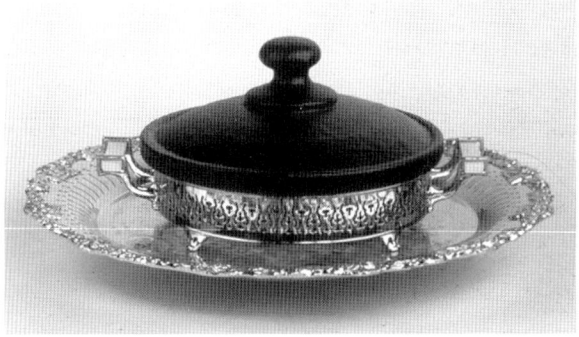

LÉOPOLD L. FOULEM, *COVERED SHALLOW TUREEN WITH METAL STAND*, 1991. CERAMIC, FOUND OBJECTS, 13.4 × 38.5 CM.
PHOTO: HUNO

Where Cindy Sherman utilized a typical Sèvres tureen to stress the genre, I used the genre as concept. An important stylistic feature of all the tureens considered in this lecture is to be found in the trays on which the vessels rest. The ubiquitous components can become very prominent attributes, as shown in this eighteenth-century *Silver Tureen* by J.N. Roettiers, in the collection of the Metropolitan Museum of Art. My *Tureen with Metal Stand* exploits this characteristic as a major component of the object. The tray is seen and used as a plinth or a pedestal to give more importance to the covered container.

Paul Mathieu's *Crucifixion Bowl* of 1984 borrows this feature to create a setting for his thrown porcelain vessel. As is the case for all this artist's work, layered and complex sets of historical citations are present. The shape of the vessel is a contemporary variation of Ogata Kenzan's *Bowl With Peony Design*. The eighteenth-century Japanese polychrome bowl is a prime key to the interpretation of this Montrealer's oeuvre. Let us recall Mathieu's large black-and-white tureen shown earlier in this presentation. The edges were cut out according to the outline of the floral motifs, similar to Kenzan's rim of the vessel presently on the screen.

The cut-out rim of the *Crucifixion Bowl* (part of a series) should not be seen as a decorative element but as an artistic endeavour in an ironic sense. The cut-out volumetric form is intended as a clear metaphor for abstract sculpture, a mainstream art commodity codified by Mathieu simply as an eccentric form with a hole through it. The proper prototype can be found in the sculpture of British artist Barbara Hepworth.

On the well of the bowl, Paul Mathieu has affixed a monochromatic self-portrait decal of the artist as crucified victim. This crucifixion is also a poignant visual metaphor for the ostracization of the so-called "decorative-art object" in the contemporary art milieu by the mainstream art establishment. It is the victimization of the media-based artists.

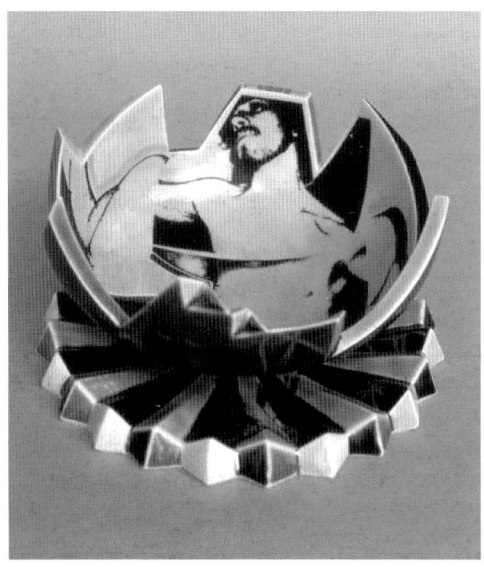

PAUL MATHIEU, *CRUCIFIXION BOWL "MÈRE ANGÉLIQUE,"* 1984. PORCELAIN, 15.0 × 30.0 CM.
PHOTO: PAUL MATHIEU

The dissected figure overlaps on to the side of the bowl, making the whole surface a single pictorial field and, by extension, equating surface with painting. By establishing a clear separation between sculpture as genre and painting as genre, and by juxtaposing these facts as no more than components for a decorative art object, Paul Mathieu affirms the complexity and independence of the vessel as concept. In so doing, he demonstrates that surface and form are autonomous concepts and that it is erroneous to treat them simply as painting or just as sculpture.

From Richard Milette's series *Museum Quality Pieces*—ironically all broken vases—I have selected an eloquent example to focus on his comments about the relativity of official art and its phobias. It is *Hydria 13 – 6294 with Apollo Temple IV*, a work created in 1991. On the belly of *Greek vase 13-6294* is substituted an image of Roy Lichtenstein's *Apollo Temple IV*, a 1964 painting.

The Greek prototype chosen by Milette for this series is a true-to-life *hydria*, a generic, stereotypical form used because of its perverse association with art museums and, more accurately, with the study of Greek painting. It is common knowledge that the study of Greek painting from the classical period implies the scrutiny and evaluation of pictorial representation on now useless pottery forms. However, what is ignored is the contradiction which exists when fifth-century BC fired surfaces are glorified as painting by intellectuals and by the art establishments, while major twentieth-century works, such as Picasso's, Matisse's and Duffy's painted pots, are excluded as modern painting.

By using faux-Greek, pseudo-restored pots and by substituting the painted narrative of the originals with a well-known contemporary easel painting, Richard Milette accentuates the contradictions of accepting painted Greek vase ceramic surfaces as high art and categorizing ceramics, per se, as decorative art. While Paul Mathieu established the autonomy of the surface and of the support, Milette, in his *Museum Quality Pieces*, admits their separateness.

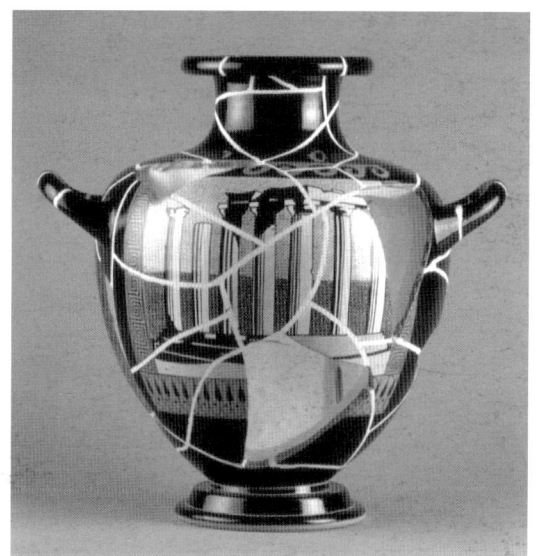

RICHARD MILETTE, *HYDRIA 13-6294 WITH APOLLO TEMPLE IV*, 1991. EARTHENWARE, PLASTER, 39.3 x 41.0 x 30.7 CM.
PHOTO: HUNO

Not only does the youngest member of this Montréal group focus on the inherent formal dichotomy of ceramic vessels, but he also emphasizes the desynchronization of the antique and the contemporary as content and as context. Whereas Cindy Sherman appropriated a Sèvres tureen as a support and then affixed her disguise as decoration on the surface, making a statement about herself as artist and Sèvres, the type, Milette utilizes the Greek vase as metaphor for all vessels and painting as a surrogate for art history.

What is particularly significant in the Sèvres approach to vessel is the distance which exists between the designer of the form and the group of makers involved in their production. A Sèvres porcelain vessel, as product, is the total of many independent steps made by a number of specialized individuals. A Sèvres object is never a craft object! It is this major conceptual difference that Richard Milette exploits in his *Vases à boulons with Leather Garlands*. Not only are these contemporary vases about Sèvres porcelain as a type, they also refer to a very precise production period in the Royal Factory of Sèvres; those soft-paste vases were made during the reign of Louis XV. The *fond vert* and *fond rose* of these objects are typical period colour combinations. The shape was appropriated from the Sèvres repertoire. Sèvres is seen here as a type of stereotypical, bourgeois collectible.

At the structural level the vases *à boulons* (listed as such in the factory inventory) and the other vases from this series, are reminiscent of the blue-and-white teapot discussed at the beginning of this lecture. The shards are individually hand made, neither imitations nor reproductions. Really, they are faux shards.

These highly decorative, soft-paste vases made at Sèvres were time consuming, rare, and expensive, and represented a type of goods comprising but a minute portion of the whole factory production. They were meant to be used for decorative purposes only. It is just this decorative aspect that Richard Milette wanted to emphasize by negating the possible function of such a ceramic vessel. The openings of his vases have been physically blocked, then glazed black to nevertheless affirm the volumetric. Negating the functional aspect of these vases decontextualizes them as containers by actually making them three-dimensional images of themselves.

The sexual narrative of this pair of vases is not to be overlooked, especially not here today. Gone are the pastoral landscapes with candid shepherdesses and other truly insipid, heterosexual erotic scenes, such as on this eighteenth-century *vases à garlands* with dark green ground from the Wallace Collection. On the white reverse of this vase, to the right side, a bare-breasted, titillating Venus is "giving arms" to a half-naked stud. The artist displaces covert eroticism with blatant sadomasochistic symbolism. In Milette's series the conventional silk, tassels, ribbons, and flower garlands have been replaced by leather, metal, and studs. This displacement has two avowed purposes. One is to stress the fetishism involved with the materiality and hierarchy of precious objects, and the second is to ridicule the stereotypical right-wing rhetoric of equating S&M with perverse, unnatural, homosexual sex.

It is no coincidence that Milette intended this series of vessels as memorial urns for AIDS victims. Whereas many original Sèvres vases were made for the court and the moneyed elite, these contemporary artifacts could have been made for the "queens" who lost their lives to the frightening HIV virus. The drastic shift in suggested cultural values, the decommodification of Sèvres as a status symbol, the mocking of the narrative, and the exploitation of the decorative as something political, and especially the negation of the "craftness" of the hand-made vessel, make such vases as his highly subversive objects.

In my 1986 *Gold Teapot with Yellow Spout*, I also used the hierarchy of materials as concept. My approach, being less literal, was more abstract than that of Richard Milette's Sèvres vases; whereas Milette questions the hierarchy of material within a ceramic context, I addressed this very issue in a broader cultural sense. This gold teapot is a synthesis of many formal preoccupations manifested in earlier series.

One predominant conceptual imperative was exploited in a 1982 one-person exhibition held in Toronto at Prime Canadian Crafts. This solo exhibition was called *Matter Doesn't Matter*. Collapsing forms, like the *Uprooted Root* on the screen, were lavishly covered in shiny gold luster, in order to confront the viewer's response to the materiality of the object. The premise was that, dependent upon the status of the material, the reaction to a sculptural form would differ entirely. For example, a bronze classification would unquestionably give the object a de facto fine-art-sculpture status, which would then imply another set of values in analyzing the object's significance. Thus the gold surface of these artifacts negates their clay materiality and therefore puts forth a really troubling conceptual peculiarity.

The yellow spout on this teapot is true plastic; the lid is a recycled metal part, and the twig handle is real wood. The *trompe l'oeil* in this vessel is the gold surface. Admittedly, it is an unusual twist, but because of the contextuality of the teapot and of the *Uprooted Root*, it is indeed *trompe l'oeil*. Not only has the "clayness" of the teapot been impudently negated but also the functional aspect of the container has been annihilated by the piercing of a structural hole through the form. The teapot is about teapots, not about function. This artistic vandalism also accentuates the decontextualization of the artifact.

Yes, again, here is that reference to the historical precedent of mounting rare porcelain in precious and semi-precious metal mounts. The mission of this ancient ritual, as previously pointed out, was to render even more precious the porcelain object. Here, the found parts modify our cultural perception of the domestic vessel by shifting the focus from the collectible as commodity to the object as concept.

The category of ceramic prototypes from which Jeannot Blackburn appropriates some of his formal ancestors is quite different from the broader, general, historical pool of his three colleagues. Jeannot sees ceramic history through a distinct prism. Whereas Mathieu, Milette, and I refer mostly to "classical" historical precedents within the ceramic tradition, Blackburn alludes to singular, recent, kitsch ceramic.

The distance between Blackburn's *Lady Vase* of 1981 and the anonymous *Lady Head Vases* on the screen is not so far as that which separates the other Quebecers from their references. It is much closer, in the literal sense, because the era when the lady head vases were manufactured, and the time of artistic interpretation of his figural vase, were not too far apart; and also, in the cultural sense, because the lady head vases are banal types of ceramics, easily found in one's own neighborhood or even around the house.

The tall, anthropomorphic flower vase depicts a high-camp Venus dressed in a black-and-white polka dot "Diorish" outfit. The black pill-box hat can be "flowered" by inserting a bouquet through the opening on top. Blackburn's vessel is about the vagaries of taste and the recognition of a notion of class distinction within ceramics.

This polarization of aesthetic extremes within the genre can be visually established by juxtaposing the *Lady Head Vases* with Richard Milette's vases discussed today, or even Paul Mathieu's *Garniture* at the Everson Museum of Art. Ceramics is much more than the "world's most fascinating hobby." The range of eloquent, creative possibilities between these two antipodes, the secular and the sublime, are innumerable.

In conclusion, I have discussed only briefly the overt use of ceramic history by a few ceramic artists from Montréal. At the beginning of my exposé, I showed you one view of Mathieu's *Garniture* (now you have the other side on the screen) without commenting on the complexity of the conceptual content. I also wanted to establish as a fact that an object can be appreciated and collected, solely as an artifact, for its aesthetic qualities recognized mostly on an intuitive approach. This *Garniture* and, as a matter of fact, all the ceramics discussed in this lecture are far more significant when properly contextualized. Ceramic history is basic literacy.

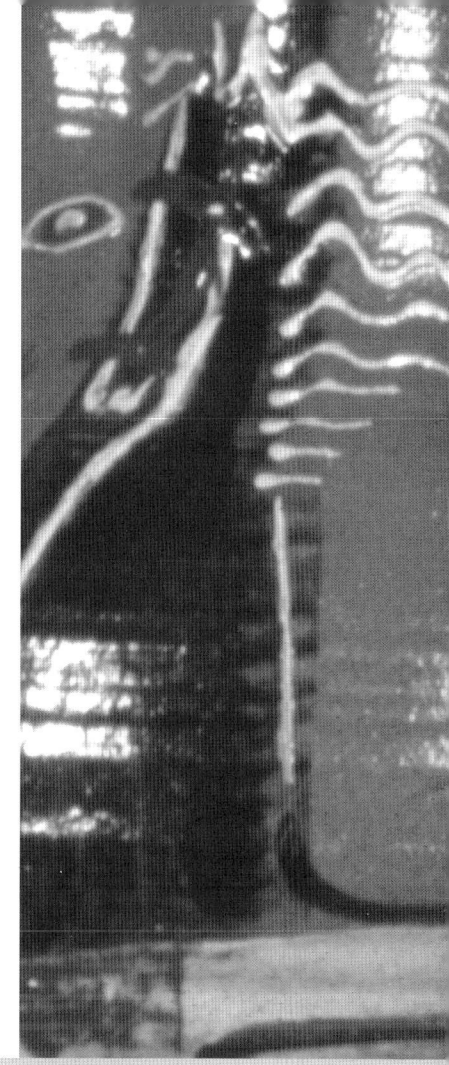

SECTION SIX
EDUCATION

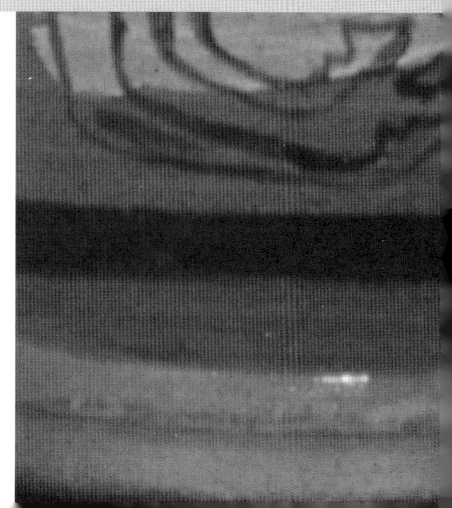

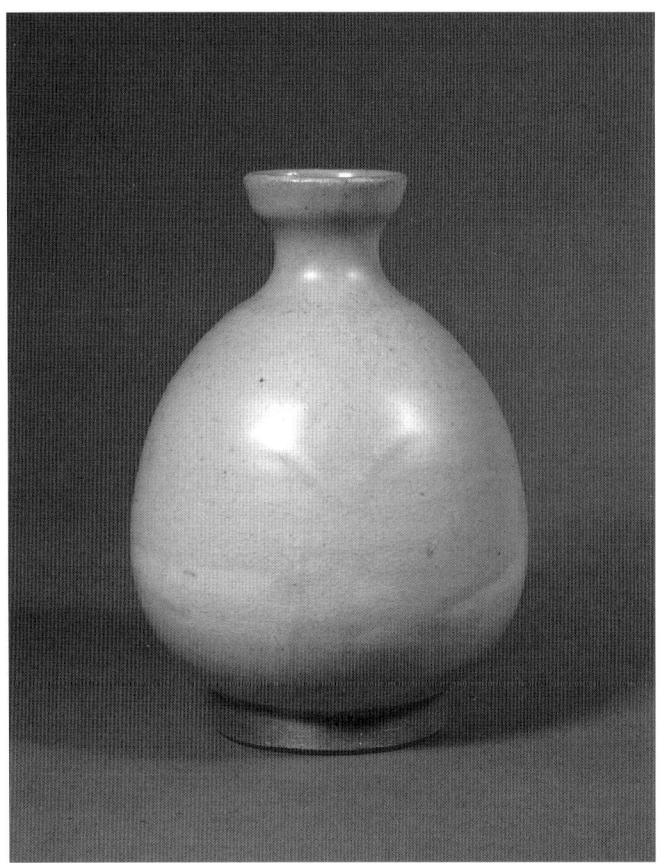

BERNARD LEACH, *VASE*, C. 1946. STONEWARE, 24.0 CM.
COLLECTION/PHOTO: CERAMIC ARTS FOUNDATION

CHAPTER 21

STILL A SURE TOUCHSTONE:
THE FUTURE OF CERAMIC HISTORY
IN ART AND DESIGN EDUCATION

DR. GRAHAM MCLAREN

"Judge the art of a country, judge the fineness of its sensibility, by its pottery; it is a sure touchstone."
Herbert Read, *The Meaning of Art* (1931)

Presented at *The Ceramic Millennium*, 1999, Amsterdam

It is one of the ironies of the period up to the millennium that it is as good a place to look back as it is to look ahead. Certainly, for the provision of tuition in the history of ceramics in higher education, the experience of the past fifty years or so offers much, both as a foundation on which to build and as a caution for the new century. This moment is also an opportunity to re-examine whether the British art critic Herbert Read's famous suggestion from the 1930s, that we should be able to "judge the art of a country, judge the fineness of its sensibility, by its pottery"[1] is still true; for, if so, it clearly presents new challenges to the present-day historian in our post modern world, with all of its uncertainties. Despite these challenges, or perhaps even because of them, a truly critical reading of contemporary activity in ceramics can only really emerge via the sure anchor provided by an understanding of its historical basis, an understanding that does not build too many fences around the still very fluid categories of "art," "craft," and "design."

This last point is important because, ceramic historians have had to "speak" to at least two constituencies during the late twentieth century: to makers (or aspiring makers) and to the wider public. Ceramic history can offer insights in so many different ways: to the lives of ordinary people as well as the elite, to the value of understanding technique as well as practice, to the value and importance of locality and community as an inspiration to makers—as well as being the bedrock of modern society. It can achieve these things in a far more meaningful and vital way than other areas of art and design history because of its historically rather humble status. If I may paraphrase Val Cushing "…the teaching of pottery helps to convey an historical context to society."[2]

The main task remains, though, to communicate this to a much wider audience. This is not so easy, as ceramic history carries with it the baggage of dry academic texts written by connoisseurs for connoisseurs. These are books which remain unread on the shelves of libraries for decades rather than years, their approach and language repelling advances from any but the most fanatically interested in a particular type, factory, or period.

One group which has been particularly disadvantaged in this way is makers, particularly during the formative years of their college and university education. The absence in these books of engagement with technical issues or with issues of meaning and intent has tended to imply to students that ceramic history has little or nothing to offer them—in effect, that it is (to use Patrick Wright's phrase) "a foreign country."[3] The emphasis on the industrial past does not, of course, match the aspirations of most students of ceramics, and as a result, the texts used most heavily are almost always those dealing with contemporary issues or with the life and work of individual makers. Whilst this is understandable, it also widens unhelpfully the gap between ceramics in its industrial and its studio contexts in the minds of students.

It was not always like this, though. It is perhaps appropriate that makers were amongst the earliest historians of their craft, and here I hope you will forgive me if I concentrate on the development of the subject in the British context for a little while. Josiah Wedgwood's interest in the history of the Staffordshire pottery industry, for instance, mapped the contribution of the immigrant Dutch-born Elers brothers to the technical development of the industry through their introduction of slip casting. His analysis had an accuracy which has only very recently come to be fully

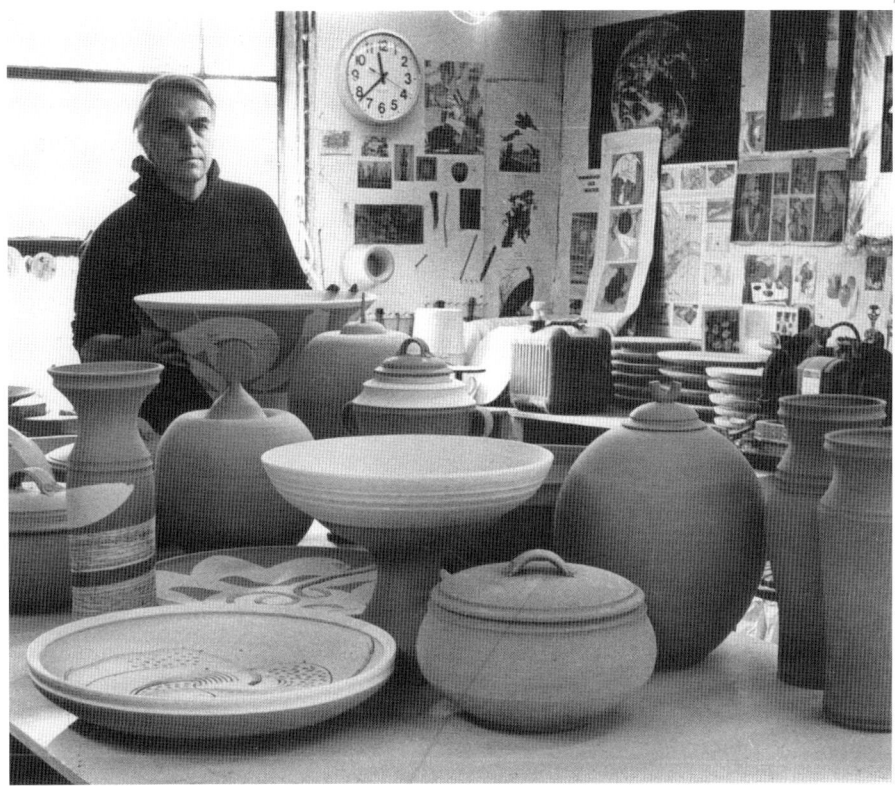

VAL CUSHING AT STUDIO IN ALFRED, NY C. 1960.
PHOTO: COURTESY THE ARTIST

appreciated. A century or so later, Wedgwood's biographer, Eliza Meteyard, published the fascinating *The Wedgwood Handbook* in which she analyzed in extraordinary detail the pieces he produced, arguing that the reader should "let the eye and finger acquire what is true as to color, grain, condition and touch, and there can be few or no errors of judgment."[4]

What these two early examples show is a concern for the material and the particularity of the object, which has been lost to a large degree in ceramic history for much of the twentieth century. Instead, the historical context to ceramic production and consumption has been pushed and pulled hither and thither, according to the whim of a variety of groups, frequently to its discredit. Most of us know of the political slant that the British potter Bernard Leach placed on the past by his emphasis on the "Sung Standard" (the use of archaic Chinese ceramic types and shapes as a basis for a twentieth-century production philosophy), but arguably, this has gained as many enemies for the study of the ceramic past as it has done friends. At the opposite end of the scale, and at the most humble level of ceramic education, a gradually evolving denial of the past to contemporary practice is to be found in the so-called "how-to-do-its" for the home potter, which became so popular during the 1950s and 1960s. It is possible to track a general decline in the amount devoted to historical context in these manuals from the late 1940s onwards.

This has also been reflected in higher education during the post-war period, and it can be put down to the fundamental changes in the teaching of ceramics that the last half century or so has seen. In Britain, a perceived "crisis" in art and design education led to an emphasis, after the war, on ceramic education being first and foremost about the education of the industrial designer; and government funding followed those courses which could demonstrate such an emphasis. This was a situation which continued until the early 1960s, with the centrally organized and examined National Diploma system prescribing the aspects of ceramic history that students should receive. Often the objects chosen were ones with a distinct moral emphasis, as in this example circulated to schools of art as part of a teaching pack by the government-sponsored Council for Industrial Design during the late 1940s. Students were advised by the caption on the back that it was "now fortunately outmoded but still to be seen, and avoided. The unfunctional handle and the decoration provide a useful cautionary study." This example came, of course, from the 1930s and "Jazz" style, a period which was attacked for its lack of a serious approach to the problems of function on the one hand, and for not demonstrating a proper allegiance to historical prototypes on the other.

In Britain, the teaching of the history of ceramics became part of a debate during the 1940s and 1950s, over the right way forward for ceramic design during the second half of the twentieth century, a debate which spun around the degree to which the ceramic past should form part of the ceramic future, a debate which is still as valid today.

Nowhere is this more clearly illuminated than in the post-war history of the Royal College of Art in London. There, the past (to the professor of ceramics newly appointed in 1948) was full of examples to aspire to in terms of both technique and design. His students received a thorough (many would say overly thorough) grounding in historical forms and techniques before being allowed to approach issues of contemporary design and manufacture during their third and final year at the college. At the heart of his approach to education was the role of the Victoria and Albert Museum just down the road:

> …I used to send them (the students) down to the V&A to find a piece to copy…so you'd get some sort of bleating about a piece of porcelain they'd picked, and we were accused of being a bit traditional, and we got all the students coming in saying they'd like to produce more modern stuff. Of course, it was all a load of garbage, because unless you've got a full compliment of craftwork and technical knowledge you can't be modern either, you can't be anything.[5]

The result of this approach was the production of pieces like these from the RBA exhibition of 1952, which were technically highly skilled but also largely indistinguishable from the museum pieces they emulated.

This approach to the use of the past in ceramic design was overtaken by the liberalizing tendency in Britain of the late 1950s and early 1960s, resulting in studio practice supplanting industrial practice as the main emphasis of art school ceramics courses. The Royal College of Art example helps to demonstrate how the subject can sometimes have a surprisingly powerful influence on the development of ceramic design, particularly in the industrial context. Analyzing the influence of ceramic history upon individual makers raises different, although not necessarily unrelated, issues. One of these is the evolving relationship between the student of ceramics and the museum as a primary resource for ceramic history.

Museums have, of course, had such a role in the education of the potter ever since they evolved into their modern form in the Western world during the mid-nineteenth century. During the twentieth century, they have had a particularly powerful influence in shaping understanding of ceramic history, not merely because some of the best known authors of texts on the subject have been museum curators, but also for reasons which have far more to do with the nature of our relationship to the real, to the artifact, and to the past itself. To Rose Slivka for instance, writing in the early 1960s of the "lonely, ambitious eclectic," who was the modern American potter, the museum was a means to draw inspiration from the ceramic history of the world, unhampered by the boundaries of national tradition: "Lacking an American pottery tradition, he [that is, the potter] has looked to the world heritage and made it his own."[6]

As a source of visual inspiration for the craft potter, the museum considerably predates the availability of relatively cheap books providing high quality illustrations. Since 1945 it has also had other, more fundamental, roles than this, which have included acting as an arbiter of the position and status of potters and as a significant patron of ceramics as an art form. During the past couple of decades in particular, museums throughout the West have risen to the challenge of what has been described as the "new museology" and shown the student that the history of ceramics can be about present-day issues as well as the deep past. They have brought a new meaning and significance to ceramic objects seen together and in context, in contrast to the individual object by itself and on its own—the tyranny of both texts and slide shows devoted to ceramic history in the past.

The absence of teaching provision for the history of ceramics can never be entirely alleviated by visits to museums, though. Warren MacKenzie's suggestion that "when a pot goes into a museum it is partially dead,"[7] does not just refer to the numbing effect of viewing objects behind glass cases. It also speaks to the huge loss of meaning and value, for utilitarian ceramic objects in particular, caused by the barrier the glass creates. These utilitarian pieces necessarily have to be touched and used in order to be able to communicate their true significance. Over the last fifty years or so, the influence of the "museum effect"—without the discursive approach to the historical context which only teaching can provide—has been to emphasize visual impact, together with immediately discernible "messages," over the tactile qualities of a ceramic piece, the relationship of a single piece to a group, and the role and context it was originally intended for.

The significance of this for the studio potter can be seen through the life and teachings of the British potter Michael Cardew. His visit to the pottery museum at Joss, in Nigeria, in the film *Mud and Water Man*, saw him lovingly cradling an Ebo palm-wine pot and extolling its utilitarian virtues—by directly handling it in a way that would only rarely be countenanced in the context of Western museums.

In retrospect, although Philip Rawson may well have been correct in asserting that potters "work in the knowledge that each piece they make amounts to a modulation within a stream of live tradition,"[8] the provision of ceramic history teaching for potters of all types has been left patchy and frequently incoherent. Were it not for the interest and influence of other disciplines, it is doubtful that it would exist today as a coherent subject area within Western higher education.

And so it is to outside the world of the practicing potter that we have to look to appreciate the full scope of the history of ceramics. Disciplines such as archaeology, ethnography and (in first the American context and now, increasingly, the European one as well) material culture studies have all had an influence in developing the subject away from its roots in connoisseurship and in museology. In Britain the development of the history of design as a discipline with a methodology, which is distinct from that of art history, has been very significant in supporting and nurturing specialist areas, such as the history of ceramics, through otherwise lean times.

It would be wrong, though, to see these problems and pressures as something entirely related to the past thirty years or so. To truly understand them, we need to adopt a larger time frame. For example, the role of the ceramic past under modernism before the Second World War was also ambiguous. In the British context, attitudes towards it were embodied by the German critic and architectural historian Nikolaus Pevsner. Looking at the Staffordshire pottery industry in the late 1930s, he could find only one or two products like this to applaud in terms of design quality, and he was severely critical of the traditionalist industry, by contrast with modern continental developments, suggesting that "The Bauhaus pots and cups may be less perfect than some of Josiah Wedgwood's, but they express one quality which Wedgwood of necessity could not bestow upon his objects—the spirit of the twentieth century."[9]

The European, modernist credo extolled the training of the architect as the most appropriate template for educating other designers because of the way in which he or she had to grapple with issues of space, utility, and context in such a complete and wholehearted manner. Within this belief system, the history of the subject is relegated to a role of justifying the contemporary.

By contrast, the effect of postmodernity over the past thirty years or so has been to sweep away the crutches of culture, industry, skill, and indeed tradition, which had previously supported studio potter and industrial ceramic designer alike, putting in its place diversity of intention and practice on a scale never seen before. In truth, Bernard Leach was probably already seeing the seeds of this revolution sprouting when he bemoaned the lack of cultural taproots in the work of American studio potters during his famous lecture tour of the United States in 1950; but it is since the mid 1960s that this revolution has really taken hold in Europe as well as in America.

In the face of all of this, the educational environment has necessarily had to change. In the industrial context, the production of graduates of ceramic design has almost always outpaced the ability of industry to employ them, but today there is certainly a shrinking market and one which frequently looks to employ designers on a part-time basis rather than to offer them a coherent and fulfilling career. All of this takes place against a background (in my country) of industrial producers like Wedgwood and Royal Doulton who have abandoned their traditional allegiances to "place" in favor of following the market and of finding the cheapest place to produce their goods, in Portugal and in Indonesia respectively.

For aspiring studio potters, the future is equally uncertain. The master-apprentice approach to education envisaged by Michael Cardew and others today seems further away than ever, and the comforting supports of community—of local, regional, and national identity—which until very recent times were the bedrock upon which individual potters could build their careers, have been largely swept away. They have been replaced by a post-modern world in which we are deluged by visual and text-based information, alongside which the "information" provided by creations in clay has to fight for attention.

Facing these pressures, it would be all too easy to dismiss the provision of ceramic history as a side issue, but I would argue that it is precisely such challenges which prompt a new approach to the history of the subject. How can ceramic history help? To understand that, one first has to understand the possibilities for the subject which have appeared over the past couple of decades.

Hugely significant amongst these are those offered by the development of new technologies, including multimedia and the Internet. The idea of delivering distance learning by utilizing these is not particularly novel, but up until now, distance learning courses have tended to concentrate on large subjects with equally large potential markets. The problem which has historically dogged the subject has been that the size of the student audience rarely justifies the provision of dedicated staffing. I would argue that ceramic history courses "online" could do much to alleviate this, and, indeed, what is often overlooked by those pushing the potential of the Internet as an educational medium has been its ability to deliver material to very specific, specialist audiences. It therefore becomes, to borrow Malcom McCullough's phrase, a "niche enabler"[10] for those wishing to broaden and deepen their knowledge and understanding of the subject.

Obviously, there are very tangible philosophical and practical issues to be overcome first. If we agree that, as some would argue, in the electronic age, the tactile and sensuous quality of ceramics is what sets it apart from other types of making, then the Internet would seem to have little to offer, and certainly, providing the tactile is what the computer is least good at. Of course, we have to ask ourselves, though, just how often students are lucky enough to get to touch historical ceramics anyway. For the vast majority, their experience of these comes via the slide or by looking through the glass of the museum showcase.[11]

Some have been concerned that the Internet can be used by the unscrupulous to hide ceramic work of poor quality, providing a medium where they are able "to exhibit even very old work already sold and gone from it's maker's control, to exhibit work with only one side worth viewing (cracks out of sight, ugly views to the back), to show work aided by epoxy or with the value of fine detail reduced to meaninglessness."[12] Perhaps these concerns have already been overtaken by what might be termed the "postmodern condition," though where issues of meaning and intent have replaced those of technical quality in the hierarchy of the modern viewer's concerns. It is ironic that, in the context of the connoisseur tradition, the "cracks out of sight" possibilities of the Internet can be positively beneficial. Frequently, the Western collector's concern with the "perfect" has meant that ceramic pieces which were full of meaning and of historical interest but which were imperfect—cracked or damaged in some way—were consigned to the trash bin. The ability of the Internet to "hide" such imperfections could have a very positive influence in "resurrecting" these pieces in the eyes of the public.

The Internet has the potential to allow a far larger and more disparate audience to examine objects as closely as they can via the images in magazines, books, and catalogues, which used to be the way in which most people got to see "elite" ceramics. Some of the most impressive sites on the Internet today, such as that of the Kyoto National Museum in Japan, offer a comprehensive, beautifully designed site, thoughtfully constructed to both educate and entertain. These also offer comprehensive illustrations with a level of resolution sometimes comparable to that found in good-quality magazines.[13]

On a practical level, copyright issues present a very significant barrier to the use of both text and images as educational tools on the Internet, and it is only to be hoped that agreements on these can be hammered out in the same way that they were for dealing with photocopied texts.

All of this should not blind us to the fact that the Internet and allied technologies offer so much that is positive. The sheer number of people now "logging on," with the medium moving from being the preserve of the technically minded to being accessible to those who a few years ago didn't believe it had anything to offer, signals its general potential. The increasing power and decreasing price of computers makes this an especially exciting time for those of us concerned with the visual image, because such developments mean that we can download images from around the world ever more quickly and easily. The possibility now also exists to "tumble and turn" images of ceramics on the Web, holding out the possibility of making the Internet a more effective way of looking at ceramics than peering through a museum case.

The development of the Internet as a tool for viewing images redresses an imbalance which was particularly clear during its early years. Then, the power of the Internet search engines to define which sites people were able to visit exerted a powerful influence on the way in which the text introducing both sites and makers was worded. In essence, what the maker said tended to be more important than what they showed, and as Kevin Murray points out, "The story of a craftsperson's life seems more important when their work is reduced to images."[14]

All of these issues relate back, in one way or another, to that of "quality." Anyone who has used the Internet to any degree will know that the quality of information available is hugely variable. How can we ensure quality whilst at the same time coping with the tendency of this new medium to break down local, regional, and national boundaries, to lump the work of makers into one more or less homogenous whole? I ask this because, although many would see the trans-nationalism of the Internet as a wholly positive thing, appreciating the variety within regional and national ceramic traditions provides real substance for the study of ceramics. The geography of regional and national boundaries also supplies an (admittedly imperfect) map for navigating our way through history. Surely this is what Herbert Read referred to in "judge the art of a country, judge the fineness of its sensibility, by its pottery," written at a time when the internationalism of the modern movement was at its height, and yet this was against a disturbing backdrop of gathering clouds of extreme nationalism in Europe.

Is there any way to reconcile issues of quality and of particular ceramic traditions with the fickle creature that is the Internet in order to deliver education in the history of ceramics in a new way? We think that there is; and at Staffordshire University, we are building on more than twenty years of experience in delivering the history of ceramics at undergraduate level, and six years experience with our unique MA in the history of ceramics to bring distance-learning packages in the subject to the Internet.

Of course, there are all sorts of technical and legal issues to be overcome first, but these are surmountable. Of more immediate interest are the issues of implementation that the initiative raises. First amongst these must be developing a programme of ceramic history, which can be disseminated via the Internet and, at the same time, be appropriate to a world-wide audience. Part of the answer, a large part I think, lies in the methods and approaches provided by material culture studies, a discipline first developed as a way of examining and explaining the historical development of America as an entity. Material culture had its beginnings in the early years after World War II when America broke many of its cultural and intellectual bonds with Europe. Its methods are particularly significant when allied to those of other disciplines, such as post-medieval archaeology, has helped to legitimize the study of fragments of our recent past, breaking down the connoisseur emphasis on the "perfect" and the "whole."

What this synthesis offers is a new toolkit of methods for the studying of ceramics, which places emphasis on the object as an historical text, and on the real and the particular at a time when these qualities are in short supply, having been shrouded by late twentieth-century culture. At Staffordshire University we are already applying these methodologies to an amazing range of ceramic artifacts through our unique relationship with the Potteries Museum and Art Gallery. What we are most concerned to ensure is that students come away with the tools to analyze the elements of ceramic history and ceramic artifacts of all types. It is through this approach that we have recruited and trained students with a wide variety of backgrounds and an equally disparate range of interests. We have students working side by side, applying these methodologies to ceramics from the present and from the deep past, to industrial ceramics, and to contemporary studio production, and dealing with issues ranging from the technological to the philosophical and the theoretical. The beauty of this system is that once the "toolkit" is provided, students can apply it to the area of ceramic history that interests them most.

Most significantly of all, this approach to ceramic history offers a way forward for disseminating, via the Internet, a subject which has suffered in college and university curricula because it is too specialized to be adequately staffed. The history of ceramics, via distance learning, will primarily be about meanings and methods. Certainly, it will have to show historically significant examples of ceramics from around the world, and certainly, it will have to find a way to bring a sense of community to learning via the computer "at a distance." The "real," in terms of objects to touch will be drawn by the students from their own experience, their own locality, and their own interests, interpreted by them using the skills provided by the course. By these means we may eventually find a way of judging not just a country by its pottery, but the whole world.

1 Herbert Read, *The Meaning of Art* (London: Faber and Faber, 1931) 42.
2 Val M. Cushing, "An Academic View," *Studio Potter* (Vol. 18, No 1, 1989) 25.
3 Patrick Wright, *On Living in an Old Country: The National Past in Contemporary Britain* (London: Verso, 1985).
4 Eliza Meteyard, *The Wedgwood Handbook: A Manual for Collectors. Treating of the marks, monograms, and other tests of the old period of manufacturing* (London: G. Bell and Sons, 1875) 25.
5 G. M. McLaren, "The Colleges and Responses to Industry—Ceramic Design Education c.1945 - 1965: Perspectives and Policies," Ph.D. Thesis, Royal College of Art, 1991.
6 Rose Slivka, "The New Ceramic Presence," *Craft Horizons* (July/August, 1961) 37.
7 Warren MacKenzie, "Criticism," *Studio Potter* (Vol. 9, No 1, 1980) 68.
8 Philip Rawson, "Continuity and Rootedness," *Studio Potter* (Vol. 20, No 2, 1992) 24.
9 Nikolaus Pevsner, *Pioneers of Modern Design: From William Morris to Walter Gropius* (New York: Museum of Modern Art, 1949).
10 Malcolm McCollough, *Abstracting Craft: The Practiced Digital Hand* (Boston: MIT Press, 1997).
11 Despite attempts to achieve this via gloves which enable the user to manipulate "virtual environments" by hand movements or receive computer generated stimuli via pressure pads and other sensors embedded in the glove material these innovations miss the subtlety and complexity of the experience of touching and feeling the ceramic surface.
12 William Hunt, "The Pure and the Impure in Cyberspace," *Virtual Ceramics Exhibit*, October 13, 2005 <http://www.ilpi.com/artsource/vce/huntstatement.html>
13 Kyoto National Museum <http://www.kyohaku.go.jp>
14 Kevin Murray, "All Aboard for the Craft Diaspora," *Craft Victoria* (Spring 25/229, 1995: 16-19, October 13, 2005) <http://www.kitezh.com/texts/train.html>

Chapter 22

Studios, Academies, and Workshops: Ceramics Education From the Mid-Nineteenth Century to World War II

Tanya Harrod

What seems paradoxical is that ceramics, as a new kind of expressive art form (not just an elevated area of industrial design), was to enter the academies of art as a practical hands-on discipline in Britain and the United States in the first decade of the century. Previously, since the establishment of the Schools of Design in 1837, the emphasis had been on a training centred on drawing, largely intended to produce suitable surface decoration for ceramics.

Presented at *The Ceramic Millennium*, 1999, Amsterdam

In 1905 the great arts and crafts designer and socialist Walter Crane published a collection of essays entitled *Ideals in Art*. An early oil on canvas by Crane, *Love's Altar* of 1870 heralds the theme of Crane's book in that its neo-medievalism, its object-like presence, suggests Crane's ambivalence towards contemporary painting. Crane was more at ease as a designer of textiles, wallpapers, interiors, and stained glass and of vivid graphics made in the cause of socialism, such as his *Cartoons for a Cause* made in 1896 to mark the International Socialist and Trades Union Congress of that year. We do not think of Crane as a radical artist in the context of early modernism. He belongs to an earlier period; he was 60 when *Ideals in Art* appeared.

But like intelligent artists all over Europe, he was addressing a perceived crisis in the fine arts in which one of the commonest forms of artistic currency, the portable easel-sized painting, had come to be associated with decline and decadence. In Crane's view, what he called "mere easel painting"[1] lacked a serious contemporary context and had destroyed painting as an art of design, with links to architecture and a wider world.

Crane was reiterating ideas that had been at the heart of the design reform movement initiated in Britain by William Morris as early as the 1860s. Morris's own doubts about fine art were clearly articulated both in his writings and in the way in which he transformed picture-making by, for instance, integrating it into furniture or by translating the pictorial into craft media such as tapestry and stained glass. One aspect of the Morris legacy was handicrafts of the most uninspired kind. But Morris's linking of art and politics and morality and his concern with a context for art was taken up by avant-garde thinkers all over Europe and North America and in the Far East, particularly Japan. Morris's political writing led serious young artists to think how their work was consumed and by whom. Morris's imaginative valorisation of design encouraged a new interest in the quotidien, the everyday, in *things* at the expense of easel painting.

Of course, not all early modern artists rejected the activity of easel painting. For Paul Cézanne, the internal problems specific to painting were complex and demanding enough to take up all his energies without forays into the applied arts. But for other European painters, one way of questioning the skills taught by the academies of art through the systematic study of casts and copies was through self-taught experimentation in other media. In France this anti-academy approach was first pursued by Paul Gauguin and the group which admired his work—the painters who called themselves les Nabis—the prophets. Works like Gauguin's wooden carved relief *Soyez amoureuse, vous serez heureuse* (Boston, Museum of Fine Art) 1890 and Pierre Bonnard's painted screen *Women in a Garden* (Musee d'Orsay) 1891 suggest these new concerns. New media and unfamiliar methods were, in some instances, part of a strategy to alter the ways in which art was consumed, and in Gauguin's case, part of a strategy to make ends meet. For the young Bonnard, the Nabis's experiments with painted screens and fans and with stained glass and enamels and ceramics were both emblematic and political: "Our generation (who) are always seeking links between art and life through objects of everyday use."[2]

Dissatisfaction with the academy led the young architect Le Corbusier, in a polemic written in 1914, to recommend the closure of schools of applied art, while in 1905, Walter Crane had written of the teaching of art: "Well to begin with, you cannot teach it."[3] These were commonplace observations at the start of the century amongst an avant-garde who had experienced a conventional academic training. But forays into the applied arts were also inspired by another modern trope—that familiar anti-modern nostalgia for earlier cultures and non-European cultures. Anti-industrial yearnings were commonplace amongst European novelists, critics, and artists from Rainer Maria Rilke to Walter Benjamin to Le Corbusier.

On his journey around Europe in 1911—an important journey of self-education—Le Corbusier was deeply moved by vernacular craft. Significantly, he illustrated a Serbian and a Spanish pot in his magazine, *L'Esprit Nouveau*, commenting despairingly: "Finished! Replaced by the tin can." But ironically, the surviving vernacular and pre-Renaissance and non-European art were powerful models for early modernism. The ideal site of learning became the workshop and the studio, not the academy. Processes of self-instruction were favoured. High skill (or perhaps facility is the better word) was often set aside. Favoured areas for experimentation included direct carving in wood or stone (such as Brancusi's *The Kiss*, 1912 and Eric Gill's, *The Rower*, 1912) the creation of crude wood-block prints (for instance a work like Ernst Ludwig Kirchner's *Women Bathing Between White Stones*, 1912), and the decoration and occasional creation of ceramics.

In the case of ceramics, were these esssentially private experiments? Some were, some were not. Gauguin's ceramics certainly differ from the activities of neo-Orientalising figures like Auguste Delaherche, Ernest Chaplet, Emile Lenoble, and Emile Decoeur, who are regarded as the pioneers of French studio pottery. Gauguin's ceramics, made between 1886 and 1895, were not particularly well received—even today his ceramics still seem "difficult" and adventurous. But he clearly hoped for an audience and was bitter about the way in which the public appeared to prefer safer kinds of experimentation in the form of Delaherche's monumental neo-Oriental pots.

The ceramics decorated by the painters known as Les Fauves around 1907 similarly tended to be little discussed when they were exhibited. They were made, in most instances, with the encouragement of the dealer Ambrose Vollard, who suggested that his artists work with the self-taught tin-glaze potter Andre Metthey at his studio north of Paris in 1907. Despite the lack of public interest, these tin-glaze plates, plaques, and pots were clearly valuable to their creators—to Matisse, to Rouault and Maurice Vlaminck and Andre Derain, for example. Rouault had, in fact, started working independently with Metthey before 1907. On one level, involvement in making or decorating ceramics alerted artists to deficiencies in industrial design. Gauguin had been particularly critical of the historicist production at Sèvres for instance—he called it "the death of ceramics." The potter Andre Metthey—an interesting figure in his own right—had a horror of what he called the "cold, pompous and static" productions of the French ceramics industry.[4]

But an involvement with ceramics worked in other ways too. In the case of Matisse, in his early work he created little worlds of objects. His own ceramics, small sculptures, and the textiles and carpets which he collected animated his interior scenes, portraits, and still lifes. His 1911 *The Red Studio* (MOMA) and his *Girl with Green Eyes* of 1908 (San Francisco Museum of Modern Art) both include examples of his ceramics. At that early date, Matisse was also depicting archetypal figures against empty, flattened backgrounds, as in *La Danse* of 1910 (Hermitage). Again, his ceramic experiments can be seen as important; his painting on pots suggested a new kind of dancing figure inhabiting a new kind of space. Andre Derain, on the other hand, combined the decoration of pots with the making of woodcuts and direct carving during this Fauve period. He used these other media because they lent themselves to the heightened colour and flattened space he was pursuing in paintings like *The Dance* of 1906.

Apart from Gauguin, none of these painters seem to have left accounts of what ceramics meant to them, and for each artist, it seems likely that ceramics played a different role, ranging from spatial to colouristic experimentation. The best exegesis of the possibilities of ceramics was provided after the Second World War by Pablo Picasso, in a letter to the sculptor Henri Laurens. Picasso explained to Laurens that while painting should create a sense of space, he had found that by painting a ceramic form, he was able to create the multiplicity of flattened viewpoints which he demanded from sculpture. As Picasso's dealer Kahnweiler astutely observed, some of the paradoxes which Picasso first explored in sculptures like the 1914 *Glass of Absinthe* series were again investigated in the unique ceramics. But again, I stress, the possibilities were many and complex.[5]

What I have outlined here is ceramics being used as an area of experimentation, a medium outside the academy. But how much of the vigour of what we more commonly see as "studio" pottery (the trajectory from French potters like Delaherche to the Martin Brothers to Bernard Leach, if you like) derives from a self-taught, experimental approach? What seems paradoxical is that ceramics, as a new kind of expressive art form (not just an elevated area of industrial design), was to enter the academies of art as a practical hands-on discipline in Britain and the United States in the first decade of the century. Previously, since the establishment of the Schools of Design in 1837, the emphasis had been on a training centred on drawing, largely intended to produce suitable surface decoration for ceramics. What I want to discuss now is the ways in which figures who actively described themselves as studio potters—unlike the Paris-based artists I have mentioned above—viewed the role of ceramics in the academies. I also want to analyze the uneasy position occupied by ceramics within the academy up until the Second World War. To summarize very crudely, it seems to me that in Britain in the first part of the century, ceramics operated at its best outside or in opposition to the academy, whilst in the USA there was debate but also fruitful synthesis.

To begin in Britain, the kind of experimentation by painters, which we saw in France, was really only matched by the ceramics produced by the Omega Workshops set up in 1913 by the painter and critic Roger Fry. But in England (as distinct from Scotland), pottery practice was soon to become much more of an end in itself. A definition of studio pottery might be the artist's involvement in every aspect of making, from creating a clay body and glazes to forming and decorating. Nonetheless, the very earliest studio potters in England do seem to have seen clay as a resolution for other artistic problems—like their French painter and sculptor counterparts. For instance, Reginald Wells employed ceramics as an abstract alternative to the small-scale figurative sculpture he was making in the first decade of the century. Similarly, William Staite Murray's rather more adventurous experiments of around 1915 at the Yeoman Pottery in London appear have been part of a process of self-education in which this escapee from a family seed-and-bulb firm moved in Vorticist circles, cast in bronze, studied Buddhism, and was informed by the remarkable series of exhibitions of advanced European art held in London from 1910 until the outbreak of the Great War. Murray might have seen ceramics by Matisse, Derain, Vlaminck, and others, which Roger Fry chose to include in his exhibition, *Manet and the Post-Impressionists* of 1910 or he might have seen the graphic work

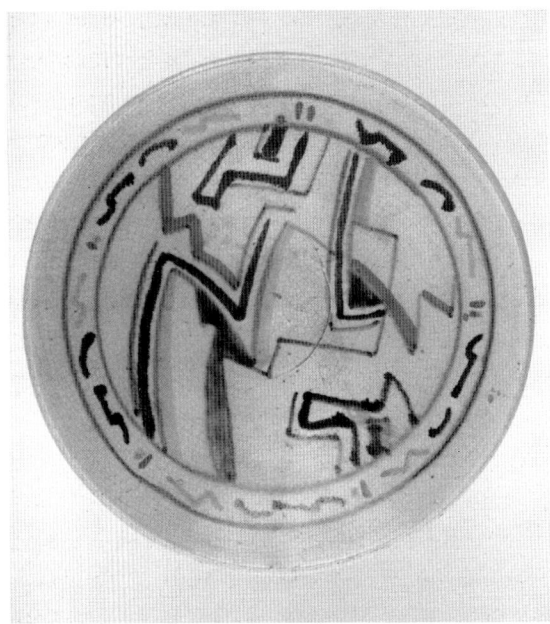

WILLIAM STAITE MURRAY, *BOWL*, YEOMAN POTTERY C.1919.
EARTHENWARE WITH GLAZE DECORATION,
17.9 CM.
PRIVATE COLLECTION

of Vassily Kandinsky, who since 1909 had been a regular exhibitor in London with the Allied Artists' Association.

But from 1925 Murray joined the academy. He was appointed pottery instructor at the Royal College of Art in that year by the principal, the painter William Rothenstein. What is interesting is at that date, the role of a pottery instructor in an art school in England was an uncertain one as regards relations both with fine art and with industrial design. What was the point of learning ceramics in an art school? The first object might seem to be to train students to design for industry, and this had been the aim since the formation of the Schools of Design in 1837. Not surprisingly, this was the emphasis at the Stoke-on-Trent art schools headed from 1920 by Gordon Forsyth. At Stoke there was a strong system linking primary, secondary, and further art education. But away from the heartland of the pottery industry, the situation was less clear cut.

A carefully posed photo, taken at the Central School of Arts and Crafts in London in the late 1930s, shows ceramics as then taught in the School of Painted, Sculpted and Architectural Decoration. There is evidence of slip casting, of hand building inspired by a North African model. The pot held by a woman in the foreground was probably thrown. We will return to questions of gender suggested by this image later. In London in 1923, it was possible to learn pottery at four LCC art schools: at the Central School of Arts and Crafts, at Camberwell School of Arts and Crafts, at

Putney School of Art, and at Woolwich Polytechnic. Camberwell was where both Roger Fry and Murray went to learn the rudiments in 1914 and 1909 respectively. But in all these places there was an emphasis on designing on paper and on creating moulds, and there was a lot of intervention from technicians that, I would argue, reflected the social make up of these ceramics classes. They were made up of, on the whole, middle- and upper-middle class students who would have accepted such assistance as inevitable and natural. At the Royal College of Art, Walter Crane introduced demonstrations of pottery in 1898. By 1901 pottery was taught there by Richard Lunn, who claimed that this was "the first attempt to make pottery in a school, carry out all the processes of making, drying and firing biscuit, decorating, glazing and firing glazed ware in the classrooms themselves." [6]

Ceramics, as taught at the Central School, was limited in 1914 to china painting, but by 1919, it became an adjunct to architecture and sculpture. A full range of craft and industrial techniques were on offer—from throwing to jigger and jolleying. From 1944 ceramics was taught in two schools—that of Drawing, Painting, Modelling and Allied Subjects and in the School of Furniture and Interior Decoration. In 1947 pottery was in the School of Interior Decoration, Pottery and Stained Glass. As a named subject, it had in a sense arrived and heralded the remarkable majolica revival at the Central, which peaked in the 1950s.

For most of this time, the craft was taught principally by Dora Billington, whose father and grandfather had worked at Stoke-on-Trent and who had herself trained there at Hanley School of Art. Billington was a rational woman, who saw no conflict between industrial and studio pottery and who disliked any kind of narrowness. From about 1920, this very new art form of studio pottery had been taken over by a modernist orthodoxy in which the studio potter turned from decorative eclecticism to the study and, up to a point, emulation of early English pottery and early Chinese wares and Japanese and Korean pottery. Mixed in with this was a good deal of religio-philosophical thinking. Dora Billington disliked this narrowing of the field, but she was unable to provide the kind of workshop atmosphere dominated by production skills (as opposed to design skills) which neo-Orientalists like Bernard Leach were able to create.

For instance, despite Billington's structured and informative course, the Central did not suit the young potter Ursula Mommens in the 1920s. Mommens, who is now ninety-one, recalls the Central as:

...hopeless, really very, very bad. Nobody could throw there and...30 people in a small room, three dreadful kick-wheels.... The clay was very dirty, lumpy and hard and I once found a dead mouse and all its bones incarcerated in it. The teachers were only interested in teaching you how to paint on pots.[7]

Nor was the aristocratic Katherine Pleydell-Bouverie particularly impressed, though she learnt to throw from "a potter from one of the potteries.... He didn't have much idea of shapes but he could throw anything."[8] Mommens moved on to the Royal College of Art where, as we saw, William Staite Murray was head of the Pottery Department from 1925. At the Royal College of Art, Murray promoted the status of studio pottery as an area of experimental fine art by keeping technical instruction to the minimum. In effect, he de-academicised the academy. Instead, his students—who went over to the Central to learn about clay bodies and glaze technology—became aware of his interest in the vitalist ideas of Henri Bergson, the writings of Lao-Tsu, and the koans of Zen Buddhism. His students rapidly made an impact in the London art world and formed a recognisable grouping, hailed in 1930 by Herbert Read as "canvas-free artists."

Towards the end of his life, Murray wrote that "a pot is born not made." It was a phrase also used by the potter Bernard Leach in his memoirs. This is an ancient high-art idea, previously applied to sculpture. We find a form of it in Cicero's *De Divinatione*, in Ovid, and in the writings of Michelangelo and Vasari. They suggest that the work of art has some kind of pre-existence, that the artist's specialness consists in an ability to uncover or unlock beauty. It was an idea as remote as possible from the practicalities of tooling up for jiggering and jolleying. Indeed, Murray's approach to the teaching of ceramics at the RCA was profoundly anti-industrial. "You can't make love by proxy,"[9] he told a studio potter who proposed to design for industry.

Murray functioned as a subversive force within a college of art whose identity, in any case, was constantly being questioned in the 1930s. But the chief critic of the art school within the studio pottery movement was Bernard Leach. His own background is of interest. Leach had trained at the Slade and more informally at the London School of Art with Frank Brangwyn in the first decade of the twentieth century. He could, as a result, draw fluently and beautifully. But when Leach came to write his classic, *A Potter's Book*, during the Second World War, he warned against art schools and art students, and he makes no mention of drawing, still then the mainstay of an education in art. Part of his antipathy may have been to do with a half promise, quickly rescinded, of the job at the Royal College of Art given ultimately—as we have seen—to Murray in 1925. That disappointment was old history by 1940, and it seems more likely that Leach believed that art students were in some sense "spoilt" for the kind of work he had in mind.

In *A Potter's Book* he explains that:

> …the people who are attracted today by the hand crafts are no longer the simple minded peasantry, who from generation to generation worked on in the protective unselfconsciousness of tradition, but mainly self-conscious art students. They come to me year after year from the Royal College, or the Central School or Camberwell, for longer or shorter, usually shorter, periods of apprenticeship. As soon as they have picked up enough knowledge, or what they think is enough, off they go to start potting on a small scale themselves. Very few have proved themselves as artists.

Nor could art students be recommended as mere assistants. In Leach's view they lacked what he called "horse sense," and Leach advised any potter contemplating sharing a workshop to choose "untrained local labour." As he explained "likely boys learn the jobs quickly."[10]

By 1948 Leach's feelings about art schools were still more dismissive. They were places "where crafts such as ours cannot be learned" and "where there is not basic production for use, where there are not nearly enough teachers who can find and prepare clays, who can throw proficiently, who can design and build a kiln and make their own pigments and glazes."[11] For Leach right making was hard won from "pure" exempla, for instance by studying medieval pots or by looking at surviving vernacular potters at work (such as Mr. Pascoe of the Truro Pottery, whom Leach visited in 1923), or by travelling far from industrialized Europe. It was an aristocratic, colonial approach to learning.

Leach's pupils were not all so critical of art schools. Norah Braden, lacking independent means, taught from 1936 at Camberwell and Brighton Schools of Art, but it was at the expense of her own work. Others continued the search for the unspoilt workshop and unspoilt pupils. Michael Cardew took this quest to some extremes, and his activities form an interesting footnote to colonial art training. Earlier twentieth-century efforts by colonial powers to teach potters from other cultures had proved tragic. Two photographs, published in the *Pottery Gazette* of 1911, show a pottery training scheme at Ibadan in West Africa. In one image we see the highly skilled women potters of Ibadan, all hand builders, and, as an almost laughable point of comparison, a group of boys standing with their European instructor behind a selection of lumpy vases, candlesticks, and teapots made for, presumably, an expatriate market.

During and after the Second World War, Cardew worked and taught in West Africa. Cardew did not see himself as a fine artist like Murray, but he set a special value on pottery, seeing it and pottery instruction as having a far-reaching social role. Here he is, writing to his wife Mariel in 1945 from West Africa about his dreams of a pottery for the Gold Coast which would;

> …make potters as well as pots, to build a tradition; and I can do so much more with Africans than with English…at least they are not mean in spirit, they have the stuff, the instinct, only waiting to be guided, helped and developed…the flower of their sense of form has never been crushed by the slavery of Puritanism.[12]

These Rousseauesque outpourings are embarassing to read today, but what seems evident is that Cardew wanted to make pots as "naturally as a tree makes leaves or fruits," and he believed that this could only properly happen in a workshop far from any kind of metropolitan centre. His dreams for studio pottery were extreme and in many ways unrealizable.

For the last part of this talk, I want to look at ceramic education in the United States. I'm nervous of attempting a crude summary, and I'm going to restrict myself to discussing two schools of art where I have done some primary research: the New York School of Claywork (now the New York State College of Ceramics) at Alfred University in New York State, and Cranbrook Academy of Art in the lush Bloomfield Hills outside Detroit. As in Britain, ceramic education at both institutions suggests the fragile nature of the crafts, and we see ceramics being pushed this way and that—towards architecture, towards sculpture, and towards design. But firstly, it seems to me that the early history of studio pottery in the USA has a quite different flavour to developments in Britain. This was partly because of the important contribution made by a succession of strong-minded women whose initial focus was the amateur craft of china painting, but who subsequently in different ways developed to encompass a range of sophisticated ceramic skills. The emphasis on simplicity and non-European culture, which hardened into an orthodoxy centred on neo-Orientalism in England, did not exist to the same extent in North America. Figures like Mary Louise McLaughlin, Maria Longworth Nichols, Adelaide Alsop Robineau, and Mary Chase Perry Stratton all became highly professional art potters, whether producing unique virtuoso pieces or running what amounted to small factories. Their exact counterparts do not exist in Britain.

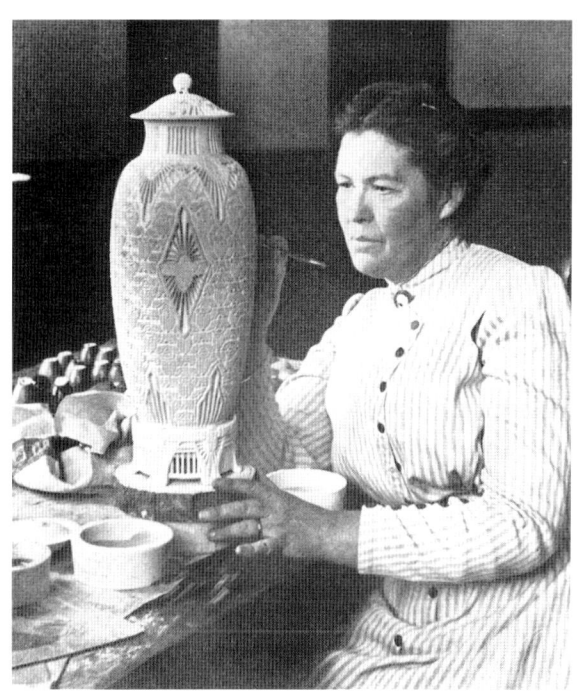

ADELAIDE ALSOP ROBINEAU IN STUDIO AT THE PEOPLE'S UNIVERSITY, ST. LOUIS, MO, WORKING ON THE *SCARAB VASE*, C.1910.
PHOTO: EVERSON MUSEUM OF ART, SYRACUSE, NY

Nor do we find the ideological antipathy to the academy or to industry which characterised the inter-war studio-pottery movement in Britain. Even though ceramic practice was often linked to utopian communities, these had none of the exclusivity of, say, Leach's interventions at Dartington Hall, and often had a strong philanthropic aspect—linking up, for instance, with the settlement-house movement, which attempted to alleviate the plight of poor immigrants in Chicago and New York.

But this is not to say that there was not a visionary side to the practice of ceramics, and nowhere do we find it more than at Alfred under the leadership of the English potter Charles Binns. Binns's approach has little in common with the techniques and underlying philosophies of British studio pottery between the wars. Binns's background was in the ceramics industry in England, as images of him using a jigger and jolley to form a bowl or throwing a complex pot form in three carefully measured sections using calliphers suggest.

The setting up of a school of clayworks at Alfred in 1900 was a fairly pragmatic step for a small liberal arts college in financial difficulties and from the start, ceramics at Alfred encompassed ceramic engineering *and* ceramics as a design and art course. Both courses were highly gendered—men doing engineering and a virtually entirely female intake doing ceramics as design and art. The same was true of ceramics in British art schools and at Cranbrook where it was taught intermittently from 1931. There, men took the graduate architecture course while women wove and potted. By the early 1930s, in a time of global economic crisis, this came to seem a "problem."

Support for Alfred from the state of New York was science inspired and was partly dependent on research into local clays and shales. Useful pioneering took place, and Binns prepared one hundred samples of fired clays of the USA for the 1900 *Paris Exhibition*. There was also moral purpose. The cloudy mixture of Far Eastern thinking which imbued the English studio pottery movement was, at Alfred, recast by Binns in a powerfully biblical fashion in which the art of pottery came to have a strong spiritual symbolism. Binns explained, in a speech of 1929, that clay:

> ...has a complicated nature upon which the fire can operate, but without the fire it remains mere earth. In this, as in other ways, the analogy to human nature is evident. Emergencies are a test of character. The path to quality, strength and beauty in life leads through the furnace and there is no other.[13]

As regards practical instruction, Alfred appears to have been ahead of its British counterparts. As we have seen, in Britain, rigid class divisions were operational in art schools, and much practical work was carried out by technicians. Those who sought practical knowledge had, in effect, to go outside the class system, often to the surprise and embarassment of the flowerpot makers and country potters from whom they sought advice. In the United States a democracy of activity appears to have prevailed.

Then again, Alfred's influence was facilitated by its summer schools. Again, Britain had nothing comparable to these kinds of idyllic summer colonies where the well-off combined nostalgic pioneering, craft activity, and a rest from "getting and spending." At the beginning of the century, an artistically minded vacationer could visit Arthur Dow's summer school at Ipswich, Mass., from 1900 to 1906, and Ernest Batchelor's summer school at Minneapolis from 1903 to 1908, and Chautauqua, New York, founded in 1874 and still going strong today. Some of the key female figures in the world of ceramics attended the Alfred Summer School in search of technical knowledge: Adelaide Alsop Robineau, Mary Chase Perry Stratton, Elizabeth Overbeck, and Maija Grotell (a highly trained Finn who wanted to familiarize herself with American ceramics).

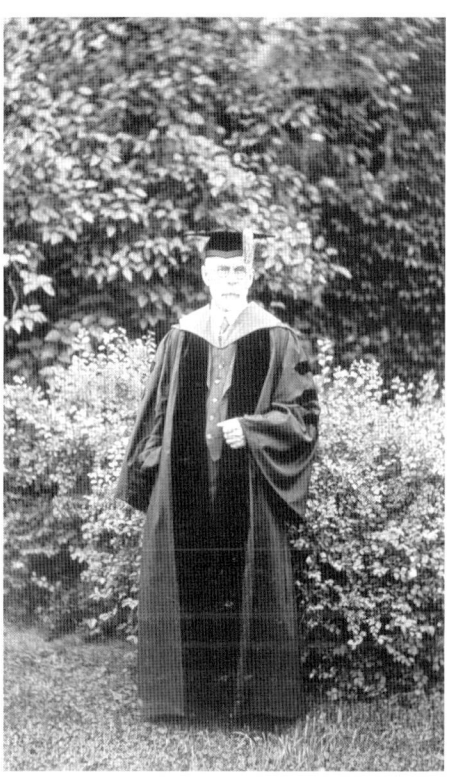

CHARLES FERGUS BINNS, GRADUATION DAY, 1910

But by the early 1930s (Binns was to retire in 1931) there was a sense of crisis concerning ceramics at Alfred, recorded by Charles Harder who taught there from 1927 and was head of the renamed Department of Industrial Ceramic Design from 1938 to 1941. Edward Holmes, Binns's replacement as dean or director, wanted to push the ceramic art and design course in the direction of industrial design. This was a specifically 1930s crisis in which world-wide economic recession made the individual self-expression associated with studio pottery seem indulgent, even immoral. Thus in England we find the art critic Herbert Read denouncing the

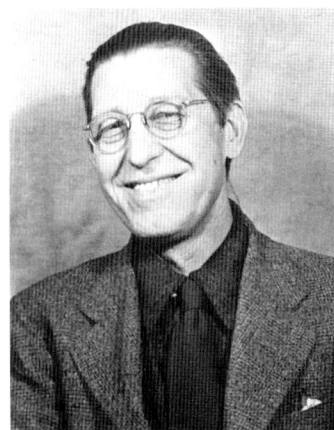

CHARLES HARDER, PORTRAIT, 1940

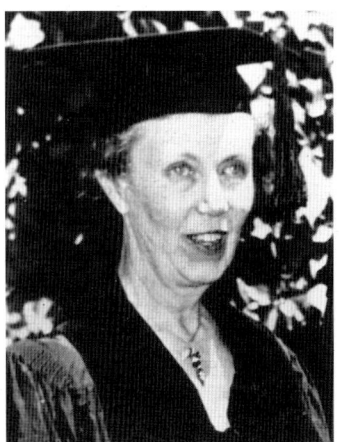

MARION FOSDICK, GRADUATION DAY, 1930

handmade object and Leach planning a small factory at Dartington and Michael Cardew planning to design for industry. Harder, who spent the year 1935 touring industrial works and studying other ceramics courses, was affected by this moral shift towards industrial design. He wanted to shake up what he called "a finishing school run by spinsters" (an unkind reference to the two women on the Alfred staff, one of whom, Marion Fosdick, was an exceptionally gifted potter) and put more emphasis on industrial processes and contact with industry. In his view, the mainly women students on the full-time ceramic art and design course sought a liberal education rather than a ceramic education; they had their taste honed and were, in effect, being trained to teach in primary and secondary schools and on philanthropic projects. The photos of the department taken when Harder was head underline his aims. They show plenty of men throwing, men designing wares to be slip cast and male-dominated industrial visits.

Harder was a visionary who perhaps lacked the artistry to realize his vision. It is of interest that, just as our period ends, he took on an unlikely figure as his first graduate assistant in design. This was Sam Haile, a surrealist painter and William Staite Murray's most brilliant pupil. At Alfred, Haile offered few solutions but preached a kind of anarchic versatility. And after the Second World War the problems of ceramic training and its relation to industry were largely resolved at Alfred and elsewhere by the extraordinary upsurge in adventurous studio ceramics which embraced the kind of distinctly fine-art freedoms only possible in a period of extreme affluence.

The built utopia of Cranbrook Academy of Art was a contrast to the rugged and remote little Alfred campus, but ceramics teaching there faced some of the same problems of definition. Ceramics at Cranbrook was initially to have an uncertain identity. It first took the form of ceramic sculpture under the leadership of Wayland DeSantis Gregory. He arrived in 1932 to join a group of craftsmen brought together by George Booth, the Detroit newspaper magnate who funded Cranbrook. But Gregory's stay there was short. Conditions in utopia were difficult: he had no salary other than what he sold and fees from students he had to seek out himself. Cranbrook between the wars was, in effect, the fiefdom of the Finnish architect Eliel Saarinen and was dominated by the needs of the graduate course in architecture and design that he established in 1930. In 1933 Gregory departed, followed by other craftsmen—a silversmith and a bookbinder—all of whom Saarinen saw as not sufficiently part of "the spirit of our time."

From 1933 ceramics was taught by Marshall Fredericks, a former pupil of the sculptor Carl Milles, another key, privileged figure at Cranbrook, whose voluptuous bronzes adorned the campus at every turn. Fredericks went on to teach ceramics and modelling, but with the emphasis on modelling in the Milles spirit. Students who wanted to make vessels were not well catered for. At the end of the 1930s, Lilian Swann Saarinen, the wife of Eero Saarinen (Eliel's gifted son), worked on fired clay architectural details for various Eero buildings. But ceramics was not one of the three key disciplines taught at the postgraduate level in the 1930s. These were: architecture

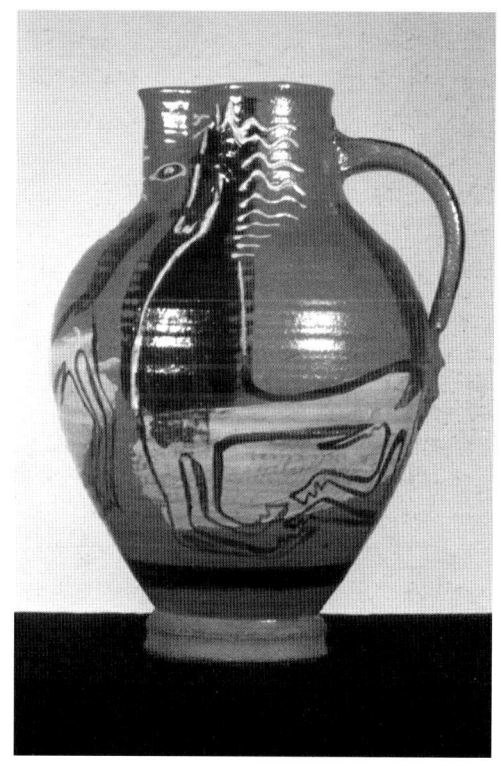

THOMAS SAMUEL HAILE, *PITCHER*, C.1939, STONEWARE WITH SLIP DECORATION.

PHOTO: ALFRED UNIVERSITY, ALFRED, NY

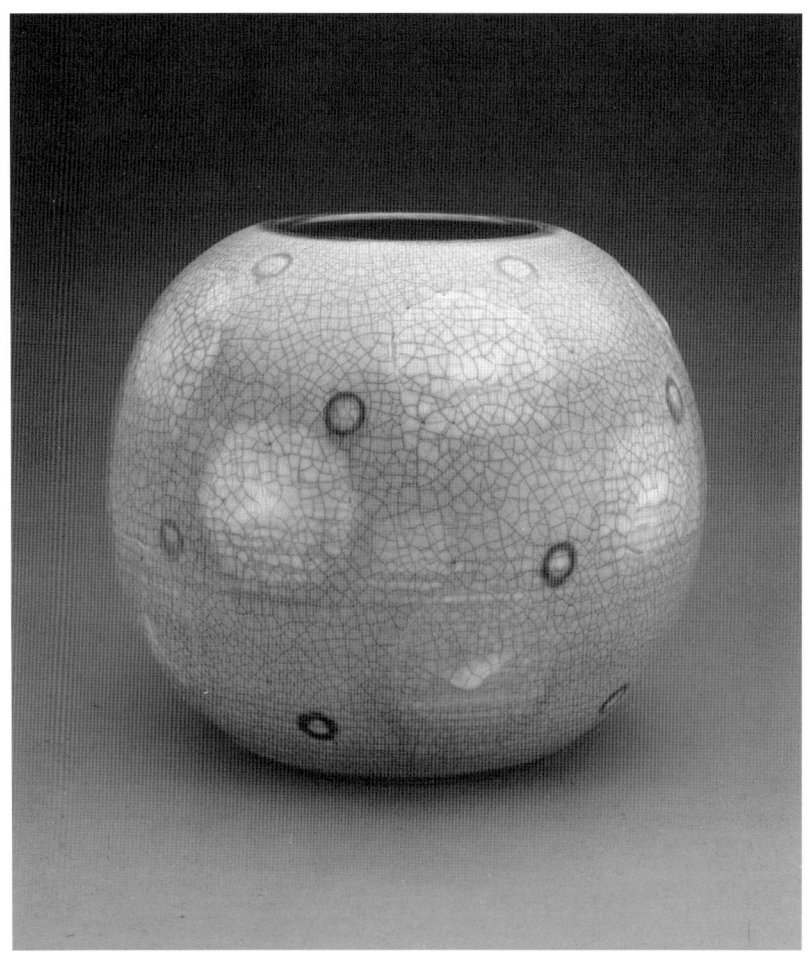

Maija Grotell, *Green and Tan Crackle Vase*, c. 1948. Stoneware, 30.5 cm.
Photo: John White

taught by Saarinen, sculpture taught by Milles, and painting taught by the Hungarian Zoltan Sepeshy. Instead, ceramics came to be a subject offered in the Intermediate School set up in 1936. It was hoped that fees from the Intermediate School would finance the graduate courses and, as with the ceramic art and design course at Alfred, was largely made up of women students. Thus in 1937 at Cranbrook, thirteen women and three men were studying ceramics, and eleven men and one woman were studying architecture.

So, finally, what did the teaching of ceramics in art schools stand for between the wars? It is impossible to give one answer, especially as regards the United States, where I have barely touched on the diversity of approaches. But it is striking that ceramic practice was constantly questioned in Britain and in the USA. After the Second World War there was an explosion in the number of courses and a huge increase in students. Some of the awkward, important questions—to do with context and relevance—ceased to be asked as men and women embraced a discipline which seemed to offer so much hope for personal fulfilment after the disciplines and limitations of the war years. Ceramics now stood for everything that was joyful and accessible.

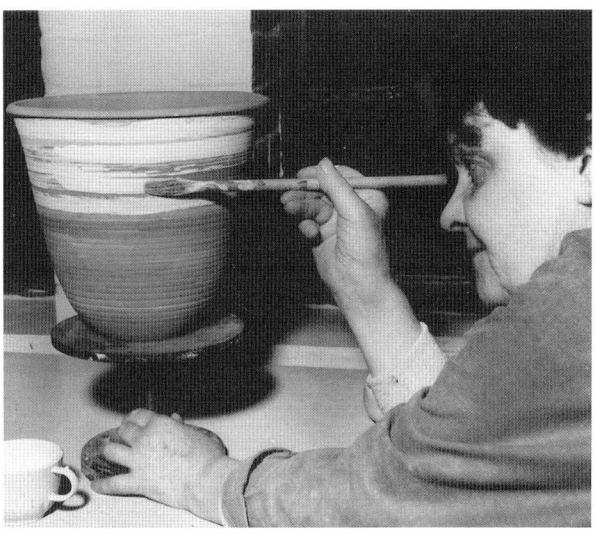

MAIJA GROTELL AT CRANBROOK ACADEMY OF ART, BLOOMFIELD HILLS, MI, 1950.

PHOTO: CRANBROOK ACADEMY OF ART MUSEUM

1   Walter Crane, *Ideals in Art* (London: George Bell and Sons, 1905).
2   Source not available.
3   Walter Crane, *Ideals in Art* (London: George Bell and Sons, 1905).

4   Source not available.
5   Daniel-Henry Kahnweiler, *Picasso Kermik, Ceramic, Ceramique* (Hanover: Kacketrager Verlag, 1956).
6   Richard Lunn, *Pottery: A Handbook of Practical Pottery for Art Teachers* (London: Chapman and Hall, 1903).
7   Source not available.
8   Source not available.
9   Garth Clark, *The Potter's Art: A Complete History of British Pottery* (London: Phaidon, 1995).
10 Bernard Leach, *A Potter's Book* (London: Faber and Faber, 1940).
11 Bernard Leach's presentation to the Royal Society of Arts, London, 1948.
12 Michael Cardew, *Michael Cardew - A Pioneer Potter* (London: Ceramic Review Publishing, 1988).
13 Source not available.

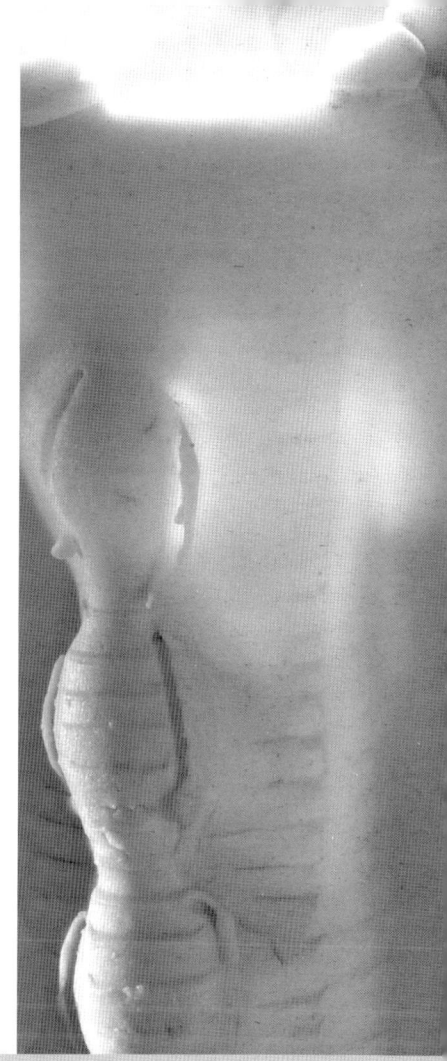

Section Seven
State of the Art

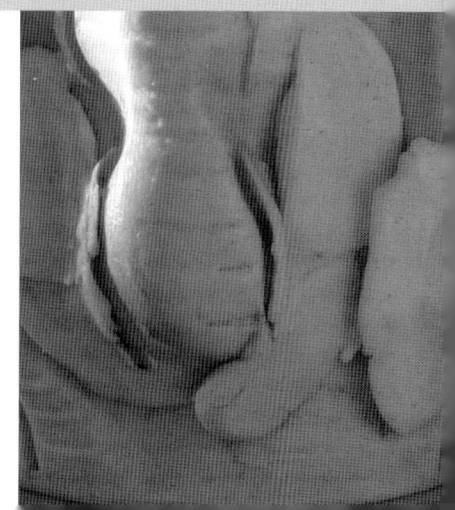

CHAPTER 23

CERAMICS AND ART CRITICISM

JANET KOPLOS

Ceramics is a visual art, although it's not painting, and it's not sculpture. It has its own identity. The position of ceramics today is not a problem. If there's a dilemma, it's that ceramists, having learned their trade at art school, lust after the perceived status of painting and sculpture, whether or not they want to follow the practices of those arts.

Presented at *The Ceramic Millennium*, 1999, Amsterdam

My subject is criticism, and although I will mention a few artists, my focus is on words more than work. I must warn you that I'm going to be saying some things that some of you won't want to hear. I have two main points to make. One will probably find no disagreement: ceramics criticism is weak if you compare it with art criticism. But my second assertion is that ceramics is not the same as painting and sculpture, and never will be. The situation is complex, and that's what makes it fascinating. But I hope to speak simply about it.

Garth has given me three charges. I'll give my perspective on the present state of ceramic art and its relationship to the art world. This is a basic consideration on which all criticism relies. I'm also going to evaluate the quality of ceramic criticism. And I'm going look at some options for the future.

I will be talking about examples and issues in American ceramics. But the similarity of the issues in other places I know a little about, such as Holland, Japan, and

Britain, lead me to believe that the discussion will be relevant to other places as well.

On the one hand, clay is just a material. It can be used to make beautiful things, useful things, thought-provoking things. There is no barrier that keeps clay out of the art galleries. In fact, one sees a considerable amount of work in clay in the museums and galleries of New York and elsewhere. Anthony Caro, Lynda Benglis, Thomas Schutte, Beverly Semmes, Antony Gormley, Charles LeDray, and lots of other contemporary artists work with clay. The Kruithuis Museum here in Holland did a show of great modern and contemporary artists who've worked extensively in clay, from Picasso to Fontana to A.R. Penck. Clay is among the materials that an artist may use to make a form or express a notion in a finished work, not to mention its traditional role in modelling for bronze casting. So there is no stigma to using clay. It's a non-issue.

But ceramics is something else. In the sociological sense, ceramics is a community based on a material and shared attitudes toward working with it. Ceramics has its own teaching programs, its own residency sites, its own publications, its own technical jargon, its own politics, its own galleries and museums, its own history of makers and styles, its own international symposia. This world is, to a degree, independent of the art world, but it brushes up against it all the time, which produces some friction.

Just as the ceramic world is distinguishable from the art world, ceramic art is distinguishable from painting and sculpture—and I'm using that cumbersome phrase "painting and sculpture" as a broad heading, because I dislike the term "fine art," which seems to me to imply that everything else is not fine. The aesthetic of ceramics is far from being a single thing, yet there are typical and atypical types, and there are qualities that identify it as a particular and interesting field in itself. So let me venture a few generalities.

Nearly always, a work of ceramic art is an object. Usually it's of throwing size, related to human body scale, even if it's made by some other technique. Most often it is a hollow volume—that is, a vessel. Although it is usually three dimensional, ceramics tends to concentrate on the embellishment of surface more than on the invention of form, and on detail more than on large gesture. Surface and form are often separate considerations in ceramics, which is seldom the case in mainstream sculpture. In general, surface is more important in ceramics than in sculpture.

And ceramics has the additional dimension of an inside contributing to its character, so that it involves a topological transformation of a bulge on the outside being a recess on the inside—a quality that open vessels particularly exploit. Vessels pull vision and imagination into themselves. They focus inward, centered on that interior void, rather than reaching outward to command the surrounding space.

Ceramics is often purely formalist, developing relationships of part or colour for their own inherent satisfaction, rather than for the expression of an external meaning. These relationships of parts typically play on a spectrum of unity or disunity, probably because of that capacity of form and surface to operate independently. It also often incorporates, as a sort of subtext, the history of decorative or utilitarian form, conveying multicultural references. Ceramics has always been richly multicultural encompassing rather than exclusionary. Ceramics may be representational as well. Although political subjects are possible, they have never been so important as in painting. Humour is found more frequently in ceramics than in painting or sculpture. This, I think, shows a wish to follow the practice of painting and sculpture to violate expectations, but without provoking hostility—or taking itself too seriously. Ceramics tends to be easy going as a statement—almost embarrassed to be excessive—yet intense as a demonstration of skill.

Looking at the field as a whole, it's possible to recognize a certain manner. One can also recognize that different character when gallery hopping. If you've been looking at paintings or installations, and you walk into a ceramics show, you have to narrow your focus to smaller scale, attend more to detail and subtler interests. Ceramics seems to ask for intimate address more than painting and sculpture do. Nevertheless, the whole twentieth century drift in ceramics is for the work to be analyzed and understood in terms of expectations adopted from painting and sculpture. Both inside and outside the field, it's the deviations from this typical character that get attention.

While there is no hostility toward clay in the art world, there are negative stereotypes about ceramics in general and assumptions that it is not as interesting, not as adventurous, not as important as painting and sculpture. Often the ceramics field itself seems to share this skepticism! In fact, ceramics, for the most part, operates under a sensitive aesthetic that has more in common with prints and drawings than painting and sculpture. The labour of processes, the vulnerability of the material, do not seem to encourage the grand gestures or flamboyant outrages that our celebrity-obsessed and media-driven contemporary culture responds to. Leading-edge art today tends to challenge traditions and to respond to the world—with social engagement or with irony.

Art has been defined by materials and format. That is, a painting is art whether it is good or bad; it's art by definition, and quality is a separate question. More recently, art is defined by manner and mindset or by context: that is, anything shown in an art gallery is art, even cooking a big pot of food to share and not cleaning up afterwards, or setting out a giant ashtray full of cigarette butts. Skill may be demonstrated, and some recent art even takes virtuosity and obsessive labour as its subjects, but it's the treatment of a subject, not the skill or the labour per se, that makes it art today.

Clay, of course, may match these art characteristics and fit the definition of art without strain. Even works in clay that take the vessel form may do so. Even vessels produced by people who come from a ceramics background by training and socializing may do so. It becomes art by accolade, because it's so good. Thus Betty Woodman, who started out as a production potter, is discussed in art magazines in terms of her innovative and challenging painting, which moves through three-dimensional space discontinuously around the surface of an object or several objects in combination. Thus Robert Arneson is praised by art critics for his irreverent wit, for his skill at mimicry, and for grasping archetypal forces that animate the collective American psyche, as one of them put it. Thus art critics looking at Ken Price's recent vessels respond to their sensuousness, their anthropomorphic mystery, and their striking concordance with the formal insouciance and eye-grabbing colour of a much younger generation of Los Angeles artists, as another critic said. Thus Daisy Youngblood has impressed a succession of art critics with her eerie fragmented animal and human figures with empty eye sockets that seem to give a view into their bleak souls. Clay is not an impediment to art status in any of these examples. Woodman, Arneson, and Youngblood in New York and Price in Los Angeles show at important mainstream art galleries, not in specialized craft or ceramic galleries.

Considering how different the work of these four artists is, it seems clear that ceramics criticism can not be reduced to a simple formula or set of expectations. Once there was talk about truth to materials, but we've come to realize that one of the truths of ceramics is that it's a chameleon. It can be pretty much whatever the maker wants it to be. Figural, decorative, tactile, architectural, painterly, gestural, pictorial, usable, symbolic of the long continuity of time, symbolic of the fleet passage of time, and so on and so on. It can be formalist, it can be metaphoric. Archaic or space age, sensuous or cold.

Ceramics is a visual art, although it's not painting, and it's not sculpture. It has its own identity. The position of ceramics today is not a problem. If there's a dilemma, it's that ceramists, having learned their trade at art school, lust after the perceived status of painting and sculpture, whether or not they want to follow the practices of those arts. Young art students today, as a legacy of conceptualism, learn that the idea is the important thing, and they should use whatever medium works for it. But ceramics artists don't want to use whatever medium. The clay comes first, as a precondition. Many of them isolate themselves in the ceramic world and don't know what's going on in painting and sculpture. Yet their complaints reveal that they think that the art world is better than their own, and they want access. Actually, they hope that the art world will discover them, come around to their thinking, buy their work for the high prices paintings sell for. They want to be appreciated not by the public but by these elites. If I were being unkind, I'd say that they don't want to play the game, yet they want to win the prize. This is ambition in word but not in deed.

I must emphasize and re-emphasize that the "otherness" of ceramics, this non-paintingness, non-sculptureness, is a good thing. Ceramics should be accepted and celebrated for its own attributes. What would be gained by every medium trying to adopt the expectations of painting? Art, you know, goes through fads and aberrations, follows social change more often than it foreshadows it, and has lately become so dependent on language and video that one wonders if its simply going to turn into literature and movies and nothing else! Art does not have a stranglehold on wisdom, and a lot of artists come up empty. So why is there this endless whining about the art status of ceramics as a field? Ceramics is a second-tier aesthetic activity or marginalized *only* if you believe that painting and sculpture define the terms of worthiness; and if you believe that the goals and means of painting and sculpture are the proper ones, then why are you in ceramics? The question is less one of aesthetic hierarchies or exclusion of a material than of identification and self-confidence.

Exactly the same paradox applies in the case of ceramics criticism. If you're comparing it to art criticism, ceramic criticism often isn't very good. It sometimes sounds as unnatural as a speech delivered in a foreign language, and sometime it's just clichéd, because it borrows an established art vocabulary without sufficient regard for appropriateness. This problem has been recognized, so now we have conferences about the need for a language of criticism for clay. But that's still using art criticism as the model and assuming that if we select some nouns and adjectives, by gosh, we'll have our own critical language! But in fact, art words fit styles and visual dynamics just fine, and ordinary language does a good job too. Only art and literary theory and social and political terms seem misapplied. What's needed is not new words, but a framework that adjusts to the specifics of the situation and responds to the particularities of ceramics.

Unfortunately, it's easy to mimic the form of art criticism without the substance. If you act like a critic, you are a critic. All you have to do is use a few popular words, such as "narrative" or "hegemony" or "discourse," or others borrowed from writing in other fields. You can get away with almost anything, because there's no certification process. Who can measure a critic's performance? Peers could, but professional courtesy tends to keep the lid on that. One might think that editors would put a stop to bad criticism, but for reasons I'll get to in a moment, that doesn't seem to happen. So a lot of nonsense gets written about ceramics. But do remember that a lot of nonsense gets written about all art, and there's a lot of excruciatingly boring writing and a lot of impenetrable stuff. That got really bad in the eighties with theoretical writing based on literary criticism and employing dense, scholarly jargon. The difficulty is compounded in ceramics because of the multiple purposes and goals of clay, and also because of a lack of support structure, such as programs of study that would give a critic a historical and philosophical background and bases for comparison. (Britain, maybe because of its literary orientation, has a stronger recent history of serious, provocative, substantial, and continuous consideration of craft issues and history by scholar/critics such Tanya Harrod, the late Peter Dormer, and others. This exemplary activity has no equal in the USA.)

Ceramics looks to art for the style of criticism, and sometimes for the practitioners as well. Just as there are visitors to ceramics, there are visitors to ceramics criticism. Craft periodicals and catalogues solicit art writers. That has the appeal of broadening the field and getting fresh perspectives. It's sometimes really just a means of seeking legitimation, but if it introduces art critics to ceramics, that can be useful. When writing by outsiders is bad, that may be because they don't know enough, and the writing is superficial—sometimes overly impressed with the fact that clay is a craft material, while not sufficiently examining what's being done with it. Other bad ceramics writing by art critics is that shaped entirely by the idiosyncrasies and established agenda of the critic, whether it's politics, theory, or psychology.

When it's good, writing by outsiders opens new doors. Arthur Danto has applied philosophical questions to the nitty-gritty of clay, using comprehensible language. Other good writing by outsiders genuinely cross-fertilizes, which is the case in recent analysis of Betty Woodman's work by the painter and critic Robert Berlind, writing a catalogue essay for an exhibition in Iowa.[1] He takes a theme of "between" in addressing Woodman's work. He describes geometric against organic, fact against metaphor, invention against reinterpretation, as well as figure-ground reversals and the relation of the work to both sculpture and painting. He compares her spontaneity to action painting (Abstract Expressionism), and he discusses thinking through the act. Berlind brings a particular painter's sensibility to his essay, producing a rich, rewarding piece of critical writing.

Another institutional or structural problem with ceramics criticism is that the field is narrow, and therefore the pay is too little for anyone to make a living as a ceramics critic. Financial hardship can deter capable writers from pursuing the subject, unless they're really driven to do it, regardless of the lack of reward. Too often criticism is expected to be a charitable donation of time and effort! Another problem is that publications don't develop critical thinking by pushing writers, by sending manuscripts back with challenging questions that require critics to reach more deeply into their resources, both factual and imaginative.

I'd like to look briefly at the magazines, American, plus a few others. *Studio Potter* has always presented serious, insider consideration of a certain range of ceramic work, but it depends upon makers to do the writing, and does not pay for writing. Thus, although it supports thinking, it does not foster the development of criticism from objective writers. *Ceramics Monthly* is both a technical publication and, in a way, an academic one—it's a place where teachers can get visibility to please their university's administration. *American Ceramics* is a sad case, because it once seemed so promising. Under the considered editorship of Michael McTwigan it once presented the most consistent critical exchange the postwar American ceramics field has known. Since McTwigan's departure—for work that would pay well enough to support a family—this magazine has come to owe so much money to so many writers and to have alienated so many gallery advertisers by its undependable publication schedule that it's amazing that it persists in its decrepit state. It's still beautiful and usually worth reading when it does come out. Also on this playing field is *Ceramics Review*, the British technical magazine. The strength of the Australian magazine *Ceramic Art and Perception* is beautiful pictures and international focus. The texts are often light and more character oriented than critical. There seem to be problems with finding writers who are not in some way involved with the people or places they're writing about. Perhaps that's because the pay is so modest that critics can't afford to do it, so friends and associates do. One can't be sure of the critical independence and objectivity of what one reads.

There are also general crafts magazines that include ceramics, such as *American Craft* magazine. Years ago, when it was called *Craft Horizons* and was edited by Rose Slivka, it presented an important bridge to the art world through Slivka's personal acquaintance with such artists as David Smith, Elaine and Willem de Kooning, and the poet and translator Richard Howard. Slivka's own writing emphasized the capacity of craft objects to carry poetic feeling; she took it for granted that ceramic objects can be metaphoric, which is a short-form explanation of what makes something art. Since her time, *American Craft* has been more of a coffee-table magazine than a critical one. The review section was discontinued. The articles are intelligent, but they rarely challenge. The only critical content is one or two single-page reviews. The British magazine *Crafts* also has drifted in a more populist, less critical direction since the days when Martina Margetts was editor, though it still has lots of reviews. It has an inventive visual style and a concise, breezy, and informational verbal style, but the articles are fairly short, and there's less sense nowadays of urgently arguing important issues. The editorial staff of most of these magazines consists of professional editors who are not active as critics, which is different than the pattern of many art magazines and may, in part, explain the different tone of craft publications.

One can look elsewhere for coverage. During the years that Derek Guthrie was publisher of the *New Art Examiner*, that magazine consistently paid attention to ceramics. And the major American art magazines—*Art in America*, *ArtNews* and *Artforum*—have all given feature treatment to significant ceramic artists, as well as publishing many reviews of clay shows. Ken Price's work has been on the cover of *Art in America*. There are also design magazines, such as *Metropolis* in New York, that include contemporary crafts and take an intelligent, critical approach. Ironically, though, these sources of critical writing don't particularly serve the makers of ceramic art as a group, because not so many ceramists read them regularly thus supporting my point about ceramics being a separate community.

Now, all my comments on these publications have been based on the assumption that an art-type criticism is a need or a desire for ceramics. If that's the case, this publication situation is lamentable. But maybe not. Maybe, like water seeking its own level or a time getting the style it deserves, maybe this writing is what ceramics needs—even if not what it says it wants. Before I go on to consider what criticism might be, let's pause to enumerate the forms of writing about ceramics. I can name the types in just a few words: technical, lifestyle, work documentation, experiential, historical, and theoretical, probably in descending order of frequency. I think that tells us something, and I'll come back to this idea at the end.

Do consider the value of various kinds of writing, now and in the recent past. There are books, whether about ceramics specifically or not, that can be profitably applied to thinking about ceramics. Bernard Leach, despite the fact that he's getting kicked around nowadays, is still useful. He attempted to identify values for ceramics, and that's still stimulating. Books like David Pye's *The Nature and Art of Workmanship* enrich the discussion of labour, which is significant in ceramics. Philip Rawson's historical treatment in his book *Ceramics* tells us how the work can be analyzed and understood, and what ceramics has meant and therefore what it has the potential to mean. M.C. Richards made ceramics a metaphor for living.[2] Henry Petroski's *The Evolution of Useful Things* makes us think about the forms and purpose of objects and tools around us. Garth Clark mapped out contemporary American ceramics history and fearlessly evaluated work, something that's very difficult to do in such a small world. This variety points to the possibilities and maybe identifies the needs. Stop to think: if there consistently is so much writing about technique and lifestyle, maybe that's in fact what's important. Maybe that's the meaning of this activity.

Well, I'm not really a believer in forecasts of anything having to do with humans. You can predict the weather, maybe, but people, and especially artists, tend to come up with options more fascinating than any I could imagine, which is why I hang around them. But I think I can confidently predict that ceramics as a field is not going to be taken up wholesale by the art world. If that's your hope, I'd recommend that you get over it. I don't think it's something to wish for. It would just mean that things would be regarded as poor sculptures rather than good pots, faulted for not being spatially interactive, or on the edge, or whatever.

The situation of photography is a relevant comparison. Photography, like clay, is a medium used by artists to suit their purposes. Yet there continue to be photography galleries and photography departments in museums; "pure photography" by people who devote their lives to traditional-format documentations of existence in this medium tend to be concentrated in these specialty galleries, rather than being taken up by mainstream painting-and-sculpture galleries. So it is with ceramics, and will continue to be.

The most traditional forms, those that make reference primarily to the ceramic tradition itself, remain in the specialty galleries, outside the usual routes of art critics. This work is covered by specialty criticism, which follows the model of art criticism—but is not the same. It is softer and more sympathetic. (One might note, however, that photography has been more successful than ceramics in establishing itself as an academic field of historic and aesthetic study.)

What should ceramics criticism be? What makes good criticism? My feeling is that learned and intellectual criticism certainly has a place, and that place is academia. Such writing is too specialized and too difficult to be useful in the ordinary consideration of ceramic art in magazines and newspapers. I prefer to think of criticism as a translation service for what is otherwise a nonverbal form of expression. The critic mediates between the work and the viewer, and helps the viewer to see. The critic may have special knowledge, or the critic may simply be a person who looks carefully at art and thinks seriously about it—an ideal viewer who also has writing skills. It has been said that the essential critical activity is not having an opinion, because everybody has opinions; the essential critical activity is giving reasons for those opinions.

If criticism is regarded that way, it surely is an important part of the ceramics world, even if ceramics is not painting and not sculpture. Criticism should be just good, clear thinking, communicated to others. Every field needs that. The problems come when critics think that ceramics should be something other than what it is and turn the heads of the makers. Critics should not write rules, and makers should remember that no one ever did a great or original thing by following what other people claim is important.

I can see four things that ceramics criticism can be. One is analysis of the big picture, ceramics in its context. Another is, contrarily, the intimate consideration of the work as a reflection of the maker and the making. Another is simply the verbal expression of the visual—this is the poetic sort of writing. And another is comparison, the grappling with standards, based on whatever seems important in our time or the past, or commercial considerations or personal goals. All these are forms of criticism. The only things ceramics criticism must adopt from art criticism are seriousness, care, and good writing, not pedantry or pompousness, and not the foolish assumption that what's difficult to understand must be important!

It's essential to think about what the specific nature of ceramic works require as a response. I would argue that in contrast to painting and sculpture, greatness and originality are not essential to the vast majority of the uses and pleasures that derive from ceramic work. Maybe function is important. Maybe virtuosity is important. Maybe perpetuating traditions is important. We all know that there *is* a place for clay that carries metaphor and meaning. That place is the art gallery. And clay in the art gallery will find consideration in the same vocabulary and against the same standards as any other contemporary art.

But I worry, in any discussion of criticism, that we will forget that there have always been other places for clay, too, where criticism is irrelevant—the dining table, the kitchen and the garden, among others. Clay has always occupied the space between art and life, although that's a space that the art world only discovered a few decades ago. It seems to me that the major issue for ceramic artists to face is resolving their identity and maintaining *plural* choices. The major issue for ceramic criticism is to intelligently support that pluralism.

1   Robert Berlind, *Betty Woodman* (Fort Dodge, IA: Blanden Memorial Art Museum, 1999).
2   Mary Caroline Richards, *Centering in Pottery, Poetry, and the Person* (Middletown, CT: Wesleyan University Press, 1964).

CHAPTER 24

OF THE UNDEAD AND DESIRES: ABOUT THE UNDEAD AND DESIRES FOR A DEFINITION OF THE CRAFT ARTS. FOR EXAMPLE: CERAMICS, AN EXAMPLE OF FUTILITY.

GABI DEWALD

As we know, the craftsmen-labourers who formerly carried out the necessary tasks are no longer affordable. This sector, too, is now governed by rationalization and monopolization. In many a case, craftsmen's firms are reduced to qualified assembly firms. In this way knowledge of materials and technology, of regional traits and individual solutions is lost. The same is also true in the world of ceramics: What was once turned is now poured; what was once painted is now decorated with a decal. Articles which used to be dipped by hand are nowadays put in the spray booth—always imitating handcrafted pieces. The result: stillbirths, utterly superfluous kitsch. To clarify matters, I have nothing against the technique of pouring, nor against ceramic print techniques or spray glazes. I do, however, object to deceit and visual stultification.

Presented at *The Ceramic Millennium*, 1999, Amsterdam

Late summer last year—it was early evening when we arrived in the secluded valley high up in the mountains. We had taken a small detour on the way from Bologna to Frankfurt and driven up here for the evening, up to the point where all the roads finally came to an end. A walk through the countryside: the air was fresh after the thunderstorm, the sunlight was already tinged with red, the green meadows were shimmering wetly, a few beetles came out from under dripping leaves and scuttled away in a hurry after the downpour. Someone was herding cows past us. I stopped in front of the house, an abandoned farmhouse. A new, modern house had been built next to it. The old farmhouse was decaying—the roof was already cracked, the stonework was damp, the wood was musty, the windows dark, blind hollows.

Suddenly the place comes to life. It's as though I see the family, the inhabitants of the house, their suntanned South Tyrolean farmers faces. I can feel the scratchy, untreated cotton fabric of their shirts and skirts, smell the kitchen range, which gives off smoke in the corner, where soup is cooking and socks are drying. They quarrel and they laugh; I can hear their songs. I hear the sound of spoons scraping against rough bowls. I breathe in the stuffy air in the room, where a handful of people seek protection and security, try to fence themselves off from the outside world, to define a part of the human world for themselves, to create a piece of culture in the midst of all-powerful nature. I see how they strip the bark from chopped tree trunks, how they grease the animals' harnesses, how their cracked fingertips ruffle their children's hair.

All this had been yesterday. This was what life was like here just fifty years ago. Situated in an inaccessible location, the village community was self-sufficient, and it was a sensation if someone left the valley, or what you could learn listening to the first radios, for example, was unimaginable. All of a sudden I start to understand: there are worlds of difference between then and now. And it is all irretrievably lost. No one can lay hands on it anymore. There it is, buried deep down, as though sealed up under a thick layer of ice, somewhat blurred, only just recognizable.

Suddenly it occurs to me how ridiculous museum attempts are to show people today something of this submerged—or should one say rapidly buried—world, to keep it alive, or even preserve it from being forgotten. In the village, committed citizens tried to pick up on the individual characteristics of regional architecture and maintain them. Taking, for example, the widespread use of wooden balcony railings in Alpine countries, one can study the complete phenomenon and the futility of the attempts at preservation: the imitation of a tradition is at best a kind of helpless worship of the past. The proportions are wrong, the patterns are uniform, the varnish lies like a skin of plastic over the wood. The colours aren't right; the high degree of precision turns a meandering decoration into a martial parade what was once an attractive, relaxed decorative adornment is now a cartridge belt surrounding the house. Do the people in the village see this? Does it bother them?

For centuries, the wood for the houses grew in forests surrounding the village; the trees were felled in winter, brought back to the village using horses and sledges, dried out over several years, then finally smoothed down and used by local builders and craftsmen. Now these balconies are made from Scandinavian, Spanish or maybe even German wood, which is all machine finished somewhere in Europe. They came to the Italian mountain village in a big container, shrink-wrapped in plastic.

As we know, the craftsmen-labourers who formerly carried out the necessary tasks are no longer affordable. This sector, too, is now governed by rationalization and monopolization. In many a case, craftsmen's firms are reduced to qualified assembly firms. In this way knowledge of materials and technology, of regional traits and individual solutions is lost.

The same is also true in the world of ceramics: What was once turned is now poured; what was once painted is now decorated with a decal. Articles which used to be dipped by hand are nowadays put in the spray booth—always imitating hand-crafted pieces. The result: stillbirths, utterly superfluous kitsch. To clarify matters, I have nothing against the technique of pouring, nor against ceramic print techniques or spray glazes. I do, however, object to deceit and visual stultification.

Let's go back to the example from the South Tyrol. What also suddenly became clear to me was that the main reason for our rapid and irreversible rupture with our own tradition is our completely changed understanding of time. Our daily rhythms have altered completely, as has the rhythm of our lives. We are living in a time-lapse world. And the unit of time—which once was called day or year or also event or celebration—is now summed up in dates and deadlines. Time is no longer measured in periods comprising processes within which growth is possible, where something can rest, germinate, mature, ferment, and soak. Time is the relentless, breathless, and uniform staccato of standardized production processes. The hammering, propelling rhythm is set by international finance and interest policies. What remains, is a longing for natural rhythms, for time spaces, for comprehensible processes, for contexts that can be experienced. Yet traditions and customs are no longer maintained—who would have enough time for that? They are merely quoted. Living tradition has, at its best, been replaced by a sentimental worship of the past, often enough by a retrospect, diffuse longing for yesterday. (Which we all left behind us readily and for easily understandable reasons. Neither you nor I would believe that any of the farmers from the mountain village mentioned at the beginning would want to live again as they did in the last century.) Only artists and artist-craftsmen, it seems, have placed themselves persistently, albeit rarely with economic success, outside the time dictates of modern life and have successfully defended the main ingredient of their products: they are long lasting and enduring.

Once again, back to the roots. Why? Simply take it as a plea against boredom. Take a look at the many international ceramics competitions, for example. Entries from California will be no different to those from Great Britain, South Africa, or New Zealand: "global art" is what bored art critics called it—and I share their irritation. I believe—and infinitely regret—that our world is losing both variety and colour as a result of the levelling out of cultural differences. I am speaking of the uniqueness and, at the same time, variety of the philosophies of life; how they developed over the centuries in relative seclusion and how they bring colour into our contemporary world. I am speaking of the peculiarities of each people, developed from the respective landscapes, the light, the climatic conditions, the smells and the fruits of a country, specific and unique for every region. What I am interested in is a kind of protection of an endangered species of creativity. Protect the variety of individuality from the cultural uniformity of internationalization!

On the European continent which—thank goodness and at long last—is politically and economically taking shape and, indeed, growing together, people are at present perhaps particularly sensitive towards the topic of an individual profile within the community. Being German, born in the time of the postwar *Wirtschaftswunder* I have, at first hand, experienced what it means to be cut off from one's own roots. Due to the abuse by the National Socialists, folk art in particular had become virtually untouchable. Branded by the German crimes, the Germans trusted no one less than themselves, their longings, emotions, and intuitive subjectivity. With perseverance, modesty, and objectivity they tried to gain trust and re-enter the international community. I want to ask you to look at German ceramics, which has often been labelled as boring and stiff.

Frightened to death by their own identity, the Germans regarded intellectualism, objectivism, and internationalism as guarantors for art which is to be taken seriously and which is accepted. Abstraction was taken as point of departure. The painters and sculptors made advances in the informal, in Art Brut, in Arte Povera. The aesthetic legacy left to the arts based on craft media was the Bauhaus. Beyond that, ceramists looked to Japan, be it directly or via the England of Bernard Leach. In the search for integrity and a definition of themselves, they withdrew into their heads. Modern German ceramics started to surpass itself with abstractions and un-sensuous creations of mind. The suspicion of everything figurative is just one symptom of this.

The subsequent search for identity took decades. It may be inconceivable to other nationalities that, for example, a young pottery should give up the production of traditional Bunzlau ware (a simple, strong domestic ware, mainly used for storage and preservation of food), because its customers placed them in a right-wing, nationalist corner. Under these circumstances it is not easy to be uninhibited and to understand that derivation means roots and life instead of tentacles and paralysis. I am, indeed, convinced that the substance, the uniqueness and the independence of a creative idea decisively depends on the knowledge of one's own background and how one deals with it.

In addition to the losses of national profiles and artistic variety we are, however, confronted everywhere with the challenge of disappearing techniques and knowledge of materials and thus with the disappearance of the knowledge of what our visible, tangible world is composed of. In a world which is getting more and more virtual, alienated from the earth and nature on which and in which we are living, doesn't that sound pathetic, almost embarrassing? We no longer know how things are related. We have no knowledge of the basic elements and materials of which our environment is composed. The crafts, often enough practiced after the day's work or, for seasonal reasons, as a side occupation, have kept this knowledge alive and passed it on, far away from specialization and division of labour. Just attempt to ask a group of adults and children to kindle a fire and keep it going. You will ask yourself how the human species ever came to develop a space program or even not to starve. Who still knows something about fire today? About water and wind? About sowing and harvesting? How paper is made, or cloth to keep us warm? When did you last stroke the animal from which you feed?

No, you need not worry. I don't want you to wear rough cloaks and carve wooden shoes in the light of a pinewood torch. I am, however, convinced that the survival of our species is largely dependent on our ability to maintain access to the simple, elementary things of life. One can only protect what one knows. If we (and our offspring) keep losing the knowledge of the natural connections at this speed, we will lose the appreciation and the protection not only of our natural but also of our cultural resources. And, as I already said, one can only protect what one knows. To my mind, in view of the relentless, global dictate of economy in our fast-moving age, the craft arts assume a new role that should not be underestimated.

What craft alone can no longer deliver because it is not able to remain competitive, and what art does not want to deliver because it primarily operates on an intellectual level, must now be done through arts based on craft media and by the artist-craftsman. It is what we call *Kunsthandwerk*, the highly developed artistic craft. Concerning the problem of languages and interpretation, these craft-media-based arts or artistic craftsmanship shall be called further and from now on "craft arts." With regard to ceramics, craft arts describe functional and decorative work made from clay/porcelain and made by a ceramist in his or her studio. The craft arts start—like craft—from the material, but they are positioned outside the constraints of production processes. Here the inherent potential of the materials is merged with the skills of craftsmanship and design innovations to form objects of everyday life.

Whether this disdained genre will succeed in achieving a self-confident, even prospering position will, however, largely depend on the support system, thought leaders, opinion makers and financial backers in our society. There is increasing evidence of the hopes that are today placed in the craft arts. Let me quote the Japanese Toshiyuki Kita from his paper "Tradition and the Modern Age":

> The collective knowledge of thousands of years is concentrated in an artistically crafted object of high quality. Such objects are, so to speak, the floppy discs of the past.... The development of new concepts for modern products in the electronics and automobile industry should really draw much more from an understanding of old traditions and ways of life. In order to create designs of a better quality we shall have to find a certain balance.

Continuation of the plea: For the craft arts, I know that all ceramists would like somehow to be artists. However, while pears and apples are both equally delicious, they are not the same thing. To clarify: when referring to craft arts, I mean everyday objects, which are useful in a functional and/or decorative sense and are put to use.

I know that the designation of craft arts—with few exceptions worldwide—is tantamount to an insult and a slight. I know that the genre of functional ware is condescendingly rejected and mocked as distasteful and frivolous. Ceramists suffer from this social rejection much more than goldsmiths, glassblowers, or even carpenters. I became embroiled in a fully blown argument when I—in my capacity as curator for a European craft arts exhibition—refused to acquire the work of ceramic sculptors for this presentation. Am I backward looking? No. However, here too, in this context, I do not believe in the blessings of egalitarianism, but much more in the sense of difference. And I actually believe that we need artist-craftsmen, in the true sense of the word, today more than ever before. After all, it is here that solutions provided by craft arts and creative innovations merge with the intrinsic potential of a material in an everyday object. In dealing with these objects, we learn in a casual, pleasant way; we train our senses and satisfy our aesthetic desires.

Liberalization was one of the great slogans of this century: down with dividing boundaries, taboos and ghettoization, freedom from narrow mindedness and conservative patterns of behavior, seeing the other person's perspective, understanding it or at least placing it without prejudice beside your own—these were the priorities. What could have been more necessary, after industrialization had turned upside down working processes along with the old code of values? In radio, and soon afterwards on television, the world approached us at racing speed, and this deadly mixture of narrow-mindedness, bigotry, and megalomania transformed Europe into a slaughterhouse.

Liberalization means: freedom from restrictions. It doesn't, however, mean the superfluity of definitions. On the contrary, it calls for an examination of existing definitions and, as a second step, to reformulate them. I think that this task—independently of the turn of the millennium—is a particular challenge with which we are confronted right now. And I also think that this is a task of exhibition organizers, for example, or of curators and jurors, not as dogma, but as an understandable concept which can be discussed. If exhibitions, like that of the international World Crafts Council in Vienna last autumn, are acknowledged as having good intentions but no orientation, this is an unfortunate judgment which could be made of craft arts events by the dozen. Out of a fear of appearing restrictive and without inner vision, the crafts side is regarded as obsolete, and the creative side is attributed to art—end of discussion. This is how the undead are produced.

As long as we consider the craft arts as secondary art or merely a traditional form of expression handed down to us, which does not have an independent future of its own, we will not be able to get out of this lull in which the craft arts are languishing. It obviously offers little advantage to sail in the shadow of the frigate of the fine arts; it would be much more useful to draw on the desperate need for the craft arts and what they can provide, formulate this and use it as a driving force. Like no other discipline, the craft arts are in a position to fulfill our tactile, visual, and intellectual desires for the materials which make up our world. In this sense the craft arts are a very integral medium for imparting knowledge, a knowledge with which—for the aforementioned reasons—no other discipline is dealing with any more.

I think that the past decades provided sufficient proof that the attempt to declare the craft arts categorically, and in the name of the above-mentioned liberalism, as art, has accomplished nothing more than to lead a host of erring souls to suddenly start naming their rose vases *Hommage a Giacometti* or, bewilderingly, call a tray lined with sheepskin, bearing seven cups, the *Meret Oppenheim Installation*. This is neither humorous nor original but helpless and annoying. It simply confirms all of the prejudice that confronts the craft arts.

The Austrian ceramist and sculptor Kurt Spurey writes: "Where is the self-consciousness of the craftsman? Why do they all flee to 'sublime art'? Can't they exist alone by virtue of their own works, must they first have the blessing of art to feel acknowledged? There appears to me to be a serious lack of support." I share his judgment and challenge all curators, gallery owners, journalists, teachers, and museum directors here to reconsider their positions and statements. When the professor of a Norwegian university informs me, with pride and a wink of the eye, that the tiresome discussion about the craft arts and the disdain associated with this has finally come to an end simply by striking the term "craft arts" from the name of the school and the department, and that the institution is now purely an art school, I find this type of cunning compromise not only futile and naive, but I am infuriated by the short sightedness of people who are part of the support system and shape opinions and careers.

Please allow me at this point to add as an explanation of the terms—an attempt at a definition, in which I would like to introduce, in their distinctiveness—the three terms: art, design, and craft or the craft arts (which are all too often thrown into one melting pot).

Art is a discipline that is orientated towards insight, free from purpose, and under an obligation to nothing but the artist's world view. Works of art derive their significance from the fact that they overcome the self-referential, opening themselves up to the recipient's own, exclusively individual insight. Art is by nature visionary.

Design is a service. It combines in functional objects the purpose which they serve with a design corresponding to the spirit of the age. Design conceives functional objects anew. In this process of conceiving anew or re-conceiving, design takes into account the requirements of today while anticipating those of tomorrow. Design is by nature urban.

Craft (craft arts) is a primarily material-oriented discipline in which there is a balance between design, choice of material, and will to conceive. The artist-craftsman is primarily bound to his or her material, which was chosen in preference to others to explore and use in a specific manner. This material is binding—also with respect to the possible results. Craftsmanship is by nature tactile and intimate. The process of defining is not restrictive in itself. What is restrictive, however, is the associated categorization into hierarchies. I refuse to lump these three things—the craft arts, design and art—together or order them in any kind of graduated hierarchy; this is indeed boring, obsolete, and superfluous! It fails to appreciate the needs and demands which we have to recognize and formulate, especially at the end of a century where we should be correcting previous courses and beating new paths.

I consider it completely senseless to avoid the term craft arts, to dress it up as something else, or to want to eliminate it. The craft arts have their own profile and their own unmistakable purpose. Self-confidence and an offensive strategy are needed here. The world's largest consumer goods trade fair in Frankfurt doesn't sponsor craft arts annually with a six-figure budget for nothing. I quote the press speaker of the Frankfurt trade fair: "The craft arts exhibitors are the creative cell. They make up the creative center at the trade fair. New ideas and innovative tendencies can be found here much earlier than in any other area."

Of course, the craft arts find themselves in a much more difficult position than design because of its very nature: design—in accordance with its function (production in large quantities)—promises the modern person a certain degree of individualism by keeping him distinguishable without becoming open to attack. A design article does protect me; it proves my prosperity, contemporary spirit, and my affiliation to an upper caste. The message is here: I am not a conformist, but am floating in the middle of the stream of events. A crafts object now endangers me, for it is not a streamlined design, but an individual, personal statement. Design is an evidence, craft is a confession. Here, one person produces something and another can buy it. Design is public, crafts is private. Design slips something upon me while crafts uncover something. Design keeps me impregnable while crafts expose me. It is the crafts insistence on the intimate view of the world that today's society rejects as embarrassing, awkward, and out-of-date. Design is so successful because it knows how to take the innovative derivatives from the craft arts and combine this distillate with the right amount of understatement and mass acceptability.

I would like to just quickly prevent any misconception that I might be of the opinion that people who work with ceramics should stick to the craft arts sector and ideally produce tableware. Clay is a material. It can be used for interior design, for example, for things for the table and the household, structural ceramics, technical ceramics, ceramic sculptures and reliefs, etc. This is each individual's decision, for which he or she, in consequence, is responsible.

But please allow me to make a brief observation on the subject of "ceramic art," an expression that I believe to be an unhappy one (how would it be if we had "bronze art" or "wooden art"?). Anyone who wants to work as a sculptor should be trained as a sculptor. If they also have an interest in clay, they can undertake additional, special training for this material. Anyone who applies for special ceramics education shouldn't act as though they didn't know that they would be taught as a rule by specialists in ceramics—with jobs involving ceramics—and not by painters and sculptors. One is trained here as a ceramist and not as a sculptor, which is the case at academies of fine arts. Why do these students wonder at the fact that they can't exist in the fine arts market when they have undergone specialized training in ceramics? One hears time and again that this problem of acceptance of ceramic art in the art market doesn't exist in the USA. But as a rule you'll have to search long and hard even to find names like Voulkos or Saxe in the relevant art magazines.

I don't think that it is merely the ignorance of the media, critics, and gallery owners if they seldom show enthusiasm. I admit that I have only rarely seen sculptures made of clay which I understand. Anyone who is fully aware of what he or she is doing and has retreated for years into a niche in the ceramics greenhouse should not be surprised when he or she withers faster than imagined when venturing into the acid rain of the fine arts market and doesn't find acceptance. However, I have intentionally chosen not to make this bleak chapter the topic of today's talk.

Instead, I would like to turn my attention to a stepchild of the scene, which I find has unjustifiably been rejected in ceramic circles and has been dismissed as base: tableware. It is a regrettable misjudgment of reality that it is considered more dignified today to create some dust, collecting object instead of conceiving and producing objects that are actually needed! It is considered an insult to artistic potency to work on the development of tableware, which people will then use daily for their meals, but it is seen as a challenge to build some gigantic installation which, apart from the artist and possibly his or her three best friends, won't interest another soul, and which the art scene has already been subjected to on at least thirty other occasions in some similar shape or form. Again, the teachers and training concepts also come into the line of fire here.

Why is it seen as an unbearable humiliation to work, for example, with crockery? The industry and design sectors make big names for themselves with these things. Are people unaware of the subversive power of ordinary everyday life? Advertising, as an example, uses the effect of the subliminal in a blatant and effective way. In the morning, when I'm still half asleep and long before my visual sense, never mind my brain, has started to function, and I reach for one or another of the cups in the cupboard, pour tea into it and lift it with both hands to my mouth, I am taking in so much information, unspoken, subconsciously. I let myself be led, I acquiesce, I respond to suggestion, and I am influenced in such a way, that in the end, I don't understand why the production of tableware, even in its artistic challenge and potential for expression (especially in the sense of a dialogue with the user/onlooker), is rejected as being banal. The tactile quality of the material, the possibilities of making a meal (not only a feast for the palate but also for the eyes) a pleasure to the sense of touch, an aesthetically pleasing experience, a celebration of food as a baroque event, as ascetic architecture, as a marriage of the inner and the outer, to school the senses, to waken the consciousness of the whole everyday experience as the essential and substantial act and ritual—what is banal and boring about this?

Here, gallery owners and exhibition organizers as well as organizers and sponsors of competitions and the media are called upon to arouse more attention and appreciation among the public. Incidentally, where prizes are concerned: the craft arts are expensive because exclusivity can by no means be cheap. It is up to us to create awareness and forums for it, to think up forms of presentation and events which clarify this interaction of these different cultural assets and their indispensability to our lives. The classic gallery, with spotlights and white pedestals, does not (not only in this context) belong more to the obsolete bourgeois forms of presentation. Artist-craftsmen need support from external sources. I would like to quote Garth Clark at this point. When I interviewed him in February, he commented that "for an artist to make a career, he or she needs some ten, twenty or a hundred authors, curators, dealers, collectors, photographers, exhibition organizers, and restorers." I completely agree.

Someone, for example, who seriously advises a man like the French Claude Champy to finally, and in God's name, give up on the idea of the vessel and the functionality of his ceramics, completely fails to recognize the rhyme and reason of his work and that of many other ceramists, who devote their work to the concept of the vessel, one of our oldest cultural assets: it serves the holding, collecting, storing, and the proffering of the contents. Vessels only reach perfection by being used and become complete through their respective uses, which is completely beyond the control of the artist as author. The artist's influence ends with the stimulating effect with which he imparts to the vessel its individual character. But the vessel, even the ritual vessel, is always communicative and open for use by other actors and, for this reason, is also irreplaceable as a metaphor and symbol in the human community. How marvelous it is that there are always people who devote themselves to this subject, in keeping with the times.

In this sense I also perceive this conference as a vessel, in which I place my theories and thoughts—a bit like fruit. I hope that they will awaken your interest, curiosity, or even your desire. Maybe you will pick up one or another of these. I hope that you will savour them, that they will refresh or strengthen you, and that you will extend this palette of intellectual food with further, perhaps completely unfamiliar, forms of nutrition for a new millennium.

Chapter 25

Patronage

David McFadden

We will look at the ways in which ceramics, and particularly porcelain—I've really narrowed it on this field—have interacted with individuals, cultures, institutions, and systems of values, and how the complex story of these interactions provides a suitable background for a new paradigm of creativity in the field today, one constructed from new interdependencies among craft, art, design, and technology, which I believe may be the most important artistic, cultural, and intellectual shift of our times.

Presented at *The Ceramic Millennium*, 1999, Amsterdam

Collecting and connoisseurship, although in the same family of behavior patterns, are not necessarily sympathetic or mutually supportive. Collectors assemble groups of things; connoisseurs establish hierarchies of meaning within groups of things. As early as the eighteenth century, it was Voltaire who said, "The best is the enemy of the good," establishing a hierarchical relationship of quality between objects. The writer John Windsor calls collecting "man's fatal attraction to objects," and he goes on to say it's the primary determinant of human culture. As we all know, the objects of affection for collectors can range from what can only be described as "sublime" to what can only, with great kindness, be called "trash." Werner Muensterberger, in his 1994 book called *Collecting: A Unruly Passion*, introduces the psychology of collecting. He says,

> Observing collectors, one soon discovers an unrelenting need, even hunger, for acquisitions. This ongoing search is a core element of their personality. It is linked to far deeper roots. It turns out to be a tendency which derives from a not immediately discernible sense of memory, of deprivation, or loss, or vulnerability, and a subsequently longing for substitution closely allied with moodiness and depressive leanings.[1]

What makes a collector and what turns a collector into a connoisseur? What is this fatal attraction to stuff that somehow expresses inner states of thought, being, and belief? In 1993 (and I apologize for those of you who already know this famous quotation) British writer Martin Kelner penned what has become a very often-quoted function of the meaning of life for the collector. Kelner's theory states:

> Life is all about acquiring stuff, then acquiring more stuff, maybe changing your stuff around a little, then acquiring even more stuff, then getting a bigger place because there's no room for all your stuff, getting rid of some stuff, then getting a smaller place because you haven't got as much stuff, then you die.[2]

What do our collections mean? Are there standards of excellence that are understood by all collectors within a field or are the vagaries of connoisseurship and taste as undependable and as changeable as artistic trends in fashions? As we are all here to examine aspects of ceramic culture at the end of one millennium and the beginning of another, it would be a more than serious oversight to ignore the fascinating and sometimes perplexing history of collecting, patronage, and connoisseurship in the field.

At the same time the subject is one fraught with many uncertainties and gray areas. While the history of collecting has been extensively researched and written about, it is curious to find that even recent books, like Munsterberger's, do not even address connoisseurship or patronage as an extension of collecting. This brief talk must necessarily skim lightly over a history of connoisseurship, collecting, and patronage.

To examine connoisseurship and its relationship to patronage, I have chosen certain areas for closer examination and, needless to say, a great many more are over looked. Today we will look at the ways in which ceramics, and particularly porcelain—I've really narrowed it on this field—have interacted with individuals, cultures, institutions, and systems of values, and how the complex story of these interactions provides a suitable background for a new paradigm of creativity in the field today, one constructed from new interdependencies among craft, art, design, and technology, which I believe may be the most important artistic, cultural, and intellectual shift of our times.

In discussing connoisseurship, I am treading on dangerous ground, since connoisseurship, supposedly the home base for all museum curators, is supposedly based on timeless qualities and characteristics that allow one to make flawless pronouncements of taste. But is the situation truly that simple? Are the standards of excellence and quality ultimately focused within materials, techniques, and process, or are these standards determined and analyzed according to purely formal qualities? The nurture versus nature debate in the worlds of biology and social sciences are paralleled by our own dichotomy.

Connoisseurship may be either a matter of content or context. Context and content are often difficult, if not impossible, to separate, particularly the end of this millennium. In our own epoch—I'll start here—ceramics have served many masters. At one extreme, we take ceramics for granted as the accoutrements of our daily lives. They are our trusted and silent servants. They are with us at our most private and intimate moments. The inherent banality of the material—silent, dependable, affordable, even disposable, as we saw yesterday—makes it the ideal house guest. In the past millennium, however, ceramics have also served on a higher plane, speaking to our most profound and persistent need to create, possess, preserve, and enjoy beauty. Our multilayered relationship with ceramics includes work of exceptional refinement, elegance, and visual provocation, such as the *Light Gatherer* by Rudy Staffel (1979).

The movement of ceramics over the past millennium can be compared to the shifting of tectonic plates in the earth itself: the field moving, colliding, sometimes collapsing, but reforming as social, cultural, commercial, political, and artistic imperatives change. On one hand, we continue to believe in the intensely private inner life, the soul, the content of art, a legacy delivered to our century by thinkers such as Sigmund Freud. At the same time we know that art has also shifted its focus dramatically because of events outside of our own control. Einstein's flexible and

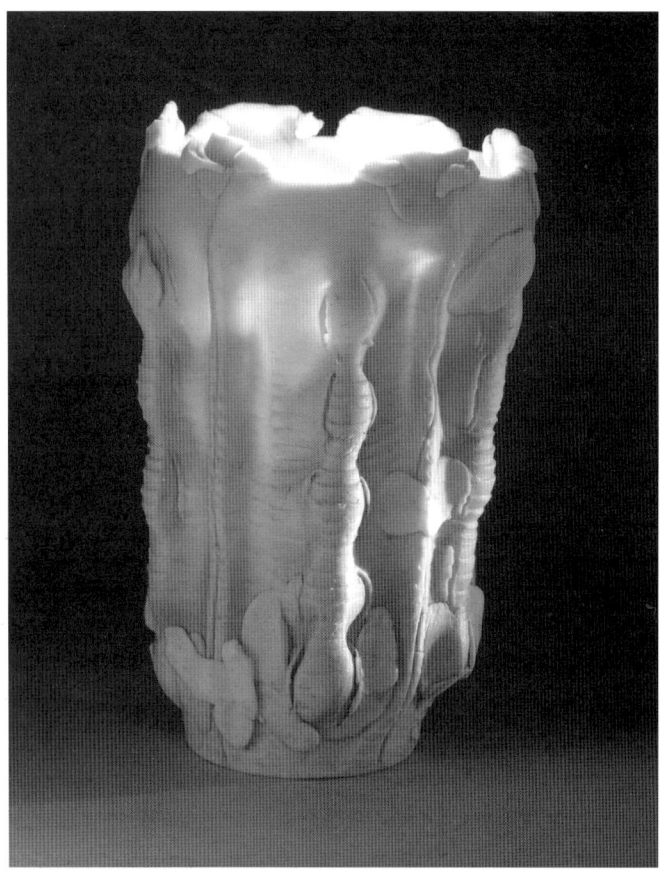

RUDOLF STAFFEL, *LIGHT GATHERER*, 1976. PORCELAIN, 22.9 × 12.7 CM.
COLLECTION/PHOTO: HELEN DRUTT GALLERY, PHILADELPHIA

changing universe reminds us that our understanding of the external world can be as deceptive and as changeable as our own psyches.

We're obsessed with the relationships we have constructed between internal and external events, filling our world with objects that speak to our timeless, prenatal existence. While these comparisons are simple and obvious, our own century has changed the way we view objects and how we view our own points of view about them.

We are a global culture that loves the external, making things into seductive fetishes and making images of those things into the substitution for the real. We assign internal values to these external symbols in the belief that what we see and what we own is who we are. Material culture studies of our century have changed the way we read and understand objects. Things once viewed as objects that remind us of our prenatal existence also remind us of strong political systems and sentiments, such as the chess sets issued as part of the Soviet propaganda porcelain era in the 1920s. The chess pieces, by the way, depict the communists and the capitalists, and, of course, it's the capitalist in chains, the white figure at the right.

But the way we have changed our understanding of objects is that we have shifted our focus away from pure function, function that might have symbolic and cultural meaning, such as King Tut's Throne, into objects of cultural and artistic meaning that may or may not have function. The history or, more properly, the prehistory of ceramics gives us ample evidence of the duality of inner and external realities, exemplified in the use of clay as a medium for figural sculpture, such as the work from Iran, or Mesopotamia in the sixth to fifth millennium BC, objects of symbolic, religious, and spiritual value as well as ornamental, but essentially functional works. This duality continues to be recognized and exploited effectively by ceramic artists, reminding us of the deeply felt, emotive, and even haunting world of signs, symbols, and memories that bring us face to face with other realities. Through art, we're able to record our external world and begin to describe our complex network of relationships to our society, our epoch, our culture, and to ourselves. Art, however, does not stop there, but leads us into the present by reminding us where we came from.

If history has one essential purpose at the close of this millennium, it may be to provide the raw material for our cultural future. It the future will ceramics have a role? While this brief talk is not intended to provide a final, pretentious answer to such a pretentious question, I do believe that a look backwards at the social, political, and cultural context of ceramics in the West gives us some important insights into the current state of affairs we're all here to talk about in this conference.

In a very limited amount of time, I would like to look back over the past millennium, noting some of the high points in the history of connoisseurship in ceramics (and specifically porcelain, as defined by a small number of examples in collecting and patronage) and then to explore some of the relationships that developed between makers and consumer, between potters and patrons, between art and society as they were drawn into the sphere of this unusual material. It is my belief that the history of patronage of ceramic artists and enterprises in general has a distinctive profile from that of many other art forms.

This difference, it can be argued, is primarily due to the fact that patronage in the field of porcelain has a notably secular and commercial basis that has coloured our understanding of ceramics as an art form in our own time. At the same time porcelain is the only ceramic body that, for centuries, was revered as precious, rare, ethereal—a double-edged sword for those working in the field today. Finally, it is a material that's proven its ability to move with memorable grace and alacrity among the fields of art, industry, and craft. As such, it may have an instructive value as we look at current trends in the visual arts.

One thousand years ago, Lief Erickson may have discovered America. One thousand years ago, gunpowder was invented by the Chinese. One thousand years ago, the poet Omar Khyyam was born, and one thousand years ago, Europe was in the throes of millennium fever and agitation. In the East, developing alongside gunpowder and an elaborate court culture were new ceramic forms and mixtures. The brilliant earthenwares of the Tong Dynasty, with their rich palette of brilliant green and amber glazes, were produced at the same time as highly refined white-bodied stonewares and proto-porcelains. By the time of the Song Dynasty, from the tenth century until 1279, true porcelain, lustrous, white, resonant, and increasingly translucent, was manufactured at a growing number of kiln sites. Many of the finest of these Songwares went directly into the imperial collection. New designs and changes in techniques were carefully supervised and monitored by a master potter appointed by the emperor, who was at once the patron and the connoisseur of the finest wares, with no hierarchical distinction being made between art and craft.

Chinese porcelain flourished in an atmosphere of what I can only describe as "enlightened cupidity" and among the highest standards of excellence in material, concept, and execution. Nor was this trend or development limited to China alone. It should also be noted that, at the same time, a millennium ago, it was the period of the great Koryu Dynasty in Korea, where ethereally beautiful ceramics were created and collected. It was also a time when superbly potted and glazed wares were emanating from Islamic centers of production in the Middle and Near East. Dynastic stability underpinned and supported artistic innovation and creation in all media, but especially so in ceramics. Ceramics of this quality would not, however, reach Europe in substantial numbers for centuries.

A thousand years ago in the West, as I mentioned, it was a time of millennial religious fervor, territorial competitiveness, and growing ecclesiastical power. Around 1000, an extraordinary campaign of cathedral building was launched across Europe; impressive and imposing structures built to glorify God and his church on Earth began to take shape in cities such as Strassbourg, Wurzberg, Exeter, Winchester, London, Parma, Pizza, York, and Santiago de Compostella, to mention only a few. Patronage of artists and artisans in many fields followed in the wake of ecclesiastical supremacy.

Painters received commissions for altar pieces in churches and chapels, in the homes of the wealthy clerics and aristocrats. The decorative arts in general blossomed, with lovingly crafted and brilliantly coloured enamel, such as those created at Limoges as reliquaries and crismatories; delicately carved cryptics and book covers made of rare imported ivory in Parisian workshops, avidly sought by collectors throughout Europe; or glorious examples of the goldsmith's art, a craft which has held primary place in the hierarchy of decorative arts since the ancient world.

The importance of the church as a patron of the decorative arts at this period cannot be underestimated, however. Ecclesiastical patronage rarely extended to the humble and ordinary medium of clay, a particularly surprising development in the light of numerous references to clay and the use of pottery as a metaphor throughout the Bible. Because clay came from the earth, was it somehow debased or polluted? Even secular paintings, showing tables of the wealthy from the first half of the millennium and as late as the fifteenth and sixteenth centuries rarely show ceramics in use. Ceramics and painting at this time are often seen within the context of peasant life, such as in the detail of a three-handled jug in the famous peasant wedding scene painted by Bruegel.

At the upper end of the spectrum in the production of ceramics of this period

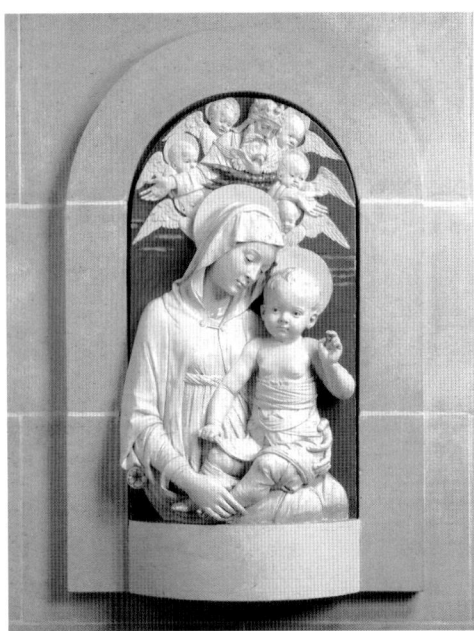

ANDREA DELLA ROBBIA, *VIRGIN AND CHILD*, FIFTEENTH CENTURY (C. 1470–75). RELIEF GLAZED TERRA COTTA, 94.9 x 54.9 CM.

COLLECTION/PHOTO: THE METROPOLITAN MUSEUM OF ART, NEW YORK. GIFT OF EDITH AND HERBERT LEHMAN FOUNDATION INC.

was the production of salt-glazed stoneware, which was then the most elegant ware available in Europe. Not that ceramics, or more specifically, glazed earthenware, could not aim for higher artistic goals. By the fifteenth and sixteenth centuries, lively pottery traditions were flourishing in Italy, as seen in this Majolica Deruta charger made in the early 1500s, or the superbly modelled and glazed *Madonna and Child* by Andrea della Robbia from the Metropolitan collection.

In France at this same period, and due primarily to the direct patronage of Catherine de Medici, Bernard Palissy created his striking chargers and platters, overlaid with ornaments taken from the world of flora and fauna. For true collectors and connoisseurs in the West, however, there was one goal in mind: the acquisition of porcelain. Porcelain, imported from great distances and at great expense, captured the attention of Europeans who had financial resources sufficient to feed their collecting frenzy. Early connoisseurs of porcelain were drawn first by the material itself, something obviously man made, but with qualities not unlike the rarest and most refined works of nature, pure in colour, translucent, resonant when struck. Beyond the material were the exceptional forms and brilliant colours of Chinese porcelains with an elegance, refinement, and delicacy totally unknown in the West.

The economics of the porcelain trade, which combined with exotic imports of luxury materials, ranging from silks and lacquer to tea and spices, founded a wide network of East India trading companies. From this juncture forward, links between porcelain and money were forged that were to hold sway for well over two centuries.

For true connoisseurs, those in the know, porcelain was a curiosity in the seventeenth century meaning of the word. As Kenneth Hudson has so eloquently pointed out in his book, *Museums of Influence*, connoisseurship, as we know it, grew out of the seventeenth and eighteenth century meaning of curious and curiosities. Connoisseurship was, in fact, not used widely at all in the literature until the early years of the eighteenth century, the same time as the blossoming of porcelain in Europe.

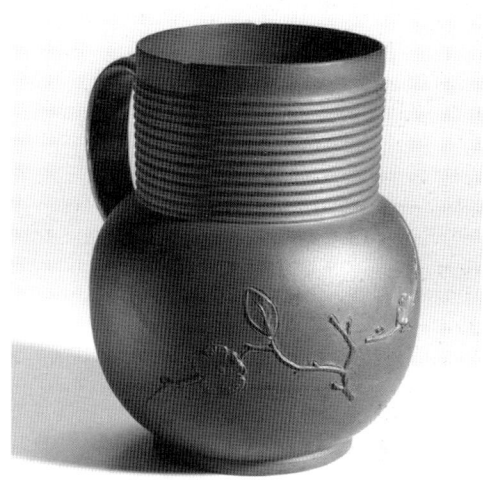

ELERS BROTHERS, STAFFORDSHIRE, *MUG*, LATE SEVENTEENTH CENTURY. STONEWARE, 10.2 CM.

PHOTO: JONATHON HORNE, LONDON

"Curious" had several related meanings. To paraphrase Hudson, it meant "careful to produce or recognize first-class workmanship, to be able to learn and to be able to excite interest by quality or novelty." All of the elements of modern connoisseurship were there in the word "curious." As Hudson stated, "The person of intelligence and learning who was not curious was almost impossible to conceive."[3]

For Europeans in the latter half of the seventeenth century who wished to join the growing number of amateurs who collected Chinese porcelains, if you couldn't join them, you could always try to beat them at their own game. It was in this period that the great flowering of imitation porcelains, mostly tin-glazed earthenware, occurred throughout Europe. Some of the best known examples such as in the collector's cabinet from Hampton Court of Queen Mary was designed by Daniel Marot, and we can enjoy it today in a contemporary reinstallation of what one of these display elements would have been like.

Last night I had a very interesting discussion with Edmund de Waal, who'll speak after me, about this idea of display and the theater of collecting, the theater of ownership, and this whole idea of displaying porcelain en masse as part of architecture. It is a fascinating idea that I think has some interesting ramifications for installation of today.

But some of the pieces that were made in imitation of porcelain included works like the superb flower vases created at the Greek A Factory in Delft for Queen Mary and her own collection at Hampton Court. All of these designs were inspired by the work of the ornamental engraver and escaped Huguenot, Daniel Marot, who was a court artist in England.

An important side effect of patronage from the community of rich collectors was the encouragement of experiments into new ceramic bodies as part of this quest for porcelain with the hope of discovering the heretofore unknown secret of making true or hard-paste porcelain. Notable was a short-lived factory in Florence patronized by the Grand Duke Francesco the First for about thirteen years, starting in 1575.

The translucent paste developed at the Medici factory was basically white clay, but combined with powdered rock crystal and other ingredients. While the forms, as we see in these slides, were often of European origin, the glazes lacked the brilliant whiteness of true Chinese porcelain. For connoisseurs and collectors in Europe, this was the closest equivalent yet produced in the West.

The passionate patron of porcelain is best exemplified, however, by the imposing figure of Augustus the Strong, elector of Saxony, and king of Poland. The romantic and dramatic history of Augustus's passion for porcelain has been told and retold for decades and does not bear repeating once again. However, that said, it should be noted that it was Augustus's personal passion and financial support—sometimes to the detriment of his own lands and people—that made the research possible that eventually broke open the secret of manufacturing true porcelain in the Chinese manner. The key figure in this discovery is the familiar Johann Friedrich Böttger, an erstwhile alchemist turned ceramic engineer. He was patronized by Augustus the Strong.

Patronage and the word "patron" has an interesting etymology. The Roman term "patron" referred to a former slave owner who had made his slaves free men. A patron in the modern sense, Augustus eventually kept Böttger under house arrest, so he was not really free. In this case Böttger, after promising Augustus he could create gold from base metals and failing, he was re-assigned to work alongside the court scientist to break the code of porcelain.

Early products produced at what was to become the Meissen Factory, were a hard, red stoneware, hard enough to be cut on the lapidary wheel, and by 1709, true white porcelain had been developed. While the early styles of Meissen were imitative of Chinese models, the aesthetic rapidly changed to embrace a wider range of European models, some based on natural forms, such as the shapes and decorations of the famous Swan Service, and others on baroque ornament. An important shift in the aesthetic was to bring three-dimensional sculpture within the sphere of porcelain, extending its function to that of tableware, lighting fixtures, and vases.

Augustus the Strong's taste in porcelain underlines the great flexibility and potential of the material in the hands of capable sculptors or painters. The preciousness of the rare material was emphasized by its elaborate and complex ornamentation, viewed by later commentators as fussy and over decorated. As a blank canvas, porcelain proved its worth as a ground for painting, for colour, and for ornaments, features that became the hallmark of the second greatest porcelain enterprise in Europe, the manufacturer Royale de Sèvres of France, which operated under the patronage of Louis XV. Founded in 1738 at Vincennes by two workman from another factory, by 1793, the manufacturer had been taken over as the royal factory, with the heavy investment from both Louis XV and his mistress, Madame de Pompadour. From its earliest days, the factory at Sèvres, which at that time produced only a soft paste (or artificial porcelain), set the standard for artistic excellence in Europe. Connoisseurs, collectors, and merchants recognized the high standards of design and execution set at the factory. Technically and artistically superior to its rivals, the ware of Sèvres also served as a major source for diplomatic gifts from the king to foreign heads of state and important dignitaries. The porcelain rapidly became a saleable item in the marketplace, an expensive and valuable commodity.

The progress of porcelain throughout the eighteenth century was shaped by powerful patrons, who provided an economic base of support for innovation, who took advantage of the social, artistic, and financial opportunities or liabilities that came with the ownership of a factory, and who made best use of the products by distributing and promoting them effectively. In the case of Sèvres, substantial losses at the end of the year were written off by the king himself in the belief that

French porcelain buttressed the political, diplomatic, and cultural profile of the nation.

The same attitude holds today, even at Sèvres, where standards of excellence in design and execution remain paramount, even when financially regressive. As Hudson, whom I quoted earlier, has pointed out, patronage and secular power work hand in hand. He states: "The humble and the meek may occasionally riot, strike, and protest, but they rarely experiment. Change usually comes from those who have a taste for innovation and the money and security to indulge it."

In eighteenth-century Europe, porcelain cannot be viewed outside the context of money, influence, and personal and secular power. Secular patronage assured survival of the material and extended its usefulness in truly innovative ways. To cite one well-known example, the Danish court merged the worlds of art and science by way of their patronage of the Royal Copenhagen Factory and, specifically, the production of the Flora Danica Service, consisting of 1,802 pieces of table porcelains, each painted with a unique representation of one of the wildflowers, grasses, mosses, and mushrooms found in Denmark. Science and art were brought together in this extraordinary service.

Works such as this raise important questions about connoisseurship, particularly in regard to innovative forms and designs. Here, the aesthetic of the design cannot be separated from its botanical and scientific context. While the botanical volumes illustrating the same plants are significant and self-referential, the porcelain in the Flora Danica Service takes on its aesthetic meaning only because of its scientific context. Connoisseurship of pure form in this instance must follow contextual function.

By the early decades of the nineteenth century, porcelain had lost its favoured place in the ceramic world. With the knowledge of its secrets of manufacturing completely broadcast to virtually every country in Europe, and especially to England (where there was no royal patronage but a number of independent entrepreneurs who founded and took over the factories, eventually creating one of the great ceramic industries of the world) the material entered a new period of economic competition as more and more firms entered the marketplace.

While some of the newcomers in the nineteenth century produced elegant, refined wares that were redolent of the golden age of the eighteenth century, others launched into a series of stylistic revivals that embraced styles as diverse as the Rococo and the Gothic. By mid-century, porcelain had made its final transition from what had been an aristocratic and royal concern into the mainstream of middle-class markets and tastes. By the 1850s, the once-revered factory of Meissen was issuing overwhelmingly dense catalogs of their tablewares and other ornamental products. Porcelain in many forms was marketed at an international scale at the many great, universal, international exhibitions throughout Europe and that proliferated in major cities, such as London with its Crystal Palace and even in the United States.

The aesthetics of porcelain made specifically for exhibitions were immediately apparent. These were highly decorative and often pretentious objects, primarily for display. It was this kind of ceramics that gained the scorn of many reformers such as William Morris. The tide of taste and connoisseurship had shifted dramatically. For the arts and crafts movement, porcelain was not the favoured material. Instead, there was a return to humbler earthenwares and stonewares, rustic pottery, and even salt glazes. Like any material limited only by the talent and ingenuity of those who use it, however, porcelain did not disappear at the end of the century but began to regain its stature as an art medium at the turn of the century at factories throughout Europe, producing work in the new Art Nouveau style.

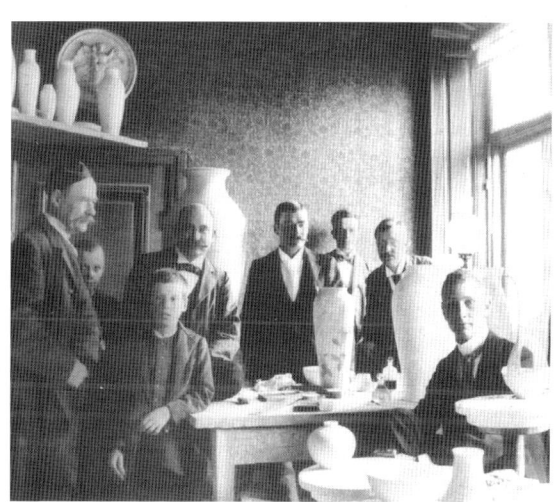

ALF WALLENDER AND STUDIO, RÖRSTRAND, SWEDEN C.1900

Yesterday, Paul Greenhalgh mentioned the factory at Rörstrand. I would like to highlight for you here Alf Wallender, the artistic director of the factory and his studio workers at Rörstrand, where some of the most beautiful Art Nouveau pieces were produced. Studios created within the factory (with the specific goal of creating new patterns that were not based on past styles but on the new art form) were established in far-flung Sweden, such as the one at Rörstrand, and it was works like this that gained recognition at the Exposition Universale in Paris in 1900. Even the French commented how wonderfully refined and elegant these Swedish porcelains were. Likewise, at Royal Copenhagen, marvelous wares were produced in porcelain as part of the studio lines, and numerous factories, particularly in Limoges, also contributed to the revival of interest in porcelain as an artistic medium.

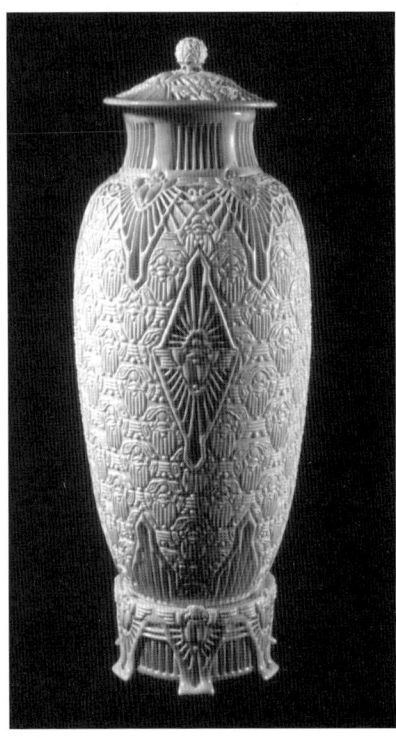

ADELAIDE ALSOP ROBINEAU, SCARAB VASE, C.1910. ENCISED AND CARVED PORCELAIN, 42.2 CM.

COLLECTION/PHOTO: EVERSON MUSEUM OF ART, SYRACUSE, NY

Two directions evolved from the situation at the turn of the century. One important one for the medium was the introduction of new designs for porcelain from talented designers for industry. From 1900, and especially in the 1920s and 1930s, a separate line of development for porcelain occurred at the great factories. Here, Trudi Petri's service from 1930 made at the Berlin factory. All of these designs exploited the inherent industrial characteristics of the material to create an aesthetic of modernism with which we have all become very familiar.

These characteristics, purity of form, surface and colour, thinness and translucency, durability and clarity of surface, and certainly malleability in moulding in production gave porcelain a new lease on life, projecting it forward into the mainstream of modern functionalism. At the same time (and, here, another service from later on, Eva Zeisel's service from 1952, I believe it is), developments in ceramic studios and manufactories around 1900 also underlined the artistic value of the material for the artist creating one-of-a-kind, unique works of art. This second avenue of aesthetics for porcelain leads in a somewhat logical progression from singular figures, such as Adelaide Alsop Robineau, who worked at the University City Pottery on her famous *Scarab Vase* of 1910, down to our own day and people like Jacqui Poncelet.

A third avenue, however, needs to be explored, and that is designers from other fields who cross over into the world of porcelain, creating models for serial production, some of it quite limited in numbers, others in extensive production, people such as Matteo Thun whose porcelains were marketed alongside the furniture, lighting fixtures, and fabrics produced for Memphis Milano in the 1980s.

The same integration of art, craft, and design is paramount at factories such as Sèvres, where an artist-in-residence program continues today, which has brought production tablewares by the Czech-born designer Boris Sipek to fruition, but also has introduced work by sculptors Charles Simmons and by the well-known Louise Bourgeois, also working at Sèvres. At the same time, the studio artists who are bridging the worlds of craft, art, and design—I should mention one of those that I think has developed some very interesting things recently, and that's Marek Cecula, who, in his most recent series called *Violations*, has created new porcelain forms that take traditional shapes and modify them radically. He took a small plate, a seemingly ordinary plate, the center of which, however, is set with a pottery chard he picked up which reveals its Nazi porcelain origin. It's a rather dramatic and moving installation piece. This change with artists from other fields working in porcelain is, in many respects, a new paradigm for the arts in general, a seamless integration and merging of fields that had traditionally been separated into hierarchies.

This, as I said earlier, may be one of the most important developments of our time. Makers of objects, like Bobby Silverman and Edmund de Waal, are testing new definitions of what porcelain, art, craft, and design are all about. These aesthetics are based on liberated experimentation, but experiments that are tempered by a knowledge of history that gives it special power and seductiveness. Redefining our material and our relationship to the object is also the territory explored visually by people like Babs Haenen and Adrian Saxe, while at the same time these works remind us that beauty is not something to be ignored or cast aside. These artists delight in beauty and see surface, form, colour, and texture almost as moral virtues.

Are standards of connoisseurship meaningful for our age emerging today? I, for one, would have to say yes. We're living in an exception time, when history and tradition have become allies of innovation and experiment, when we can appreciate the splendour of a table set with elaborate porcelains and silver from the mid-eighteenth century alongside Judy Chicago's *Dinner Party* celebrating the role of women in history, art, and culture. Who are the patrons, collectors, and connoisseurs who will defend, support, and nurture creativity in the field today?

The days of royal patronage are behind us, which I illustrate with the famous Royal Porcelain Room made at the Capodimonte Factory in Naples in 1757. Private patrons are few and far between in the field of ceramics, as any gallery can attest. However, industry continues to keep traditions alive, relying on the ability of porcelain to bring the world's art and commerce into line with each other, much as they did in the past. And in a strange way, installations at museums are trying to do the same thing. It's not necessarily the ideal situation, but it is a form of patronage that is encouraging experimentation.

Connoisseurship must reflect today a new paradigm of creativity in which art, design, and craft are merged. These roads are converging into an interesting and often confusing super highway. New road signs are needed, but also new skills, to understand what's happening in the field. If objects are to continue as metaphors for ourselves, we need to re-examine our own internal and external standards of quality and meaning. In 1869, Charles Baudelaire wrote: "Nearly all of our originality comes from the stamp that time impresses on our sensibility." It's my hope and my belief that porcelain, at the end of this millennium, has entered a new period when history is truly preparing us for a very exciting and very provocative future. We, as the collectors, the museum curators, the connoisseurs have to think about these standards and what they're going to mean to the artists who are going to come at our time and after our time. The field is not only healthy, but I think it's extraordinarily healthy at the moment. I, for one, am delighted to be living at a moment when so much change is occurring around and in the field.

1   Werner Muensterberger, *Collecting: An Unruly Passion* (New York: Harcourt, Brace & Company, 1994).
2   Martin Kelner, "Meaning of Life, The Importance of STUFF," *The Independent Newspaper* (May 15, 1993).
3   Kenneth Hudson, *Museums of Influence* (New York: Cambridge University Press, 1987).

CHAPTER 26

HOMER, CERAMICS, AND MARKETPLACE ANXIETIES

GARTH CLARK

There is an argument common amongst some ceramists, particularly those in universities, that if we push for a strong market, we are "going for the money" in its pejorative figuring. Before this criticism there exists only one question in retort, "What exactly should the ceramics market do, strive for poverty?"

Presented at *The Ceramic Millennium*, 1999, Amsterdam

Even though the marketplace is crucial to any professional ceramists life, and always has been, I have never attended a single conference where this has been the subject of a serious paper or discussion. It is as though talking about this subject will pollute the purity of the creative spirit, yet the issues of sales and galleries are the constant, unspoken subtext of anxiety and desire whenever artists gather. This ambivalence is a modern attitude, what writer Maya Angelou terms a "learned affectation."[1] The ancients were untroubled by sales and saw it as part of the process. The mysterious Greek poet Homer, of the eighth and ninth centuries BC, is the attributed author of a poem entitled, *Kiln*, a meditation on the importance of marketability and its potential threat to the potter's integrity:

> If you will pay me for my song, O potters,
> Then come, Athena, and hold thy hand above the kiln!

> May the kotyloi and all the kanastra turn a good black,
> May they be well fired and fetch the price asked,
> Many being sold in the marketplace and many on the road,
> And bring in much money, and may my song be pleasing.
> But if you (potters) turn shameless and deceitful,
> Then I summon the ravagers of kilns….
> May they hit these pots hard, and may the kiln collapse.
> And may the potters wail as they see mischief.
> But I shall rejoice at the sight of their luckless craft.
> And if anyone bends over to look into the spy-hole, may his whole face
> Be scorched, so that all may learn to deal justly.[2]

Against the backdrop of such an admonition, we can proceed to look at how ceramics, art, and money have come together at the end of the second millennium, and specifically at the arrival and mechanics of a fine arts market for ceramic art. This is examined against painting, the gold standard for the visual-arts marketplace. Canvasses by modern masters such as Picasso fetch $49 million and wet-art by living artists, sell for up to $18 million. This is an intimidating standard. Yet, before we castigate ourselves for not having reached the same lofty fiscal plateau, let's place this in perspective. The painting market is about six hundred years old and has been developed shrewdly and uninterruptedly throughout these centuries, beginning in the Renaissance, when painters considered themselves, first and foremost, businessmen. This market is bolstered by hundreds of thousands of academics, dealers, consultants, and museum specialists, all directly or indirectly working to maintain the status quo.

The ceramic market, by comparison, is minuscule, underdeveloped, and still in its infancy. As a field for individual artists, it is little more than one hundred years old and the so-called fine-arts market for ceramics is less than fifty years old, in real terms maybe only twenty five years. But the market for ceramics is nonetheless a remarkably resilient organism. With the barest of resources, practically no academic support, and only slight museum interest, it has, since the late nineteenth century, survived all kinds of vicissitudes—periods of indifference and a vulnerable, underfunded support structure—to emerge in the last decade of the twentieth century with surprising strength and promise.

This paper deals with the art market for ceramics in the West. Although I work internationally, my primary sphere of activity is the art market of New York City, and that will be the central focus of the second half of this paper. The first half deals with the history of the modern ceramic marketplace until 1950. As New York remains the market leader for art, developments there often signal new trends. This does not ignore the fact that other markets are important as well and may be more so in years to come, but they will need to be the subject of another study.

The Eighteenth Century: Porcelain, Kings, Queens, and Wedgwood

The modern trade in ceramics as art in the West begins to take shape in the late sixteenth century with the collecting of Chinese porcelains by the aristocracy. These became so sought after that King Augustus the Strong, one of the most passionate collectors, even exchanged his personal bodyguard for a set of Chinese vases, now appropriately know as the *Dragoon Vases*. Attempts were made to produce porcelain in the West, but it was not until 1810 that the alchemist Böttger stumbled onto the porcelain formula, while he was the "detained guest" of Augustus. It was an ironic circumstance. Böttger was trying to turn base metal into gold so that Augustus could afford his porcelains, amongst other extravagances. Instead, he came up with porcelain itself, and so Augustus set up the Meissen Porcelain Works, the first makers of "true" porcelain in Europe.

Soon kings, queens, and princes throughout continental Europe were following his lead, opening Sèvres, Nymphenburg, and other manufactories. To give the work added cachet and aesthetic importance, favorite court painters and sculptors were employed to design and paint the elaborate and costly wares. The Sèvres porcelain pictured above is from 1813, a disastrous year for restraint and good taste, it seems; but more pointedly, it shows that porcelain was regarded more as an indication of wealth than as art. Earlier Chinese connoisseurs loved the purity of the porcelain body itself, while in the West, the ware was covered in gold to mimic the plate of royal tables, more evidence that the court porcelains were a form of currency rather than considered an art form.

The real credit in establishing a broader ceramic market goes to Josiah Wedgwood. Possessing a genius for marketing, Wedgwood created a "vase mania" amongst Britain's ruling elite, playing on the then, fashionable interest in antiquities.

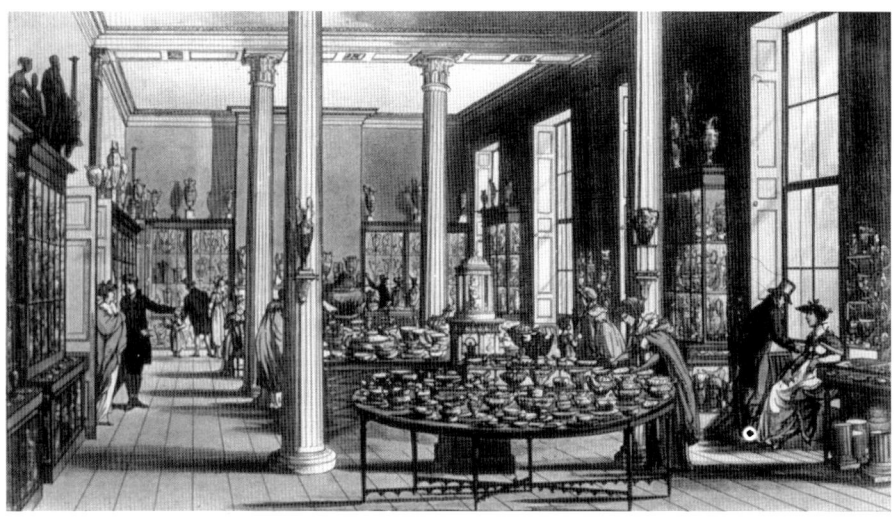

THE WEDGWOOD AND BYERLEY YORK STREET SHOWROOMS. REPRODUCED FROM R. ACKERMANN'S *REPOSITORY OF ARTS*, 1809.

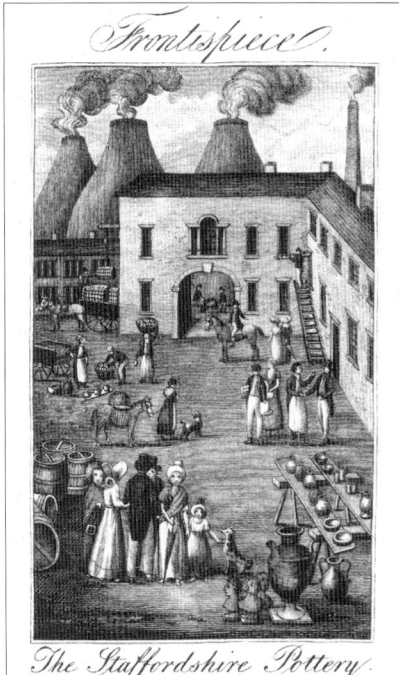

STAFFORDSHIRE POTTERY COPPER PLATE ENGRAVING SHOWING THE PROCESS OF MAKING EARTHENWARE AND CHINA POTTERY. PUBLISHED IN 1827.

Wedgwood took the *lowliest* of clays, earthenware, and improved it to be fit for the table of Queen Charlotte as well as the Adam-style, neo-classical interiors of the nobility. Like the porcelain houses, Wedgwood also selected known artists, such as John Flaxman, to design forms and even had William Blake illustrate his catalogue. Wedgwood's shrewd and tasteful marketing sold the idea that ceramics was an ancient, revered art.

In comparison to the rude, traditional markets of Staffordshire potteries, Wedgwood opened an elegant London gallery where London's beau monde could socialize, browse and shop, to run up debts they rarely paid. Wedgwood even issued the first numbered ceramic art multiple: his translation in jasperware of the Portland Vase, a Roman glass vase, one of the most famous antiquities of his day. He exhibited his "copy" of the Portland Vase in his Greek Street, Soho showrooms, issuing tickets to view the work and also sending the vase on a tour to the royalty of Europe. By the end of the eighteenth century, the modern market for ceramics had been well and truly launched, even if this was under the aegis of industry.

Arts and Crafts Movement

In the late nineteenth century the Arts and Crafts Movement evolved out of a desire to reform design and counter the decay of taste resulting from industrialization. This movement rescued ceramics from the anonymity of industry and returned it to the individual artist, even though, unlike the Martin Brothers, most were potters only in the white-collar sense, doing glaze science, designing pots on paper, and perhaps painting wares. The bulk of the work was still done by nameless "labourers" who did the "dirty" crafts—they mixed clay, threw pots and fired the kilns—activities not compatible with the image of a Victorian gentleman-artist. William Morris, a founder of the Arts and Crafts Movement, was also a pioneer of the British socialist movement that introduced uneasiness into the world of crafts with its free-market solutions, and he also generated a certain antipathy towards elitism within the arts.

Individual potters and potteries found different ways to reach the growing Victorian market for decorative arts. Exhibiting in the various salons of the Arts and Crafts Exhibiting Society was one outlet. Some potteries were represented by progressive design boutiques that were set up at the turn of the century, such as La Maison Moderne and La Maison Bing de l'Art Nouveau in Paris, Tiffany's in New York, and Liberty's in London. Other potters created their own showrooms. Some were lavish affairs, like the London showroom for Burmantofs. Others were modest, such as the small, crowded store, also in London, for the eccentric Martin Brothers, run by Charles Martin.

Unfortunately, Charles was mentally troubled and while mild insanity is not a disqualifier for dealing in art (some might even say it is an essential quality), he suffered serious paranoid delusions and would hide the best pots under the floorboards of the store, fearing that if they were on display, other potters would copy

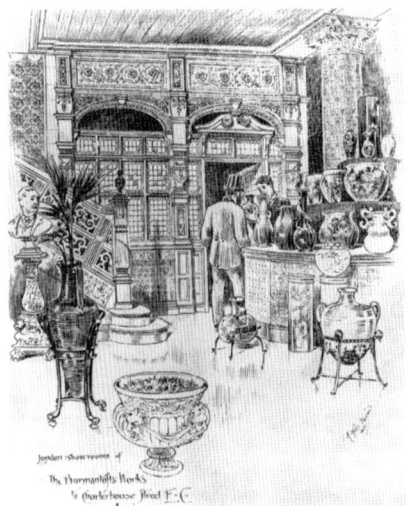

ILLUSTRATION OF THE LONDON SHOWROOM OF BURMANTOFTS POTTERY BY T. RAFFLES, 1888.
COLLECTION: LEEDS CITY MUSEUMS, UK

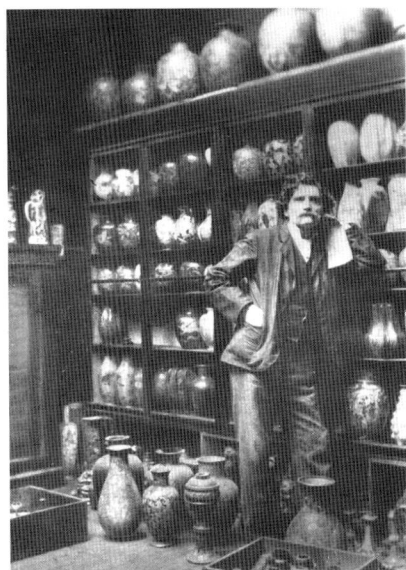

CHARLES MARTIN IN THE MARTIN BROTHERS SHOWROOM IN LONDON, C.1900.
PHOTO: SOUTHALL PUBLIC LIBRARY, UK

them. While an extreme example, this highlights the point that potters were not necessarily the best salespeople for their own work, and having to keep an entire store constantly stocked with new and exciting ware was an arduous and commercializing pressure that could lower the aesthetic quality of the work.

World Fairs and other expositions of decorative art were crucial in marketing high-end decorative ceramics. The major potteries created elaborate booths for these events, as one sees in the case of Bing and Grondahl and the Royal Worcester porcelain works (both exhibitors at the 1900 Paris Exposition). Smaller potteries took part in group exhibitions and juried competitions. The point of the exercise was to win one of the fiercely contested medals, which was then ostentatiously publicized to increase the prestige and marketability of the pottery.

It was also common amongst potters who were less commercially successful to pursue one or more related activities to make ends meet. Mary Chase Perry Stratton, who founded the Pewabic Pottery in Detroit, was also a partner in the Revelation Kiln Company for china painters. Adelaide Alsop Robineau, one of America's first studio potters, could not sell her exceptional incised vases for her asking price of only $30 to $40.

Ironically, these works made between 1904 and the 1920s are valued today at as much as $500,000. But Robineau made a good living nonetheless, publishing *Keramik Studio*, a magazine for the armies of women china painters. As her daughter remarked, "Every summer mother would say that we would end up in the poor house, but we always went to the South of France instead."³

George E. Ohr, the greatest of America's early potters, survived by making and selling sewer pipes and water coolers to the households of Biloxi, Mississippi. Again, Ohr was not his own best dealer, announcing that he would sell his beloved art pots, his clay babies, for their weight in gold. This approach discouraged buyers. He also sold novelties, souvenirs, and gimcracks, like humorous brothel tokens for tourists. His second pottery—an architectural curiosity, kind of Canton-meets-Bayou—was designed to attract this tourist trade. Looking at this strange building makes it seem all the more appropriate that Frank Gehry will be designing Ohr's museum in Biloxi.

It became increasingly common that the ceramist's secondary occupation was teaching, although for most, it soon evolved into their primary occupation. From

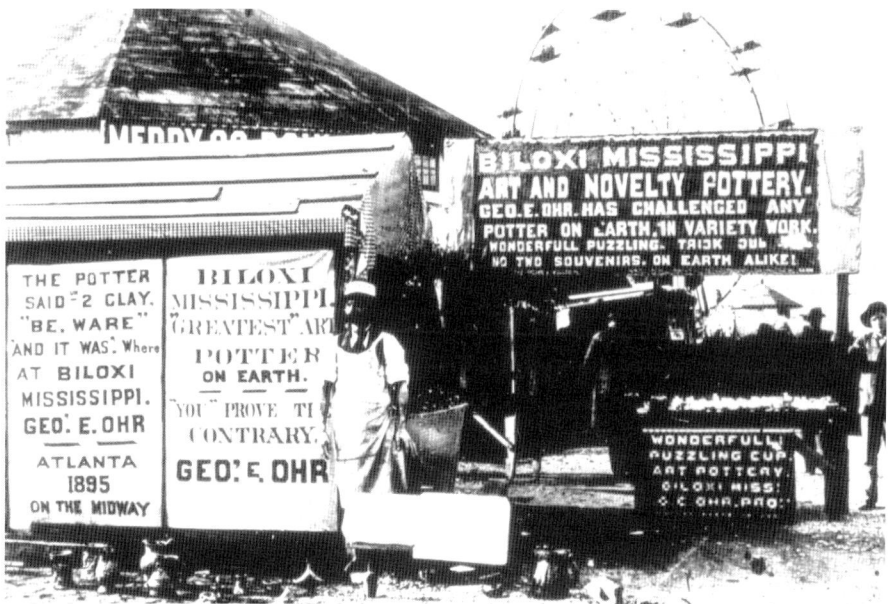

GEORGE E. OHR AT THE COTTON STATES AND INTERNATIONAL EXPOSITION IN ATLANTA, 1895.
PHOTO: SOUTHALL PUBLIC LIBRARY, UK

1900 on, ceramic departments became more common, and soon institutional education was ceramics' dominant patron. Charles Fergus Binns was the founder of the New York State College of Ceramics and Clayworking at Alfred University, America's largest ceramics school. There is a historical photograph of him with his summer school class in 1901, the year in which the college was founded. In both Britain and America, a teaching post became the economic lifeline for the precarious role of the ceramic artist. Schools did not buy the artists' work, but they paid a regular salary, and often provided a studio, materials, and a venue for exhibition. This grew modestly throughout the first half of the twentieth century and then, after World War II, increased dramatically as we will explore later.

Industry was another patron. One could find artists' workshops in the Lomonosov State Porclain Factory in Leningrad, Bo Fajans and Gustavsberg in Sweden, Bing and Grondahl and Royal Cophenagen in Denmark, and Arabia in Finland. Other Scandinavian potteries created artist studios within their factories, and paid their artists stipends and commissions on their sales, which were made through the company stores around the world. This was a progressive approach but had its drawbacks: artists had to conform, to some extent, to the corporate culture of their sponsor. Also it compromised any reality that ceramics was an independent art-making activity. Such collaborations, however, did facilitate production of the sensual, organic, and reductive Scandinavian pottery of Wilhelm Kage, Axel Salto, and other highly collectible artists. Their work, dating from the fifties, sixties and seventies enjoys tremendous vogue in today's marketplace.

Lastly, there is the matter of state sponsorship of the arts, including ceramics. This system is found mostly in Europe. In the 1920s and 1930s such plans were introduced into the Soviet world, ostensibly to promote culture and free artists from the marketplace. Instead, it served to control artists' subject matter and pressured their style to conform to the political party platform. After the War certain countries in Western Europe introduced artist subsidies that allowed a freer and more idealistic agenda. But one must question whether it did anything to increase the quality of the arts and whether, in actuality, its legacy merely produced a generation of artists without survival skills. Certainly, in the Netherlands, one witnessed great anxiety and confusion when the system of artist stipends that guaranteed a minimum income each year in return for artworks, was terminated. The surplus works from this defunct program now pack state warehouses. No one wants nor sees the art, not even the artists themselves. Makers who were born into this system simply had no concept of how to engage their marketplace. In Eastern Europe the shift from Communism to democracy did away with the Artist Unions and left ceramists high and dry, without any network of galleries or having provided practitioners with any experience selling their work. Moreover, Unions had a strange effect on aesthetics, disconnecting the artists from their community. As subsidized artists, they could make work that was so personal and introverted that it had no relevance to their culture at all. In other cases it did allow for work to be created that the marketplace might not have rejected. These instances of socialized art programs are always double-edged swords but seemed to cut more deeply on the negative side of both creative liberty and commerce.

THE STUDIO POTTER

Around 1920 the market for studio pottery began to take over as the art pottery movement declined. Leach, arguably the most influential single figure in twentieth-century ceramics, took the insistent position on pricing by contending that pots should be affordable. There was no economic reasoning behind this position; rather, it was a moralist stance with a dubious and decidedly political motive. Why should pots be cheap when painting and sculpture could be expensive, particularly when industry was providing every man and every woman with excellently made and affordably designed tableware and decorative wares? Moreover, Leach collectors were by and large a somewhat affluent group. But his ideas about the ethics of pricing took hold. Why anyone would take business advice from Leach is beyond understanding.

He established a pottery with a wood-burning kiln in St. Ives, an area totally devoid of trees. His main market was in London, and shipping costs from Cornwall were extremely high. The *coup de grâce* was that St. Ives had one of the shortest and least profitable seasons of any resort town. It took Leach from 1921 to 1950 to get his pottery to run profitably, and its post-War success was not his own doing but the result of careful restructuring of the pottery's standard wares by his son David.

In the 1920s Leach was caught up in the ubiquitous art/craft debate with his nemesis, William Staite Murray. In theory, Leach stood for craft: repetitive wares made to be affordable, functional and accessible. Murray stood for art: made to be expensive, unique and beyond issues of function. The prices for Murray's pots were unparalleled in his day: up to 190 guineas in 1935, a time when a forty piece handpainted dinner service by Clarice Cliff cost only four guineas. Leach's prices were costly as well, but at thirty guineas, relatively low. Murray showed in art galleries with sculptor Barbara Hepworth and painter Ben Nicholson and was regularly and favorably reviewed by Britain's art critics. Leach, by contrast, showed with the Red Rose Craft Guild and at Muriel Rose's Little Gallery, amongst other places.

Leach actively promoted his ideals of humble craft as the counterpoint to Murray's elitism and, one might argue, with the purpose of undercutting Murray's stature, because he was resentful that Murray had been chosen to be head of ceramics at the Royal College of Art, a post Leach coveted. Leach soon began to sway the critics, a dangerous game that played on their inherent unease about the marginality of ceramics as an art form. He attacked artists such as Murray who Leach claimed worked by hand to please themselves as artists first, and therefore produced only limited and expensive pieces, that were supported by collectors, purists, 'cranks' or 'arty' people rather than by the normal man or woman. Yet Leach's patrons constituted largely the same "cranks" and "arty" people who supported Murray.[4]

Critics who had once been supportive of Murray now began to turn against him using Leach's ersatz humility to challenge Murray's prices. In 1932, when Murray showed works with prices at a new high, the critic Charles Marriott offered the view in the *London Times* that Murray was perhaps getting too big for his boots and was "in some danger of forgetting that a pot is just a pot."[5] Later Leach confessed to Murray that the whole thing had gotten a little out of hand and complained that, "we seem to be in an exaggerated phase of functionalism which is pushing live handcrafts out with the dead."[6] But the damage was already done.

Leach's impact on ceramic pricing was both unfortunate and dishonest. He regularly sold the best of his pots in Japan for prices as high as those of Murray, while keeping the prices low in Britain. Yet by 1950, his views had spread through the commonwealth and to the United States, and expectation of cheap pots became, whole-cloth, a requisite of the potter's identity and caused further damage, as low prices were instilled as the birthright of every collector; it built into the nascent ceramic market an expectation that a pot should be necessarily cheap. Collectors were encouraged to buy in volume and fill their shelves, which demoted the potter's art into a delivery system for handmade crockery.

A far better condition existed in Japan. Functional wares in Japan were accorded an elevated market by virtue of the tea ceremony, around which wares were implemented towards concerns of aesthetics, religion, and ritual. The Japanese "pot" enjoyed wholeness within its generative culture. The leading potters regularly destroyed all but their best work, and this kept prices high. This provided the correct arena in which careful editing, craftsmanship, beauty, utility, clay, glaze, weight, balance, spirituality, and tactility could be savoured, all of this within a generous and supportive market. Tea bowls by the earliest sixteenth-century master potters sell for well over a million dollars. Contemporary works by national living treasures are sold for as much as $100,000. But the issue is not just money, as we will discuss, but how the market resonates within the entire arts structure.

The British model, by comparison, was based on educated middle-class craftsmen imitating the working rituals of poor country potters. This was not quite Marie Antoinette playing at being a shepherdess, but it came painfully close. Either way, it was an artificial construct. While one can argue that these decisions were unfortunate and that their long-term impact has been harmful, I do not want to suggest that these market stances were insincere. In the 1920s and 1930s many artists were Socialists; indeed it, was practically *de rigeur* in bohemian society. Michael Cardew, for one, was deeply concerned that his handmade wares, even though inexpensive, were not properly serving the people. He championed their total accessibility from cost to use to overall social practicality. These views were morally correct but simply not a realistic strategy in the *realpolitik* of the arts marketplace and so only served to further marginalize the potter.

The Fifties

By 1950 ceramics had emerged with a thoroughly conflicted marketplace. From Socialism it had inherited unease about wealth and the exclusiveness of the art market. From education came airs of superiority; an academic, ivory-tower perspective; and requisite disdain within academe for the vulgarity of the marketplace. In some countries the belief arose that art should be funded regularly and generously by government, and in these places artists developed little if any survival skills. The impact of all this was to render selling a secondary activity, and that has built a culture of amateurism into ceramics that masquerades as principle. It is perhaps one of the more unfortunate aspects of our field and so internalized in collective ceramic identity as to be crippling.

In the 1950s the GI Bill in America and the introduction of broader art education in Britain increased the number of ceramics departments dramatically. The career routing of a ceramist now became a straight line between graduating from one university and immediately being hired to teach in another. Teachers receiving regular paychecks had neither the survival pressures nor the time to make and sell aggressively. The exhibition of their art was often in the public galleries of educational institutions.

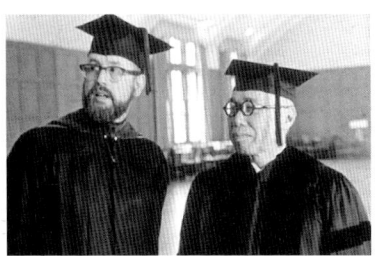

SHOJI HAMADA WITH JOHN STEPHENSON AT THE UNIVERSITY OF MICHIGAN, ANN ARBOR, 1966.

Exhibitions at commercial galleries were sought after only occasionally, for the reason that it looked good on the resume at tenure time. It rarely meant a serious pursuit of a career as a professional artist. It is not that educational patronage was inherently a negative force. What was negative was its dominance of the field, which so inhibited the development of the ceramic market. There is a photograph where John Stephenson is pictured next to a capped and gowned Shoji Hamada, while he is receiving an honorary doctorate from the University of Michigan in Ann Arbor. This incongruous image symbolizes the reach of the educational system. In this way the education system was even able to co-opt the idealized working ceramist, like Hamada, who was not at all part of their world.

1950 is a dividing line for the ceramic arts. Up until that time almost all ceramics belonged to either a craft or a decorative arts market. It was after World War II that a real fine arts market began to develop. There were a few earlier individual attempts, but for the greater part, the first significant steps to take ceramics out of the crafts milieu came in the late 1950s with the advent of the Abstract Expressionist ceramics movement. This began in Los Angeles at the Otis Art Institute and was spearheaded by Peter Voulkos with students Ken Price, John Mason, Paul Soldner, Jerry Rothman, and others. One might argue that this was a perfect example of the positive qualities of an education system able to nurture its artist-teachers. But in fact, this group's relationship with the Otis school was more like an ongoing state of war. The head of the school hated the work they were doing, thwarted them at every turn, and when one of their kilns set fire to a new school building, Voulkos was fired.

Voulkos's students tended to be older than most and arrived equipped with a desire to be practicing artists, although ultimately Price was one of the few who did not end up heading a university ceramics department. Members of the Otis group were exhibiting their work even before they left school. Ferus Gallery was the primary focus in Southern California for a combination of emerging, avant-garde and established artists. Indeed, private galleries have consistently been the driving force in bringing new ideas and risk-taking, experimental new work to the attention of the art public. Only after art has first passed through this portal does it reach museums a decade or so later. It was at Ferus Gallery that Andy Warhol had his first public exhibition. Ferus also showed Morandi and other European masters, together with ceramists Mason and Price, among others.

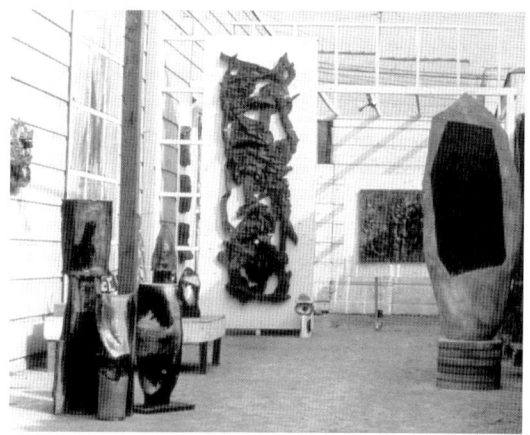

JOHN MASON EXHIBITION, FERUS GALLERY, LOS ANGELES, 1957.

Walter Hops and Ed Keinholz, who founded Ferus, saw something happening at Otis and wasted no time showing the work in 1957 in their patio gallery. One photograph shows Jerry Rothman's sculptures on steel poles and alongside them, work by John Mason. Legendary dealer Irving Blum acquired the Ferus Gallery and continued to show the work of Kenneth Price and John Mason. It was almost a decade later that museums started to show interest in the revolutionary work that took place at Otis. Voulkos was represented in the 1950s by the Felix Landau Gallery, who also showed European and American sculptors. Although its members had not

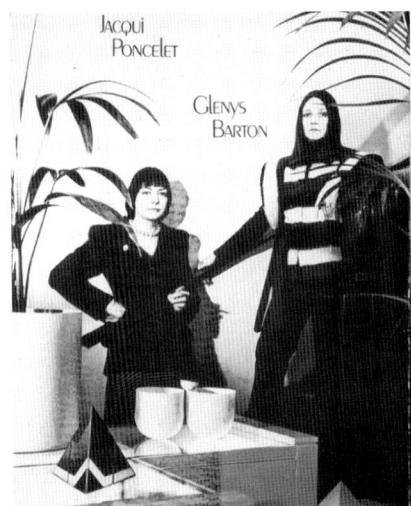

GLENYS BARTON AND JACQUELINE PONCELET,
EXHIBITION ANNOUNCEMENT CARD FOR THE
BRITISH CRAFTS CENTER, WATERLOO, 1973.
PHOTO: COURTESY THE ARTISTS

achieved a solid footing in the art market by the end of 1960s, the Otis group had established an impressive resume of exhibitions at MOMA, the Whitney Museum, and an assortment of galleries in the USA and abroad. Certainly their penetration into the fine arts market was deeper than any group before them.

In the 1970s those who believed in the field continued to push the boundaries. Specialist galleries started to appear, such as the Quay Ceramics Gallery in San Francisco and Exhibit A in Chicago. General galleries began to take an interest, notably Allan Frumkin, who held spaces in both Chicago and New York and became the main promoter of the work of Robert Arneson. But America was not the only place where changes were taking place. In England a group of ceramists at the Royal College of Art decided that they wanted to stand up and be counted as artists. The image that reflects a changing point in attitudes in British pottery is this announcement card from 1973 for the work of Jacqui Poncelet and Glenys Barton. Both the work and the stylish dress of the artists demonstrated clearly that this was no longer business as usual. Gone were the pleated cotton smocks, the clay-smeared painter's pants, and the wooden medicinal shoes. These events marked a new wave of ceramic artistic ambition, even though the escape was not complete because their venue was still the British Crafts Centre. However, Barton soon moved to one of London's better fine arts galleries, Angela Flowers.

I recall a visit shortly after this exhibition to the Centre's Waterloo Place Gallery in London to see the work of Liz Fritsch. The exhibition was magnificent but what transfixed the ceramics community were the prices. They cost from one hundred to nearly three hundred pounds each, and many had sold. At a time when a great Hans Coper could be purchased for one hundred pounds, this represented an extraordinary amount of money. It was an important moment when Fritsch's prices succeeded in breaking through a two-digit ceiling that had long loomed over ceramic market growth and held prices at a ridiculously low level. Today Fritsch's pots cost up to ten thousand pounds and those formerly "cheap" vessels by Coper have crossed into the high range of around $100,000.

The Eighties

It was in 1980 that the "pot began to boil," as the entire art world entered the greatest bull market of the century. Ceramics culture started to make its first serious inroads into a world of dealers and collectors who had previously shunned the field. It was a British artist who made one of the most dynamic entries into New York's art market, a playing field traditionally resistant, if not outright hostile, to ceramics.

Andrew Lord's first exhibition in 1981 at Blum Helman, one of New York most influential galleries, was a sellout success. Jasper Johns, Robert Rauschenberg, and other artists were amongst those who acquired the work. The critics tripped over each other in the race to lavish praise on the work and, with their total ignorance of ceramic history, credited Lord with every innovation made within ceramics in the last three hundred years. But the work was powerful and held its own against the toughest competition from the fine arts. Through its impact another benchmark was achieved. Lord has often been the subject of great resentment for his stance that ceramics must be priced and treated exactly the same as any other artwork and for his determination to make the concept stick. He opened a door; those who feared to follow have only themselves to blame.

However glamorous the Blum Hellman exhibition might have been, much of the progress was made incrementally by a small, hard-working group of dedicated ceramics dealers in the USA, Britain, Germany, Holland, and Japan who opened galleries that were unquestionably galleries of art in their design of space, presentation, and professionalism. Over time, and largely from their work, ceramics advanced its position and its profile slowly but surely.

The Nineties

In 1990, with the collapse of an overheated art market, one would have expected ceramics to be pushed back into obscurity. This did not happen. The fact that ceramics held its own and that neither did its prices collapse nor its collectors disappear the way they did for some years in the painting market, earned some serious respect and material interest on the part of the fine arts. Ceramics was more solid than the arts community expected. One does not want to create too much of a Pollyanna scenario, because even the top end of ceramics still exists in a marginal zone; however, it is now marginalized within the fine arts rather than without. This may sound like a shift in degree rather than a substantive change, but it is in fact the beginning of whole new paradigm. It has many ramifications, including the reality that New York's critics are taking time to bone up on the history of the field before rushing to print. The review of the Picasso show at the Metropolitan Museum of Art by Roberta Smith actually devoted a portion documenting the views of major ceramists in regard to Picasso's work, including Arneson and the ubiquitous Leach.

This opening up of the ceramics market is not all good news. When ceramists so eagerly sought entrance to the fine art galleries, they did not realize the extreme selectivity of the art market's mechanisms. Many felt that, one day, ceramics would be pronounced art and that there would be a blanket change of designation for all ceramists. They did not realize that the art market would only allow a small group of ceramists to cross over from crafts to art, leaving most of the field still excluded and much more frustrated and embittered than before. As Truman Capote warned, "Beware of answered prayers, they are the cause of the greatest pain."[7]

To demonstrate how this market has broadened and increased, I have prepared a scrapbook of images: slides, announcements, and advertisements that show a selection of many of the ceramics exhibitions that took place in New York in only one season, from September 1998 to June 1999. The purpose is for one to feel the texture, the diversity, and the heft of this relatively new market. One needs to look at these with the understanding that, as late as 1985, New York was considered a hostile environment for ceramics. Unlike now, ceramic shows then were reviewed by the *New York Times* in the "Home" section, next to recipes for coconut cream pies. So the change has been real and dramatic.

A look at some price tags reveals just how much the fine arts market has grown. Taking the American market as a guide, the price of an average handmade pot by a good, if not historically famous, potter (I hope that Jeff Oestreich won't mind his pitcher serving as the prototype) selling in the crafts market has increased in value

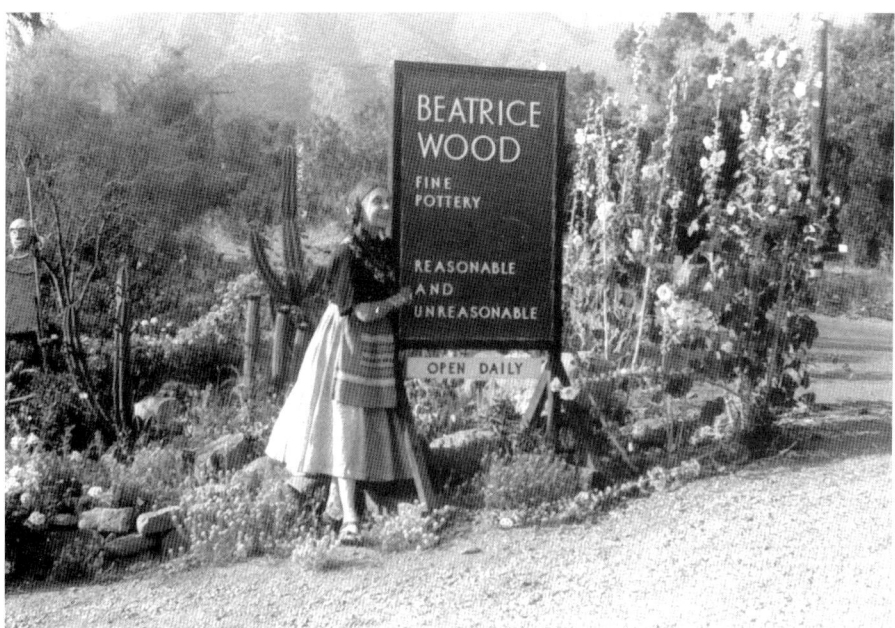

BEATRICE WOOD OUTSIDE HER STUDIO ENTRANCE, 1956.

from around $200 in the sixties to today's high of about $1500. That is an impressive growth of 750%. But if we look at those artists who function in the fine arts market, the figures are very different. Over the same period of time, the values of Peter Voulkos's works have risen from $1000 to $200,000, an increase of 20,000%. A Betty Woodman *Pillow Pitcher* that cost $250 in 1975 is now $18,000, an increase of 7,200%. A major work by Adrian Saxe has jumped in value from $600 in 1980 to $30,000 in 1999, an increase of 5,000%. Beatrice Wood's work went from $1,000 in 1980 to as much as $45,000 in 1999, an increase of 4,500%. Then there is Arneson, whose work has fetched the top price for contemporary ceramics of $250,000. This represents a growth from his 1960s days (when $1500 was a high price) to the tune of a whopping 166,000% increase. Arneson's market values continue to increase strongly as work disappears into public collections. In certain bodies of work, notably the portraits of the 1970s, only a handful of Arnesons are left in public hands, so the competition when one comes up for sale is fierce.

All this discussion of money may appear to be a vulgar recital of greed. But that is really just a superficial, simplistic criticism and usually a dishonest one. One of the old saws about the arts is, when bankers get together, they talk about art. When artists get together, they talk about money. Everyone has to pay his or her way and everyone worries, just like the potter of 100 BC, that the fire will be kind and that the finished ceramic will not only fetch its price but find a buyer. Why is this top end of the market important? Before engaging this inquiry, it bears re-emphasizing that the art gallery is not the only market, and that in most countries, it either does not exist or else is so small as to be immaterial. Craft shops, crafts fairs, and studio sales are still the major market for the majority of ceramists.

Why the focus on this market? Is it a focus on wealth, fame, and power? Seeing as I know few artists and no dealers in this field who can claim to have achieved any combination of these goals, it really seems to be about something else—the reality of cultural mechanisms and how their wheels turn. The top end of the market does have a disproportionate effect on how the rest of the medium is viewed. It is the needle-sharp, uppermost point of the market triangle. Painting is not presented to the world at large through secondary and tertiary artists. Its most public face is through primary artists. The stature of those artists, which is established for better or worse in the marketplace, in many ways determines how seriously painting is taken, how much money is spent on exhibiting that work in museums, what kind of scholarly research ensues as the consequential fallout of low market demand, and how much money can be spent on publications. If one is almost invisible in the food chain, all of these resources are reduced, denied, or altogether negated.

Is there a direct, causal relationship between market profile and the allocation of resources to a field? Yes, there is. Ceramics has suffered from being allocated a very small part of the total pie, precisely because its top end is so small. It is this part of the ceramics world that generates most of the mainstream reviews in the press and, in turn, makes the field visible and apparently viable. Such material is, in turn, seen and read by those who sit on the boards of foundations. If we are not seen to be players in the art world, we are extended neither the lifeline of funding nor the gesture of due consideration.

There is an argument, common amongst some ceramists—particularly those in universities—that if we push for a strong market, we are "going for the money" in its pejorative figuring. Before this criticism there exists only one question in retort, "What exactly should the ceramics market do, strive for poverty?" Would such a response provide a solution? I think we have done that for long enough and realize that it has kept ceramists in indentured servitude. A very strong market for ceramics at the top end, if even for a small group of artists, lifts price ceilings and raises the profile and the glamour of the entire field.

Those who complain most loudly about the evils of selling art are usually those who take home regular paychecks via academia. Their attitude flies in the face of pervasive truths for art survival. They seem determined to trap ceramics in an economic cul-de-sac, whereby they claim some specious moral higher ground. One notes, however, that members of this group do not suggest that their friends in the world of painting should follow the same route and are indeed often proud of their colleagues' market success. Nor do they reason that for ceramic faculty to get paid less than their colleagues who teach in other wealthier areas of the arts is right.

This sackcloth market is reserved for the clay-dobber. It's the throwback to Leach's hypocrisy, to William Morris's dilettantism, and to the supposed ethical superiority of academia over the free market. These bouts of idealism have repeatedly failed ceramics culture and will continue to do so. Yet in the wake of these failures, sounds emanate from the droning voices of the spoilers, masking with false humility their insecurities, perhaps hiding a fear of being tested in this ruthless proving ground and failing, or sadly, an even deeper fear of success.

But the fine arts market is not for everyone. Firstly, access is extremely difficult. Secondly, most ceramists do not fit. It's a very particular aesthetic, and only particular artists will survive in this world. It demands a high level of professional input from both artist and dealer. This means that to progress, ceramists have to give up their cherished culture of amateurism or what one dealer scathingly referred to as a "hobbyist-wanker" mentality. Remember, there is a difference between a professional artist who takes his or her income seriously and a commercial artist who panders (and one finds the latter in every market, high and low). Professional artists (perhaps "working artist" is a less loaded term) confront the responsibility that their art must sell if they are to afford another day in their studio. All artists do, and probably must, feel ambivalence for the admittedly artificial mechanisms for selling art, but they still have to come to terms with being professionals. Some of them do this superbly, without any compromise to their art, while others hide behind the shibboleth that artists are congenitally incapable of any kind of efficiency or direction.

Now that artists from other media (i.e. sculptors Tony Cragg and Thomas Chutte) are entering the ceramics field in increasing numbers and often with good and ambitious work, the market paradigm, once dominated by the specialist ceramist, is in flux. Good? Bad? It does not matter, it is happening. So ceramists, per se, are not alone in the ceramics market any more. They are not protected in a discreet, controlled marketplace, and increasingly, they are being pushed out into the cut and thrust with competitors whose signatures alone give them a head start over most ceramists, before you even consider their powerful marketing networks of international dealers.

One needs to juggle all the issues, finding time for teaching, if that is part of a career choice, finding time to make the art in sufficient quantity to be a player, looking into how the art can find a voice in other media aside from ceramics, and learning to work in the rough and tumble of a furiously competitive art market. Ceramists love tools. The time has come to provide—or history conspired to offer—such new tools within the marketplace, that if ceramists can learn how to use them, they might compete

1   Maya Angelou, "Power moves: A conversation with Maya Angelou and Eleanor Holmes Norton," *Essance* (August 1998).
2   Attributed to Herodotus, *Life of Homer*, 2nd or 3rd century AD. Adapted in Joseph Veach Nobel's *The Techniques of Painted Attic Pottery* (New York: Thames and Hudson, 1988).
3   As recounted to the author by Peg Weiss, Curator of the Everson Museum of Art, Summer, 1980.
4   Bernard Leach, *A Potter's Outlook* (London: Handworkers Guide, 1928).
5   Charles Marriott quoted in Malcolm Haslam, *William Staite Murray* (London: Crafts Council, 1984).
6   Letter from Leach to Murray quoted in Haslam.
7   Truman Capote, *Answered Prayers: The Unfinished Novel* (New York: Random House, 1987).

CHAPTER 27

GUESS WHO'S COMING TO LUNCH

LÉOPOLD L. FOULEM

The works in clay (made by ceramists I would define as "transient-artist potters," including Picasso) that are being discussed in this paper are in no way exhaustive examples. The objects presented, rather, should be understood as being representative of formal prototypes used to clarify the characteristics of various types of objects or of various standpoints. Actually, they are "facts" brought forth for the sake of argument. The real question I will deal with in this discussion is: do big-name artists bring anything more to ceramics than just their bankable signatures?

Presented at *The Ceramic Millennium*, 1999, Amsterdam

This paper will examine some ceramic objects made by a few mainstream artists (mostly painters and sculptors) to evaluate the kind and extent of their contribution to ceramics. The premise I use to gauge the intrinsic value of their production in clay is to consider ceramics as a generic group. This implies, therefore, that we are dealing with specific laws, language (terminology), and idiosyncrasies. In regard to intrinsic value, I mean the aesthetic or formal significance of the completed image itself. Not many occasional visitors, even if they were well-known artists, made even a lasting ripple in the larger pool of ceramic history. A good proportion of these aficionados came out for a good free lunch.

This paper is divided into three principal conceptual parts. At first I will establish a rudimentary overview of the state of the situation regarding such artists' ceramics. In the next section I will construct a proper context for evaluating ceramics. The final part will be devoted to the assessment of the contribution of a few of these so-called "major" artists to ceramics as a discipline.

From the start, it is truly impossible at this point to list all the protagonists from the major art field, who have, at one time or another, made a thing or two in clay during their careers. In fact, many more have dabbled in clay than historical research has shown. Consequently, an accurate assessment of the contributors to the field of ceramics (as an independent and autonomous art form) is to date unfeasible. Nevertheless, it is, for the sake of argument, possible to proceed to a valid appraisal based on the information or artifacts that have been published, even though the findings are non-comprehensive.

To give you an idea of the condition of scholarship in this highly specialized area, consider the troubling fact that (even in the case of Pablo Picasso—one of the most formidable major artists of this century) ceramics have not yet been properly assessed. What can we say for the others? Picasso worked in clay at various times during his illustrious career. According to Dominique Bozo, the first Director of the Musée Picasso in Paris, France, there were 3,222 of his ceramic works in the estate inventory.

Of course there are numerous picture books and exhibition catalogues devoted to the subject of Picasso and ceramics. Among these, there is little serious analysis and rigorous investigation being done. Most of the writings on the ceramics of Picasso can actually be viewed as press releases—and press releases of press releases. I have been following this issue for over twenty-five years now, but to my chagrin, I can say that the situation has not progressed much.

The works in clay (made by ceramists I would define as "transient-artist potters," including Picasso) that are being discussed in this paper are in no way exhaustive examples. The objects presented, rather, should be understood as being representative of formal prototypes used to clarify the characteristics of various types of objects or of various standpoints. Actually, they are "facts" brought forth for the sake of argument. The real question I will deal with in this discussion is: do big-name artists bring anything more to ceramics than just their bankable signatures?

Only a few comprehensive ceramic history books, and even fewer art history books, cite that artists have, indeed, made any ceramic objects. *Ceramics of the 20th Century,* by Serge Gauthier and Tamara Préaud, published in 1982, is one tome that comes to mind. Monographs on collections, or groups of artists, are more frequent. One could cite a text published in 1998, pertinent to this subject: *The Unexpected: Artists' Ceramics of the 20th Century*, the Kruithuis Museum collections. This catalogue, however, is skewed, as artists' ceramics are not really represented as part of a lineage, but rather as freak incidents in artists' careers or blips in the continuum. These two publications could be used to stand for many, showing the status of the situation regarding the literature pertaining to twentieth-century ceramics. These are the models: monographs on collections, monographs on groups of artists, and monographs on artists, where *some* clay works are featured.

On the one hand, you have some so-called ceramic book specialists who include works by transient-artist potters, usually as a separate chapter within a compendium; and on the other hand, you have audacious writers who publish essays, books or catalogues, who ignore completely the general ceramic production of a period as a totality of a culture, as if clay works by major artists were made outside of a creative or historical complexity. In both types of publications, however, there is a similar trend: the interest in the artifacts lies in the status of the maker rather than in the intrinsic value of the object itself. So objects are not compared to each other with any great insight. After all, we know that, in regard to graphics, formal components such as the illustrations for the text are the major consideration. For example, Préaud and Gauthier include an illustration of *Plaque* a macramé and stoneware specimen made in 1981 by a major Canadian-born artist, known internationally, mostly for his abstract paintings: Jean-Paul Riopelle. Most of us would undoubtedly agree that this suspended thing is at best a C minus project in a ceramics 101 class. Riopelle is one of that group of transient artist-potters who worked with Hans Spinner in a Grasse studio in Southern France over the years. This banal work is just included, shall we say, because Riopelle did some ceramics, and therefore they're good because they are Riopelle's. Major artists in one medium are not necessarily adept in another. Of course, Picasso is an exception.

Some fine artists who have worked in clay have utilized various strategies to make a production at all. Canadian painter and writer Emily Carr went all the way. She dug her own clay and built her own kiln and set up shop in the basement of her Canadian West Coast house. In the 1920s she made pottery, hooked rugs, and she even raised dogs and took in boarders to supplement her scant income. Carr's handiwork was directed toward the tourist trade. Women potters living in the area were encouraged to decorate their pots with Indian motifs. Emily Carr signed her pottery under her pseudonym—Klee Wyck, the name of one of her famous books. The more common approach for visitors who have worked in clay was to work in collaboration with potters or ceramists in already-organized studios, a practice already prevalent in ancient Greece. Some of those couplings resulted in highly successful ventures. Just think of the visits of Paul Gauguin to Ernest Chapelet's studio, of the visits of Raoul Dufy and Jean Miró to Llorens Artigas's studio, and Picasso and the Madoura Pottery.

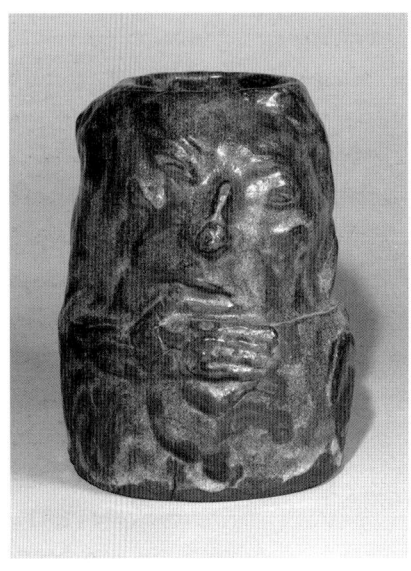

PAUL GAUGUIN, CERAMIC VASE WITH A GROTESQUE SELF-PORTRAIT, 1889. STONEWARE WITH GLAZE, 28 CM.
MUSÉE D'ORSAY, PARIS (OA 9050). PHOTO: ART RESOURCE NY / RÉUNION DES MUSÉES NATIONAUX, HERVÉ LEWANDOWSKI

A third form of collaboration is the association between artists and factories such as Rosenthal and Sèvres. In this instance the customary approach is to decorate vessels with images emanating from well-known artists, such as Serge Poliakoff, a Russian emigré living in Paris. Poliakoff's plate from the *Service Diane* of 1968 is simply a Sèvres factory blank on which Poliakoff's designs have been painted in his typical geometric polychromatic compositions.

Probably, it is the Parisian art dealer Ambroise Vollard who, at the beginning of the century, started to understand, encourage, and promote the commercial advantages of ceramics made by artists. We know that Paul Gauguin had worked with Ernest Chapelet, making singular stoneware vessels and sculptures such as *Vase with Mask: Portrait of a Woman*, made between 1887 and 1897. Gauguin's handling of clay can be characterized as intuitive and raw. This approach to the material gave a primitive allure to the vessel. In this work, the artist not only acknowledged the plasticity of the medium he was working with, but also the specificity of the formal repertoire he was involved in. The spout-like structure at the back of the human face is reminiscent of pre-Columbian Mochica stirrup vessels from Peru. Gauguin could have known about those highly distinctive forms, either from his mother's collection of Peruvian artifacts, or perhaps through some Parisian collections that he might have seen. The crudeness of the object could, more than likely, be interpreted as a manifestation of Gauguin's rebellious stance regarding the state-subsidized porcelain production coming out of the Manufacture Nationale at Sèvres.

Now the process of acquiring ceramic objects, sculpture, and art as collectible (and now we are looking at art from the point of view of the consumer) can be a complex or simple affair, as easy as deciding whether to eat lunch at McDonald's or at a very select Michelin five-star restaurant. Both are restaurants indeed, but needless to say, the choice, the service, the price, and the quality are different. You might think the example just suggested is far fetched, but not really, if what we are purchasing are simply commodities. All things are not equal. Even free lunches are not equal.

However, the fact is that ceramic objects can be more than just mere commodities. In the art field, the "quality control," if I can use this business term, is a well-entrenched process. Curators, museums, galleries, and magazines play a crucial role in weeding out what they consider to be the chaff from the wheat. It is practically inconceivable that a serious anthology or even an art history book would include, in a survey of twentieth-century Western-art watercolours by one Prince Charles, Prince of Wales, or a landscape by English statesman, Sir Winston Churchill. Instead, perhaps these amateurs should have made or decorated ceramics. Then they would more than likely have had their creations published in colour, in nothing less than a World Ceramics Overview, maybe even published by Abrams. The public that is aware, however—and there is one—knows what is happening in this specialized sphere of activity. Serious collectors, to their credit, not only take note of the trends but also (some of the most committed ones) add, on top of knowledge, clairvoyance, that special intuition that will end up with a small collection being built into a great collection.

However, ceramics and art are not in the same generic group. Consequently, scholarship and insight are not necessarily transferable. In the McDonald's comparison, we compared restaurants. To assume that ceramics made by respected and well-known major artists can be de facto credible ceramic objects is preposterous. I should also point out that to build a ceramics or an art collection on the premise of permeability or transference of competence from one medium to another is clearly a tightrope act. Imagine the dilemma if you are a collector. Do you acquire a bad pot by a major artist or a good pot by a second-rate painter or sculptor? The danger here is that the "signature" becomes a quality symbol, a bar-code, and a bankable resource. Unfortunately, that is often what is happening in clay. Some people actually make a lot of money out of this. It must now be obvious that the premise for analyzing something, whether restaurants, art, or ceramics, is that a context must be circumscribed.

This leads me to the second section: establishing a context. At the very beginning of "Guess Who's Coming to Lunch" I stated clearly that I saw ceramics as a generic group with its own set of rules, specialized terminology, and distinctive characteristics. Once the basic tenets are defined, categories can then be formulated. For the purpose of this talk, let me suggest that ceramics by visiting artists should be partitioned in two predominant groups based on two entirely distinctive approaches to ceramics.

The first grouping is material oriented. Here we can find works in clay by Paul Gauguin, Lucio Fontana, and Antoni Tapies. The second cluster might be formed with artists who use concepts as their bases. This latter group of protagonists perceives and exploits ceramics as a generic group. By using ceramics' intrinsic idiosyncrasies, they achieve highly significant and independent images. The singularity of their objects, in this case and in this category, resides in the fact that the object is not simply concerned with the transfer of imagery or pictographic style, as it was, say, for Poliakoff's plate; nor is it the expression of an angst-ridden ego, such as in Fontana's expressionistic work. The epitome, the graphic symbol to describe visually this second particular group is—now hold on to your seat—Marcel Duchamp's well-known *Fountain* from 1917, originally a plebian bathroom fixture, bought in a plumbing supply store and found in most public washrooms.

Once these two dominant conceptual approaches have been established and compared, we also have to consider (as a component in the evaluation process of ceramics) Western civilization's cult of the cultural categorization of art, of craft, of design, and of decorative art into distinct typologies. Blurring and blending are difficult to deal with in Western art; whereas Eastern art approaches these issues with totally different considerations. Analyses of painting and of sculpture are, by these criteria, totally different. Usually, when dealing with art, the fundamental question is always: Is it good? In ceramics, that question might be, is it art, which is a much more difficult question to answer.

We can say that the vast majority of pottery forms executed or decorated by transient-artist potters can easily belong within the boundaries of decorative art objects. In this particular instance, I am being fairly specific and am not including terra cotta sculpture such as the portrait bust of Charles Gounod from 1872 by French nineteenth-century sculptor, Jean-Baptiste Carpeaux, in the collection of the Hirshhorn Museum in Washington, the capital city of the U.S.A. That sculpture is considered a work within a completely different generic group, which is fine art. This being said, there will also, nevertheless, be some sculptures included in that classification that show strong and undeniable conceptual affinities with the field of ceramics. Again, I must stress that it is only by using a precise contextuality, with an appropriate grid, that objects can be rigorously analyzed and contributions assessed before we can say, what is art? What is the category?

An eighteenth century Sèvres *Porcelain Breakfast Set,* decorated with highly sentimental motifs (after the French painter, engraver, and decorator, François Boucher) perfectly fits the standard decorative art category. Calling the 1753 *Déjeuner Hébert,* with Boucher's blue vignettes, (in the Pierpont Morgan Collection) a craft object would be as ludicrous as classifying Duchamp's famous porcelain urinal within the decorative arts. Both artifacts, we can agree, are in no way—either at the semantic or conceptual levels—craft objects. Nevertheless, we can agree that they have an undeniable ceramics commonness. Decorative arts, crafts, and art are not essentially media-based classifications, unlike ceramics, which always is.

Let us return momentarily to the suggested classification I made, pertaining to the material-oriented group of ceramics in order to clarify the notion and exemplify the situation. There are subtle but real semantic and conceptual differences between material-oriented and media-based ceramics. The first term, the material-oriented, has to do with the tangible. For instance, the physicality, the plasticity of clay, the direct involvement of the artist with the immediate creative process can be attested by Lucio Fontana's terra cotta *Plate* of 1957. Here the vessel's integrity has been overwhelmed expressionistically and reduced to anonymity. The surface treatment takes precedence over form; the artistic expression is the raison d'être, the viscerality its manifestation. Whereas the second definition, the media based, encompasses the idea of channelling, here the primary image itself is the message, as in Pablo Picasso's oval platter *Corrida* (dated 1951) depicting a bullfight, a piece formerly in Jacqueline Picasso's collection. Here, contrary to Lucio Fontana's *Concetto Spaziale Piatto*, not only is there an accountability for the inherent particularities of the specific vessel shape, but also, the volumetric is pictorially intensified. The transposition of a round, three-dimensional stadium into a two-dimensional narrative space is masterly.

While in the earlier formal prototype made by Fontana the vessel becomes simply another surface to be decorated, punctured, and slashed, in Picasso's oval platter, the role of the singular shape of the vessel is determinant in the elaboration of its final image. There is a definite formal and conceptual symbiosis. The plate as a plate becomes a channel, a precise format for artistic fecundity. As it stands now, I am utterly convinced that it is especially in the conceptual area, namely media based, that there is to be found the most significant, provoking, authentic, and progressive cluster of works made in the field; and there, contributions by some visiting artists are potent. In the conceptual category, a serious observer can, without too much difficulty, differentiate tourists from masters, artists from decorators, Art from any kind of souvenir ware.

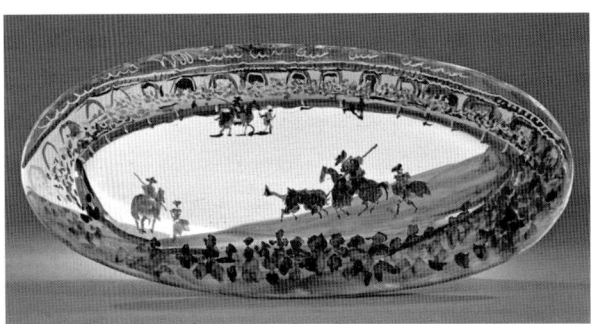

PABLO PICASSO, *DISH WITH BULLFIGHT SCENE*, 1951. WHITE EARTHENWARE WITH WHITE GLAZE PAINTED WITH OXIDES, 29 X 65 CM. PRIVATE COLLECTION (56946). © PICASSO ESTATE/SODRAC 2005

Yes, you heard me correctly. I really said—and I really do mean—Art with the proverbial capital A. There is also absolutely no doubt in my mind that the output, within the confines of ceramics as a whole, does indeed include some very liberated works transcending all the categories we have discussed. The difficulty of establishing and accepting and giving credit to those deserving recognition for their meaningful contribution—as either fine ceramists or exceptional visiting artists—is unfortunately due to intellectual imperialism, ignorance, and chauvinism. There is this structural problem in the field of ceramics, and I will recapitulate a few of the major problems once again: A) Ceramics is art on its own terms. B) A pot can simply be a pot, regardless of the status of the maker. C) Art is a concept, and craft is a process.

"Crossing the Rubicon": Now that a framework for evaluation has been somewhat set in place, we can proceed to the analysis of a sampling of ceramics made by transient-artist potters to appraise their contribution to the generic group, which is essentially the raison d'être of "Guess Who's Coming to Lunch."

Before going further in the discussion, perhaps the notion of contribution should be rationalized. There are not only various angles to interpret what is meant by this term, but also degrees in the extent or importance of the contribution to the generic group. For instance, is a visiting artist who made over three thousand ceramic objects contributing as much, or more, to ceramics than another who has produced only a few pieces in clay? Is Dada artist Meret Oppenheim's iconic of twentieth-century *Object (le Dejeuner en fourrure)* of 1936 a banal cup and saucer lined with fur (now in the collection of New York's Museum of Modern Art) a valid and acceptable example in the field?

Earlier on in this presentation, I put forward a few questions regarding what was at stake in the notion of assessing the contribution to ceramics by mainstream artists. I attempted to situate the debate and foresee the eventual dénouement of the process. Now it seems appropriate, before going further in the last stretch of this talk, to enunciate as clearly as possible what will be considered a contribution to ceramics as a whole, regardless of the birthright of the usurper.

Since what is being gauged is the intrinsic quality of the image itself, the signature or identity at this stage is obviously of no value to the process. Now, I am not saying that the privileged status of a maker has no role to play in the classification, marketing, and diffusion of a product by a transient-artist potter, but this fact will not be a criteria. Nevertheless, the sampling will be taken from the corpus of ceramic objects produced by some fine-art protagonists. The standard, the paradigm, to take into account in measuring the scale and proportion and/or value of the contribution, should be (as it also should be when evaluating any ceramics) the intrinsic quality of the image itself. Does it suffice? Is it significant? Does it really bring something singular to the generic group, either at the formal or conceptual level? And, even better still, does the image transcend the boundaries of the category it belonged to? Does the image cross the Rubicon? Oh yes. Furthermore, another part of the quandary should be resolved right now. This is the aspect related to the number of pieces needed to be considered admissible to the Pantheon. Only one, babe! But it better be good.

Let me illustrate this idea with two archetypes, again from the formidable Picasso clay corpus made with the assistance of the Madoura potters, located in the picturesque region of the French Riviera. This was a collaboration that started in 1947 and lasted some twenty years. I intend to prove more securely my argument that it is possible to divide ceramic objects into two inclusive groups—one based on the premise of a material-oriented proposition, and the other, media-based—and to show, as well, that, even within the clay œuvre of one artist, we can find and identify both dispositions, since we are in the process of evaluating the morphology of ceramic objects and are not categorizing artists into period, style, and genre. You have to admit that such a stylistic eventuality is far from being eccentric.

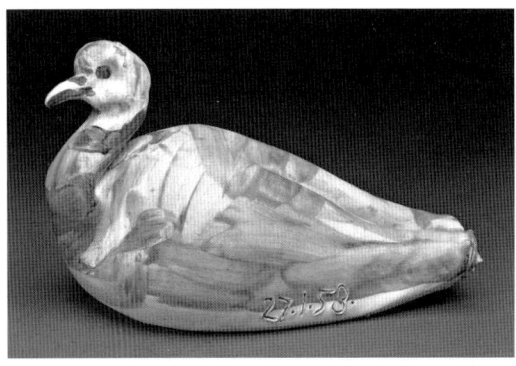

PABLO PICASSO, *Dove*, 1953. WHITE EARTHENWARE PAINTED WITH SLIPS, 15 X 20 CM.
COLLECTION/PHOTO: MUSEUM FUR KUNST UND GEWERBE, HAMBURG (1967.222), © PICASSO ESTATE/SODRAC 2005

Pablo Picasso's *Colombe à la Roue* dated 1953, formerly in Jacqueline Picasso's collection, would fit in the material-oriented category. The plasticity of white earthenware clay has been exploited creatively in the construction of the image of the *colombe*. The black defining brushstrokes are intuitive and aggressive. There is a ceramic materiality in the finished sculpture that is partly its meaning.

However, in *Pitcher* made in 1954, and with the same provenance as *The Colombe à la Roue,* the materiality now has been pre-empted by the dominance of the pictorial sign. This pitcher is one of the truly great ceramics by Picasso. The complexity of the image is breathtaking, and the object functions on numerous semiological levels. Not only are there a series of multilayered images, but also the physicality of the original pitcher as vessel has been annulled and deconstructed and not overpowered as a form, as was the case with Lucio Fontana's plate discussed earlier. By covering the surface of the true pitcher in black, and then painting in white the silhouettes of generic ceramic forms (which are pitchers and drinking glasses located under the spouts of all the pitchers), Picasso not only recognized the dichotomy of form versus surface, or form as form and surface as surface, but he also established the potency of the ceramic sign as message, and in this particular case, the specificity of ceramics as a visual and as a conceptual language.

What is so radical here—and it is the case for several of Picasso's greatest vessels—is that "l'objet va changer de destination et devenir lui-même sujet." This brilliant synthesis of Picasso's conceptual framework concerning his ceramics output was made by Georges Ramié in his book, *Céramiques de Picasso,* published in 1974. Ramié's insightful contention was that, while a visiting artist at the Madoura Pottery, Picasso inferred that a pot could either be an image or a concept. This revolutionary insight into pot making resulted in the birth of the true conceptual ceramic object.

Hey, babe! Remember I said that it only took one good piece to be admitted into the Pantheon of artists who have made singular contributions to ceramics? Here is a perfect example. Any contributor who can present a proposition of this magnitude should be unequivocally accepted into the Ceramic Hall of Fame.

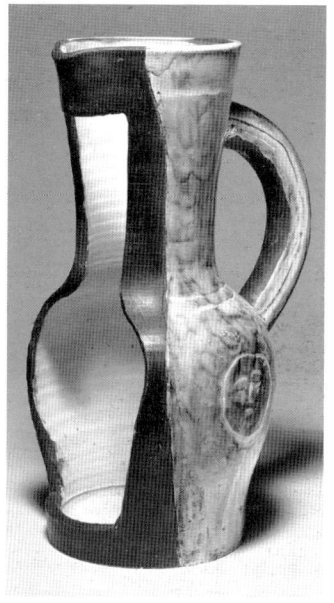

PABLO PICASSO, *PITCHER WITH OPEN VASE*, 1954. EARTHENWARE WITH SLIPS AND GLAZES, CARVED. 38 CM. PRIVATE COLLECTION (57682).
© PICASSO ESTATE/SODRAC 2005
PHOTO: PATRICK GOETELEN, GENEVA.

To suggest that the ceramics of Picasso are simply the result of an artist playing with clay, and even worse, to include his work in such a condescending category (as was done recently in an essay to be found in *The Unexpected: Artists Ceramics of the 20th Century,* the Kruithuis Museum collection catalogue mentioned at the beginning of my talk) is a gross misunderstanding, not only of the scope of the

Picasso clay œuvre, but also of the specificity of ceramics as an independent art form.

American artist Cindy Sherman's *Tureen with its Platter* is a remarkable addition in the media-based category and also an extremely successful result of a wedding between an art-edition project and an artist's collaboration. The channel she uses for her artistic intervention is an appropriation of a tureen-and-platter-set originally made in 1756 by the Sèvres porcelain factory for Madame de Pompadour, mistress of French monarch Louis XV, and a well-known devotee of the fine and theatre arts. This particular ensemble was made between 1988 and 1990 by the Ancienne Manufacture Royale in Limoges, a renowned porcelain centre situated in the Limousin area in France. This edition, made for Artes Magnus, is limited to twenty-five copies in four colours: yellow, pink, green, and blue. In this yellow *Tureen with its Platter*, Cindy Sherman uses the idiosyncratic (as Picasso has done in the pitcher just anatomized) to affirm the existence of the new art group she was now visiting and to confirm at the same time the potency of the genre as a precise, conceptual context for unique artistic contribution.

At the bottom of the scale, measuring the extent of the contribution from big-name artist to ceramic vernacular, is American artist James Brown's *Gefäss* of 1987: a crude, basket-shaped vessel; a vintage flea-market trinket whose only reason for being shown in a serious exhibition would be the value of the signature. Brown was not only coming to the field to get a free lunch, he even made his own lunch pail.

It has so far been established in this talk that artists' ceramics are not a cohesive entity. What we are dealing with are incoherent groupings, loosely assembled and vaguely defined, which have been conveniently and randomly organized for the purpose of cataloguing, collecting, exhibiting, and marketing certain works in clay by some painters and sculptors. These works have emanated from larger and more varied sources than are usually acknowledged.

It has also been convincingly demonstrated, I hope, that any object has to be properly contextualized in order to articulate its relevance and demonstrate the extent of its significance to the field of ceramics. This sounds self-evident, but it has not been adequately demonstrated in texts or exhibitions. The purpose of this paper was to inquire into the scale, value, scope, form, and extent of the contribution by transient-artist potters to the field of ceramics in order to confirm or to dispel the argument regarding the worth of their signatures. It is even fair to say, after this very short overview of the terrain, that a surprising number of good mainstream artists did make significant investigations that resulted in unique and arresting ceramics, which, without question, enriched the ceramic repertoire in a period and expanded the categories of an age.

However, I have to point out that, had the sampling studied been more traditional in scope, for instance, I could have discussed only studio ceramics as the mainstream prototype rather than include also media-based ceramics made by famous artists. The outcome possibly would have had a different conclusion and my presentation would have been less thought provoking and far more standard. But I must say once more, we haven't gotten past the standard. By deciding to expand the categories of eligible artifacts to include those magnificent anomalies found particularly in the media-based group of artistic interventions, such as Duchamp's famous *Fountain* or Meret Oppenheim's fur-lined cup and saucer, I circumvented the traditional dialectic. The discourse would have been more predictable and familiar but, undoubtedly, less challenging.

Finally, to review, let us recall that I stated at the beginning of the lecture that I would present ceramics as a generic group. Unfortunately, this is still a utopian goal. Ceramics is rarely discussed as an encompassing conceptual entity, despite the survey texts, monographs, etc., and other ambitious undertakings by galleries or museums.

At the dawn of a new millennium, I think that there is an urgent need for a radical shift regarding fresh critical and cultural approaches to our field, perhaps by using the system I have just identified. Otherwise we will continue to validate clay as art without changing the parameters and continue to be impressed by a pot signed by a big-name artist or one shown in a so-called "world-class museum" under false pretensions. That is not to say that some objects are not perhaps, beautiful in themselves. I hope that "Guess Who's Coming to Lunch" has convinced some of you that art is not about material or about signature or signatories, but it is about concept, babe. Ceramics is its own concept.

CHAPTER 28

NOT IN IDEAS BUT IN THINGS

EDMUND DE WAAL

Rebus: Non Verbis Sed Rebus—Not by words but by things

Presented at *The Ceramic Millennium*, 1999, Amsterdam

Michel de Montaigne wrote in his essay *On the Vanity of Words*,

> I don't know whether it happens with others as with me, but when I hear our architects puffing themselves out with those big words like pilasters, architraves, cornices, Corinthian and Doric work and such like jargon, I cannot keep my imagination from immediately seizing on the palace of Appolodon; and in reality I find these are the paltry parts of the kitchen door. When you hear people talk about metonymy, metaphor allegory and other such names in grammar, doesn't it seem that they mean some rare and exotic form of language? They are terms that apply to the babble of your chambermaid.[1]

How can we talk about the paltry parts of the kitchen door, those quotidian objects we encounter, without succumbing to the vanity of Montaigne's architects? How can we respond to the "babble of the chambermaid," the demotic language of those around us, without the pretensions of grammarians? Is it possible to address these silent and, to some, ineffable objects that we call ceramics, pots, ceramic art, art, and not fall into the closet codifications, those ever-helpful bits of shorthand that seem to arise when aficionados are gathered together? Is it possible to believe, with passion, that there is a great value to theory and to the practice of theory and still respond in interesting ways to objects? And if all these possibilities are genuine and not the whimsy of Montaigne's grammarians, why aren't more makers of ceramic art writing about their work? Why this great exercise in cultural ventriloquism on our/their part? Does our critical language disempower the growth of their critical language?

My first contention is that ceramics is an art whose practitioners have become peculiarly suited to silence. That is that their silence about their own work, that of their peers, that of aesthetics or the cultural life that sustains them, has become an iconic marker for their seriousness as artists in a way that is radically different from other arts. The truly authentic and serious potter is the one who unknowingly makes her pots, whose silence allows a critical space to open up into which the critic, the curator, and collector can step, who allows what could be described as an interpretative vacuum. A silence or a vacuum allows for aestheticizing encounters. Rilke writes in a letter of

> ...the hours I was able to stand in Rome watching a rope-maker repeat in his craft one of the world's oldest gestures, just like that potter in the little village on the Nile—to stand by his wheel was so indescribably and mysteriously fruitful to me.[2]

Mysteriousness, indescribability, ineffability, conjoined with ancient craft: the heady mixture of the encounter between the over-cerebral writer and the authentically silent. The maker's silence is necessary for the poet's creativity: the reminder of physicality, of repetition, and of a gestural language that is the spur for the interpreter. If we examine this vocabulary of interpretation, we have more than a list of words to investigate; there is also a syntax: a way of putting these words to use. And we come up with an attitude and a methodology for approaching the writing on ceramics, what might be termed an ethnographic approach to the making of pottery.

It is ethnography of a very particular kind. It is based on the positioning of the (normally) Western writer-critic-ethnographer as both "the man apart," the dispassionate onlooker able to observe the goings-on rationally and impartially, and also to be the intuitive, instinctual colleague of the craftsman, to crouch next to the wheel and enact the pantomime of shared skills. This is the taxing position of the colonial encounter with authentic craft, the problem of "being there."

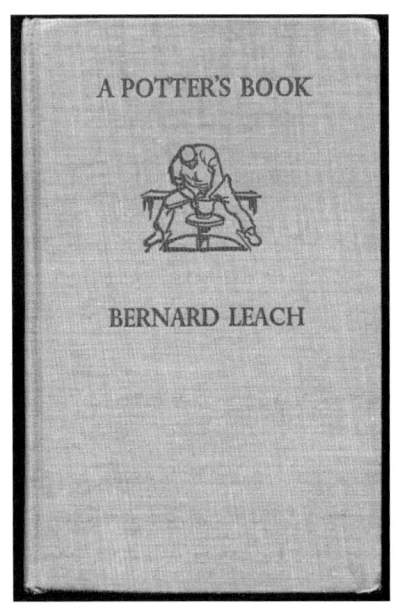

BERNARD LEACH, *A POTTER'S BOOK*. 2ND ED. HOLLYWOOD-BY-THE-SEA, FLORIDA: TRANSATLANTIC ARTS INC., 1967.

Authenticity is a pre-lapsarian condition. It is a condition discernable in other groups that have not yet experienced the rift that Ruskin defined between maker and object within industrial society. Authenticity occurs elsewhere, noticed only by the anxiously inauthentic. Thus in the most obvious of ways, it is "a form of cultural discrimination projected onto objects," and, of course, onto people.

The first marker of authenticity is that the maker of the object must not be self-aware, must be unconscious of the possibility of inauthenticity in making. Therefore, the process of making must be consuming, even self-abnegating, thereby allowing little of the destructive self-consciousness that has infected the West. Consider this characteristic piece of aesthetic ethnography by Soetsu Yanagi, the theoretician of the Japanese folk craft movement and interlocutor of Bernard Leach, writing about the Kizaemon teabowl, a bowl that a poor man would use every day:

> ...a typical thing for his use; costing next to nothing; made by a poor man; an article without the flavour of personality; used carelessly by its owner; bought without pride; something anyone could have bought anywhere and everywhere. That is the nature of this bowl. The clay has been dug from the hill at the back of the house; the glaze was made with the ash from the hearth; the potter's wheel had been irregular. The

shape revealed no particular thought: it was one of many. The work had been fast; the turning was rough, done with dirty hands; the throwing slipshod; the glaze had run over the foot. The throwing room had been dark. The thrower could not read. The kiln was a wretched affair; the firing careless. Sand had stuck to the pot but no one had minded; no one invested the thing with any dreams. It is enough to make one give up working as a potter....The plain and unagitated, the uncalculated, the harmless, the straightforward, the natural, the innocent, the humble, the modest: where does beauty lie if not in these qualities?...Only a commonplace practicality can guarantee health in something made.[3]

Yanagi's Korean potter, healthily illiterate, naturally aesthetic, too busy to be self-conscious is a vivid example of "homo orientalis…by nature mystical and concerned with great ideas," the peasant craftsman who underpins the creation of Leach's authentic Orient. That great list of descriptive words—the harmless, the straightforward, the natural, the innocent, the humble—is a lexicon of Orientalist language. These are the words that, with their antonyms, occur and re-occur throughout ceramics criticism. They tell of the Rilkean moment of the encounter between the silent maker and the incisive critic. To call it patronizing is too facile. Listen to the language of Leach when writing on the feeling of glazes to the touch:

Unconsciously our fingers are invited to play over the contours, thereby experiencing pleasure through the most primitive and objective means. Children play with pebbles with a similar awakening of perception, and Orientals have lost touch with the fresh wonder of childhood less than we have.[4]

Authenticity is indeed pre-lapsarian.

The Edenic fall into self-consciousness, the fall into language that comes in childhood, is particularly dangerous for the Korean bowl maker or the young Japanese potters (counselled by Leach) who wanted to escape their traditional roles:

A young "individual" potter protested that our advice to stick to good old traditions was cramping. Yanagi and I, each in our own way, replied:

"Be modest. These results of wild experiment show indigestion. Launch out into new only as you can understand it and feel it." In any case only a few have this natural creative capacity in my country.[5]

The quotation marks that frame the word "individual" say much about where authenticity is sited and where it is held to be absent in this encounter. For the second marker of authenticity is that of tradition. An easily identified and extensive tradition is a safeguard against the novel. Tradition means knowing your place. Experimentation is transgressive. For the writer-ethnographer it means knowing one's place: the infantilizing of the maker is part of the equation.

The third requirement for the authentic object is that it should be made in quantity, preferably for quotidian local living. As we have seen, this was a principal definition for Yanagi, as it was for Cardew in West Africa. Quantity protects the object from the possibility of transformation into a self-conscious art object. That transmutation is only permissible in that object's assimilation into a collection: the valuing or endowing of it with aesthetic meaning is the province of the collector, not the original maker. It is important that the maker cannot talk of aesthetic value or see aesthetic value as clearly as the critic. It is, of course, the Japanese tea master who aestheticizes the Korean tea bowl. This may be the reason that there is such anxiety about objects made for display or with a superabundance of decoration: such objects extend the possibility of the original maker's intentions in making, beyond the site of authenticity.

Making merely for local, everyday life rules out the dangers of transgression into complex trade relations and delimits the obvious commoditization of the craft object. Making in this way also reinforces

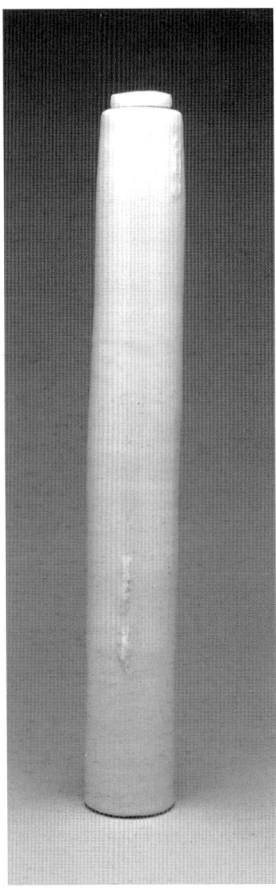

EDMUND DE WAAL, *TALL PORCELAIN LIDDED JAR*, 1998. PORCELAIN, 63.5 CM.
PHOTO: COURTESY THE ARTIST

the possibility of the craft-ethnographer aestheticizing the whole culture in which the object is made. As Cardew wrote:

> In West Africa, art has not yet been separated from ordinary life; it is still the air that everyone unconsciously breathes. Every man and woman is by nature a poet, a stylist, an aesthete, though outsiders like ourselves may sometimes disagree with or disapprove of the ways in which it is expressed. West Africans do not need to make a cult of art—still less, of what we call "good taste"—because they live with it all the time and, unlike ourselves, have not made the mistake of treating it as a separate department.[6]

Finally the authenticity discerned must be capable of being transferred in easily communicable ways. When Ezra Pound published his versions of Chinese poetry in 1916 entitled *Cathay*, the exotic or "Other," nature of the original Chinese verse was always apparent. They always seemed Chinese, even in translation. This was a tendency vividly remarked on by George Steiner: "The more removed the linguistic and cultural source, the easier it is to achieve summary penetration and a transfer of stylized, codified markers."[7] These are the codified markers of authenticity, and the markers of having "been there" in ethnographic terms. Thus the anthropologist Clifford Geertz, writing on the seductive stylistic fluency of the patrician British ethnographer Sir Edward Evan Evans-Pritchard, "assured, limpid, measured, equanimous, effortless, superior, conversational, and further noting the constant row of promulgatory declarations" identified this transference. Geertz continues: "The outstanding characteristic of E-P's approach [sic] to ethnographic exposition and the main source of his persuasive power is his enormous capacity to construct visualizable representations of cultural phenomena-anthropological transparencies." This kind of flashing-up of "magic-lantern images" demonstrates that "the established frames of social perception, those upon which we ourselves instinctively rely, are fully adequate to whatever oddities the transparencies may turn out to picture." That is to say, the "stylized markers" are both easily identifiable as strange, exotic, and Other, but crucially, their difference from us, however dramatic, does not finally count for much.[8]

When we read Cardew or Leach, in their limpid and assured prose, the summary, repeated flashing up of a few images of the authentically exotic in their encounters is always without the mediation of any surprise, astonishment, wonder, or bewilderment at what they see. It is as if they had already been there: the Korean potter waiting for his Yanagi, the Nile potter waiting for Rilke. In some ways they had: what they see fits in with what they want to see and with what they went to see. The critical position is close to essentialism, to a belief that there are necessary properties to things, that these are logically prior to the existence of the individuals who instantiate them. The makers are channels for the fulfilment of various sets of conditions.

But it is also important to register that it is the nature of the "magic lantern images" of ethnography to fragment a culture into digestible morsels. To paraphrase Barbara Kirshenblatt-Gimblett, the "artfulness of the ethnographic object is an art of excision, of detachment, an art of the excerpt." Like the ruin, the "ethnographic fragment" is informed by a poetics of detachment. Detachment refers not only "to the physical act of producing the fragments," but also to "the detached attitude that makes the fragmentation and its appreciation possible."[9]

That is, as readers of this particular craft ethnography, we give ourselves up to the authorial decision about the removal of particular objects from complex material cultures and their re-presentation to us as "craft objects."

Authentic ethnic craft validates the critical abilities of those who have spotted it, just as Sir Edward Evan Evans-Pritchard's fieldwork acts as a bulwark for his ethnographic insight. But it also points up our own inauthenticity: it suggests both a "more strenuous moral experience than sincerity does, a more exigent sense of the self, and what being true to it consists of,"[10] and also, crucially, a way to overcome this. "Losing one's tail" is how Leach put it: the passage through self-consciousness back into childlike, transparent making; the strenuous moral experience; the elective submersion into repetition and process.

The exhausting of self, whether in the studio or, in the case of Cardew (and Conrad's Marlowe), in the bush, is the hallmark of the Western craftsmen after their encounter with the authentic. One of the more fanciful early etymologies of "authentic," after all, is that of perpetrator, murderer, and suicide: the destruction of self lies deep within its cultural meaning. And it is this view of the self that is predicated on authentic silence: a self that could verbalise the reasons surrounding the making of objects would be "unreal." Thus Cardew can call the large stoneware oil jar he made at Abuja in Nigeria in 1959 *Heart of Darkness*. This jar was a composite of West African decorative repeat incising into the clay under an Oriental mottled tenmoku glaze. It stands as a hybrid of authentic markers, symptomatic of the confusion that the transfer of coded meanings leads towards.

This is our inheritance: a collapsing together of words, ethical positions, and attitudes to ceramics, centering on an idea that some pots are more "real" than others. When we read the literature of ceramics, that great and unruly mass of tracts, pamphlets, catalogues, monographs, surveys, plain-speaking essays on how to reduce, public quarrels about good practice in magazines, the innumerable murmuring of glaze recipes, this is the vocabulary that underpins the edifice. In the language of praxis, the discourse on technique that occupies the huge majority of the writing about ceramics, this is the foundation stone. For if, as I suggest, the language of authentic making necessitates silence on the part of

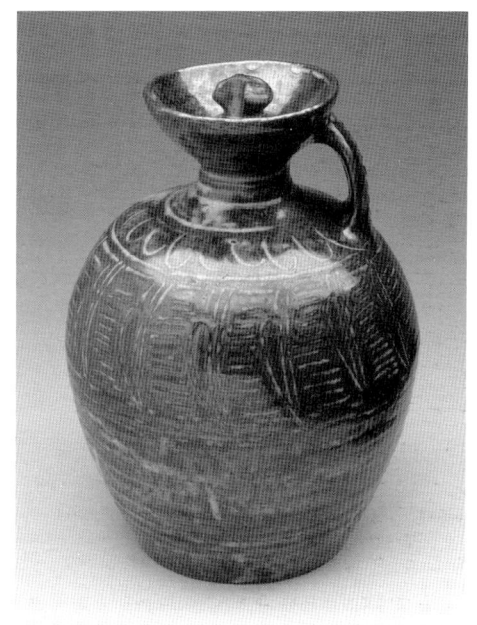

MICHAEL CARDEW, *JUG WITH STOPPER*, C. 1960.
EARTHENWARE, 33.0 × 25.4 CM.
PHOTO: JOHN WHITE

makers, then how do artists who use clay, makers of pots, ceramicists converse except through that low level noise that could, and should, be called "potchat"? Interpretation, curation, display go on elsewhere. Makers mistake their reverential silence when confronted by the quiddity of their own objects; the involuntary lapsing into wonder about their own ceramics for the authentic ineffability of the pot speaks for itself. Except that it doesn't, and others do.

What can we do about this situation? In other disciplines the call has been for deconstructive attacks on canonical works and on the very idea of the canon itself. There have been clarion calls to reflexivity, to dialogue, heteroglossia, linguistic play, rhetorical self-consciousness and performative textuality, as if by becoming textually self-critical we will escape the philosophical limitations of our critical inheritance. Of course there is value in this, as I hope I have shown in examining one element of this vocabulary. Attacks on canonical works continue to give me great pleasure, as my work on the construction of *A Potter's Book* shows. But the mere additions of neo, post, anti, or meta to an argument does not qualify as intelligent rethinking of agendas. The scattering of a little postmodern birdseed round ceramics is not going to change the status of theory within our discipline, let alone encourage the *rare avis* of art criticism to take an interest in pots. And the risk is that the gulf between the makers of ceramics and critics will widen. The commonplace that there is already one language for critics and another for makers will become true.

My contention is that we have to reground ceramics within the material cultures from which they come, that is in the materiality of their making and in the matrix of their commoditization as objects. Both of these aspects are crucial. If we can take the complexity of the making of objects more seriously, rather than regarding their creation as an essentialist outcome of various cultural factors, then we may find that there is more to talk about in these ineffable objects than we thought. When we overhear anthropologists, ethnologists, or other writers on material culture talking, what do we learn about the ability of objects to change their meanings? Due to the widely appreciated collection of essays edited by Arjun Appadurai, we are familiar with the proposition that things have social lives, that is, that the same object is successively recontextualized and that its meanings are radically contingent. As Nicholas Thomas has written, the problem, of course, is that the artafact is never just "a thing in itself." Artifacts and technologies alike are more than physical forms and machines: they cannot be dissociated from the bodies of knowledge, practices, and values, through which they are animated and given social life. However deliberately we choose to engage with the materiality of things, it will never be possible to invent a rigorous or pure study based on deductions from forms. Our strategies may fail because an object's meanings are only weakly or partially inscribed in it. Social life is surely a succession of gambles on the bad chance that things will be received in the spirit in which they are given.

This is more like the language of material culture, of ethnography, with which we might want to be associated: bad chances, a succession of gambles, the weak inscription of meaning. This is not the limpid colonial assurance of a Leach or Yanagi, secure in their aestheticizing removal of objects from the complex of their making, happy to believe that rigorous and pure studies were possible. This is more an acceptance that all objects are entangled objects, entangled in the values of the maker, in that maker's appropriation of ideas and images, as well as the values of those through whose lives it is successively animated. If we believe this, then we have to find a critical language that is lithe enough to cope with objects that do not stand still, objects whose contingency is also the play with the metaphorical references to which any object is susceptible.

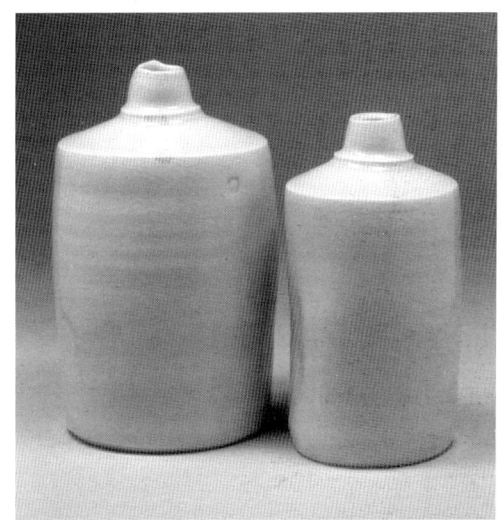

EDMUND DE WAAL, *PAIR OF BOTTLE FORMS*, 1998.
PORCELAIN, 30.5 AND 25.4 CM.
PHOTO: COURTESY THE ARTIST

And if we believe this then we have to find a critical language that can map the influences and relationships between objects that "map of misreading"[11] that has proved so useful within literary criticism. "Misreading" is more than the passing on of images and ideas. It is the critical act of interpretation that allows one artist to make space for his or her own work. Makers of objects do "misread" in this way, do make those critical decisions about where to work amongst the cloud of presences, do decide about difference or similarity with other objects. If we can learn from the new ethnography that any biography of an object will reveal that that object's meanings will not stay still, we can learn from some aspects of the new literary criticism that it is often the things that remain unsaid that are most revealing. That on any "map of misreading," it is those areas left blank that are so intriguing.

Within the contemporary sculpture of this century, from Duchampian readymades, through Pop Art, to the affectionate interventions of Richard Wentworth, there has been a substantial body of art where the imperative has been to explore how the language of objects can be used. There has been no great anxiety on the part of critics in dealing with this sculpture. Because it has often been an artistic intervention on a readymade object rather than its creation per se, there has been no expectation of an authentic approach to materiality. If you believe, as I do, that in making something, it is possible to enrich even further the possibilities for exploring ideas, then the critical lacunae around ceramics seems even more heartrending.

I am a potter who writes, not a writer who pots. My writing is a response to areas of difficulty or anxiety within my life as a potter. It is a way of making conceptual space for my work and conceptual space for the interpretation of my work. I was brought up within the Leach tradition. The profound disjunction that I felt between the work I wanted to make and the work I felt I should make, the Orient I saw and the Orient I read about, the canonical pots I was aware of and my own personal canon felt unbridgeable to me. I had studied literature at university and knew my Orientalism and knew my structuralism, but this did not seem to help. And then I started to learn how to write about ceramics. I broke the pact of silence. I first wrote about my apprenticeship, then about Leach: early writings as "slash and burn." And since then, there has been a profound symbiosis for me between my growth as an artist and my increasing discovery that it was possible to write about other areas that matter to me, from display and curation, to my uneasy love affair with modernism. Hence my slightly zealous attitude.

In *Gulliver's Travels* Gulliver meets a group of people who have given up on language. They carry a great weight of objects on their backs and produce them, gesticulating and miming, in order to converse. It is an image to haunt us.

1 Currently available from Penguin Classics, Michel de Montaigne, *The Complete Essays* (New York: Penguin Classics, 1993).

2 Quoted in "Rilke and Things" by Idris Parry from *Obscure Objects of Desire: Reviewing the Crafts in the Twentieth Century*, University of East Anglia conference papers edited by Tanya Harrod (London: Crafts Council, 1997) 13.

3 Soetsu Yanagi, "The Kizaemon Teabowl", from *The Unknown Craftsman* (Kodansha International, 1972).

4 Bernard Leach, *A Potter's Book* (London: Faber and Faber, 1940) 37.

5 Bernard Leach, *A Potter in Japan* (London: Faber and Faber, 1960) 88.

6 Michael Cardew, *Michael Cardew - A Pioneer Potter* (London: Ceramic Review Publishing, 1988) 203.

7 George Steiner, *After Babel* (New York: Oxford University Press, 1976) 361.
8 Clifford Geertz, "Slide Show: Sir Evans-Pritchard African Transparencies," *Raritan 3*, (No. 2, Fall, 1983) 62-80.
9 Barbara Kirshenblatt-Gimblett, "Objects of Ethnography," in Ivan Karp and Steven Lavine (eds), *Exhibiting Cultures: The Poetics and Politics of Museum Display* (Washington, DC: Smithsonian Institution, 1991) 386-443.
10 Lionel Triling, *Sincerity and Authenticity* (Cambridge, MA: Harvard University Press, 1982)
11 Harold Bloom, *A Map of Misreading* (New York: Oxford University Press, 1975).

Chapter 29

The Aesthetics of Function

Edward Lebow

The thing we're really good at as a species is usefulness.
Lewis Thomas, c.1993

We cannot possibly call an object beautiful, no matter how lovely the ornamentation, if it totally fails or only partially succeeds in fulfilling the function for which it was intended.
Joseph-August Lux in 1910

Presented at *The Ceramic Millennium*, 1999, Amsterdam

The duality of usefulness and beauty—the aesthetics of function—is an old and luminous topic. This twin tower of philosophical reckoning has drawn the likes of Aristotle, Plato, Burke, Coomaraswamy, Emerson, Yanagi and Octavio Paz, to name-drop a few. Their responses have ranged from riddles to calls for action. "Beauty must come back to the useful arts and the distinction between the fine and the useful arts be forgotten,"[1] Emerson wrote in the mid 1800s. If only he could see us now, engulfed as we are by style and expectations that every imaginable product have the eye-popping magic to tinkle the ice and jewellery at gatherings like this one. Yet what has happened to the idea of "usefulness"?

"The thing we're really good at as a species is usefulness," Lewis Thomas (the physician and biologist who wrote *Lives of a Cell* and *The Snail and the Medussa*) told a reporter shortly before he died in 1993. "If we paid more attention to this biological attribute, we'd get a satisfaction that cannot be attained from goods or knowledge."[2] His pairing of usefulness and goods, and his distinction between achieving one and acquiring the other is an ancient coupling: meaning and material. By usefulness, do we mean practical utility or poetic function? Objects or symbols? Things or expressions?

Anyone who spends any time around infants can tell you, as the cultural historian Lewis Mumford once did, that babies babble and gesture long before they crawl or walk. Their first work is communication, expression. It is a fundamental human urge. Yet not one that's so exclusive it forces a choice between pure use and pure expression.[3]

Ceramics and other media have always alternated between the two, between the practical and the poetic. And, in our age of online communication, the alternation between expression and shopping, or other virtual gratifications, bounces us increasingly between what we need and what we want, between what we desire and what we can afford.

What's clear is that the aesthetics of function pertain as much to world views as to objects. And any view of modern objects can't avoid the elusiveness—the muddiness of values that once seemed so sure and so reliable. Not too long ago, we could still point to Sung ceramics and say they exemplified beauty in clay, the cream of the crop.

We could also say that things were useful because they were linked directly to some basic necessity or function. They performed physical labour and made life easier. In the pre-digital era, people could still see the linkages, gears, and pulleys that made things go. They could follow the progress of labour from beginning to end. They could see the role and even the vestiges of the hand and the body in work. For skilled artisans utility wasn't an end. It was a beginning: a place to begin to identify oneself through a material, and infuse objects with details that elevated the experience of practical work.

"One of the rewards of hand craftsmanship," said Mumford, "was that as workers developed their technical skills, they could pass from the operational to the expressive parts of their job." In school we call it learning the vocabulary. Once artisans learned it, handicraft, in Munford's works, "became the mediating factor between pure art and pure technics, between things of meaning that had no other use and things of use that had no other meaning."4 The rhythmic flow of throwing rings around forms, or the floating world of surface decoration that covered them, or the fluent gesture of spouts and handles, all of these aspects revealed the extraordinary range of ways in which artists sought to enlarge the meaning of useful things and to have them communicate something besides their actual task.

But that was before the great abstractions of this century took hold. I don't mean the abstractions of art. I'm thinking of the abstractions of effort and purpose that transformed the way in which work fulfills our basic needs. Clear connections between needs and labour, cause and effect have been replaced—as we have witnessed by elaborate systems: systems that convey water, power; and fuel systems that carry off waste; ones that bring us food, communications, and information; systems that mass produce every conceivable need, by the thousands and millions, without pause. We can't begin to count the advantages of these advances. Yet, as Lewis Mumford noted almost fifty years ago, it comes with the "terrible new burden of having to constantly consume what's produced."5

In the past half century, shopping has become the central work of advanced civilizations. It keeps economies afloat. It legitimizes things whose only real function is to create sales, a region where taste and desire come "bundled," as we like to say in the computer store. We want the sizzle, but we want the product to work too. That's a measure of our progress. When Marinetti proclaimed that the rumbling motor car was more beautiful than the Victory of Samothrace, I suspect he was considering at an old roadster, not a modern ad proclaiming the beauty and fine lines of this automobile.6 But I'm getting ahead of the practical, the useful.

The architect Adolf Loos caught the spirit of modern usefulness about one hundred years ago, when he heralded the plumber as the state's top tradesman, "the pioneer of cleanliness," the "quartermaster" of civilization. He went on to say: "Every English wash basin with a tap and plughole is a mark of progress" and "only nations that matched the English use of water could keep pace with them economically."7 There's a certain Dr. Strangelove ring to his preoccupation with water use. Yet every madness has its meaning. On a broad public level, Loos's preoccupation with plumbing had less to do with water than with the efficiency and control modern systems brought to culture. Civilizations that mastered the flow of water and waste could avoid pooping where they ate. They could stay healthy, thrive, prosper, become powerful. On an individual level, this hygienic step provided fixtures that turned bathrooms into domestic nirvanas, private rooms where one could hunker down with a good read and relieve the woes and lower-tract baggage of the day.

The systems devised by good plumbing reflected the highest values of efficiency. Along with other magnificent systems, they reduced physical effort, increased comfort and, ultimately, transformed needs into conveniences that took on new forms and generated new aesthetics. Ceramics, of course, were there to answer nature's call, with forms that followed bodily functions: potties and sinks and tubs with integrated pipes carrying away the waste. The forms were somewhat crude at first. But ergonomic studies eventually led to designs whose simplicity and ease would have delighted Leonardo and Archimedes. Loos and other moderns believed that industrialization would usher in a higher civilization, a higher form of art. A form as visually clean as the new hygiene that all this flowing water was bringing to modern pipes.

"New concepts of beauty have evolved in our age," wrote Joseph-August Lux in 1910. Lux had joined the Deutscher Werkbund in 1908. He said the new concepts could be attributed to the idea of harmonious practicality and functionality: "We cannot possibly call an object beautiful, no matter how lovely the ornamentation, if it totally fails or only partially succeeds in fulfilling the function for which it was intended."[8]

Forms that followed functions were hardly a modern idea. More than anything, they marked the return to one of the truly ancient standards of utilitarian design, a standard that the high end of European culture had set aside to pursue neoclassical and regal ornamentation. It is a gift to be simple, the Shakers believed. "The line of beauty is the result of perfect economy,"[9] wrote Emerson. And Vitruvius—like Lux and many others—suggested that "the perfection of all works depends on their fitness to answer the end proposed."[10] The standard, the principle, of course was that of nature.

"In nature, all is useful, all is beautiful,"[11] wrote Emerson. For thousands of years, nature had been mankind's world and inspiration, the proving ground not simply for the forms and proportions of things, but for their colourings, their variations, the very idea that great designs—like successful forms in ceramics—endure and recur, time and again. That's obvious in the nimble structure of insect wings, or the distinctly streamlined shapes of things that swim and fly.

What these beautiful things shared, wrote Horatio Greenough (the American sculptor, who in the mid 1800s, coined the phrase "form follows function") was "the principle of unflinching adaptation of forms to functions."[12] Botanical forms frequently were more than just the precedents for design; they served as the materials and objects themselves. The tops of gourds and other growing things could be lopped off and scooped out to make useful vessels: ones with an organic simplicity that have always made potters swoon. Ceramics represented a substantial advance in what societies could do to provide for themselves. Clay also marked an advance in thought. Instead of accepting the given natural forms, artisans could invent and refine their own.

That course of refinement and development of useful ceramics followed the same aesthetic arc seen in other media and technologies. New works step on the heels of the old. Potters simply followed nature's lead. And why not? Natural forms are fully resolved. Their beauty is so wound up in function that they evince the kind of perfection that drives artists nuts. "I am studying after nature and it seems I am making slow progress,"[13] Cézanne wrote to a friend shortly before he died. Little wonder. He was trying in relatively few years to perfect a mountain, and not through rigorous verisimilitude that nature had built over millions of years.

It's a perfection that proves itself by surviving and reproducing. Josiah Wedgwood's grandson Charles Darwin attributed that to natural selection. The fittest and most durable forms survive. They look their purpose, even when the purpose is to camouflage their identity.

The designer Christopher Dresser understood this better than almost anyone. He started out as a botanical specialist before becoming one of the early wizards of modern design. He grasped that what was good for nature was also good for design. The rule of the jungle was the rule of art. The fittest forms functioned well, adapted well, and were stable and proven enough to accommodate change and variation without losing their identity or compromising their purpose. This is key. The basic forms of teapots, pitchers, bowls, cups, plates, and other utilitarian vessels manage to keep their jobs because they can be adapted to changes in style and circumstance.

The same is true of many non-ceramic forms. Look at the centuries of remarkable letterforms modeled after the roman letters on the Trojan column. They encompass thousands of different shapes. Yet that variation doesn't alter the basic intelligibility or meaning of the alphabetic letter it represents. Such variations of form give artists the ideal means to personalize experience and expression. Whether the artists are children drawing their own versions of Abe Lincoln, or Alvar Aalto elaborating on the idea of chairs, this push and pull between form and function remains much the same.

In the realm of strictly useful things, basic ceramic forms arrived at their fitness—just as natural forms did—through gradual evolution and refinement. Charles Harder, who headed the New York State College of Ceramics at Alfred University from the 1930s through the 1950s, characterized that evolution as a patient one, occurring "at the hands of thousands of individual makers, whose works were criticized and corrected over generations."[14] Dresser encouraged designers to "do as nature did," to consider the purpose, material, and eventual surroundings of objects, and to be true to the forms and processes. "Let there be no shade of hypocrisy about any part of the production," he said. Let every line "go to express and give force to the intention of its every part."[15]

His pitch for "truth to materials" echoed Ruskin's earlier demand for honesty in the use of materials and creation of forms. It also joined a chorus of admonitions by other thinkers of the day against concealing and disguising architectural members with any kind of borrowed features. He urged designers to study growing forms, to look at them from above and from the side. From above, one could look down and see what he characterized as the "great principle in the vegetable world... the centralisation of power," the exertion of centrifugal force, "which gives a marvelous oneness to the structures of this kingdom."[16]

This centralization doesn't apply just to botanical forms. It exists across the spectrum of living things. Things as varied as artichokes and sea shells grow from the inside out, repeating their patterns. It is a practical matter, a physical matter. It enables forms to conserve energy, concentrate resources, and deliver nutrients where they're needed.

The same can be said for some of our better cities. Paris spiraled itself outward from the banks of the Seine. In ceramic terms, this dynamic helps forms to act their size and perform their practical and poetic work. Modern potters might resist the rules of proportion and optimal decanting angles that Dresser laid out in his *The Art of Decorative Design*. His standards attempted to optimize the grunt utility of forms, and they turned the pot into an engineering project.

Yet he wasn't alone. The vast history of useful pottery is filled with forms that embody such rules about the finest ceramic physique and pose. Plain physics guides shapes and proportions. Pitchers and teapots generally pour more easily when their spouts angle off at about ninety degrees from the handle. The forms are easier to handle when the elbow of that angle runs through the pot's center of gravity. That configuration gives you the leverage to tip the central weight. You can even do it with one hand. In-turned rims make it easier for mixing bowls to contain the mix. Flaring bowls give better access to the mix, especially when you want to scrape off the sides. Mugs with narrow openings keep liquids warmer. Slightly flared rims are slightly easier to drink from than straight-sided ones. And stackable forms conserve space—on the shelf or on the floor—a modern concern that defines the shape of many things, from chairs to plastic cups.

Each variance gives potters fresh opportunities for expression, a fresh chance to articulate their own voice. In an evolutionary sense, the repetition of functional features, from one generation to the next, substantiates their viability. Their particular fitness becomes the tradition, the standard by which subsequent forms are judged. What was startling about Dresser's forms (made late 1800s) and other modern designs was that they altered the common view of simplicity. They made ancient truths about natural and man-made design seem to be utterly new. Part of that was due to the fresh way Dresser and others tapped new materials. Yet this new aesthetic wouldn't have been viable or evolved into the dominant style of the century if it hadn't conveyed something vital about the spirit of the age.

The irony of this aesthetic newness is that it evolves from conservatism, one tweak or tuck at a time. Like natural forms, the designer George Nelson once wrote, the evolution of design resists mutations. And when mutations occur, their survival depends on outside forces.

The evolution of the modern chair is a good example. The old four-legged post-and-beam structure evolved into the Thonet bentwood configuration, which gave chairs a flowing line. That line sparked ideas about what new materials could do to advance the idea of visual flow. As Nelson and many others have pointed out, tubular metal, plastics, laminated wood, and other modern materials enabled designers to cantilever seats above legs, to decrease the mass and achieve a visual lightness of being. It is a gift to be simple.[17]

Was this new simplicity better, more original than the simplicity of traditional folk craftsmanship? Probably not. But industrial production made it possible to distribute the same make and model of a form to many more people. This new simplicity transformed the chair without compromising its practical virtues. As in other areas of modern design, new technology was key. It helped to reinvent an old structure. Moreover, it ushered in a fundamental change of taste, a new aesthetic for that particular function. I have spent a good deal of time talking about the parallels between the efficiency and simplicity of modern and natural design, the aesthetics of the usefulness we've lived with for much of this century. What I haven't mentioned is how technology has increasingly separated the two, how it has changed our view of our surroundings, our sense of usefulness and form.

Up until this century, nature has dominated the human outlook. This century has changed that. We live increasingly in a realm of manufactured or artificial influences. I don't mean that in the pejorative sense. Thanks to post-war productivity and distribution systems—remember Loos's plumbing—we've been able to surround ourselves increasingly with our own "nature," our own inventions. Industry has introduced materials and techniques that have freed forms from having to follow function, or even the appearance of function. We no longer need to mimic nature as we once did. We mimic ourselves and our inventions. We perpetuate our own designs. The centralization of form that Dresser was so keen on has become the model for corporate efficiency (but not corporate creativity) and modern systems of mass production and communication.

Occasionally, functional pottery has surfaced in the modern style, taking on the streamlined look of things made to resist the wind, or the fragmented chunkiness of abstract art. But, on the whole, technology hasn't altered the nature of utilitarian ceramics to the extent it did when Wedgwood went industrial. It hasn't directly affected forms in clay to the extent that it has affected furnishings or image making through photography. However, it has certainly changed the terrain surrounding the production of clay.

In many parts of the world, technology has assured the obsolescence of hand made utilitarianism, nudging it toward irrelevance. That's one of the reasons why studio ceramics as a field of art has built its stature as an alternative to technological products. Compared with modern industrial techniques, hand labour was, in Thorstein Veblen's words, "wasteful and imperfect." He considered Morris's and Ruskin's applause for handicraft an "exaltation of the defective," and "propaganda of crudity."[18] But, as I've said, the aesthetics of function involve more than mere utility, more than fulfilling practical goals. It is about giving voice.

In the 1920s, Lewis Mumford and others challenged what they considered to be the "unesthetic and life-denying quality of utilitarian philosophy." By failing to balance imaginative vision with practical technique, he warned, a society could easily stifle the "alternating rhythm of dream and deed" that enables it and its artists to invent new symbols and forms.[19]

Bernard Leach said the functionalism of the mechanical age overlooked the irregular and irrational element in making pottery. Charles Harder agreed. Machines had no nervous system, no flexibility to allow artists to interact, moment by moment, thereby impressing what he characterized as "the irrelevant details of his personality on the things he makes." Compared with the factory worker, the artist-craftsman was distinct, for the simple reason that "he exercises the responsibility of making things for full human use."[20]

Leach's friend Charles Harder knew that, too. Although he was an advocate of industrial design and believed that the practice and aesthetics of utilitarian handicraft were at an end, he worried about the conformity of an increasingly canned culture whose mechanization "frees the individual from the necessity of making judgements and choices,"[21] actions that were central to the human spirit, actions that became central to the function of works by the likes of Peter Voulkos and the rest of the post-war rabble. "When you come right down to it, I have a very selfish attitude," said Voulkos. "I don't really make pots for people, but to satisfy myself." He said his functionalism was that of the human spirit.[22]

That has been the reigning function, the reigning aesthetic and purpose of ceramics in the post-war years. Expression superseded strict practicality. Communication became the specialization of clay. There's no doubt that, in a technological sense, less continues to be more. The systems driving our culture are becoming ever smaller, more powerful. They're slipping out of sight, but not out of mind. If anything, they are slipping deeper into the mind-like powers, into the inscrutable details of micro-circuits, computers, and software that produces things that seem to appear out of thin air. Modern technology hasn't left much room for nineteenth and even twentieth century talk about truth to materials and structural honesty. The only truth that emerges from new materials, new media, and new technologies is their defiance of physical realities. Their appearance reveals little about the work they perform. What do the guts of the latest computers tell us about how they work, what they can do, what they can make?

These new materials and technologies are overturning old assumptions about function, what we thought useful materials were, how usefulness should be produced, and how we thought usefulness should appear. The irony of the current change is that its sales pitch counters that of the industrial revolution. It is selling itself as the means to gain greater personal creativity and control—an opportunity, as Malcolm McCullough puts it, to combine "the skillful hand with the reasoning mind."[23] It is a reversal of industrialization's withdrawal of materials and processes from the direct control of workers. This new technology is personalizing the very idea of aesthetics, changing it from an established ideal to a shifting state of mind—a matter of channel surfing for desires.

As new technologies often do, digital ones are raising the question of what is useful and what is necessary. We are in the midst of the greatest exploration and reinvention of usefulness that we have seen since the beginning of industrialization. I don't know whether this new technology marks the profound shift "in the ancient craft of the Beautiful" that the poet Paul Valéry envisioned in the pre-war heyday of modernism. But it has certainly delivered on his prediction that it would become possible one day "to send or recreate anywhere a system of sensations... a system of stimuli, provoked by some object or event." He called it "home delivery of Sensory Reality," whose works of art would "acquire a kind of ubiquity." All we'll have to do is summon them, he said, and they'll "appear and disappear at a simple movement of the hand, hardly more than a sign."[24]

1   Ralph Waldo Emerson, "Art," in *Ralph Waldo Emerson: Essays and Lectures* (New York: Library of America, 1983).
2   Roger Rosenblatt, "Lewis Thomas," *New York Times Magazine* (November 21, 1993).
3   Lewis Mumford, *Art and Technics* (New York: Columbia University Press, 1952).
4   Lewis Mumford, *Art and Technics* (New York: Columbia University Press, 1952).
5   Lewis Mumford, *Art and Technics* (New York: Columbia University Press, 1952).
6   Filippo Tommaso Marinetti, "The Futurist Manifesto"
    <http://cscs.umich.edu/~crshalizi/T4PM/futurist-manifesto.html>.

7   Adolf Loos, "Plumbers" (first published in Neue Freie Presse, Vienna, 17 July 1898) in *Adolf Loos, Pioneer of Modern Architecture* by Ludwig Münz and Gustav Künstler (New York: Frederick A. Praeger, 1966).
8   Source not available.
9   Ralph Waldo Emerson, *Essays and English Traits* (New York: P.F. Collier & Son, 1909-14).
10 Ralph Waldo Emerson, "Art," in *Ralph Waldo Emerson: Essays and Lectures* (New York: Library of America, 1983).
11 Ralph Waldo Emerson, "Art," in *Ralph Waldo Emerson: Essays and Lectures* (New York: Library of America, 1983).
12 Horatio Greenough, *Form and Function* (Berkeley: University of California Press, 1947).
13 John Rewald, ed., *Paul Cezanne Letters* (New York: Hacker Books, 1985).
14 Charles Harder Papers, Scholes Library Archives, New York State College of Ceramics at Alfred University
15 Christopher Dresser, *The Art of Decorative Design* (London: Day and Son, 1862).
16 Christopher Dresser, *Rudiments of Botany* (London: James S. Virtue, 1859).
17 George Nelson, *Problems of Design*, 4 ed. (New York: Watson-Guptill Publications, 1979).
18 Thorstein Veblen, *Theory of the Leisure Class* (New York: Penguin Classics, 1994).
19 Source not available.
20 Charles Harder Papers, Scholes Library Archives, New York State College of Ceramics at Alfred University
21 Charles Harder Papers, Scholes Library Archives, New York State College of Ceramics at Alfred University
22 Source not available.
23 Malcolm McCullough, *Abstracting Craft: The Practiced Digital Hand* (Cambridge, MA: MIT Press, 1996).
24 Paul Valéry, "The Conquest of Uniquity, Collected Works of Paul Valéry," Volume 13: *Aesthetics* (Princeton, NJ.: Princeton University Press, 1964) 225-226.

The Ostracon Awards

Ceramic Arts Foundation has been giving awards for distinguished service to the ceramic arts since 1979. In 2005 the award was renamed, The Ostracon Award. Ostracon is an ancient Greek word for pottery shards that were used to write notes, to send messages, or as ballot "cards" for voting. They were the Post-Its of the time. This relationship between a ceramic fragment and language seemed perfect for an award that is given primarily for writing and criticism. In the future the Ostracon Award will be given exclusively for achievement in critical writing on modern and contemporary ceramics. The sixth and seventh Symposium awards were chosen by the Everson Museum of Art. All other awards were chosen by the various organizing committees of Ceramic Arts Foundation. The 2001 Awards were given without a symposium.

FIRST INTERNATIONAL CERAMICS SYMPOSIUM, 1979
A Century of Ceramics in the United States 1878-1979
Syracuse University, Syracuse, NY
Coordinator: Ann Mortimer
AWARDEES:
Michael Cardew
Jean Delius
Bernard Leach
Fred Marer
Anna Wetherill Olmstead
Daniel Rhodes
Rose Slivka

SECOND INTERNATIONAL CERAMICS SYMPOSIUM, 1981
Ceramics and Modernism
Waldorf-Astoria, New York, NY
Coordinator: Mark Del Vecchio
Awardees:
Helen Drutt
David Queensbury

Ted Randall
Philip Rawson
Gerry Williams

THIRD INTERNATIONAL CERAMICS SYMPOSIUM, 1983
Historical References in Contemporary Ceramic Art
Contemporary Art Society / Nelson Atkins Museum of Art, Kansas City, MO
Coordinator: Lennie Berkowitz
AWARDEES:
Beatrice Wood

FOURTH INTERNATIONAL CERAMICS SYMPOSIUM, 1985
Edges: In Thought, In History, In Clay
Ontario Institute for Studies and Education, Toronto, ON, Canada
Coordinators: Marge Malouf and Ann Mortimer
AWARDEES:
Ruth McKinley
Les Manning

FIFTH INTERNATIONAL CERAMICS SYMPOSIUM, 1986
American Ceramics Today
Victoria and Albert Museum, London, UK
Coordinator: John Huntingford
NO AWARDEES

SIXTH INTERNATIONAL CERAMICS SYMPOSIUM, 1989
East and West
The Everson Museum of Art, Syracuse, NY
Coordinator: Barbara Perry
AWARDEES:
Martin Eidelberg
Kenneth Ferguson
Daniel Jacobs

SEVENTH INTERNATIONAL CERAMICS SYMPOSIUM, 1993
History and Its Role in Contemporary Ceramic Art Criticism, Scholarship, Education
The Everson Museum of Art, Syracuse, NY
Coordinator: Tom Piche
AWARDEES:
American Ceramics Magazine
Takako Araki
Garth Clark
Anne Mortimer
Judith J. Schwartz

EIGHTH INTERNATIONAL CERAMICS SYMPOSIUM, 1999
Ceramic Millennium: A Leadership Congress for the Ceramic Arts
RAI Congress Centre, Amsterdam, The Netherlands
Coordinators: Dawn Bennett, Garth Clark, Mark Del Vecchio
AWARDEES:
European Ceramics Work Center
International Academy of Ceramics
National Council on the Education for the Ceramic Arts
Carlo Bonjani
Richard Dennis
Tanya Harrod
Dr. Yoshiaki Inui
Janet Mansfield
Susan Tunick
Henk Trumpie
Ettore Sottsass
Jan van der Vaart

2001 AWARDEES (NO CONFERENCE)
Jimmy Clark / Clay Studio
Emmanuel Cooper
Gabi DeWald
Yvonne Joris

Biographies

Compiled with Christopher Dowdell

GARTH CLARK (PRETORIA, SOUTH AFRICA, 1947)
Clark was the youthful industrial editor of *Business South Africa* in 1972, when he decided to move from Johannesburg to London shortly after completing his first book, *Potters of Southern Africa* with his then wife, Lynne Wagner. After a year of travelling to museum collections of ceramics throughout Europe, he settled in London and was accepted for a degree by thesis at the Royal College of Art under David Queensberry and David Hamilton. After receiving his master's degree in modern ceramic history from the Royal College of Art, London, he moved to the United States in 1976, settling with his wife and son Mark (later joined by a new arrival, Kellam) in Claremont, California. From the outset, he was a lightning rod for competing philosophies in ceramics, arguing that the field lacked self-confidence and a sense of its own history. His annual national lecture tours drew large and lively audiences, but it was his role as co-curator, with Margie Hughto, of *A Century of Ceramics in the United States 1876-1979* that established his presence in the US. In 1979 he founded the Ceramic Arts Foundation (CAF) to host a symposium in conjunction with the Everson exhibition and has directed its since then, overseeing six of the eight International Ceramic Symposia. He is currently at work on the ninth, *Ceramic Canon*, which will involve scholars across the world in defining the artists who were the primary figures in twentieth-century ceramics. In 1981, now divorced, with his business and life partner, Mark Del Vecchio, he opened the internationally known Garth Clark Gallery, where he has presented over five hundred exhibitions in its several venues in Los Angeles, Kansas City, London, and New York City. The Gallery celebrates its twenty-fifth anniversary this year. Clark's efforts have attracted a number of awards, beginning with the Art Critics Award from the National Endowment for the Arts in 1981. In 1996 he was inducted as an Honorary Fellow of the Royal College of Art, London. He has received honorary doctorates from Staffordshire University and the Kansas City Art Institute, with his partner Mark Del Vecchio. He was the recipient of the Art Book of the Year award from the Art Libraries Society of America and received the Art Critics Fellowship from the National Endowment of the Arts for his book on George E. Ohr, *The Mad Potter of*

Biloxi (1989). Together with Del Vecchio, Clark was also recognized by the Museum of Arts and Design, New York City, with its Visionaries Lifetime Achievement Award in 1999. Recently he has received the 2004 Achievement Award from the American Immigration Law Foundation. The hydra-headed Clark continues to shift among his roles as curator, writer, historian, and gallerist. He has now either written or contributed to nearly forty books and has produced two hundred catalogue essays and magazine articles. His most recent book, *Shards: Garth Clark on Ceramic Art*, has been received enthusiastically by both the craft and fine art press. It resulted in him receiving the College Art Association's Frank Jewett Mather Award, one of the most prestigious awards for critical writing on art. This is the first time that this award has gone to a writer from a craft-based discipline. Clark is currently at work on a major history of ceramics since 1900 and on *Free Spirit*, an exhibition and book on the avant-garde movement in Native pottery of the American Southwest.

JUSTIN CLEMENS (HONG KONG, CHINA, 1969)
Clemens received his doctorate in philosophy from the University of Melbourne. His resume lists many titles, including musician, martial arts teacher, fashion model, and university lecturer, with the latter drawing attention to the author, critic, and eclectic professor. Clemens continues to lecture both at the University of Melbourne and at Deakin University, also in Melbourne, Australia. Lecturing in cultural studies, aesthetics, and literature, Clemens combines contemporary theory, pop culture, and world history to evaluate the current trends in marketplace dynamics. In 1996 he co-authored with Mark Pennings, *Cultural Theory and Craft Practice*, a slim document that has become required reading. His writings include *Infinite Thought: Truth and the Return to Philosophy* co-written with American theorist Oliver Fetham (2003), *The Romanticism of Contemporary Theory: Institutions, Aesthetics and Nihilism* (2003), *The Mundiad* (2004), *Ten Thousand Fucking Monkeys* (2005), and his newest work, *Avoiding the Subject: Media, Culture and the Object* (2005). Recently Clemens has been proposing what he calls the Infernal ©raft Gymnasium. His proposal for a craft gymnasium is that craftspeople should get together to design and build it:

> The perfect craft gym would not be a finished place or product; it would rather be the process of its own design, discussion, organization, and

construction. Or, again: training at the Infernal ©raft Gymnasium would be about the fraught relationship between process and product, to the point where means and ends are no longer easily distinguished. If you think about what's involved in the architecture, materials, and technologies at any gym, you'd realise that it offers unbelievable opportunities for craftspeople. Glass, wood, metal, textiles, and even ceramics are key features of gyms; the possibilities for building a gym—whether full size or scale model, fully functioning or absolutely decorative—are legion. Would a craft-dumbbell fit the hand more or less snugly than the machined metal of standard equipment? Would the mirror reflect in a verisimilitudinous fashion? What muscle groups would it exercise?

EDMUND DE WAAL (NOTTINGHAM, UK, 1964)

Edmund de Waal has a degree in English literature from Cambridge University (1986) and received his post-graduate degree in Japanese studies from Sheffield University (1991). As he makes clear, de Waal wears two hats: "I am a potter who writes; the reason for writing is to make conceptual space within my own work." De Waal is the chair of the Crafts Study Center, a member of the editorial board of *Crafts Magazine*, and a professor at the University of Westminster. He is a celebrated ceramic artist with works in numerous public collections such as the Victoria and Albert Museum, the British Council, and the Contemporary Arts Society in London. He is a fellow of the Royal Society of Arts.

His other hat is as a provocative writer of numerous essays, reviews, and books. Amongst the latter are *Bernard Leach* (1998), *Ceramics Design Source Book* (2000), and *20th Century Ceramics* (2003). He has also contributed introductions and essays to several other books. His book on Leach is a tough, unflinching indictment of Leach's narrow appreciation of ceramics and his misunderstood vision of Asian ceramics and philosophy. When de Waal presented the 2002 Peter Dormer Lecture at the Royal College of Art, London, he explained that his search for:

> the experiential in clay [of the last quarter of the twentieth century] lies in its valorizing the non-canonical. Its search for beginnings is one of the great themes of the ceramics of this century, with a legacy that echoes

the land art and environmental art movements of the 1970s and 1980s. Most importantly of all, however, I want to try and recover playfulness (indeed the digressive) as important and exciting.

GABI DEWALD (WORMS/RHINE, GERMANY, 1956)
Dewald, who studied at Gutenberg Universität, Mainz, is a peripatetic, multitasking whirlwind: journalist, lecturer, critic, freelance author, and (since 1993) editor in chief of the internationally recognized specialist journall *KeramikMagazin /CeramicsMagazine*. She is also a member of the *Journalistinnenbund* (Women Journalists' Association), where she works to raise the bar for her fellow writers. In addition to being one of the founding members of *Interactive Ceramics*, the electronic ceramics publication, Dewald is a founder of the Think Tank: A European Initiative for the Applied Arts, which includes some of the speakers featured in this anthology: Edmund De Waal and Tanya Harrod. She is a recipient of the 2001 Ostracon Award from the Ceramic Arts Foundation, New York, and is honoured for her vigour in expanding the critical dialogue for ceramics and encouraging the development of a more meaningful analytical language. She lectures actively in Europe and abroad. Dewald's focus is in analyzing global trends in contemporary ceramics and crafts. She travels extensively through Europe, Asia, and America, lecturing and serving as a juror for international ceramic competitions. She has written and contributed to numerous catalogues and publications, including the book, *Gertraud Mohwald: Keramik* (2005) published in conjunction with a touring retrospective of the late artist's work.

LÉOPOLD L. FOULEM (BATHURST, NEW BRUNSWICK, CANADA, 1945)
Foulem received his BA from the Alberta College of Art and Design, and later received an MA (1988) from the Indiana State University. From the outset, his conceptual approach to ceramics, his careful scholarship, and his outspoken opinions have made him a conspicuous figure and a prominent voice in the ceramics community.

Garth Clark remembers seeing Foulem for the first time in 1975, during an annual meeting of the National Council for Education in Ceramic Art in Louisiana. At the end of a particularly poor lecture, Foulem leapt from his seat and, in a breathless rush, listed the numerous historical errors the speaker had made in his presentation. Foulem then denounced him for insulting the audiences' intelligence and not doing his homework. This was classic Foulem. He is also a meticulous scholar, and his carefully researched paper on Picasso's ceramics, presented at the 1983 symposium in Toronto, was one of the high points of the event, revealing a depth and subtlety in the best of Picasso's ceramic work that had not before been revealed. Foulem was one of an international team of contributors to *Picasso and Ceramics*, the definitive book on the subject, published in conjunction with an exhibition organized by the Musée national de beaux-arts du Quebéc, the Gardiner Museum in Toronto, and the Musée Picasso Museum in Antibes. Like so many of those in this anthology, Foulem is also an artist. He inspired the formation of Québécois Clay, a group of like-minded French-Canadian artists that included Richard Millette, Jeannot Blackburn, and Paul Mathieu, who all exhibited together. His works have been acquired for many prominent collections across North America, Europe, and Asia and he has shown in more than twenty solo exhibitions worldwide and in literally hundreds of group shows. Foulem's role as a critic and scholar dovetails perfectly with his work, which incorporates analysis of values, mores and traditions in the medium. His works are often provocations to taste and fixed ideas about utility and clay. "I am not dealing with the real thing," says Foulem, "but with the idea of the thing itself." He has received some of Canada's most prestigious awards, including the Jean A. Chalmers National Crafts Award (1999) and the Saidye Bronfman Award (2001). Both awards highlight his achievements in furthering Canadian culture and crafts. In addition to being an artist and writer, Foulem teaches in Montreal.

CLEMENT GREENBERG (NEW YORK, NEW YORK, USA, 1909 - 1994)
Clement Greenburg graduated from Syracuse University with a BA in 1930. Once back in his hometown of New York City, he began to write about art and culture. *Partisan Review* was the first to publish his criticisms on politics and art, and within a year, he became a contributing editor for the publication. It was his article, "Avant-Garde and Kitsch" that catapulted Greenberg to public attention. In this piece, Greenberg argued that Modernism and the avant-garde constituted the first line of defense against the dumbing down of culture by consumerism. From 1941, *The Nation*, a weekly publication on political and social issues, also began to publish his art criticism, and in 1944 he became their full-time art critic. From here Greenberg rose as one of the twentieth century's most influential critics. In 1955,

his essay, "American Type Painting," he advanced the idea that Jackson Pollock, Willem de Kooning, Hans Hoffman, and others from the New York School represented the next stage in Modernism.

In 1960 Greenberg wrote his critique, *Modernist Painting*, which was read later that year on a Voice of America radio broadcast, allowing the world to hear his thoughts on Modernity. His book, *Art and Culture: Critical Essays* (1961), and later articles, such as *Avant-Garde Attitudes* (1968) and *Modern and Postmodern* (1979), have also become standard advanced academic texts in the fine arts. Greenberg's absolute rejection of postmodernism left him more and more isolated as a critical voice, and rejection of his ideas—known as "Clembashing"—became a popular activity. But Greenbergian theory has survived, and it was the gravity of his writing that encouraged serious journals in America to begin publishing art criticism for the first time. Shortly after his death, Hilton Kramer (critic and editor of *The New Criterion*) was asked, "How will history remember Greenberg?" His reply is interesting, since Kramer is an arch right-winger, and Greenberg represented the far left: "In my opinion, Clem was the greatest art critic of his time. And for art critics writing in the English language in this century, I would say he was the greatest critic since Roger Fry. He resembled Fry in many respects by placing aesthetic values above sociological interpretations of art."

PAUL GREENHALGH (BOLTON, LANCASHIRE, UK, 1955)
Greenhalgh trained and practiced as a painter but became increasingly attracted to art theory and history. He has taught history and theory at the Royal College of Art, been head of art and design history at Camberwell College of Arts (London Institute) and first deputy curator of ceramics and glass and later head of research at London's Victoria and Albert Museum (V&A), the world's largest museum of fine, decorative art and design. In 2000 Greenhalgh curated the outstanding exhibition, *Decadence and Dreams: Art Nouveau 1890-1914*, for the V&A. In explaining his fascination for Art Nouveau in an interview for the V&A website, Greenhalgh summarized what he finds compelling in the best of contemporary craft:

> There's also something about Art Nouveau that is perhaps an antidote to the irony that permeates contemporary practice. Art Nouveau is based on very positivist principles. It's not critique and irony. It is cele-

bratory art; it can be shocking, but it's celebratory. And perhaps we've had too much irony for the last twenty years. Postmodernism is essentially ironic, and its glib commentary on the condition of the world is now mainstream. While this point of view is quite legitimate and important, it is appealing to think that we could return to simply trying to produce the most beautiful objects humanly possible for the largest possible audience at the highest possible quality. This has always been difficult, but it is clearly what the Art Nouveau designers were trying to do, and I think it's about time we tried to do it again.

Since 2001 he as been the president of NSCAD University in Halifax, Canada. He lectures across the world and has published articles in numerous journals and magazines with a special fondness for ceramics. When Greenhalgh gave the fourth annual Dorothy Wilson Perkins Ceramic History Lecture at the Schein-Joseph International Museum of Ceramic Art at Alfred University in 2001, he dealt with another one of his themes, the absence of canon:

> Ceramic presents us with fascinating historiographic problems. Unlike other key arts it has never had a consistent historiography created for it. (We must remember of course that historiography does not equal truth. It is an invented version of the truth. However, it does have the odd ability to become a surrogate truth for the majority of people). As such, many things are yet to be resolved in the history of ceramics.

He has produced seven books, including *The Persistence of Craft* (2002), which received acclaim for its definitive search into the vocabulary and issues of crafts, and a major opus, *The Modern Ideal: The Rise and Collapse of Idealism in the Visual Arts from the Enlightenment to Postmodernism* (2005).

DAVID HAMILTON (LEEDS, YORKSHIRE, UK, 1940)
Hamilton studied at the College of Art, Bradford (1957-61), and Goldsmiths College, London (1961-62). He is an artist, educator, and design consultant. While he is modest about his accomplishments, he has had strong influence on British design and studio pottery as a maker, writer, teacher, organizer, critic, administrator, and

activist. He taught at the Lancaster College of Art and Portsmouth Polytechnic before being made head of ceramics at the Royal College of Art in London in 1974. During his tenure there as head and as professor of the Department of Ceramics and Glass (from 1983-1989 and from 1992-2000), Hamilton, a caring and connected teacher, assisted in developing many careers including those of Martin Smith, Phil Eglin, Magdalene Odundo, and Garth Clark, among others. He became the head of the RCA's School of Applied Arts in 1993, its pro-rector in 1996 and professor emeritus of ceramics in 2000. He is the author of *Pottery and Ceramics* (1974), *Architectural Ceramics* (1978), and *Stoneware and Porcelain* (1982), all by Thames and Hudson. Hamilton was one of the founders in 1983 of NACHE, the National Association for Ceramics in Higher Education and was group design director of the Wedgwood Group from 1989 to 1992. Since 2004 he has been a design consultant for Simon Harrison, Ltd. Amongst his pubic commissions are several works for the London Transport, London Underground, and the Newcastle Metro.

TANYA HARROD (BETCHWORTH, SURREY, UK, 1951)
Tanya Harrod trained as an art historian. Her doctoral thesis (1978) examined English interest in early Italian art in the nineteenth century. Harrod is Britain's foremost critic, author, and speaker on modern and contemporary crafts. She has been responsible for raising the quality of research and writing in this field with a steely intellect that filters out the excessive romanticism prevalent in the crafts while, at the same time, always framing her work in humanist terms. Tackling what has been acclaimed as one of the most significant historical endeavours of craft history, Harrod recently published her prize-winning book, *The Crafts in Britain in the 20th Century* (1999). She continues to lecture globally, has curated numerous exhibitions, and writes regularly for *The Burlington Magazine* and *The Times Literary Supplement*. Her interests include the vernacular in relation to modernism, art education in colonial sub-Saharan Africa, notions of wealth and poverty in early twentieth-century Britain, and the effect of the new media on the applied arts. Harrod is professor of design history at the Royal College of Art, London, serves on the advisory panel of the *Journal of Design History* and *Interpreting Ceramics*, and is advisor to the Craft Lives Project based at the National Sound Archive of the British Library. In addition, she is a member of the International Association of Art Critics, Critics Circle, and is a fellow in critical appreciation of craft and design, University of East Anglia. In 1999

Harrod received the Ostracon Award at the *Ceramic Millennium* for her work on ceramics and, in 2001, the Design History Society honoured her as their inaugural recipient of the Award for Scholarship. She is currently at work on a biography of the potter Michael Cardew for Yale University Press and is researching a broadly-based study of the meaning of the handmade for Reaktion Books.

JANET KOPLOS (CALIFORNIA, USA, 1946)

Koplos first started writing about art in 1976. Her first editorial position was with *Craft Connection*, a periodical published by the Minnesota Crafts Council. She received her art history master's degree from Illinois State University in 1984 and her MA from Illinois State University in 1986. She has written extensively about the fine arts, ceramics, and crafts in general, including several books, many catalogues, and more than two thousand reviews and articles in about four dozen magazines and newspapers. Articles by Koplos have appeared in *Afterimage, American Ceramics, American Craft, Art in America, Arts, Crafts* (U.K.), *Fiberarts, FlashArt* (Italy), *Glass, Hand Papermaking, Horizon, Japan Times* (Japan), *Metalsmith, Metropolis M* (Holland), *Minichi Daily News, Museum News, New Art Examiner, Public Art Review, Sculpture, Studio Potter, Surface Design Journal, Surfacing Journal* (Canada) and many more. Koplos is the author of *Contemporary Japanese Sculpture* (1991) and co-author of *The Unexpected: Artists' Ceramics of the 20th Century* (1999). The indefatigable Koplos is the most important activist in American crafts, raising the intelligence, credibility, and standards of the field through her critical writing, lecturing, and behind-the-scenes work in many arts organizations, including the College Art Association. Moreover, her encyclopedic knowledge of modern and contemporary fine arts and crafts has given her writing a uniquely authoritative tone, particularly in ceramics, where writing is often too inward and hermetic. Her awards include the National Endowment for the Arts' Art Critic's Fellowship. Koplos is senior editor at *Art in America*, where she has been on staff for fourteen years. Koplos and her co-author, Bruce Metcalf, are currently at work on *20th Century Studio Craft in America*, a textbook intended for use in art history programs. The book will introduce and explain the sociopolitical and stylistic changes in crafts over the century, as well as such matters as government support, education, and publications.

EDWARD LEBOW (CHAMBERSBURG, PENNSYLVANIA, USA, 1953)
Lebow studied at the New York State College of Ceramics, Alfred University, where he received a BFA. He has since worked as a proofreader, editor, freelance writer, and curator. He worked in public art for the Phoenix Arts Commission from 1989 to 1996 and then as a multiple-award-winning journalist, first for the *Phoenix New Time* and, more recently, for the *Daily Press* in Newport News, VA. He has just been appointed senior arts specialist in the Office of Arts and Culture for the city of Phoenix. The city's notice of his appointment states that he brings to the post, "[prior] understanding of the evolution and principles of the city's current public art master plan, global knowledge of the field of public art, and a working knowledge of Phoenix city government and the larger community from his experience as a city employee and journalist." Lebow has written extensively on all aspects of the arts but maintains a specialist interest in ceramics writing for *American Craft*, *Studio Potter*, *American Ceramics* and other publications. He has written on William Perry, Edwin and Mary Shire, Lidya Buzio, Kurt Weiser, and Ken Price. His paper on Price at the 1983 International Ceramics Symposium in Toronto was one of the event's highlights. Lebow then went on to co-author, with Walter Hobbs, the catalogue for *Ken Price*, an exhibition organized by the Walker Art Center in Minneapolis and the Menil Collection in Houston, with the catalogue published by Houston Fine Art Press. His writings on Price are among his best and reflect a singular writing style that is much like a stoneware clay: laden with grog—tight, tough and gritty. He does not praise his subjects so much as he objectively deconstructs their achievements (both their strengths and weaknesses, which the artists often find disconcerting, expecting hagiography), and Lebow leaves it to the reader to feel the weight of each subject's art and career. As he says about his approach to art, "I'm just assuming artists will find surprises in what I write because my view is as subjective as their own." He was curator of the meticulously organized *Ken Ferguson: A Retrospective* at the Nelson-Atkins Museum of Art in Kansas City and is currently at work on a exhibition surveying the history of ceramic education at the 92nd Street YMCA in New York City.

JOHN BENTLEY MAYS (LOUISIANA, USA, 1941)
Mays is a journalist, novelist, and critic known for his articulate, informed, and occasionally controversial opinions regarding international art practice and cultural

issues. Particularly drawn to photography, he has covered numerous exhibitions in Toronto and abroad. From 1980 to 1998, Mays was the visual arts critic for *The Globe and Mail*, and from 1998 to 2001, he was the cultural correspondent for the *National Post*. Mays has received the National Newspaper Award and four National Magazine Awards for his work as a journalist. In addition, he has written several books, including *Emerald City: Toronto Visited*, *Power in the Blood: An Odyssey of Discovery in the American South* (which was short listed for the Viacom Canada Writers' Trust Non-Fiction Award and was named a 1997 Notable Book by the *Globe and Mail*), *In the Jaws of the Black Dogs: A Memoir of Depression*, and *Arrivals: Stories from the History of Ontario*. He is currently working on *Eminence: Toronto's Elite*, for Random House, Canada. He is currently a weekly columnist at the *Globe and Mail*.

DAVID R. MCFADDEN (DEVIL'S LAKE, NORTH DAKOTA, USA, 1947)
McFadden graduated magna cum laude in art history at the University of Minnesota, where he also received an MA. McFadden is both chief curator and vice-president for programs and collections at the Museum of Arts and Design. Prior to this, he was in Taos, New Mexico, acting as executive director of the Millicent Rogers Museum. Earlier he was with the Cooper-Hewitt National Design Museum in New York, initially as curator of decorative arts/applied arts and then as assistant director for collections and research. He is also president of the International Council of Museums Decorative Arts and Design Committee. McFadden's work has been widely honoured. He has recieved the Order of the Lion of Finland First Class (1984), Knight Commander of the Order of the Polar Star of Sweden from King Gustav VI (1998), and Chevalier de l'Ordre des Arts et des Lettres from the Republic of France (1989). McFadden is a three-time winner of the Presidential Design Award for Excellence (1994, 1995, and 1997). He has curated numerous groundbreaking exhibitions, including *Hair*, a landmark exploration of the visual and design history of human hair; *Toward Modern Design: Revival and Reform in Applied Arts 1880-1920*; *Structure and Style: Modernism in Dutch Applied Arts 1880-1930*; *Scandinavian Modern Design 1880-1980*; *Wine: Celebration and Ceremony*; *Changing Hands*; and *Rörstrand: Swedish Art Nouveau Porcelain from the Robert Schreiber Collection*. In 2002, he curated *Art without Reservation: Contemporary Native American Art from the Southwest* with Ellen N. Taubman and

edited the excellent book that accompanied the show. In all, McFadden has written over seventy articles and has written and edited numerous books and catalogues. In addition he has delivered over two hundred lectures and papers to national and international audiences.

GRAHAM MCLAREN
McLaren received a degree in the history of design and the visual arts from North Staffordshire Polytechnic, followed by a PhD in history of design at the Royal College of Art. He is senior lecturer in the history of art and design, and course leader of the MA in the history of ceramics, the only program of its kind in the Western world. Begun in 1993, the course has recently expanded to an off-campus, on-line program, acknowledging that those interested in pursuing the specialty are scattered across the globe. McLaren has worked in a number of museums, including the Victoria and Albert Museum, the Brighton Pavilion Museum and Art Gallery, and the City Museum and Art Gallery, Stoke-on-Trent. His teaching appointments include Winchester School of Art and West Surrey College of Art and Design, and he has lectured nationally and internationally including in Ireland and America. He has published extensively in such publications as *The Burlington Magazine*, *Crafts Magazine*, and *The Times*. He is currently completing a major text, *The Culture of Ceramics*, for Manchester University Press.

MICHAEL MCTWIGAN (LINCOLN, NEBRASKA, USA, 1948)
McTwigan studied at Lake Forest College, Illinois, before moving to New York were he held a series of editorial and writing positions: assistant editor, *Craft Horizons* magazine (1972, 1974–78); writer, Time-Life Publications (1978); assistant editor, *The Art Quarterly*, the Metropolitan Museum of Art (1978–79); senior editor, Watson-Guptill Publications (1979–1981), where he guided several notable ceramic books into press including *Porcelain, Traditions and New Visions* (1981) by Jan Axel and Karen McCready, *Low Fire Ceramics* (1981) by Susan Wechsler, and *American Potters: 20 Modern Masters* (1981) by Garth Clark. After a short stint as editor in chief of *ID* (International Design) (1982–83) McTwigan became the co-founder and editor of the New York based magazine, *American Ceramics*, from 1982 to 1993. His role at *American Ceramics* was a seminal one for the field at large, bringing a new era of sophistication to writing on ceramics and establishing an editorial policy that

excluded all technical or process articles and focused exclusively on aesthetics, criticism, and appreciation. Writing for the inaugural issue (Summer, 1982) in an article entitled "First Things First: Some Second Thoughts on How We View Clay Today," McTwigan made the call for a more formalist approach to ceramic literacy: "There are many ways in which ceramics must be first be understood before they can be appreciated and this requires the viewer to understand the ceramist's formal vocabulary, the myths, memories and other cultural traditions" specific to an particular artwork. A prolific writer on American ceramics and the American crafts movements, Michael has produced numerous essays and catalogues for significant exhibitions, including *Heroes and Clowns: Robert Arneson* (1979); *In the Eye of the Beholder: A Portrait of our Time* (1985); and *Ron Nagle: A Survey Exhibition 1958-1993* (1993) with Mills College Art Gallery. He is now a freelance branding consultant.

MARK PENNINGS (MELBOURNE, AUSTRALIA, 1960)
Pennings received his PhD from the University of Melbourne, Australia, and lectures at the Royal Melbourne Institute of Technology and at Queensland University of Technology in Brisbane. His primary teaching interests are modern and postmodern art, consumer culture, and video art. He is an executive member of the Australian Art Association in Queensland and is currently working on a book on the history of Australian video art. He is a skilled writer and has written over fifty catalogues on a wide variety of artists and art media. He is a critic, book reviewer, and curator as well as an active lecturer at conferences throughout Australia and abroad. He first came to the attention of the international ceramics world in 1996 when, together with Justin Clemens, he co-wrote the influential booklet, *Cultural Theory and Craft Practice*, based on their papers given at a five-week seminar series organized by Craft Victoria. This modest document, only fifty six pages in length, deals with the still vexing relationship of ceramics to modernism and its more cozy, but still poorly defined, relationship with postmodernism.

PHILIP RAWSON (LONDON, UK, 1924 - 1995)
Rawson's original research into the aesthetics of Middle Eastern art secured his position as an influential scholar, critic, and artist of his time. Rawson travelled internationally, though his focus was primarily within Oriental and Middle Eastern cul-

tures. Centering his studies on the aesthetics of those cultures, Rawson published numerous essays and books on his findings. Author of titles such as *Indian Painting* (1961), *Japanese Buddhist Painting* (1963), *Indian Sculpture* (1966), *The Art of South East Asia* (1967), *Indian Sword* (1967), and *The Erotic Art of the East* (1968), Rawson became an expert on the subject of the decorative arts within Asian and Middle Eastern countries. Rawson authored two titles for Oxford University Press in the series, *The Appreciation for the Arts*. The first book, *Drawing* (1969), was followed up by *Ceramics*, published in 1971. *Ceramics* was the most significant study on ceramics and aesthetics in the 1970s and 1980s. In the foreword to the 1984 edition by Penn Press, Wayne Higby wrote: "It is rare to find a book on art that presents complex aesthetic principles in clear readable form. *Ceramics*, by Philip Rawson, is such a book. I discovered it ten years ago, and today my well-worn copy has scarcely a page on which some statement is not underlined and starred." National Council on Education for the Ceramic Arts Newsletter noted:

> With the unassuming title of *Ceramics*, Rawson has presented a very clear, orderly and thought-provoking guide for discussion. He provides words for those nebulous, or nonexistent, thoughts that students avoid talking about in critiques, and our professional associates talk all around, using whatever art language is being worn out at the time—"Is your work postmodernist yet?" Now we have no excuse to complain that there is no vocabulary.

The book revealed the glory and the surprising (to some) complexity of the ceramic aesthetic. In addition to his numerous texts and essays, Rawson was curator of the Gulbenkian Museum of Oriental Art at the University of Durham and an assistant keeper in the Department of Eastern Art at the Ashmolean Museum in Oxford, England. For the latter part of his career he held the title of Dean at the School of Art and Design at Goldsmith's College of the University of London.

NANCY SELVAGE (NEW YORK, NEW YORK, USA, 1945)
Known for her extensive public art commissions throughout the United States, Europe, and Asia, Selvage has taken her works public creating well-crafted ceramic and mixed media works for site-specific locations internationally. Currently program

director for Harvard University's Radcliffe College Ceramic Program, Selvage has also held teaching positions at Massachusetts College of Art, the University of Massachusetts, the Boston Museum School, the Rhode Island School of Design, and the Ewha University in Seoul Korea. Among her awards and achievements are her commissions for the Grand Canyon Visitor's Center (2002), a National Endowment for the Arts grant (2001, 2002) and the Massachusetts Arts Council New Works Commissions (1982, 1987). Selvage has been on the board of directors of the magazine, *Studio Potter*, for many years. Selvage is currently writing a book for A & C Black Publishers, Ltd., London, on public art projects that use ceramics, and she is serving with a team of artists who are developing public art projects for a new government building in Hangzhou, China.

DORIS SHADBOLT (PRESTON, ONTARIO, CANADA, 1918 - 2003, VANCOUVER, BRITISH COLUMBIA, CANADA)

Shadbolt studied fine arts at the University of Toronto. She then took jobs at the Art Gallery of Ontario, the National Gallery of Canadam and New York's Metropolitan Museum before moving to the Vancouver Art Gallery, where she eventually became associate director and then director. There she met and married artist Jack Shadbolt after World War II. Shadbolt had two primary focuses. She received much acclaim for her widely read books on Emily Carr: *The Art of Emily Carr* (1979), *Emily Carr* (1986), *The Emily Carr Omnibus* (1993), and *Seven Journeys: The Sketchbooks of Emily Carr* (2002), which describe the artist's visits to isolated Aboriginal villages on the BC Coast, her visits to eastern Canada, and two metaphorical journeys. Shadbolt was also an early advocate of Native art and a champion of the Native artist Bill Reid. She is credited with having changed Canada's perception of art by the Northwest Coast Aboriginal peoples. Shadbolt argued that their creative work was indeed art and not simply anthropological artifact. While Shadbolt was acting director of the Vancouver Art Gallery in 1967, she created a groundbreaking exhibition, *The Art of the Raven*, about which Martine Reid, the widow of native artist Bill Reid, said "This was a turning point [and] deepened our sensibility toward Northwest Coast art." Later Shadbolt published a book on Reid himself, *Bill Reid* (1986). In 1999, when former Governor General Roméo LeBlanc and the Canada Council for the Arts created the Governor General's Awards in Visual and Media Arts, Shadbolt was one of the inaugural winners, recognized in a category honouring volunteerism, philanthropy, board governance, and community outreach activities. "All my adult life I have been aware of how fortunate I have been to be engaged, whether gainfully or not, in the varying fields of art," Shadbolt said on CBC News shortly after receiving her award. "I do believe that it is the arts which speak to the whole person, that is, to the spirit and the emotions, and to the mind and body alike…which are the most important components in the formation of culture." Later teaming up with her husband Jack Shadbolt, she established the Vancouver Institute for the Visual Arts and its VIVA awards to honour emerging artists.

SUSAN TUNICK (NEW YORK, NEW YORK, USA, 1946)
Tunick received her BA and MFA from Bennington College in Bennington, Vermont. She is an artist, writer, and activist. Among her titles on ceramics and architecture are *Terra Cotta: Don't Take It for Granite* (1995), *George & Edward Blum: Texture and Design in New York Apartment House Architecture* (1996), *George and Edward Blum: Field Guide to Apartment Building Architecture* (1993) with Andrew Dolkart, and *Paris and the Legacy of French Architectural Ceramics* (1997) with Susan Montgomery, Patrice Goulet, Bernard Marrey and Anne-Laure Goulet. In 1997 *Terra Cotta Skyline: New York's Architectural Ornament*, a remarkable work of scholarship and erudition, was published to rapturous reviews and several awards including the 1997 Book of the Year Award from the New York Society Library. In addition, she has published dozens of articles and catalogue essays. Tunick has received numerous other awards, including the Tile Heritage Foundation Award, 1997; Municipal Art Society: Brendan Gill Award 1998, 1999 International Ceramics Symposium (Ostracon) Award at the Ceramic Millennium in Amsterdam and the Grassroots Preservation Award, Historic District Council 2004. Along with her artistic accomplishments and writings, Tunick is an international force in the preservation, documentation, and study of architectural ceramics and tile worldwide. She is the founder of Friends of Terra Cotta, a non-profit organization, and she is known as New York's most passionate and public defender of the city's huge legacy of ceramic-clad buildings. She has almost single-handedly transformed the city's understanding and appreciation of these buildings after decades of neglect and ignorance.

GERRY WILLIAMS (INDIA, 1926)
Williams grew up in India, where his parents worked as missionaries. He attended

Cornell College in Iowa and then moved to New Hampshire shortly after World War II. Here he was influenced by Edwin and Mary Scheier as well as other notable potters. Williams founded the quarterly journal *Studio Potter* in 1972 with his wife and served as editor until 2004. The magazine is a work of remarkable integrity, and while it reflects the tastes of its editor, it is, at the same time, neutral ground for the discussion of all kinds of issues facing the studio potter. Each issue is so lovingly assembled that it can almost be viewed as a hand-made work. A practicing potter for over fifty years, Williams works both in utilitarian vessels and also in more sculptural aspects of ceramics, often evoking socio-political overtones in some of the work. The work shows several influences in his life: his upbringing in India, the American Crafts Movement, and the post World War II rebirth of craft-based studio practices. But the influence that formed him most indelibly was Gandhi's emphasis on the practical and symbolic role of basic craft practice. This has lead Williams to take on a leadership role in encouraging apprenticeship in the crafts. He has taught, given workshops, and lectured throughout the world at such venues as the World Craft Conferences in NYC, Japan and Australia, the Foshan International Ceramics Conference in China, several International Ceramics Symposia (including the first in Syracuse), and numerous other venues around the world. Williams is New Hampshire's first state artist laureate.

GEORGE WOODMAN (CONCORD, NEW HAMPSHIRE, USA, 1932)
Woodman studied painting and philosophy at Harvard. As a painter he emerged as an important member of the Pattern and Decoration (P+D) movement. His paintings are in many private and public collections, including the Guggenheim Museum, New York, and the Denver Art Museum. Woodman was a long-time faculty member of the University of Colorado in Boulder and, since 1996, has been professor emeritus of art. His writing on art and aesthetics has an incisive, analytical quality, part of what made him such a valued and effective teacher. His study of philosophy under Ivor Armstrong Richards at Harvard has equipped him both in his art and writing to confront and make sense of conundrums. Woodman has continued to work as an artist, but in 1987 he shifted his focus to photography, creating multi-layered exposures of black-and-white images in varying allegorical compositions. His photographic images are highly constructed, with elements often double exposed or reversed and layered over other images of objects, people, or nature. Woodman's

photography is in many public collections, including the Denver Art Museum; the Museum of Modern Art, New York; the Solomon R. Guggenheim Museum, New York; and the Whitney Museum of American Art, New York. Woodman and his wife, the renowned ceramic artist, Betty Woodman, have had a studio and home just outside Florence, Italy, and for forty years have divided their time between this studio and their homes in Boulder and, currently, New York City.

Aalto, Ivar, 367
Abstract Expressionism, 19, 125, 328
Acquaviva, Giovanni, 109
Adorno, Theodor, 124
Aeroceramica, 108
Aesthetic
 domestic & industrial life, 146
 ethnography, 352
 meaning and metaphor, 36
 of everyday life, 125
 of the machine, 13
Albers, Josef, 82
Alexei Sotnikov Dulevo Factory, 95
Alfred University. *See* New York State College of Ceramics
Allied Artists' Association, 264
Almiral, Raymond, 183
American Ceramics, 284
American Craft, 285
Ancienne Manufacture Royale Limoges, 348
Andre, Carl, 82
Angelou, Maya, 317
Anselmo, Giuseppe M., 109, 111
 Vase in Form of Cyclist, 14
Anthropomorphic, 39, 42, 50, 85, 213, 222, 244
Appadurai, Arjun, 358
Appalachian Pottery, 198
Aquaviva, Giovanni, 111
Archimedes, 365
Architectura Razionale, 105
Architecture, 169-194,
 ceramic decoration, 275
 European Ceramic Form, 145
 Postmodern, 77
 See Terra Cotta
Arguelles, Jose, 226
Aristotle, 158, 362
Arneson, Robert, 16, 21, 126, 151, 281, 330, 333
 Bird, 127
 Crazed, 22
Arquero, Juanita, 197
Art Deco, 93, 105
 Italian, 105
Art in America, 285
Art Nouveau, 64-75, 93, 104
 Italian, 105
 porcelain, 313
Art Object, 232, 354
 classification of, 166
Art Pottery, 70
 Gallé (France)
 Grueby Company (US)
 Rookwood Company (US)
 Teco Company (US)
 Tiffany (France)
 movement, 146

Art vs. Craft Debate, 3-4, 10-23, 24-25, 31, 96, 116-17, 122, 135-36, 165-66, 203-4, 279, 288, 296, 306, 325-26, 328, 332, 341-43, 344
Artforum, 285
Artist, 14, 90
 definition of, 10
 engineers, 79
 myth of genius, 12
 professional, 328
Artist Unions, 325
Artist's Workshops, 324
 Arabia (Finland)
 Bing and Grondahl (Denmark)
 Bo Fajans and Gustavsberg (Sweden)
 Lomonosov State Porclain Factory (Leningrad)
 Royal Cophenagen (Denmark)
ArtNews, 285
Arts and Crafts Movement, 12, 13, 14, 18, 21, 69, 120, 122, 321
 rustic pottery, 313
Ashbee, C.R., 21
Assenza, Enzo, 112
Astarte Goddess Syria, 40
Astrologers (Babylon), 54
Augustus the Strong, King of Poland, 310, 319
Avant-Garde, 19, 93, 126, 164
 ideology, 116
Baccarini, Domenico, 105
Bacerra, Ralph, 156
Bampi, Richard, 103
Banham, Rayner, 13
Barton, Glenys, 330
Batchelor, Ernest, 271
Battock, Gregory, 84
Baudelaire, Charles, 7, 78, 316
Bauhaus, 14, 19, 36, 96, 97, 122, 164, 253
 Art and Technics, 100
 ceramic studio (Dornburg), 97
 Das Staatliches (Weimar), 96
 Dessau, 102
 earthenware/stoneware, 99
 education, 15
 folk art, 98
 industrial production, 14
 machine production, 122
 pottery workshop, 103
 United States, 14
Bauman, Zygmunt, 130, 132
Beastie Boys, 130
Bell, Clive, 223
Benglis, Lydia, 279
Benjamin, Walter, 261
Bergson, Henri, 266
Berlind, Robert, 284
Bertelli, Renato

 Black Pottery Head of Mussolini, 112
Billington, Dora, 265
Bindesboll, Theodor, 71
Binns, Charles, 270, 324
Blackburn, Jeannot, 231
 kitch ceramics, 244
 Bride Teapot, 235
 lady vases, 244
Blake, William, 226, 320
Bloomsbury Group, 224
Blum Helman Gallery, 331
Blum, Irving, 329
Bogler, Theodor, 14, 98-102, 123
 Double Spout Coffee Pot, 99
 Kanne Pot, 15
Bohemian Society, 327
Bonnard, Pierre
 Women in a Garden, 260
Booth, George, 273
Booth, T.C., 181
Böttger, Johann Friedrich, 310, 319
Boucher, François, 343
Bourgeois, Louise, 315
Bozo, Dominique, 338
Braden, Norah, 267
Brancusi, Constantin, 261
Brandjes Factory (Holland), 70
Brangwyn, Frank, 266
British Crafts Centre, 330
Brown, James, 348
Browne, Sir Thomas, 86
Browning, Robert, 223
Bruegel, Pieter, 307
Bucci, Anselmo, 105
Buddhist, 227
Burton, Scott, 155
Buzio, Lydia, 193
 Skyline Pot, 192
Camberwell School of Arts and Crafts, 264
Cantatore, Sirio, 112
Capodimonte Factory, 316
Capote, Truman, 332
Cardew, Michael, 205, 223, 226, 252, 254, 268, 272, 325, 327, 354, 355
 Heart of Darkness, 356, *357*
 Mud and Water Man, 252
 West Africa, 268, 354
Carlyle, Thomas, 57
Caro, Anthony, 6, 279
Carpeaux, Jean-Baptiste, 5, 343
Carr, Emily, 339
Carrara Ware, 171
Carries, Jean, 71
Cégep du Vieux Montréal, 232
Celoria, Francis, 170
Celula, Marek, 315
Central School of Arts and Crafts (London), 264

Ceramic Art and Perception, 285
Ceramics
    art criticism and, 283
    as an art form, 5, 7, 17, 20, 25, 27, 32, 43, 45, 72, 82, 93, 103, 104, 136, 338, 346
    concern with technique, 27
    contemporary, 78, 130, 144
    critical language, 359
    criticism, 28, 278, 287
    definitions of, 351
    description, technique, 279
    high art, 138
    history, academic texts, 248
    history, development of, 168
    international symposia, 279
    literature of, 357
    objects and use value, 118
    photography, 4, 287
    representational, 280
    reviews of, 334
    studio ceramics, 348
    tableware, 299
    visual art, 282
    writing on ceramics, 100, 351
Ceramics Monthly, 284
Ceramics Review, 285
Ceramists, 5, 25, 329
    compared to other artists, 29
    contemporary, 26
Cézanne, Paul, 15, 260, 366
Chaco Canyon, 41
Champy, Claude, 300
Chaplet, Ernest, 70, 261, 340
Chasnik, Ilia, 79, 96
Chicago, Judy, 316
China Painting
    ceramic education, 265
    Keramik Studio magazine, 323
    United States, 269
Chinese, 41, 44
    brush arts, 216
    calligraphy, 42
    dragon vase, 51
    ink paintings, 42
    linear tradition, 46
    painting, 43
    porcelain, 306, 308
    collecting of, 319
    ritual vessels, 216
Chiswick Press, 41
Chutte, Thomas, 335
Cicero, 266
Clark, Garth, 4, 5, 6, 7, 35, 37, 45, 92–113, 219–29, 278, 286, 317–36
    and an artist's career, 300
    contemporary history, 286
Clemens, Justin, 128, 129–39
Cliff, Clarice, 326

Coalport, *Cabbage Tureen Form with Underdish*, 47
Cobra Group, 113
Cochiti, New Mexico, 197
Coleman, Tom, 199
Communism, 325
Confucian, 60
Connoisseurship, 253, 309
    art, 222
    collecting and patronage, 302
    curators, 303
    curiosities, 309
    porcelain, 308
Contemporary Ceramics, 144
    modernism, 77-78
    Soup Tureen show, 151
    in the university, 221
Contemporary Culture, 281
Contemporary Theory, 130
Constructivism, 79, 82, 83, 93, 99, 110, 164
    influence on Bauhaus, 100
Coper, Hans, 53
Cup Form, 55
Pair of Coronation Pitchers, 59
    pricing, 330
Cordero, Helen, 197
Cosimo Medici II, 204
Council for Industrial Design, 250
Craft Horizons, 19, 285
Crafts, 285
Crafts Council (British), 174-175
Cragg, Tony, 335
Cranbrook Academy of Art, 204, 268, 272, 273
Crane, Walter, 261, 265
    Cartoons for a Cause, 259
    Ideals in Art, 259
    Love's Altar, 259
Crete, 41, 52
    Snake Goddess, 40
    Octopus Vase, 51
Crystal Palace, porcelain, 313
Cubism, 164
    geometric forms, 81
    influence on ceramics, 93
Cubo-Futurist style, 107
Currier, Anne, 86
    Box, 87
Cushing, Val, 248
D'Albisola, Tullio, 13, 107
    Half Pot, 110
    Pitcher, 107
    Stile Futurista magazine, 109
da Vinci, Leonardo, 365
Dada, 164, 345
Daley, William, 38, 85, 87, 147
    Onegas Passage, 85
    Our Turn, 85
    Taos Procession, 85
    Untitled, 38

Dalpayrat, Pierre-Adrien, *Vase*, 70
Dangar, Anne, 93
Danko, Naralia, 96
Danto, Arthur, 284
Darwin, Charles, 366
Davis, Harry, 203
Davis, Ron, 81
De Benedetti, Carlo
    Il Futurismo in Liguria, 113
de Duve, Thierry, 135
de Kooning, Elaine, 285
de Kooning, Willem, 147
de Morgan, William, 69
De Porceleyne Fles, 183
de Stijl, 117, 164
de Waal, Edmund, 315, 350–60
    installation of porcelain, 309
    Pair of Bottle Forms, 359
    Tall Porcelain Lidded Jar, 354
Decoeur, Emile, 261
Decoration
    artist images, 340
    China, symbolic, 45
    Cochiti sytle, 198
    decals, 291
    decorative art, 142
    hakeme, 29
    indian motifs, 340
    Korean tea bowl, 354
    painting, 144
    peony, 45
    Phoenix, 45
    sentimental motifs, 343
    surface, 344
    visual language, 67
Decorative Arts, 64, 307, 321, 328
Degas, Edgar, 5
Delaherche, Auguste, 70, 261
    Vase, 70
Deleuze, Gilles, 134
della Quercia, Jacopo, 107
della Robbia, Andrea, 70
    Madonna and Child, 308
    Virgin and Child, 308
Derain, Andre, 262
Design, 253
    evolution, 368
    natural forms, 367
    service, 297
Deutscher Werkbund, 97, 365
DeVore, Richard, 147, 227
Dewald, Gabi, 289–300
di Puglia, Nicolo, 107
Dianan of the Ephesians, 39
Dill, Guy, 82, 83
Dillingham, Rick, 147, 156-157
    Globe, 156
Diulgheroff, Nicolay, 109
Doat, Taxile, 70
Dormer, Peter, 136, 283
Dow, Arthur, 271

Dresser, Christopher, 366, 367, 368, 369
　Art of Decorative Design, 367
Driesch, Hans, 98
Duchamp, Marcel, 20, 121, 214
　Fountain, *20*, 21, 342
　Large Glass, 139
Duffy, Raoul, 241, 340
Education, 103, 261, 265, 324
　artist-teachers, 329
　British, 263
　contemporary practice, 250
　co-optation, 328
　design, 264
　female enrollment, 270
　GI Bill, 328
　history of ceramics, 247
　　via distance, 258
　influence on the market, 335
　master-apprentice, 254
　museums, 251
　role of the university, 204
　United States, 268
Egypt, *Egg Pot*, *61*
Eighteenth Century, 131
　aesthetics, 136
　craft and capitalism, 119
　ceramics, 145
　Chinese porcelain, 209
　French pottery, 237
　porcelain, 311
　sculpture, 5
　terra cotta, 171
Einstein, Albert, 204, 303
Elers Brothers, 248
　Mug, *309*
Eliot, T.S., 187, 227
Elozua, Raymond, 193
Emerson, Ralph Waldo, 362, 365
Engelman, Richard, 103
Erickson, Leif, 306
Erotic Imagery, 235, 242
Ethnography, 253, 351
Eugene, Winton and Rose
　Cow Pens Studio, *200*
Europe
　colonialism, 137
　middle ages reliquaries, 192
　painters, 260
Evans-Pritchard, Sir Edward, 355
Everson Museum of Art (Syracuse), 6, 7, 8, 231, 244
Fabbriche Riunite Ceramiche Faentine, 105
Factories, 68-71, 79
Fafard, Joe, *Cow*, *30*
Falk, Gathie, 30
Farfa, Francesco, 110
Featherstone, Mike, 126
Feininger, Lyonel, 96
Felix Landau Gallery, 329

Ferus Gallery (California), 329
Figurine Tradition (Russia), 96
Filarete, Antonio, 77
Fin de Siècle, 64-76
Finland Potteries, 70
Flaxman, John, 49, 119, 320
　Portland Vase, *48*, *119*
Focillon, Henri, 41, 42, 86
Folk Pottery, 18
Fontana, Lucio, 91, 109, 113, 147, 279, 342-344, 346-347
　Cavallo, *110*
　Concetto Spaziale Piatto, *147*, *Plate*, 343
　Sèvres Manufactory, 111
Form, 205
　follows function, 123, 369
　　Horatio Greenough, 366
　modern functional, 104
　typography, 25
　variations, 366
Forsyth, Gordon, 102, 264
Fosdick, Marion, 272
Foucar, Li, 98
Foulem, Léopold L., 231-46, 337-49
　Covered Shallow Tureen With Metal Stand, *239*
　Gold Teapot..., *243*
　Matter Doesn't Matter, *243*
　Rhyton From The Tropics, *236*
　Shallow Tureen..., *238*
　Uprooted Root, *243*
France
　cave paintings, 16
　ceramics, 65
　Franciscono, Marcel, 98
　Grasse Studio, 339
Frankfurt School, The, 124
Fredericks, Marshall, 273
Freud, Sigmund, 303
Frey, Viola, 226
Friedlander, Marguerite. *See* Wildenhain, Marguerite
Frimkess, Michael, 158
　Casa Gloria, *157*
　Ecology Krater II, *158*
　Melting Pot, *223*
Frimkess, Michael and Magdalena
　Rouleau, *234*
Fritsch, Liz, 330
Frumkin, Allan, 330
Fry, Roger, 224, 263, 265
　Cubist influence, 93
　Omega Pottery, 93
Function
　aesthetics, 362
　communication, 370
　definition (art and craft), 11
　forms, 93
　industrial production, 369

mechanical age, 370
painting and ceramics, 78
vessel, 27
Futurism, 13, 36, 96, 107, 108, 164
　Aeroceramisti, 93
　influences, 109
　Italy, 78, 106
Gabo, Naum, 82
Galerie del Milione (Milan), 111
Galerie Jeanne Boucher, 111
Galleria Sproviera (Rome), 107
Galleries, 328-330
Gambone, Guido, 112
Gauguin, Paul, 70, 71, 260, 261, 262, 340, 342
　Ceramic Vase with Grotesque Self-Portrait, *340*
　Soyez amoureuse, vous serez heureuse, *260*
　Vase with Mask..., *340*
Gauthier, Serge & Tamara Préaud
　Ceramics of the Twenieth Century, 338
Geer, Walter, 177
Geertz, Clifford, 355
Gehry, Frank, Ohr Museum, 323
German, 14, 190
　ceramic identity, 292-293
Gilbert, Cass, 181
Gill, Andrea, 152
Gill, Eric, 261
Gill, John, 153
Gilman, Sandor, 137
Ginori, Richard, 105
Gladding McBean & Co., 184
Gladstone Pottery Museum, 170
Glaze, 103
　development of colour, 181
　feeling of, 353
　Japanese, 143
　lustre, 107
　majolica, 92
　overglaze, 43
　reduced copper, 49
　tenmoku, 357
　Tung-yao celadon, 47
Gleizes, Albert, 93
Glick, John, 153
Goldin, Amy, 145
Gordon, Rae Beth, 137
Gormley, Antony, 279
Gradl, Hermann
　part of a fish service, *69*
Graves, Michael, 83
Greenberg, Clement, 3-9, 229
　formal analysis, 125
Greenhalgh, Paul, 64-76, 163-68
Greenough, Horatio, 365
Gregory, Wayland DeSantis, 273
Gropius, Walter, 14-15, 96-97, 122
　Art and Technics, 99

Grotell, Maija, 271, 275
  Green & Tan Crackle Vase, 274
Guattari, Felix, 134
Guillory, John, 137
Habermas, Jurgen, 130
Haenen, Babs, 315
Haile, Sam, 272
Haile, Thomas Samuel
  Pitcher, 273
Hamada, Shoji, 18, 45, 328
Hamilton, David, 170–75
Han Dynasty
  Storehouse, 187, *189*
Hanley School of Art, 265
Harder, Charles, 271, 367, 370
Harrod, Tanya, 259–75, 283
Harvey, David, 134
Haviland Porcelain, 70
Hegel, Georg W. F., 118, 138
Hepworth, Barbara, 240, 326
Herakleion Museum, 41, 51, 210
Hettner, Rolando, 105
Higby, Wayne, 147, 152, 157, 160
  colour, 86
  Imaginary Bay, *150*
Hildbrand, Adolfo, 107
Hirsch, Rick, 227
Hirshhorn Museum, 343
Hoentschel, George, *Vase*, 70
Holmes, Edward, 271
Homer, *Kiln*, 317
Hops, Walter, 329
Horkheimer, Frank, 124
Hudson, Kenneth, 5, 309, 312
Hughes, Robert, 28
Hughto, Margie, 6
Huysman, J.K., 89
I Ching, 60
Ibstock Hathernware Ltd., 184
Illian, Clary, 198
Imperial Porcelain Factory, 95
Impressionism, 78
Industrial
  companies and artist, 212
  craft, 136
  design, 14, 126, 370
  economics, 119, 121
  production, 369
  society, 11, 352
Industrial Revolution, 371
  Thomas Wedgwood, 119
  William Morris, 96
Institute for Ceramic Studies, 112
Internet, 254-256
Iron Age, 39, 213
Italy, 104
  Aeroceramisti, 93
  painted design, 143
Itten, Johannes, 97, 99
James, William, 192
Jameson, Fredric, 130, 134

Japanese, 45
  brush arts, 216
  folk craft movement, 352-353
  functional wares, 327
  I-Hsing & British imitation, 157
  lacquerware, 215
  market, 326
  prints, 18
  Zen raku, 214
Jasperware. *See* Wedgwood
Johns, Jasper, 331
Johnson, Philip, 77
Joost Thooft & Labouchere, 183
Judd, Donald, 82
Jung, Carl, 37, 193
Kage, Wilhelm, 324
Kandinsky, Vasily, 93, 99, 264
Kang Hsi, 227
Keats, John, 223
Keeps, Rose, 103
Keinholz, Ed, 329
Kellner, Martin, 302
Kelly, Ellsworth, 81, 82
Kenzan, Ogata, 38, 237, 239
Kirchner, Ernst Ludwig, 261
Kita, Toshiyuka, 294
Kobyletskaya, Zinaida, 96
Koetsu, 47
Kok, J. Juriaan
  vases and coffee pot, 65
Königliche Porzellan Manufaktur
  (Berlin), 102
Koons, Jeff, 139, 236
Koplos, Janet, 278–88
Koryu Dynasty (Korea), 307
Kraus, Liz, 198
Krehan, Max, 98, 102, 122
Kruithuis Museum, 279, 347
  The Unexpected..., 339
Kubler, George, 227
Kung Hsien, 44
Kunsthandwerk, 294
Kuznetsky Bridge (Moscow), 95
Kyoto National Museum, 255
La Maison Bing (Paris), 321
La Maison Moderne (Paris), 321
Lao-Tsu, 266
Lash, Scott, 131
Laurens, Henri, 82, 262
Le Corbusier
  L'Esprit Nouveau, 261
Leach, Bernard, 18, 45, 71, 117,
  123, 127, 146, 151, 214, 223,
  249, 253, 263, 265, 266, 269,
  272, 286, 325, 326, 335, 352,
  353, 355, 356, 358, 370
  A Potter's Book, 266, 358
  Anti-Modernism, 124
  apprenticeship, 360
  art schools, 267
  assimilation, 215

Bowl, *246*
Cornwall, 198
decoration, 124
pricing, 325, 326
tradition, 360
Vase, *123*
Lebow, Edward, 186–94, 362–71
LeDray, Charles, 279
Leningrad State Porcelain, 94
Lenoble, Emile, 261
Les Fauves, 261
Les Nabis, 260
Levy, Gertrude Rachel, 41
Li Po, 42
Liang K'ai, 42
Liberty's (London), 321
Lichtenstein, Roy, 110, 126, 240
Lieu Ouest Gallery, 235
Lilly, William, 54
Limoges Porcelain, 307, 314, 347
Lindig, Otto, 98, 100, 102, 103
  Coffee Pot, *99*
  High Cover Pot, *98*
  Stoneware Pitcher, *102*
Lissitzky, El, 12, 14, 99
Lomonosov Pottery, 96
London School of Art, 266
Loos, Adolf, 364, 365, 369
Lord, Andrew, 331
Lowes, John Livingstone, 209
Luhmann, Niklas, 130, 139
Lunn, Richard, 265
Lux, Joesph-August, 365
Lyell, Charles, 182
Lyotard, Jean-François, 130, 133
Maberry, Philip, 87
  Striped Bowl, *88*
MacKenzie, Warren, 252
Madame de Pompadour, 238
  Royale de Sèvres, 311, 347
Madoura Pottery, 340, 345, 347
Malevich, Kasimir, 50, 79, 93, 94
  Suprematist Teapot, *12*
Manet, Edouard, 7, 263
Manufattura di Doccia, 105
Marcks, Gerhard, 97, 99, 102, 122
  Double Spout Coffee Pot, *99*
Margetts, Martina, 285
Marinetti, Tommaso, 13, 364, 108
  Manifesto of Futurism, *106*
Market, 317-336
  collecting, 244, 301
  commodity and art, 126
  consumerism, 26, 124
  specialized galleries, 281
Marks, Graham, 89, 91
  Untitled, *90*
Marot, Daniel, 309, 310
Marriott, Charles, 326
Martin Brothers, 70, 321
Martinez, Maria, 203

Martini, Arturo, 107
Marx, Karl, 117, 121, 130
Mason, John, 83-84, 328-329
  Monolith, 83
Mass Production, 116, 117, 119, 122-126, 364, 369
Material Culture, 257, 305, 358
Mathieu, Paul, 232, 237-240
Matisse, Henri, 241, 262, 263
Mayakovsky, Vladimir, 79, 95
Mays, John Bentley, 53–61
Mazzotti, Giuseppe, 106-112
  Bullonvaso, 106
McCluhan, Marshall, 133
McCracken, John, 82
McCullough, Malcolm, 255, 371
McFadden, David, 301–16
McLaren, Graham, 247–58
McLaughlin, Louise, 269
McTwigan, Michael, 77–91, 284
Mei-Ping, *dragon vase*, 44
Meissen Porcelain, 68, 159, 167, 190, 311, 313, 319
Melandri, Pietro, 112
Meteyard, Eliza, 249
Metropolis (magazine), 285
Metropolitan Museum of Art (New York), 239, 332
Metthey, Andre, 261, 262
Mexico, 51
  Two-level House Model, 187
Middle East, 307
Milette, Richard, 232-235, 240-244
  Hydria 13-6294 with Apollo Temple IV, 241
  Teapot, 233
Milles, Carl, 273
Mimbres Indians, 223
Minimalism, 82, 84
Minton Pottery, 70
Miró, Jean, 12, 16, 19, 340
Modernism, 7, 15, 21, 78, 93, 360
  and ornamentation, 65
  ceramics, 36, 118
  definition, 116
  design, 366
  European, 164
  the machine, 122
Modernity and Postmodernity, 130
Mogelin, Ellen, 98
Moholy-Nagy, L., 99
Mommens, Ursula, 265
Mondrian, Piet, 82, 117
Monet, Claude, 78
Montaigne, Michel de, 350
Morris, Robert, 82
Morris, William, 13, 69, 96, 120-121, 138, 146, 313, 321, 335
  art, politics and morality, 260
  industrial capitalism, 117

Moscow Higher Technical Institute, 95
Mrs. Coade's Manufactory, 171
Mumford, Lewis, 363, 364, 370
Munari, Bruno, 109, 111
Munsterberger, Werner, 301
Murray, Kevin, 256
Murray, William Staite, 263, 264, 265, 266, 272, 325, 326
  Bowl, 264
Musée Picasso (Paris), 338
Museo della Ceramiche Internationale, 112
Museo Nazionale degli Abruzzi (Torino), 155
Museum of Modern Art and the Otis group, 330
Nagle, Ron, 87, 89, 155
Nancy, Jean-Luc, 133
Nardis, Fulvio, 105
NCECA, 204
Natural History Museum of London, 174
Nature
  designers, 367
  forms, 181, 366
  in ceramics, 20
  of art, 20
  of clay, 24
  of metaphor, 36
  painting, 78
Nelson, George, 368
Neo-Cubism, 110
Neo-Orientalists, 265
Nepal, 223
Nevsky Prospekt (Petrograd), 95
New Art Examiner, 285
New Ceramic Order, 129
New Clay Project, 6
New York School of Claywork, 268
New York State College of Ceramics at Alfred University, 204, 268, 270, 324, 367
New York Times, 332
Newman, Barnett, 82
Nichols, Maria Longworth, 269
Nicholson, Ben, 326
Niderviller Surfaces, 237
Nietzsche, Friedrich, 35, 36
Nineteenth Century, 7, 41
  porcelain, 312
  style, 72
  technologies, 132
Noguchi, Isamu, 91
Noland, Kenneth, 82, 155
Nolen, Matt, 234
Nonni, Francesco, 105
Non-Utilitarian, 13, 19
Northwest Coast Indian, The Tlingit, 31
Novacento (Art Deco), 105

Nymphenberg Porcelain, 68
Oestreich, Jeff, 332
Ohr, George, 71, 74, 75, 121, 323
  Handled Vase, 121
  Pitcher, 73
Olitski, Jules, 82
Omega Pottery, 93
Omega Workshops, 224, 263
Opie, Jennifer, 65
Oppenheim, Meret
  [*Le Dejeuner en fourrure*]
  Object, 17, 18, 345
Ornament
  art noveau, 64
  floral, 41
  function, 365
  porcelain, 311
  terra cotta, 180
Otis Art Institute, 328, 329
Overbeck, Elizabeth, 271
Overdieck, Eva, 98
Ovid, 266
Pacetti, Ivos, 111
Painting, 44
  visual-arts marketplace, 318
  on ceramics, Matisse and Picasso, 262
  three dimensional, 82
Palissy, Bernard, 308
Panofsky, Erwin, 77
Paps of Anu, 213
Paris Exposition
  Binns, Charles (1900), 322
  Futurist ceramics (1925), 107
  Grand Prix Vase (1937), 103
Pastiche, 134
Patronage, 302
  Catherine de Medici, 308
  education, 204, 328
  porcelain facotoires, 68
  secular power, 312
  the church, 307
Penck, A.R., 279
Pennings, Mark, 115–28
Petri, Trudi, 314
Petroski, Henry, 286
Pevsner, Nikolaus, 253
Pewabic Pottery, 322
Picasso, Pablo, 12, 16, 19, 78, 81, 82, 155, 213, 226, 241, 262, 279, 318, 332, 338, 340, 344, 346
  Dish with Bullfight Scene, 344
  Dove, 346
  Pitcher with Open Vase, 347
Piché, Tom, 231
Plato, 362
Pleydell-Bouverie, Katherine, 266
Poliakoff, Serge, 340, 342
Polygnotos (Attr.), RedFig pelike Perseus, Medusa, 229

Poncelet, Jacqui, 315, 330
Pond Farm Pottery (California), 103
Ponti, Gio, 105
   Pair of Lamp Bases, *104*
Poons, Larry, 82
Pop Art, 21, 126
Porcelain
   Chinese, 137
   East India Trading Co., 308
   patronage, 303
   resonancy, 207
   secret of making, 310
   serial production, 315
Porcelain Factories, 68-69
Portland Stone, 171
Portland Vase, 49, *119*, *211*, 321
Post-Impressionists, 263
Postmodernism, 129, 358
   aesthetics, 127, 134
   authoritative texts, 130
   diversity of intention, 253
   economics, 131
   informatics, 133
   techno-science, 132
   the subject, 134
Pottery Workshop, (Bauhaus), 99
Pound, Ezra, 355
Prampolini, Enrico, 106
Pre-Columbian, 8, 235, 341
   Price, Ken, 80, 82, 89, 155, 281, 285, 328, 329
   M. Violet, *80*
   Untitled Cup Form, *81*
Prime Canadian Crafts, 243
Propaganda
   Communist, 305
   Fascist, 111
Ptolemy, Claudius, 56
Pueblo Indian Potter (Cochiti), 197
Pueblo Pottery, 157, 215
Punin, Nikolai, 79
Putnam, Edward H., 180
Putney School of Art, 265
Pye, David, 286
Quay Ceramics Gallery, 330
Québécois ceramists, 232
Queen Charlotte, 320
Rady, Elsa, 227
Raku, 45, 123, 147
Ramié, Georges, 347
Rauschenburg, Robert, 28, 151, 331
Rawson, Philip, 35–52, 207–18, 222, 252, 286
Read, Herbert, 12, 32, 219, 247, 256, 266, 271
Redgrave, Richard, 72
Regout Factory (Netherlands), 102
Rembrandt, 4
Renaissance, 15
Revelation Kiln Company, 322

Richards, I.A., 151
Richards, M.C., 286
Rie, Lucie, 45
   Teapot, *46*
Rilke, Rainer Maria, 261, 351
Riopelle, Jean-Paul, 339
Rittweger, Otto, 123
Robineau, Adelaide, 71, 269, 271, 322-323
   Scarab Vase, *314*, 315
Rococo, 313
Rodchenko, Alexander, 79
Roettiers, J.N., 239
Rolt, T.C., 172
Rörstrand Porcelain Factory, 68, 313
Rose, Barbara, 154
Rosenberg Porcelain Factory, 68
Rosenthal Factory, 340
Rossi, Franco, 107
Rothenstein, William, 264
Rothko, Mark, 82
Rothman, Jerry, 328, 329
Royal College of Art (London), 250, 264, 265-267, 326, 330
Royal Copenhagen, 314
   Flora Danica Service, 312
   porcelain factory, 68
Royal Doulton, 70, 245
Royal Worcester Porcelain, 322
Ruess, Gusso, 103
Ruskin Pottery, 70
Ruskin, John, 13, 352, 367, 369
Russian Revolution, 79
Saarinen, Lilian Swann, 273
Saarinen. Eliel, 273
Salto, Axel, 324
Sariputra, 56
Saxe, Adriane, 121, 126, 157, 160, 315, 333
   Parisienne Chainsaw Massacre, *160*
Scheidig, Walter, 98
Schellink, Samuel
   vases and coffee pot, *65*
School of the American Craftsman R.I.T., 103
Schutte, Thomas, 279
Schwarz, Peter, 132
Schwarzburg Porzellan Manufaktur, 97
Sculpture, 6, 16, 42, 288
   and ceramics, 80, 144
   ceramics, 5, 26, 31
   compared to ceramics, 279
   contemporary, 359
Selvage, Nancy, 10–23
Semmes, Beverly, 279
Semper, Gottfried, 72
Sepeshy, Zoltan, 275
Severini, Gino, 111

Sèvres, 68, 70, 160, 343
   criticism by Gauguin, 262
   painted vignettes, 238
   porcelain factory, 68
   porcelain vessel, 242
   Royal Factory of Sèvres, Louis XV, 242, 311
Sèvres Manufactory, 111, 341
Sèvres Museum, 232
Sezessionstil, 93, 105
Shadbolt, Doris, 24–34
Shaw, Richard, 17, 148
   Camden Passage #4/5, *17*
Shaws of Darwen Ltd., 184
Shchekatikhina-Potoskaya, Aleksandra, 96
Shep, Larry, 10, 20
Sherman, Cindy, 237-241, 348
Shills, Edward, 205
Shire, Peter, 82
   Pan Pipe Scorpion, *83*
Silverman, Bobby, 315
Simmons, Charles, 315
Sipek, Boris, 315
Slivka, Rose, 32, 251, 285
Smith, David, 82, 285
Smith, Roberta, 332
Smith, Tony, 82
Soldner, Paul, 125, 147, 328
   Bottle, *149*
   Plaque, *148*
   Vase, *201*, *202*
Solon, Leon, 182
Song Dynasty, 306
Spinner, Hans, 339
Spode, blue-and-white wares, 214
Spurey, Kurt, 296
St. Augustine, 189, 193
Staffel, Rudolf
   Light Gatherer, 303, *304*
Staffordshire
   figurine, the poetry of, 166
   potteries, 320
   pottery industry, 248
   University, the Internet, 257
State Porcelain Factory, 95
Steiner, George, 6, 209, 355
Stella, Frank, 81, 82, 143, 155
Stephenson, John, 328
Stile Liberty (Art Nouveau), 104
Strada, Nino, 111
Stratton, Mary Chase Perry, 269, 271, 322
Studio Potters, 11, 201, 212, 254, 263, 284, 322, 325
   contemporary, 199
   definition, 205
   history of (United States), 269
   individual, 68, 70
Suetin, Nicolai, 79, 96
Sullivan, Louis, 190, 181

Sung Dynasty, 18, 363
  bowl, 224
  celadon bowl, 50
  Chun-ware dish, 49
  floral bowl, 50, 213
  Kuan vase, 43
  standard, 250
  stoneware bottle, 210
Suprematism, 79, 93, 96, 99
Surface, 112, 241
  and volume, 50
  contours, 50
  crackled, 14
  decoration, 18, 43, 263, 364
Surrealism, 15, 19, 105, 110, 164
Suzuki, D.T., 46
T'ang Dynasty, 42, 43
  dwelling, 187
  funeral pot, 38
Takamori, Akio, *Owl*, 162
Tao, 42, 45
Tapies, Antoni, 342
  Archeologie II, 153
Tatlin, Vladimir, 78-79, 82, 93-94
  Porcelain Feeding Bottles with Rack, 94
  utilitarian ceramics, 94
Taylor, James, 181
Taylor, Samual, 138
Teague, Zedith, 198
Terra Cotta, 40, 170-175, 176-185
  Bayard-Condict Building, 181
  Broadway-Chambers Building, 182
  Greek, 214
  Natural History Museum of London, 173
  Parkchester Building, 183
  sculpture, 5, 107, 343
  Seaview Hospital, 184
Terra Cotta Society of Great Britain, 171
Thomas, Lewis, 362
Thomas, Nicholas, 358
Thun, Matteo, 315
Tiffany's, 321
Tolstoy, Leo, 146, 189, 193
Tong Dynasty, 306
Traditional
  craftsman/potter, 11, 29, 196
  cultures, 200
  function, 32
  utilitarian, 200
Transient-Artist Potters, 344-348
Truro Pottery, 267
Tunick, Susan, 176–85
Turner, Bob, 227
Turner, Robert, 84
Twentieth Century, 11, 15
  art, 26, 78
  ceramics, 339

industrial design, 82
  style and genre, 74
Tzu Chou Pottery, 221
Union of Artists (Soviet Union), 96
University City Pottery, 315
University of California, 204
Urry, John, 131
Utilitarian
  aesthetic responsibility, 221
  ceramics, 5, 12, 369
  design, 365
  objects, 21
  objects and modernism, 116
  pottery, 198
  vessels, 15, 366
Utopian Communities, 269
Valery, Paul, 371
Valori Plastici, 107
Van de Velde, Henry, 74, 75, 97
  Blessed be Free Labour, 95
Van Doesberg, Theo, 99, 117
Van Gogh, Vincent, 215
van Rossum, J.M.
  vases and coffee pot, 65
Veblen, Thorstein, 369
Venturi, Robert, 184
Venus of Laussel, 39
Vessel, 110
  geometric progression, 85
  history and tradition, 232
  maker and sculptor, 31
  metaphor for life, 31
  organic, 366
  root and gourd forms, 71
  tripod (Mexico), 47
Victoria and Albert Museum, 65
  and education, 251
Viollet-le-Duc, Eugène E., 72
Vollard, Ambroise, 261, 340
Von Beek, Bontjes, 103
von Schiller, Friedrich, 86
Voulkos, Peter, 19, 84, 125, 147, 151, 177, 219, 226, 328, 329, 333, 370
Wallender, Alf, 313
Warashina, Patty, 150
Warhol, Andy, 126, 139, 155, 329
Waterloo Place Gallery
  British Crafts Centre, 330
Weber, Max, 82
Wedgwood Pottery
  industrial production, 254
  jasperware, 49, 211
  Jasperware Vase, 48
  Portland Vase, 49, *119*, *211*, 321
Wedgwood, Josiah, 248, 253, 366
  and ceramic marketing, 319
Wedgwood, Thomas, 117, 119, 120, 121, 138
Wells, Reginald, 263

Wentworth, Richard, 359
West Africa, Ibadan, 268
Whitney Museum (New York)
  and the Otis group, 330
Wildenhain, Frans, 98
Wildenhain, Marguerite, 19, 98, 102, 103
  Teapot, 101
Williams, Gerry, 196–206
Windsor, John, 301
Woodman, Betty, 147, 152, 160, 281, 284
  Pillow Pitcher, 333
  Pillow Pitcher, 161
  Tang Pillow Pitcher, 159
Woodman, George, 142–53, 154–62
Woolwich Polytechnic, 265
World Crafts Council (Vienna), 295
Wright, Frank Lloyd, 177
Wright, Patrick, 248
Yakushiji, Nara, 43
Yanagi, Soetsu, 18, 227, 353, 354, 356, 358, 362
  Kizaemon teabowl, 352
Yeoman Pottery (London), 263
Youngblood, Daisy, 281
Yung-cheng, 44
Zeisel, Eva, 314
Zen, 17-20, 266
Zimelli, Umberto, 109
Zsolnay Factory (Hungary), 70
Zuni Indian Pot, 50